PRAISES FOR
STRONGER THAN STEEL

"There is nothing more challenging, frustrating but at the same time satisfying than being part of changing the trajectory of your city from one that was failing to one that gives hope for a future. It doesn't happen by accident. It happens because a few people in a very intentional way re-image a different future for abandoned mills and declining neighborhoods when most others see only decline. It takes a strong, strategic vision and an appetite for risk to succeed. Jeff Parks captures the challenges from the naysayers, that "there is no funding, no one will go there" attitudes that have to be overcome first before financing and design challenges really begin. It is a great read."

—**Tom Murphy,** *Urban Land Institute, Senior Resident Fellow*
Joseph C. Canizaro/Klingbeil Family Chair for Urban Development
Former Mayor, Pittsburgh, PA

"*Stronger than Steel* is a thoughtful and engaging account of the transformation of Bethlehem, Pennsylvania through community-based creative placemaking. After the city lost its major industry, it managed to survive and eventually thrive by using its creative assets to help realize its potential. An important addition to field studies in creative placemaking, this book demonstrates how creativity and relevant arts participation can build powerful social capital. That social capital can leverage economic, social and cultural vibrancy, resulting in an exceedingly livable community. Jeffrey Parks beautifully brings Bethlehem's journey of rebirth and transformation to life."

—**Pam Breaux,** *President & CEO*
National Associations of State Arts Agencies

"Even though I grew up just two hours north of Bethlehem, my first visit there didn't come until years later, when I was at the National Endowment for the Arts on a trip to understand how music and art can play a role in the rebirth of American cities. My time with ArtsQuest has profoundly informed all of my work since, and I am thrilled that Jeff is now sharing these lessons with a national audience.

—**Jamie Bennett,** *Executive Director*
ArtPlace America

"The history of Bethlehem and of ArtsQuest's role in its revitalization is an amazing story of a community coming together through the power of the arts. Its message is universal and speaks to the power of overcoming differences to realize a greater good. This tale of hard-won success is a compelling read and should be required for students of urban planning, sociology, public policy or culture and anyone living in a community that is facing economic and social challenges."

—**Mario Garcia Durham,** *President & CEO*
Association of Performing Arts Professional

"Bethlehem is a successful city today because it took a different pathway to address the loss of industry. *Stronger than Steel* demonstrates the success of open minded, consistent civic leadership. The book tells the tale of the creative strategies used in Bethlehem, the people who conceived and implemented them and how they contributed to the success of the city. Bethlehem took advantage of its history, culture and resources, and aggressively pursued opportunities, rather than accept defeat. It was my privilege to be Mayor and cheerleader-in-chief during a critical phase of this amazing renaissance that is well chronicled in this book by Jeff Parks one of those visionary leaders. "

—**John B. Callahan,** *Mayor of Bethlehem, 2004-2014*

STRONGER THAN STEEL

FORGING A RUST BELT RENAISSANCE

JEFFREY A. PARKS

Rocky Rapids Press Bethlehem, PA

Published By
Rocky Rapids Press, LLC
70 E. Broad Street
Bethlehem, PA 18018

Library of Congress Cataloging-in-Publication Data
Parks, Jeffrey A.
Stronger than steel: forging a rust belt renaissance/
by Jeffrey A. Parks
Printed in the United States of America

Jacket design by Lisa Hokans
Cover photo credit: Zachary Matthai
Author image: Olaf Starorypynski

ISBN 978-1-7320636-0-0

For Susan

—§—

CONTENTS

PREFACE

Academic studies of urban success and failure almost always focus on New York, Los Angeles, Chicago, or one of the other eighty-two American cities with populations greater than 250,000. They ignore the thousands of smaller cities or portray many of them in the aggregate as hollowed out and left behind. When studies mention these communities at all, it is usually in the context of a metropolitan statistical area, not the city at its core.

Studies of economic transitions of small industrial cities remain rare. It is true that many still are struggling as their populations and prosperity dwindle, their population siphoned off by larger cities and displaced to the South and West from the Northeast and Midwest. But some small Rust Belt cities are succeeding.

Stronger Than Steel is a firsthand account of one of those success stories. Bethlehem, Pennsylvania, home of the once mighty Bethlehem Steel Corporation, lost its major industry but managed to survive and become an economically, socially and culturally vibrant twenty-first-century city. The book chronicles how the community succeeded where others have failed. For thirty-five years residents grieved, then moved on, using the city's history, culture, and the arts to attract the people and capital necessary to thrive along with its surrounding region.

Stronger Than Steel demonstrates the direct connection between the arts and economic success. *Creative placemaking* is a term coined by the authors Ann Markusen and Anna Gadwa Nicodemus in their groundbreaking 2010 study of the role of the arts in urban redevelopment.[1] The term describes the infusion of the arts in public and private spaces, thereby contributing to the well-being of a community and to a broader agenda for change, growth, and transformation. Bethlehem's experience confirms the benefits of the practice.

The story also reveals another truth—rebirth does not happen overnight, nor is the march to success linear. Bethlehem's revival took decades and did not come easily.

Stronger Than Steel is a clarion call to artists and especially arts organizations. The arts always have drawn people together, and for centuries that meant constructing and caring for museums, galleries, and concert halls, then inviting people in. Now, however, technology has changed our habits and expectations. It has conditioned people to fast, barrier-free access to what they want. So arts organizations must think differently about how they interact with potential patrons. Although these traditional organizations deserve recognition because they continue to provide a cultural staple for their communities, they must move the barriers to access aside and connect with the community wherever, whenever, and however they can. Bethlehem's revival through accessible, relevant arts illustrates those principles.

Bethlehem was founded in 1741 by the Moravians, a Protestant sect that worshiped with music, practiced the domestic arts and painting, educated girls, and brought Native Americans and Africans into their religion and their community. As Bethlehem developed an important role in the industrial revolution, attracting workers from Europe, Mexico, and the Caribbean, those values set the tone for the city. When the City of Bethlehem was incorporated in 1917, its seal included representations of music, education, religion, sport, and industry. Those values became part of the city's salvation as it struggled in the late twentieth century against suburbanization, the loss of educated young people to places where they found greater opportunity, and deindustrialization that took one-fifth of its taxable land base and many of its residents. A generation of young people fled the city. At its darkest moment the community came together through an open-air festival and appealing arts and cultural programs.

Musikfest now is the largest free music festival in the United States, open to all members of the community regardless of financial means. Its two thousand volunteers work toward a common community purpose. ArtsQuest, the nonprofit parent organization of Musikfest, offers more than two thousand arts and education programs every year that call on the talents of hundreds of local and regional artists. In the process the arts have generated enormous social capital, bringing residents out of their neighborhoods and cultural tribes to engage with each other in public spaces.

Today Bethlehem has the highest median household income of Pennsylvania cities with a population of more than twenty thousand, the highest single-family residential housing values, the lowest poverty rate, and two thriving downtowns.[2] (The city has two downtowns because of the separate histories of Bethlehem and South Bethlehem, a borough formed after the Civil War. After the two became one city in 1917, the former South Bethlehem, which had the larger retail district along Third and Fourth streets, was called the south side, while Main Street on the north side continued to be called "downtown.") Young people are returning to find a vibrant, livable place with great employment opportunities, cultural diversity, and a palate of arts activities that many much larger cities would envy. From the concert halls, educational institutions, art galleries, neighborhood centers, parks, and plazas, accessible arts have brought this resilient community together, ready to meet the next set of challenges it inevitably will face.

This book is about using the resources at hand to convene a community and help it realize its potential. Many small cities seek a single quick fix—a new manufacturing plant, a performing arts center, a sports arena, a convention center. Most are disappointed. The people of Bethlehem took another path, one that was more complex but proved to be transcendent. This is their story.

Jeffrey A. Parks
Bethlehem, Pennsylvania
January 2018

BETHLEHEM, PA
MORAVIAN HISTORIC DISTRICT
2016

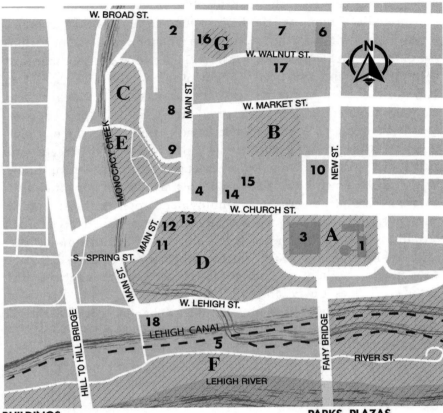

BUILDINGS
1. Bethlehem City Hall
2. Bethlehem Commons
3. Bethlehem Area Public Library
4. Central Moravian Church
5. Charles Brown Ice House
6. Former First Valley Bank
7. Former Bethlehem Plaza Mall
8. Goundie House
9. Hotel Bethlehem
10. Kemerer Museum of Decorative Arts
11. Moravian College Foy Hall
12. Moravian College Peter Hall
13. Moravian College Single Brethern's House
14. Moravian Museum (Gemein Haus)
15. Moravian Old Chapel
16. Sun Inn
17. Walnut Street Garage
18. Wooden Match (former CNJ train station)

PARKS, PLAZAS, HISTORIC SITES
A. Bethlehem City Center Plaza
B. God's Acre Cemetery
C. Johnston Park
D. Moravian College Priscilla Payne Hurd Campus
E. Moravian Colonial Industrial Quarter
F. Sand Island
G. Sun Inn Courtyard

BETHLEHEM, PA
SOUTHSIDE ARTS DISTRICT
2016

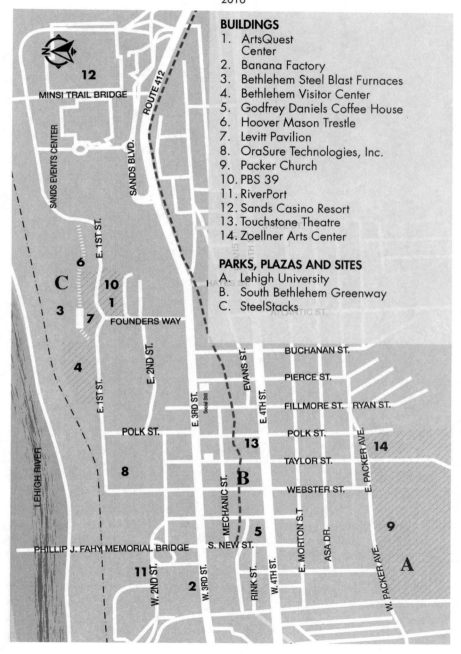

BUILDINGS

1. ArtsQuest Center
2. Banana Factory
3. Bethlehem Steel Blast Furnaces
4. Bethlehem Visitor Center
5. Godfrey Daniels Coffee House
6. Hoover Mason Trestle
7. Levitt Pavilion
8. OraSure Technologies, Inc.
9. Packer Church
10. PBS 39
11. RiverPort
12. Sands Casino Resort
13. Touchstone Theatre
14. Zoellner Arts Center

PARKS, PLAZAS AND SITES

A. Lehigh University
B. South Bethlehem Greenway
C. SteelStacks

PROLOGUE
THE DAY THE CANDLES DIED
NOVEMBER 18, 1995

When I was growing up in Bethlehem in the 1950s, two sets of candles illuminated my life—the traditional Moravian candles placed in windows at Christmas, and the giant industrial flares of the Bethlehem Steel blast furnaces that burned bright blue year-round along the south bank of the Lehigh River. The delicate Moravian Christmas lights were reminders of the founders of Bethlehem. The huge Bethlehem Steel flames were a year-round testament to the industrial might of the city and its eponymous company. They represented the prosperity that brought our parents, grandparents, and great grandparents to this city and, in many cases, to this country. They also symbolized the power and prestige of the United States. Whether we were scions of the wealthy, children of union workers, or simply residents, we were proud of "the Steel."

I remember sleepless hot summer nights when my bedroom window in our newly built tract house, less than a mile from the steel plant, was open. The clanking noises were the ambient music of a thriving community. We knew our city was an important place because the Steel had helped win World War II and was busy continuing to build America and our defense system. We knew that Bethlehem probably was a designated target of a Soviet nuclear missile. In elementary school we participated in regular drills every year: Go into the hallway, sit on the floor, put your head between your legs. When I was older, I realized the drills were useless. We were only one mile from the bomb drop zone.

Everyone always said that if those giant candles ever went out, the city would die with them. It seemed unimaginable. But as the decades ticked by, the world was changing and implacable forces were closing in on us.

The story was a national one. Inevitably, Bethlehem Steel, the company that produced the ships that literally created the modern U.S. Navy; one-third of the steel for U.S. armaments in World War II; a ship a day during the war years; the steel for uncounted bridges, including the Golden Gate and the George Washington; and the steel that built most of the Manhattan skyline, became a symbol of the agony of change.

By the early 1980s the company was suffering dire financial losses that brought layoff after layoff. We began to worry that the candles might actually be snuffed. Fear resonates through a community when something as major as its own industrial bastion is in a downward spiral. The fear at first is economic—Where will I find a job? How will it affect my business? How will it affect my taxes if the biggest taxpayer in the community disappears? As the reality sinks in, new fears arise: Will I have to move? Will my children be able to get jobs here? Will they even visit? Will my grandchildren grow up thousands of miles away?

As the years passed, dire possibility became reality. Then came January 1994, when the struggling company announced its timetable for closing the home plant during the next two years. Losses from the previous five years of operations had exceeded $100 million annually, a rate unsustainable for even a once-great industrial giant. The day set for the last "hot metal charge" at the Bethlehem plant was Saturday, November 18, 1995. By then the plant was down to 3,600 workers from a high of 23,700 at the end of World War II. All that would remain would be the coke works and some fabrication facilities with a labor force of 1,800, a futile gesture to the unions and a worried community.

The path ahead looked bleak. As postwar deindustrialization set in and worsened throughout the Northeast and Midwest, cities dependent on old-line manufacturing began to collapse. States created laws to address the needs of the failed cities, putting them under direct state control and providing them with additional support. In 1987 Pennsylvania's legislature approved the Municipalities Financial Recovery Act to address the concerns of distressed cities. By 1995 eight cities, seven of which had hosted a steel mill, had come under the protection of the law. Would Bethlehem be next?

During the weeks before the plant closed, national, international, and local reporters covered the story with varying degrees of detail. The stories were more or less the same—increased competition from imports, declining demand, and the upstart Nucor (which used recycled steel, saving the cost of creating the steel from raw materials, and new, less costly electric furnaces) were causing the steel industry to contract. The Bethlehem plant had out-of-date technology and was too costly to maintain.

The local media focused on community impact. Some of the laid-off steelworkers were ready for retirement, perhaps with a supplemental job. Others were left with anxiety about not having cutting-edge skills because they had been doing repetitive work using outdated technology. One told the (Allentown) Morning Call: "You're talking about equipment that's decades old, half a century old. Compared to the equipment outside of this plant, that's like working in the dinosaur age. You might as well be Fred Flintstone."[3]

When Bette Kovach arrived from New Jersey to attend Moravian College in 1971, she could see Bethlehem Steel's new twenty-one-story headquarters under construction from her dorm window. It made an impression. The tallest building in the Lehigh Valley looked powerful yet airy. Built as a cruciform to meet the demand for corner offices, the building exuded the power of a company that then was a staple of stock portfolios around the globe.

Kovach, who had studied marketing and public relations, was hired within two years of graduation to work in Bethlehem Steel's media relations department. At the time she was part of a tepid effort by management to diversify the workforce, one of the few women not employed as a secretary or a hospitality worker at Martin Tower, as the corporate headquarters was called.

Kovach was responsible for media relations for all aspects of the November 18, 1995, closing of the Bethlehem plant. The plant welcomed reporters during the five weeks before November 15 but not during for the last three days before the closing, to allow the workers privacy during such a difficult period. On the cold, clear Saturday morning of November 18, she got up early and headed to the plant, stopping for a snack at a minimart. "When I get nervous I get hungry, and I wanted to make sure I had something to eat," she recalled.[4]

One observer described the "last cast" as an Irish wake. The plant had relaxed its security rules so that workers could bring adult family members to observe a piece of history that was truly theirs. Kovach arrived to find a worker in a shack near the blast furnace making plenty of potato, egg, and cheese sandwiches for everyone who entered the Cast House at the rear of Blast Furnace C, the only one of the five-furnace array that had been running since the early 1980s, when decreased demand shut down the other four.

At approximately 6:30 a.m., a worker opened the tapping hole. As the molten yellow-red pig iron flowed through the narrow channels on the casting house floor, a recording of "Amazing Grace" piped through the cavernous building whose open wall faced the Lehigh River. The fluvial iron fell through the holes in the floor that allowed liquid metal to drop into the hot metal railroad cars below the Cast House. As the cast ended, the smell of sulfur pervaded the building, and the unusable slag by-product emerged from the tapping hole and was emptied into slag pots. The entire process took less than an hour. The hot metal car, known as a "submarine car" because of its shape, carried the molten pig iron through the plant for three-quarters of a mile to the next stop on its way to becoming steel, the basic oxygen furnace adjacent to the Grey mill.

By that afternoon the last batch of pig iron was ready for the basic oxygen furnace, where it would be transformed from iron to steel and rolled into various shapes for the company's customers. Dozens of people had wandered in throughout the day. In an office trailer outside the mill a clerk was quietly weeping while distributing soup, sandwiches, cakes, and beverages to the assembled group of workers, family, and friends. At about 3:00 p.m. an enormous steel ladle on a four-hundred-ton crane transferred the still molten pig iron into the basic oxygen furnace, a vat open to the ceiling. In the vat would be placed a "charge" of carbon to create the chemical reaction to make steel. As the last ladle of pig iron began its journey along the crane run, a giant American flag unfurled in its path with "God Bless America" streaming from the speakers as onlookers soberly watched history being made.

Transformed into steel, the hot metal was ladled into ingot molds for transfer to the Grey mill and other parts of the plant that made the final steel products. A portion was made into an I-beam that was cut into pieces and turned into souvenirs commemorating the day and the industry. For the first time since 1853 the city of Bethlehem was no longer producing hot metal.

As he left the plant, one worker said, "I had a good job. I raised two kids, had a house and two cars. I have no complaints."[5]

As Bette Kovach drove home that November evening, she passed the dark, silent blast furnaces and felt the ghostly atmosphere of the eighteen hundred acres of mostly vacant industrial structures, which people soon took to calling "the ruins."

I left Bethlehem for the University of Pennsylvania Law School in 1970; my goal was to take my Ivy League law degree; settle in New York, Washington, or Philadelphia; practice law; and never look back. Then the reality of living in a major American city in the early 1970s taught me about myself and about urban life. Today much of central Philadelphia is gentrified, a wonderful place to live, work, and play, with diverse urban housing, entertainment, great museums, restaurants, microbreweries and distilleries, shops, and, most important, jobs. But back then it was home to three classes of residents—rich, poor, and students (also mostly poor).

Because I was not independently wealthy, part of my law school experience was my job at the city's police headquarters, the Roundhouse, so named because of its architectural design. As an employee of the judicial system I worked either the four-to-midnight or midnight-to-eight shifts on weekends. From this vantage point I met the worst of society and learned much about both the criminal justice system and the challenges of urban America.

I realized that if I were to work in New York, Washington, or Philadelphia after graduation and have a family, I would have to have a home in the suburbs and spend hours commuting by train or car every day. I made the decision to do the unthinkable—return to Bethlehem after graduation. I realized that this small city had many of the same issues as a big city, but they somehow seemed more manageable. I would be able to live in an urban environment, although not one as exciting as in the big cities. I also convinced Susan, my fiancée, whom I had met at Penn, to join me in a community that was completely strange to her. She is a native of Tampa, Florida, and had thought we might do well in the deep South. I am sure she was right—Tampa today is an attractive, economically vibrant city. Nevertheless, we decided to take a chance on Bethlehem.

Each third-year student at Penn Law was required to participate in an exit interview by the placement director, Helena Clark. During my brief interview I informed Clark, a Philadelphian to the core, that I planned to return to my hometown where I had been offered a position in estate planning and business law. I will always remember what she said as she looked at me over her readers, head slanted forward: "We do appreciate it when some of our graduates go to *those* places." Clearly she thought I was off to the boondocks and was wasting an Ivy League education.

But I figured I could parlay my friendships and some civic engagement into a successful law career. Then I could consider public service through elected office, perhaps as a state representative, senator, or even a U.S. representative.

After a year of working for another attorney, I established a legal practice with a clientele of more than one hundred small businesses, and I wrote more than twenty-five hundred wills. I became deeply involved in civic activities, including the chamber of commerce, Kiwanis, Fine Arts Commission, and the Sun Inn Preservation Association, a non-profit that was seeking to restore a colonial inn.

I also ventured into politics. My parents' attorney, Justin D. Jirilanio, was the long-time political boss of Bethlehem and Northampton County. In 1978 he was in ill health and announced he would retire from that position. Here was my shot. I announced that it was time for a new generation to take the lead. At twenty-nine I became the youngest Democratic county chair in the history of the historically Democratic county. We were going to change the way things worked. But reality soon tempered my enthusiasm. Local, state, and national candidates expect votes and money. Democratic Committee people expect the party to cover their get-out-the-vote expenses. And everyone expects miracles. I admit that it was a heady thing to walk into Air Force 2 in 1980 to meet Vice President Walter Mondale when he landed at the local airport; to greet Roslyn Carter when she came to town; and to be invited to the White House. But with a young child, a house that was an 1895 Victorian money pit, and a growing law practice with two offices, I quickly realized that the job of county chair was too demanding. I stepped down after one two-year term and served another two years on the state committee, where I met legislative leaders from throughout the state. Politics wasn't for me, although the experience and contacts were a foundation that helped me later in ways I couldn't then imagine.

In January 1982 the Jaycees named me "Young Man of the Year." While it was a great honor, I also felt a great responsibility because my hometown was in the throes of a crisis. With the decline of the steel company, people were losing their jobs, local businesses were hurting, and the town was in a funk. I had tried to tackle the malaise by volunteering for civic groups, but solutions to the community's larger problems seemed elusive.

My family owned a stationery store while I was growing up. The store was originally on Bethlehem's thriving south side, home of Lehigh University, the steel plant, and thousands of steelworkers and their families. By the time I was in high school in the 1960s, the south side's retail district had collapsed. In desperation my parents moved the store to Bethlehem's smaller but still active north side, home of Moravian College, the city's banks, and the historic Moravian and Victorian buildings. I vowed not to go into retail, but the downtowns were deep in my blood. In 1982, I was determined to focus on my law business and cut down on my volunteer work, which included the tourism committee of the chamber of commerce. I was asked to do "one last thing" before my term on that committee ended. The committee wanted to create an event to bring people to the struggling north side downtown during August. That one last thing, and many things that it led to, became my life's work.

I was to have an adventure full of concepts that in the early 1980s did not even have definitions. In fact, what I became did not have a name. Now it does. Social entrepreneur—someone who uses the techniques of start-up businesses to address social issues. And it all was about helping to save my birthplace, my beloved Bethlehem, from the ravages of deindustrialization.

The journey has been fraught with challenges and rich with opportunities. In the process Bethlehem has become recognized as a pioneer in using arts strategies for urban redevelopment. None of us who have been part of this realized it at the beginning, but we were laying the groundwork for the Bethlehem of the twenty-first century, much as its steel magnates had catapulted the city into the previous century. Essential to our effort was the rich history of our community: founders with a reverence for education and culture; entrepreneurs who transformed the city and created a behemoth steel industry that helped win two world wars; and an ethnically complex population with a deep-seated sense of community.

That a Rust Belt city dependent on Big Steel reinvented itself to become a modern, economically diverse community with a standard of living, education levels, and cultural riches any town would be proud to have isn't the story that many current leaders of our country are telling. But it's true. It happened. Right here in a modestly sized Pennsylvania town. And it happened not because we looked back at a past that could not be recaptured. We did it by embracing new ideas with a hopeful spirit.

We were one of the first communities in the country to have a cultural tourism initiative (although we didn't know or use the term). We became involved in "creative placemaking" before the concept went national. Our team of professionals and volunteers would became experts at city branding. Before the creative class was recognized as an important economic driver, we were engaged in developing arts programs to retain and attract creative workers.

There were obstacles. Opposition sometimes came from the very people we were trying to help, including downtown business owners. A community used to industrial jobs with good wages and great benefits was not eager to embrace the service industry work offered by hotels, restaurants, museums, and the like. Few, if any, made the connection between using these amenities as a basis for a new economy and attracting the entrepreneurs, educators, physicians, and workers qualified for high-tech manufacturing, health care, education, and other fields who would be its lifeblood. But in the end the community was strong enough to take those leaps into the untried and unknown.

What has made my journey so fulfilling has been that community. I have had the opportunity to work with many people—entrepreneurs, representatives of major corporations and small businesses, public officials, and hundreds of volunteers from every part of the community who have been engaged in our quest to make Bethlehem thrive. Civic organizations, educational institutions, arts and culture organizations, businesses and entities from all areas of government have participated in the programs and projects that have created one of the most culturally vibrant communities in the country. I have worked with amazing people who have joined the staff of our arts organization so they can be a part of this great experiment in community development.

As I stepped into the role now called social entrepreneur, I brought with me a young lifetime's worth of Bethlehem culture and history. I knew instinctively that whatever we did to address our challenges had to be consistent with the culture of the then 240-year-old city. The community's identity was rooted in the founding Moravians, who brought their brand of Christianity to the Native Americans while developing a community that cherished music, art, and science. The inclusive Moravians respect all human beings as equal in the eyes of God. Then came the industrial revolution, fueled by entrepreneurs who brought the canal, railroad, iron, silk, candy, and, most famously, steel manufacturing to the city. Drawn here by jobs and hope for a better life were immigrants from all corners of Europe, plus Mexico and the Caribbean who flocked to the booming steel town in the late nineteenth and early twentieth centuries and brought their traditions, religion, and food. From the belfries of the churches to the cheesy potatoes in the pierogies, Bethlehem has heritage. In 1983 we relied on that heritage to create the future.

PART I

THE RISE AND FALL OF AN AMERICAN
INDUSTRIAL CITY
AN ABBREVIATED HISTORY OF BETHLEHEM,
PENNSYLVANIA

CHAPTER I
MORAVIANS

A community's history so deeply imbues its culture and character that traits can linger for centuries. What the founders of the city of Bethlehem bequeathed—community cohesion, inclusiveness, love of music, reverence for learning—have proved to be its salvation more than once.

Those founders were the Moravians who came to the New World, not to flee persecution—they had found safety at the estate of their patron, Count Nikolaus von Zinzendorf, in Saxony (Germany)—but to bring Christianity to Native Americans, to European settlers who had abandoned religion and Africans who had not been exposed to Christianity. The Moravians were preceded by the Quakers but joined a wave of Germans who settled in Pennsylvania. Between 1727 and 1775 sixty-five thousand Germans emigrated to Pennsylvania.[6] At the time of the American Revolution, Germans constituted 30 percent of the state's population, with the largest percentage settled in the arc between what are now Lancaster and Bethlehem. These people became known as the Pennsylvania Dutch, not because of an affinity with the Netherlands but because Dutch was an English perversion of *Deutsch*, the German language. The Pennsylvania Germans, who kept to their own communities, developed their own dialect, a combination of German, English, and original words. They became known for the colorful hex signs on their barns and for their tortured syntax, which produced sentences like "Throw the cow over the fence some hay."

I know much of this because my mother is Pennsylvania German. Both of her parents traced their heritage to that early German wave of immigrants. By the time I was born, at the end of America's second big war with Germany, it was not fashionable for city folk to speak Pennsylvania German. The only "Dutch" I learned were the swear words my grandmother used when I did something wrong. It took a little longer for the dialect to die out in the countryside around us, where canny Pennsylvania Dutch farmers would speak it when they wanted to keep clueless outsiders in the dark.

The Moravian Church has its roots in the Czech Republic, Germany, the Netherlands, Belgium, and England and at first was known by the Latin name Unitas Fratrum, Unity of Brethren in English, and Bruder Gemein in German. A group of followers of the early English religious reformer John Wycliffe and his contemporary, the Czech Jan Hus, were the founders. The sect spread through much of Europe before being heavily suppressed by the Roman Catholic Church and various monarchs. A small group of believers survived and continued the faith in the provinces of Bohemia and Moravia, now the Czech Republic. They called themselves "the hidden seed."[7] Between 1722 and 1727 some families of the hidden seed found refuge on the estates of Zinzendorf. Along with refugees of other Protestant religious groups, they created the village of Herrnhut. In 1735 a group of Moravians, eager to proselytize in the new world, left the safety of their homes to settle near Savannah, in the newly created British colony of Georgia. However, the pacifist Moravians established no permanent settlement because they refused to be conscripted to fight an anticipated Spanish incursion into the disputed territory.

The Moravians then accepted an invitation from the evangelist George Whitefield, a famous preacher, to move to Nazareth, Pennsylvania, a new settlement in northeastern Pennsylvania. After they arrived in 1740, the theological differences between the Moravians and their hosts became clear. On April 2, 1741, the Moravians received a deed for five hundred acres at the confluence of Monocacy Creek and the Lehigh River. Seventeen men and women moved the nine miles south from Nazareth to the new settlement and constructed a German-style log home and attached barn on a hill above the Monocacy Creek, the site of what is today the Hotel Bethlehem. Zinzendorf and his daughter Benigna visited Bethlehem in late December of that year. As the settlers and their patron were celebrating the Christmas Eve service, they moved into the portion of the building that housed the farm animals. They sang the Moravian hymn "Jesus Call Thou Me" (*Jesu rufe mich*), which includes the verse "Not

Jerusalem, lowly Bethlehem, t'was that gave us, Christ to save us, not Jerusalem." As he stood in the room with cattle and chickens, the count christened the new community Bethlehem.[8]

BUILDING A TOWN

The most important function of the religious settlement was worship. The first place of worship for the Bethlehem Moravians was the twenty-by-forty-foot log structure with a wall in the middle that separated the domestic animals' space from the settlers' living space, with the entire loft for sleeping. Before the first house was completed, the Moravians began construction of a large building to serve as the community center, the Gemeinhaus (today the Moravian Museum of Bethlehem). This five-story log structure was designed to house new arrivals and to serve as the office, school, and center for all other civic and community functions.[9] A central feature of the Gemeinhaus is the Saal, the worship room, an intimate room that retains a feel of the humility, piety, and energy of the Moravians. Completed in two parts in 1743, and covered in clapboard in 1868, the Moravian Gemeinhaus is the tallest continuously occupied colonial-era log structure still standing in the United States.

The Gemeinhaus served many functions, the most innovative of which was introduced by Countess Benigna. Moravians held the belief, unique in colonial America, that women as well as men should be educated. Benigna started a school open to women that eventually became Moravian Academy (a private K-12 school) and Moravian College, a liberal arts school that is the sixth-oldest college in the United States. Many members of the Continental Congress and other influential colonial leaders sent their daughters to Bethlehem to be educated. Visitors to the "house on the Lecha" (Lecha is the Native American name for the Lehigh River) praised the building as a splendid example of colonial architecture.[10]

The little community followed Zinzendorf's principles of living in a choir system, that is, with single women in one house, single men in another, married couples in a third, and widows in a fourth. The community was the support, and the retirement center, for missionaries the church sent throughout the northeastern United States and as far away as the Caribbean and Greenland. To sustain the inhabitants and support the missionaries, the Moravians established America's first industrial park along Monocacy Creek, now known as the Colonial Industrial Quarter. By 1747 thirty-five crafts, trades, and industries were located there, everything from a butchery to a clockmaker. This bustling area demonstrated the industriousness and the ingenuity of the settlers. On a hill above the quarter were the residential buildings: Bell House for married couples, Sisters House for single women, Brethren's House for single men, and the Widow's House. Women made clothing, beeswax candles, and decorative objects. The Brethren's House included the community kitchen, staffed mostly by men, and a cooperage (where barrels were made). The town's pottery and smithy were just across the way. Colonial Bethlehem also had a doctor and one of the first apothecaries in the country.

To provide freshwater for the residential buildings uphill from both Monocacy Creek and a natural well nearby, Hans Christopher Christiansen engineered the Bethlehem Waterworks in 1754, America's first municipal water distribution system. Using a system of pumps and heavy wooden pipes, Christiansen managed to pump water uphill from Monocacy Creek to a reservoir in the town square. Log pipes distributed the water from the reservoir to the Brethren's House, Gemeinhaus, Sun Inn, and the apothecary. Today Bethlehem's colonial waterworks is a National Historic Landmark. It was the first of many engineering feats for which Bethlehem would be known during the next 250 years.[11]

MUSIC, ART, AND SCIENCE

Music was central to Moravian worship and to daily life. The community's first spinet was delivered from London in 1744, followed by a small organ in 1746 and a larger organ in 1751. The first quartet of trombones (soprano, alto, tenor, and base) arrived in 1754 in time for the Christmas service. Before the completion of Central Moravian Church in 1806, the trombone choir would play from the rooftop balustrade of the Brethren's House overlooking the town square. Legend has it that in 1755, during the French and Indian War, Native Americans were poised to attack Bethlehem on Christmas. However, upon hearing the ethereal tones of the trombone choir, they thought better of attacking a place that seemed to have supernatural connections. Founded in 1754, the Bethlehem Moravian Trombone Choir is believed to be the oldest continuously existing instrumental organization in the United States. The choir still performs from the Central Moravian Church belfry on Easter Sunday and for other special events, including the opening day of Musikfest.

According to the writer Raymond Walters, "Benjamin Franklin in his *Autobiography* commented on the 'very fine music' he heard in the Bethlehem church during a visit in 1756. The orchestral players he praised were members of the Collegium Musicum of the congregation which was organized in December 1744. This early orchestra, besides its churchly participation, regularly occupied itself with secular compositions.... It is recorded that some of the Brethren on their way to harvest fields were wont, along with their sickles and scythes, to carry flutes, French horns, and cymbals." At Central Moravian Church orchestral music was a part of every important church service and in the early 1800s could also be heard at fifteen to twenty concerts every year. Moravian musicians often presented the works of Mozart and Hayden in Bethlehem before they were performed in other, larger colonial cities. Louis C. Elson, in his *History of American Music,* cites the Bethlehem rendition of Hayden's *Creation* and the earlier New York presentation of Handel's *Messiah* as "possibly the earliest oratorio performances on American soil."[12]

To this day Moravians worship in a service called the Sing Stunde, or Sing Hour. The Moravian Museum displays the types of instruments that were used for worship and entertainment. The harpsichord, early brass instruments, and strange instruments like the serpent, a squiggly clarinet-like instrument, and the wasserspiel, a collection of glass bowls filled with varying amounts of water, were used to sustain the spirit in this small community in the wilderness. Although colonial Moravians were isolated, they were in constant communication with Herrnhut and colleagues throughout Europe, which kept them apprised of the latest music, both religious and secular. Count Zinzendorf himself was a prolific hymn writer.

Art also was important to the Moravians. Decorative arts were largely the province of the women who made stitched fabrics for both decorative and utilitarian uses. The Moravian women designed a special banner for the Polish count Casimir Pulaski, a Revolutionary War hero, while he was recovering from an injury in Bethlehem. Design, whether for architecture or for everyday implements, was paramount because Moravian craftsmen believed they were doing God's work. A visit to Bethlehem's Moravian Museum offers a glimpse of these treasures and the culturally rich environment of early Bethlehem.

The most famous Bethlehem artist of the early Moravian era was John Valentine Haidt, who was born in Germany. Haidt studied at the Royal Academy of Arts in Berlin, became a goldsmith, and then acted as a lay preacher for the Moravians in London. After emigrating to the New World, he took up painting and worked primarily in Bethlehem, becoming the most prolific religious painter in colonial America.[13]

The city also was home to Gustavus Johann Grunewald (1805–1878), who studied painting at the Dresden Art Academy under Caspar David Friederick, one of the leading German painters of his time. Grunewald and his wife emigrated to America in 1831 and were accepted for residence in the exclusively Moravian Bethlehem in 1833. Grunewald lived in Bethlehem until 1866, and his residence elevated the visual arts tradition of a city already recognized for its engagement in the arts. Grunewald's intensely European style influenced generations of American painters. Prints of his paintings of Niagara Falls remain for sale today.[14]

BEER, HOSPITALITY, REVOLUTION

Beer and stronger spirits were part of the culture that the Moravians brought from Europe, where beer frequently was a more reliable source of untainted liquid refreshment than water. So important were these beverages that as early as 1749 the Moravian communities of Bethlehem and Nazareth commissioned a brewery at a new Moravian settlement near Nazareth called Christianbrunn, meaning "Christian spring." The thirty-by-fifty-foot limestone building had vaulted ceilings and an area for storing grain. By 1755 it was producing 187 barrels of beer annually and 789 gallons of whiskey for the Moravians and their neighbors. The Christianbrunn brewery was a source of revenue for the Moravians, as they sold some of the product to their non-Moravian neighbors.[15]

By 1783, with the growth of the community, the Bethlehem Moravians had built their own brewery at the bend of the Monocacy Creek before it flowed into the Lehigh River.[16] As clever as the Moravians were, they did not think about the brewery's being downstream from their butchery, tannery, and flax oil mill, all of which emptied effluent into the Monocacy upstream from the new brewery. Legend has it that the community was not happy with its own beer.

In 1803 a new brewer, Sebastian Gundt, also known as Johann Sebastian Goundie, arrived in Bethlehem to become chief brewer at the Moravian brewery. By 1811 he had become convinced that the brewery had to be moved upstream from the industrial activity along the Monocacy. A new brewery was quickly built and produced beer with a taste far superior to its predecessor, ensuring Goundie's name would be known to future generations. The position of brewer was so venerated that Goundie came to own the first private home in Bethlehem made of bricks; it is still standing on Main Street as part of Historic Bethlehem Museums and Sites.[17]

With good beer, orchards, and successful agriculture and animal husbandry operations, the Moravians also were also gracious hosts. In 1758 they built the Sun Inn as a hostelry for guests of the community and the traveling public. Because the inn was located almost two blocks from the town square and the residential buildings on Church Street (the square fronted what is now Central Moravian Church), non-Moravians could visit the village but not become too engaged in the daily routine of what was essentially a religious commune. The inn became known as a civilized place for colonial hospitality. The food was of much higher quality than what travelers expected in those days. Although the inn offered the multiperson sleeping accommodations common during that period, it also was one of the few establishments of its kind to offer private rooms and even a suite. Many members of the Continental Congress, as well as George and Martha Washington, stayed at the inn during their travels. Moravians, who were good bookkeepers, have the records to prove it.

During the difficult Revolutionary War winters of 1777 and 1778, with many casualties at Valley Forge and elsewhere, General Wash-

ington designated Bethlehem as a hospital for his army. Thousands
of soldiers were treated in Bethlehem, primarily at the Brethren's
House (now part of Moravian College). The First Avenue memorial
to these heroes of the Revolution notes that more than four hundred
American Revolutionary War soldiers died in Bethlehem during the
war. They were buried in graves near the site of the memorial.

CENTRAL MORAVIAN CHURCH AND GOD'S ACRE

As the community grew, the space for worship became squeezed.
The stone Old Chapel had been completed in 1750. This lovely
chapel is still used for worship, weddings, funeral services, and concerts, but it is small. In 1803 construction commenced on what
would be the Moravian community's architectural masterpiece,
Central Moravian Church. Designed with no interior columns to
hold the columned belfry that rises from the middle of the roof, the
church was the largest house of worship in Pennsylvania when it
was built. It seats twelve hundred people, large enough for the entire
community of the time and its missionary families.

The Moravian Cemetery, known as God's Acre, leaves a reminder
of the Moravians' perspective on the human race. The most famous
person buried in the cemetery is Tshoop, who is immortalized in
James Fenimore Cooper's *The Last of the Mohicans*, as the character
Uncas. Tshoop, who died in Bethlehem in 1746, was a Moravian
convert from upstate New York who was representative of the sect's
missionary spirit.[18] His headstone, like all the others in the cemetery, is a small rectangular piece of stone that quietly emphasizes the
Moravian belief that no person is above another. Women and men
are in different sections of the cemetery. Tshoop is buried with the
European immigrants, just another soul. Former African slaves lie
side by side with the rest of the deceased. God's Acre was the first
place in what is now the United States where Africans, Europeans,
and Native Americans all were buried together, as equal in death as
the Moravians saw them in life.

MORAVIAN LEGACY

The collection of Moravian buildings on Church Street is the largest of colonial era German-style buildings in the United States. The main reason for this is that all but the Gemeinhaus are made of stone and have been kept in the hands of the church and its related entities. More important than the buildings is the culture of the Moravians. They were educated, industrious, cultured, and civic minded. They kept copious records, in German, which was the official language of the community until it became a political entity in 1845. Today, when a colonial building in Bethlehem is slated for restoration, architects must consult the original documents that the congregation sent to the home community in Herrnhut to confirm the design of the building.

After the Revolutionary War the new United States was bursting with progress. Trade, industry, expansion, and a sense of opportunity pervaded the country. The tyranny of Europe was a thing of the past. And a village established to spread the gospel among the heathens had to adapt to being a town in a brand new country. At first the changes were slow in coming: a ferry across the Lehigh River, stage coach service to Philadelphia, trading with outsiders, renting rooms to nonchurch members, and celebrating the Fourth of July, which had been banned as a nonreligious activity in the first years after the Revolution. In 1815 the women of the community advised the elders that they would no longer wear the traditional *schneppel-haube*, a linen cap with a peak in the center of the forehead, but would now wear "English hats."[19] English services were offered in the Old Chapel, whereas the majority of residents, who spoke German, would attend German-language services in the new Central Moravian Church. By the end of the century this would be reversed, as only the elders spoke German.

Construction of the Lehigh Canal, which reached Bethlehem in 1826, brought outsiders, commerce, and dramatic change to the community. By 1828 the first piece of community property had been sold to private individuals who wanted sell provisions to canal boat operators. The church acted as civil government, landlord, cultural center, hospital, social safety net, and religious institution in what was no longer a society made up exclusively of its members.

The Panic of 1837 fully opened the community to outsiders. The financial panic started in Europe but quickly spread to the United States. By 1842 the crisis had "caused general losses for the businesses and in turn for the Society for the Propagation of the Gospel among the Heathen [the formal name for the church]," according to *A History of Bethlehem Pennsylvania, 1741–1892,* which was published in celebration of the 150th anniversary of the founding of Bethlehem.[20] By an act of the Pennsylvania General Assembly on March 6, 1845, the Borough of Bethlehem became a political entity of the Commonwealth of Pennsylvania, and the Moravian community became a part of the borough. German was no longer Bethlehem's official language. The community that the Moravians founded was about to change radically, becoming home to many newcomers attracted by the opportunities that the industrial revolution would offer.

Today the vast majority of Moravians are in Africa and the Caribbean, the result of the outreach by the European Moravians. Fewer than 5 percent of Bethlehem's residents are Moravians. What is so striking about the community that the Moravians established, and Bethlehem today, are not the differences but the similarities. Education, music, art, religion, and industry remain the core strengths of the city. Inclusion of people regardless of race, ethnicity, or economic status, is as important now as it was in colonial Bethlehem. And beer is still made, served, and enjoyed here, although residents drink much less of it than they did in colonial times.

After its first hundred years Bethlehem changed to meet changing times. The community opened its doors to new ideas, a new economy, and new residents, an openness its residents would need 150 years later.

CHAPTER 2
THE INDUSTRIALISTS

Natural resources, entrepreneurs, and location shaped Bethlehem's role in the enormous transition of the United States from an agrarian to an industrialized society during the nineteenth and twentieth centuries.

Nature prepared the Lehigh Valley for these vast changes, for it is blessed with deposits of zinc and iron ores as well as an abundance of limestone. Just to the north was one of the country's largest supplies of anthracite coal, soon to become better known as "black diamonds." All this natural wealth was only seventy-five miles from New York City and sixty-five miles from Philadelphia, the growing cities where coal powered the steam engines that ran the innovative industries and heated the buildings.

Local entrepreneurs developed the Lehigh Canal between 1820 and 1829 for the primary purpose of transporting that anthracite coal to the burgeoning commercial markets of Philadelphia and New York City. In Easton the Lehigh Canal meets the Delaware Canal, which provided access to both Philadelphia and New Jersey's Delaware and Raritan Canal; the latter was developed to move goods and raw materials to New York City. These entrepreneurs created a river of coal that passed right through Bethlehem, which still was a sleepy religious community with only twenty-eight hundred residents, less populous than the newer Allentown to the west and Easton along the Delaware River. That would quickly change.

The combination of natural resources, proximity to growing metropolitan areas, and a transportation system for delivering products made the Lehigh Valley a center of transportation, cement, iron, steel, and textiles and changed Bethlehem forever. The city at the center of the valley participated in all these industries as a result of the influence of industrialists, none of whom was from Bethlehem or was Moravian. Investors and industrialists from Philadelphia controlled, financed, or heavily influenced the transportation, iron, and steel industries. And investors and industrialists from New York heavily influenced the zinc and textile industries. Their vision and financial muscle transformed the region into one of the leading industrial centers in the country, hosting companies that became part of the American lexicon by the middle of the next century. Their stories are embedded in the fabric of today's Lehigh Valley.

SAMUEL WETHERILL AND JOSEPH WHARTON, LEHIGH ZINC COMPANY

My grandfather's family, with good German names like Miller, Garis, and Schaffer, settled just three miles south of Bethlehem, near the town of Friedensville in an area that became Upper Saucon Township in what is now Lehigh County. I have a small collection of beautiful Pennsylvania German Fraktur (milestone documents—birth certificates, marriage certificates, and *haus sagen*, or house sayings—decorated by itinerant artists) from this side of my family. The rarest and most interesting item in the collection is what's called a *vorschrift*, art that was used to teach the alphabet, with neatly written letters and decorative flowers. This treasured family heirloom is oddly connected to the development of the metal industry in Bethlehem.

Jacob Ueberroth, a neighbor of one of my ancestors, discovered ore on his farm as early as the 1830s. No one could identify the ore until Samuel Wetherill, a Philadelphian affiliated with the New Jersey Zinc Company, came to Friedensville in 1852 to check out the farmer's underground bounty. Wetherill, who had had just perfected a method of preparing zinc oxide from zinc ores for the New Jersey firm, knew exactly what Uebberoth had and its potential. By 1853, with capital provided by New York investors, Wetherill established the Lehigh Zinc Company and had leased four acres on the south side of the Lehigh River in Bethlehem near where the Lehigh Valley and North Philadelphia Railroads, then under construction, would meet. By October he had completed construction of a plant that produced four tons of zinc oxide per day and generated product worth $300,000 annually. Most of the oxide was used for white paint, although dozens of other applications, including munitions, increased demand. Bethlehem had its first successful metal business.[21]

That year Wetherill hired a twenty-seven-year-old fellow Philadelphian who also aspired to a career in mining and metals, Joseph Wharton. The man who would go on to cofound Swarthmore College, and establish the prestigious Wharton School of Business at the University of Pennsylvania, succeeded Wetherill as superintendent of the zinc operation in 1857. The enormously successful enterprise was only the second in the country to produce zinc oxide. Wharton wanted to take the next step, production of zinc spelter, a purer form of the metal that can be combined with other metals, such as copper to make brass. In 1859 Wharton contracted with a Belgian company to erect a zinc smelter in the style used in Europe. With the United States on the verge of civil war, and the North in need of munitions, the furnaces in Bethlehem were creating an especially valuable product.

When Wharton left the company in 1863, his net worth was nearly $130,000 (or about $3 million in 2016). He enrolled at Harvard to study math and later pursued a new venture in mining and producing nickel. The Lehigh Zinc Company in Bethlehem continued as a prosperous operation that employed more than seven hundred people through the end of the century. In 1897 New Jersey Zinc acquired Lehigh Zinc and three other zinc producers, then consolidated its manufacturing operations in its newly formed company town, Palmerton, Pennsylvania, about twenty-four miles northwest of Bethlehem. The Bethlehem plant was closed in 1911 and acquired by the Bethlehem Steel Corporation.[22]

Although Wetherill and Wharton were the first to start a nationally successful metal production enterprise in Bethlehem, they would not be the last.

ASA PACKER—LEHIGH VALLEY RAILROAD AND BETHLEHEM IRON COMPANY

Church Street in the 200 block, where my family has lived for forty years, is the first city street on the north side of the Lehigh River; the Norfolk Southern Railroad runs on tracks directly across the river from our home. We no longer notice the whistles and clanking of the trains, although guests invariably comment on the noise, which persists day and night. The sounds are the echo of a man whose influence on Bethlehem is impossible to miss.

His name was Asa Packer. His iron highway still carries freight trains, assembled in the Allentown yards just west of Bethlehem, through the town and on to New Jersey and New York. The railroad is only a small portion of his legacy, which includes Lehigh University and the steel industry that dominated the region for most of the twentieth century.

Packer was a poor man from Mystic, Connecticut, who moved to the anthracite coal region of eastern Pennsylvania in 1834, when he was twenty-nine. He settled in Mauch Chunk, now Jim Thorpe, a town that commands a strategic point as the Lehigh River winds through the southern ridges of the coal-laden Appalachian Mountains in eastern Pennsylvania. Ambitious and smart, he took advantage of the Lehigh Canal, first as an operator and builder of canal boats, then as a store owner with shops along various canal routes.[23] Eventually he served in the Pennsylvania legislature, two terms in the U.S. House of Representatives, and was an associate judge of the Carbon County court.

In 1851 Packer acquired the Delaware, Lehigh, Schuylkill & Susquehanna Railroad, which ran for about twenty miles between Wilkes-Barre and the Lehigh Canal at White Haven and was foundering because of undercapitalization. Aware that demand for rail transport was growing—drought or ice too often disrupted canal shipments—he began building a rail line from Mauch Chunk to Easton and renamed his holdings the Lehigh Valley Railroad.[24] His team for the project included Robert Sayre, chief civil engineer; Packer's nephew Elisha P. Wilbur, who oversaw the finances; and Garrett Linderman, Packer's son-in-law.

The new line was completed in September 1855. Bethlehem was its most strategic point because a group of Philadelphia investors was developing a second railroad, the North Pennsylvania Railroad, to profit from giving coal country direct access to Philadelphia through the Lehigh Valley. Demand for coal to heat homes and power businesses in the Philadelphia region was growing. The North Pennsylvania Railroad line came through South Bethlehem (on the south side of the Lehigh River, where the Moravians had maintained a few farms before 1850) to connect with the Lehigh Valley Railroad in July 1857. Both ventures were extremely successful. The cost of coal continued to rise during the Civil War.

As the industry boomed, Lehigh Coal and Navigation, owner of the Lehigh Canal, built its own railroad, the Lehigh and Susquehanna, on the north bank of the Lehigh River by 1868. South Bethlehem had become a railroad hub. Hotels, bars, and repair facilities flourished.[25]

As he was building his empire, Packer saw the wisdom of creating an iron foundry to serve the railroad. When Augustus Wolle, a Bethlehem merchant who was a Moravian, created the Saucona Iron Company in South Bethlehem adjacent to the Lehigh Zinc Company, Packer and Sayre invested in Wolle's business and ultimately took control. The financial resources of Packer and his associates, as well as the guarantee of having the railroad as a customer, assured the company of a position in the burgeoning rail industry; it was renamed Bethlehem Iron Works in 1861.

After 1856 the British began producing steel rails using the Bessemer method and exporting the rails to the United States. Most rails in the United States were made of iron, which was brittle and could not stand up to the increasing weight and speed of trains as they became modernized and hauled more tonnage. Because of its association with the Lehigh Valley Railroad and Packer's access to capital, only the Bethlehem Iron Company, among the dozens of other budding ironworks in the Lehigh Valley, was in a position to compete by adopting the Bessemer technology. The new plant rolled its first steel rails in the fall of 1873 and began filling orders for the Lehigh Valley and Jersey Central (which was now operating the former Lehigh & Susquehanna) railroads.[26]

Packer, Sayre, and Packer's nephew Wilbur saw an opportunity: manufacturing steel for armor plating, as well as for cannons and munitions. The United States had allowed its navy to languish after the Civil War, and by the 1880s its ships were hopelessly outdated; the U.S. Navy ranked only twelfth in the western hemisphere. In 1883 Congress authorized construction of new steel warships. Bethlehem Iron built the first open hearth furnace in the United States in 1888; it was an improvement over the Bessemer furnaces; like the Bessemer, it could use molten pig iron, but it could also use cold pig iron and scrap metal, which increased the quantity, quality, and variety of products the company could make.[27]

Bethlehem Iron won $4 million in defense contracts (the equivalent of more than $110 million in 2016) from the U.S. government in 1887, the beginning of a long history of armaments and munitions manufacture in Bethlehem. In 1899 the Board of Directors of Bethlehem Iron reorganized the company, adding more capital and renaming it Bethlehem Steel Company. In 1901 the board agreed to sell the company to Charles Schwab.[28]

Packer and his team—Sayre, Wilbur, and Linderman—constituted the Episcopalian elite of Bethlehem in their day. They were deeply engaged in the community and helped establish enduring institutions that are integral to the community today. All generously supported the fledgling Lehigh University. They helped establish and support St. Luke's Hospital. And they were the force behind the Cathedral Church of the Nativity, home to the Episcopal Diocese of Bethlehem, which covers fourteen counties to the north and west of Philadelphia.[29]

The only remnant of the original Bethlehem Iron furnace complex is the former stock house, for storing materials for iron making; thoroughly renovated, today it is the Bethlehem Visitor Center at SteelStacks. The state-of-the art Bessemer furnace and rolling mills survive as a ruin adjacent to SteelStacks, identified as "Iron Foundry," by a sign on Second Street.

The Victorian-era passenger station for the Jersey Central Railroad adjacent to the tracks in the Bethlehem Historic District (also called the Moravian Historic District) has been a restaurant for many years. The abandoned Jersey Central tracks from Bethlehem to Easton are part of the Delaware and Lehigh Heritage Corridor, a 165-mile trail through five counties that preserves the river, rail, and canal corridor, tells its history, and connects people to nature and the communities and cultures from Wilkes-Barre to Bristol.

As a center for logistics, education, and innovation, Bethlehem continues to benefit from the vision of Asa Packer and his team. The Lehigh Valley Railroad is now part of the Norfolk Southern Railroad, an active freight highway, although passenger service from the Lehigh Valley to Philadelphia ended in the mid-1970s. The rails today have made the Lehigh Valley a center of logistics for the mid-Atlantic region; the valley's intermodal rail-to-truck facility is seeking to become an inland international port.

CHARLES MICHAEL SCHWAB AND EUGENE GIFFORD GRACE—BETHLEHEM STEEL CORPORATION

Charlie Schwab is an outlier on the short list of industrialists who influenced Bethlehem during the industrial revolution. The only Catholic, a high school dropout, a philanderer, and a gambler, Schwab was born in 1862 to a humble family in Williamsburg, a small town along the Juniata River in central Pennsylvania.

Schwab had no formal education, but he apparently did have a sharp memory and the capacity to learn quickly: he rose from a stake driver on a survey team to become a protégé of the great Andrew Carnegie. He promoted Schwab to president of Carnegie Steel in 1897. In 1901 Schwab negotiated a merger with the steel interests of J. Pierpont Morgan to create U.S. Steel, the first billion-dollar corporation in the United States. Schwab, by then a part owner of Carnegie Steel, received $25 million in the new corporation's bonds and at the age of thirty-nine became its first president. He moved to New York City and built a mansion, Riverside. With seventy-five rooms, a swimming pool, wine cellar, art gallery, gymnasium, and its own power plant, the Schwab mansion, on a full block on Riverside Drive, was the largest private residence in New York City.[30]

In May 1901 Schwab purchased the Bethlehem Steel Company for himself. In 1902 Schwab leveraged his interest in Bethlehem Steel to create a new company, U.S. Shipbuilding, which combined the steel manufacturer with seven shipyards on both coasts to create a shipbuilding giant. Through a complex series of financial dealings that were vilified in the press and the courts, Schwab wound up personally controlling both the Bethlehem Steel Company and the shipyards, most of which he quickly sold off. With criticism mounting, Schwab resigned from U.S. Steel in August 1904, saying he was going to focus on Bethlehem Steel.

On December 10, 1904, he incorporated Bethlehem Steel with $30 million in capital. Schwab moved from New York to South Bethlehem to take command. "I intend to make Bethlehem the prize steelworks of its class, not only in the United States but in the entire world," he declared. Schwab needed money to build the Grey mill, a process for rolling wide-flange beams and columns in a single section directly from an ingot. The wide-flange beams would revolutionize construction, paving the way for skyscrapers and bridges of unimaginable height and length. But first he would have to gamble the company's future to get the money to build the mill. He famously told his secretary: "I have thought the whole thing over, and if we are going bust, we will go bust big." His old mentor, Andrew Carnegie, loaned him the money to complete the installation of the Grey mill.[31]

The Grey mill produced the Bethlehem beam, which became the symbol of the company and was the structural steel product that established Bethlehem's prowess in twentieth-century construction. By 1910 the company had ninety-two hundred employees, a company band, and the first of many periods of labor strife that would disrupt the company throughout its history.

To a large extent Schwab achieved his vision. By producing structural steel, armor, ships, cannons, and ordinance for the U.S. and foreign navies, Bethlehem Steel reached stratospheric production levels and profits during World War I. By the end of the war the Bethlehem plant employed thirty-one thousand people, and the city of Bethlehem, formally incorporated in 1917 to include Bethlehem, South Bethlehem, and West Bethlehem, was a newly minted industrial city of more than twenty-five thousand.[32]

Eugene Gifford Grace, also born into a humble household (in 1876), started his rapid ascent at Bethlehem Steel when, as the story goes, Schwab asked an assistant to name the company's most outstanding employee. The response reportedly was immediate and emphatic: E. G. Grace. Schwab mentored Grace, who rose from assistant superintendent to general superintendent to general manger by 1908, when the Grey mill commenced production and the company was experiencing explosive growth. By 1911 Grace was vice president and five years later, at the age of thirty-nine, president. In 1918 Grace became the country's highest-paid executive, earning at least $600,000 per year ($9.7 million in 2016) for the next two decades.

Schwab, who had moved back to New York, continued to draw a salary of $150,000 per year in the 1920s as chair of Bethlehem

Steel's board, which he and Grace completely controlled. He lived a high life in his mansion. But his stock market losses during the Great Depression and the extravagances of his New York lifestyle caused Schwab to lose his mansion to Chase National Bank in early 1939. He died a few months later after suffering a heart attack in his Park Avenue apartment. He was $338,349 in debt, which Grace had the company pay off to maintain Schwab's reputation.

Neither Schwab nor Grace believed in research, innovation, or labor unions. But on the eve of World War II, with the establishment of the National Labor Relations Board and the ruling by President Franklin D. Roosevelt's National Defense Commission that only companies complying with the National Labor Relations Act could receive military contracts, Grace had few options. He was forced to sign an agreement with the United Steelworkers in 1941.

Grace's shining hours came during World War II. A staunch Republican, he despised Roosevelt but was a patriot. Grace announced in January 1943 that Bethlehem Steel would build one ship a day for the war effort. From its steel plants and shipyards on both coasts, Bethlehem Steel became the arsenal of democracy. On December 31, 1943, broadcasting from a destroyer in Bethlehem Steel's Staten Island shipyard, Grace announced that Bethlehem Steel had built 380 ships that year, exceeding his pledge. Seventy percent of the ships produced were battleships, aircraft carriers, light and heavy cruisers, destroyer escorts, and landing craft for the Navy. The other 30 percent were cargo ships for the merchant marine.[33]

By the end of World War II Bethlehem Steel had produced 73.4 million tons of steel for a third of the armor plate and gun forgings the Navy required; 80 percent of all parts for radial, air-cooled engines on planes used by the Army Air Forces and the Navy; and untold quantities of munitions. The company also built 1,085 fighting ships, cargo vessels, and tankers, making it the largest shipbuilder in the world. Bethlehem Steel also repaired, converted, or serviced 37,778 ships.[34]

Despite these historic achievements, Grace had weaknesses that did not serve the company well in the long run. Chief among them was that, unlike Carnegie and Schwab, he saw no reason to mentor a successor. His rule is best described in "Forging America: The Story of Bethlehem Steel," the elegant obituary for the company published in 2003 by the *Morning Call*:

> But Grace also unwittingly planted the seeds of doom for this great enterprise. He was an autocrat who failed to groom a successor....He created a closed culture hostile to outsiders. He sacrificed innovation for short term profits....He paid himself and other executives exorbitant amounts that, while insignificant for a company of its size, betrayed a smug and ultimately misguided belief that the world would always need Bethlehem's steel. He treated organized labor with contempt, fostering a distrust that soured management-union relationships to the end.[35]

Grace retired in 1957, the year that an article in *Business Week* named Bethlehem Steel executives as seven of the top ten highest paid in the country.

Eugene Grace clearly thought that his greatest legacy would be the thriving steel empire he had led. To keep an eternal eye on it, he purchased a knoll in Nisky Hill Cemetery overlooking the Lehigh River and the iconic blast furnaces of Bethlehem Steel's home plant. The mausoleum is unlike the vertical colonnaded structures of his wealthy predecessors. It is a flat circle of marble partially bordered by a rose marble bench with ample seats, all of which face the steel plant. The monument will far outlast his company, which survived him by only forty-three years.

R. K. LAROS—SILK AND THE RISE OF TEXTILES

The zinc, iron, steel, and other industries were indirectly responsible for the development of the silk and textile industries in the Lehigh Valley. Workers who came from southern and central Europe were accompanied by wives who had skills in the textile arts of spinning, weaving, and sewing. The region's proximity to eastern markets also was important in the growth of the textile industry.[36]

Silk operations took hold in Allentown, Catasauqua, Fountain Hill, and Bethlehem in the late 1800s. Several were established in Bethlehem between 1885 and the early 1900s, including one at the western tip of Sand Island, in the Lehigh River. However, the mill that would have the greatest impact on the community was a late-comer. In 1919 a young Lafayette College graduate from nearby Easton, who had honed his business skills in New York, decided to go into business for himself. Between 1914 and 1919 the value of all silk products produced in the United States had almost tripled, from $254 million to $688 million. With capital from his wife's parents, who owned the Eagle Brewing Company in Catasauqua, Russell Keller Laros launched R. K. Laros Silk Company at facilities in Miller Heights, just outside the Bethlehem city limits. In 1922 Laros developed a larger facility on East Broad Street in Bethlehem and moved the business there. The building remains today.

The manufacture of silk and the availability of skilled female labor led to the development of a major textile industry in the region. Bethlehem manufacturers produced everything from brassieres (a factory on Conestoga Street now known as the Conestoga Condominiums) to blouses (now the Banana Factory Arts Center) to slipcovers. But few makers of silk expanded into the manufacture of clothing from the silk they produced. Laros recognized the opportunity and in 1926 began a line of ladies' undergarments—slips. The venture was a big success.

Laros became a leader in the industry, publishing the *Laros Data Book*, technical documents outlining measurements and grading criteria for silk thread. The annual booklet became somewhat of an industry standard. Laros went on to create the strongest woven seam in the undergarment industry, the "Perma Lokt" seam.[37]

During the Great Depression Laros remained in operation. One reason he was able to do so was that he did not have great financial losses in the stock market. The story goes that a banker advised Laros that the stock market was going to suffer a great calamity. Laros sold his stocks and put away a substantial amount of cash just before the market crashed. The money was sufficient to meet his business needs throughout the Depression and to fund the construction of Sunset Acres, his new family home in Bethlehem. The construction provided much-needed work for laid-off construction workers, who were paid in cash.

After Pearl Harbor the R. K. Laros Company, like virtually all other manufacturers in the country, was converted to wartime needs. Between 1943 and 1945 the company made uniforms, naval signal flags, and parachutes. The majority of the parachutes were for fragmentation bombs, which weighed twenty-three to ninety pounds and were designed for low-altitude bombing runs. Using the parachutes allowed the planes to escape before the bomb went off. Laros made more than 100,000 parachutes in Bethlehem during the war.[38]

Laros died in December 1955. The family sold the business and property. An established company called Sure Fit, which made slip-covers, bought the building and weaving equipment. Like many textile companies that had survived the Depression, Sure Fit continued to operate in Bethlehem until the 1980s, when far less expensive foreign labor made it impossible to continue this type of manufacturing in the United States.

Russell Keller Laros provided leadership and resources for several nonprofit organizations in Bethlehem, including St. Luke's Hospital, the YMCA, and the Bach Choir. He and his wife, Helen, also established the R. K. Laros Foundation, which has provided support for capital projects for nonprofit organizations in Bethlehem since 1952. It is the only independent foundation created by a Bethlehem industrialist to support the community

SAM BORN, AND IRVIN AND JACK SHAFFER—CONFECTIONERS

Sam Born, who was born in 1891 and grew up in czarist Russia, learned his trade in Paris and wandered the United States from coast to coast and improbably ended up in a Pennsylvania city of modest size. When he was still in Europe, he had wanted to study to be a rabbi but needed to make a living as well. In early twentieth-century Paris, Born learned the art of confection as an employee of a chocolatier. French chocolate was the rage in Europe and America. Within two years of arriving in France, Born had enough knowledge to make a living and enough savings for a steamer ticket to New York in 1908.

From New York he traveled to the west coast, staying in San Francisco long enough to invent a machine that inserted sticks into lollipops, the Born sucker machine. He then moved back to Manhattan, married Ann Shaffer, and set up his small confection factory in a loft at 8 East Twelfth Street in Greenwich Village. After a difficult experience as a chocolate retailer, in 1923 Born decided that he would focus on what he did best, making confections, and wholesale the product to retailers, including department stores, which were creating candy counters. He leased space in Brooklyn and started manufacturing and selling candy. As the business grew, he brought in his brothers-in-law, Irvin and Jack Shaffer. Irvin was an engineer and Jack was a businessman, financier, and salesman.[39]

A stroke of luck saved Sam Born's business from the Great Depression. He was in bed in his Manhattan home one evening in October 1929 when someone knocked on the door. His perplexed wife found the family's banker was calling; he insisted that Born immediately accompany him to the bank. The banker gave Sam a withdrawal slip and told him to sign it and take all his money out of the bank then and there. The bank closed the next day. Like the Laros family, the Born-Shaffer family understands that life might have been much different if not for that trusted relationship. Ross Born, grandson of Sam Born, and David Shaffer, son of Jack Shaffer, who serve as co-presidents of Just Born, told me that this history is why a principle of their business is trusting relationships.

By 1932 Just Born needed more space. Bethlehem needed a new tenant for vacant building that was to be auctioned by the bankruptcy court. A Born family member read about the bankruptcy sale and decided to take the train to Bethlehem and see what the possibilities were. In what became one of Bethlehem's early economic development coups, Born and the Shaffers decided that the building would meet their needs and allow for growth. That Bethlehem had a large immigrant population made them feel welcome. And they figured the wives of steel and metal workers might be good at the largely handmade process of creating confections. Within a few years the company was employing more than two hundred workers to hand-dip chocolates and other confections.[40]

In that factory Born and his team had room to tinker. Just Born was making "chocolate grains," tiny pieces of chocolate for use in dished ice cream. However, in the days before air conditioning, the grains were melting in the ice cream parlors before they could be sprinkled on ice cream. Sam Born made a new product with coconut oil and cocoa powder that did not melt as quickly. The name of the production line worker who made the tiny chocolate delights was Jimmy, and that is why they are called jimmies, Ross Born and David Shaffer said.

The owners of Just Born place a high priority on their relationship with their employees, caring about good people who are hardworking and want to give their best. According to Ross Born and David Shaffer, African Americans began moving to the community just after World War II. A black woman was hired to work in the factory. Two employees approached Bob Born, Sam Born's son, and said, "You don't expect us to work next to a black woman, do you?" Bob Born replied, "No, not at all. You can leave now if you want."

In 1953 the acquisition of the Rodda Candy Company of Lancaster, Pennsylvania, continued Just Born in the highly specialized world of candy manufacturing, marketing, and distribution. "We acquired Rodda because it produced "world famous jelly beans" (at least that's what the marketing materials said!) according to Ross Born. Just Born had introduced Mike and Ike, its iconic jelly bean brand, in 1940, and Hot Tamales, its hot cinnamon jelly beans, in 1950. That made Rodda a good fit. Rodda also had hollow-molded chocolate products, like Easter bunnies, which was not continued by Just Born. Rodda also produced marshmallow candy that was formed by hand into a variety of shapes, such as hot dogs in a bun, strawberry short cakes and chicks. The confection, which was produced and decorated by "women in the back room," was not a big seller, Born and Shaffer said.

Bob Born asked Sam, Jack, and Irv if they wanted to continue this product line. He said he could make a machine that would produce the marshmallows in a variety of shapes, a much less labor-intensive method. They gave him the go-ahead. After nine months of assembly and testing, Born and Joe Truse, the plant engineer, created the marshmallow production machine. Over the many years since the original machine, which was in service until 2014, was developed, Marshmallow PEEPS® has grown into America's largest non-chocolate confectionery brand for the Easter season. It was through the tenacity, creativity and desire to succeed on the part of the Born and Shaffer Families that a truly iconic brand, Peeps® was "born"![41]

CHAPTER 3
IMMIGRANTS AND MIGRANTS

A s the industrial revolution roared through the late nineteenth and early twentieth centuries, Bethlehem's location offered immigrants fleeing poverty and persecution the opportunity to seek a decent future for themselves and their children. The city is only seventy miles west of Ellis Island, and the immigrants' labor was in demand here.

The massive influx of immigrants eclipsed the steady German emigration to Pennsylvania that had been under way since the 1700s. Twelve million people passed through Ellis Island between 1892 and 1924, first the Irish, then a flood of emigres from throughout Europe, seeking any work that would improve their lives. Bethlehem received its fair share, and they became the people who built railroads and made zinc and iron. They brought with them their customs, language, food, and culture.

Each group had a place of assembly, usually a church and frequently a social hall, that facilitated communications with the old country and sending money back home. Some churches moved to other parts of Bethlehem or its suburbs as their congregants moved; some have been demolished or repurposed. With a population approaching thirty thousand in 1929, the south side (the former Borough of South Bethlehem; see the preface) was said to have had more than fifty houses of worship.⁴²

Luring immigrants to Bethlehem were the industries rising on the south side of the Lehigh River. Before World War I the Irish and Germans primarily satisfied the needs of local employers. Smaller groups of Italians and the diverse ethnicities of the Russian and Austro-Hungarian Empires also arrived at that period. The influx of immigrants increased dramatically with the dissolution of the Russian Empire and Austria-Hungary, and poverty in Italy, especially in Sicily and the southern part of the peninsula, drove mass emigration (which peaked at 900,000 in 1913).[43] As the steel plant hired men from these nationalities, it frequently segregated them by nationality, partly for convenience of communication and partly so that management could control them. Management believed that keeping the workforce divided rendered organized labor unrest difficult, a theory that proved flawed.

Europe was not the only source of labor for Bethlehem's industries. After World War I, Bethlehem Steel could not hire fast enough to keep up with production. The company also was contending with strong anti-immigrant, right-wing sentiment against allowing the flow of Europeans into the country to continue. However, in a twist on today's immigration politics, immigration from Mexico was unrestricted in the 1920s. Mexican workers became a plentiful and inexpensive source of labor. Many steel companies with plants in major metropolitan areas hired workers who had formed the Great Migration of African Americans from the agricultural South to the industrial North. Bethlehem Steel did not.

But Bethlehem Steel actively recruited from Mexico. The jobs awaiting the Mexican workers were the dirtiest and most dangerous, with long hours and low pay. Bethlehem Steel also liked that the Mexicans spoke Spanish and would therefore have difficulty communicating with the southern and eastern European workforce already in place. In 1923 Bethlehem Steel reached an agreement with the Mexican government to bring nine hundred unskilled laborers to Bethlehem.[44]

In a comment typical of the times, a company executive said that most of the Mexicans were "good steady workers. As a class, their intelligence is above the Slavish [Slovaks] and Wendish [Slovenians]....If some people think the Mexicans are dumb, they should see our Irish."[45]

Many Mexican workers were appalled at the grim existence that awaited them at the end of their long journey. They were housed in company-built dormitories with their families. By 1930 only 350 Mexicans remained in the workforce. In 1937 the roughly fifty families that had stayed in Bethlehem created the Mexican Azteca Club, which was a fixture of south side cultural life until the 1980s. The descendants of the Mexicans who arrived in the 1920s now are thoroughly integrated in the regional community through intermarriage, and, as is true of most of the European ethnic groups, there is no appreciable Mexican community to be found today.

After World War II the economy exploded in a period of enormous growth, and Bethlehem Steel's fortunes rose with the tide. Because of the baby bust of the Depression years, there were not a lot of young men eager to hire on for the hard labor of the steel plant. By 1948, as the plant was again gearing up to meet the needs of major infrastructure projects in the United States and the world's demand to rebuild all that had been destroyed by war, the labor problem was major. Just as Bethlehem Steel had turned to Mexicans in the 1920s, the postwar company encouraged Puerto Ricans to come to Bethlehem for jobs as unskilled laborers. The path was wide open because Puerto Ricans were U.S. citizens and work was plentiful.

Ismael Garcia, now a regular at the Basilio Huertas Senior Center at the Hispanic Center of the Lehigh Valley on Fourth Street in Bethlehem, left his hometown of Humacao, Puerto Rico, in 1946 to work in San Juan. In 1952 he came to Allentown with a cousin for agricultural work but got a job at a chicken-processing plant. In March 1952 he heard that Bethlehem Steel was hiring. He spoke little English, but when he walked into the employment office, he was hired immediately and started as a manual laborer the next day at the coke works, where impurities, water, coal gas, and coal tar were burned off, creating the purer carbon used in the blast furnaces, and an ash residue. The coke works was a dirty place to work.

Garcia spent the next thirty-eight years as a member of United Steelworkers Local 2600, working in the coke works and becoming a shop steward. He learned English by watching television and reading newspapers. He met his wife, Carmen, at a friend's birthday party in 1953. After they married, they rented an apartment on Hill Street (as its name implies, it's lots of fun in the winter), when only one other Puerto Rican lived in the building. They attended Holy Infancy Church, which was already ministering to the Portuguese and Irish communities. Garcia was one of the founders of the Puerto Rican Beneficial Society, which, like similar organizations formed by other groups, offers assistance to members new to the community, including financial help, access to government programs, and advice about travel, banking, and health care. He remembers that the

Puerto Rican community was well treated. The eighty-seven-year-old says, "I love Puerto Rico, but Bethlehem is my city. I would have never had the life there that I have here. This is the greatest country." Today Bethlehem is 28 percent Hispanic, and the vast majority are Puerto Rican.[46]

BEER

Another Bethlehem legacy is a devotion to beer.

The city never was a place where the concept of prohibition gained much traction. The Moravians had long manufactured a quality beer, and soon after trains began running on the Lehigh Valley Railroad, a German immigrant, Joseph Rennig, and his wife, Anna, opened a new brewery. The Rennigs had purchased land adjacent a natural spring and to a large park, soon to become the campus of Lehigh University, in 1860. Rennig built a brewery, hotel, and beer garden, which he named Die Alte Braueri (the Old Brewery).[47] The brewery attracted local iron and railroad workers and became a success. As the university grew between its founding in 1865 and the new century, students patronized the brewery as well. Lehigh's theatrical company, Mustard and Cheese, was started in the beer garden while its founders were enjoying some food with their beer. The university purchased the property in 1912.

And as the town grew, so did the desire for beer. The South Bethlehem Brewing Company opened in 1902. By 1915 it had expanded to a six-story building to accommodate the demand for its product. The brewery offered porter and ale under the brands Supreme and Heirloom. According to the evidence, the brewery was active even during Prohibition. Rumor had it that Bethlehem Steel's management believed that access to beer was important to keeping its labor force happy. And it is doubtful that the executives shunned alcohol during this period.

According to local legend, during the Roaring Twenties beer pipelines ran under Third Street, and residents didn't have to look hard to find speakeasies and "loose women." The South Bethlehem Brewing Company closed in 1954. In 1966, when the building was being torn down, workers found a trapdoor built into a baseboard behind a five-foot-high, six-hundred-pound safe. They turned over to the police what they found—1920s currency that totaled as much as $200,000.[48]

MUSIC

The city's long love affair with music, begun by the Moravians, expanded with its industrialization. Through the centuries, in good times and bad, music always was at the center of city life. This long tradition continued through the Civil War with the Philharmonic Society, which was a continuation of the Collegium Musicum of Central Moravian Church. When the Philharmonic Society dwindled in the early 1880s, J. Fred Wolle, then only nineteen, filled the musical gap by forming the Bethlehem Choral Union in 1882. During the ten years of its existence, the Choral Union gave twenty-one concerts devoted to the music of Handel, Haydn, Mendelssohn, and Bach. After performing Bach's *St. John Passion* in 1888, the members of the Choral Union rebelled at Wolle's efforts to perform the difficult Bach's Mass in B Minor, which led to the dissolution of the organization.[49]

Wolle then formed the Bethlehem Bach Choir and performed the Mass on March 27, 1900, in Central Moravian Church, a concert that is considered the first Bach Festival. The Bach Choir mounted a second festival in May 1901, followed by festivals in 1903 and 1905. Then Wolle left to chair the music department at the University of California, Berkeley, and the choir disbanded. However, in 1911 Bethlehem Steel's Charles Schwab, a music lover, worked with the community to lure Wolle back to Bethlehem to continue his work with the Bach Choir.[50] Schwab served as president of the choir for several years. He, Grace, Laros, and others continued to support this important community institution, which today remains a thriving local cultural asset.

The oldest instrumental group in Bethlehem is the Bethlehem Moravian Trombone Choir. The author Raymond Walters reports, "Band music in Bethlehem extends back to 1809, when David Moritz Michael organized a military band for the annual Whit-Monday boat ride on the Lehigh River." The town also boasted the Bethlehem Brass Band from 1839 to 1843 and a similar organization, the

Bethlehem Coronet Band, dating from 1861. The Keystone Band was active in the 1890s.[51]

Even before Schwab became involved with the choir, one of his first moves after Bethlehem Steel became successful was to create the sixty-piece Bethlehem Steel Band. The band's first official performance was on December 23, 1910, at a Christmas dinner Schwab gave for his managers. The band continued to play for special public and business events. Schwab purchased a house on Market Street as a rehearsal hall for the band. Today the house is part of Moravian Academy. New bands, orchestras, and even an opera company emerged during the early twentieth century. A private entertainment grove known as Central Park was developed on land along the major trolley line between Allentown and Bethlehem. Through the first half of the twentieth century the park featured live music, dancing, and, of course, beer.

The diverse immigrants of Bethlehem created music in their houses of worship and in their social halls. For most of the immigrants from central and eastern Europe, popular music was a dance that started in Bohemia, now part of the Czech Republic, in the early 1800s. The dance sensation of the period was polka. The captivating music with the 2-4 rhythm spread throughout eastern and central Europe and even to Italy, Britain, France, the Netherlands, and Scandinavia. Polka became deeply rooted in the United States, especially in places known for their beer.

Each culture offered its own variation of the polka. Today it is not the sensation it once was, but many still think of it as their traditional dance.

Bethlehem's immigrants and their progeny formed the majority of the local labor force during the industrial revolution and into the twentieth century. They worked hard for their pay and benefits, and, like their counterparts throughout the United States, settled into a comfortable middle-class life in the immediate postwar decades of the 1950s and 1960s. But ahead was adversity that they could not then imagine.

CHAPTER 4
SPRAWL, BLIGHT, PRESERVATION, AND RENEWAL

The United States emerged from World War II as the strongest nation on Earth and with a population eager to have kids, buy homes, and settle into a safe, comfortable life. Although geography had shielded the country from the devastation suffered by Europe and Asia, the infrastructure of the United States had nonetheless deteriorated because of the diversion of resources to the war effort. Neat but shabby described Bethlehem and many other U.S. cities in 1945.

The American dream of the postwar years was a house, with a yard, plumbing and modern appliances, and a car for Dad to drive to work, take the family shopping, and on the occasional vacation. In 1940 27.5 million automobiles were registered in the United States. By the end of the war, with production focused on military vehicles, that number had dropped to 25.8 million. By 1950 Americans had 40.3 million cars on the road.[52]

The hunger for home ownership and a desperate housing shortage caused by the demands of war led to government action. As a result of the New Deal, most communities already had a housing authority designed to provide affordable housing for low- and moderate-income families, the elderly, and people with disabilities. Fannie Mae, a major mortgage lender, had been established as a federal agency in 1938 to encourage banks to offer long-term, low-rate mortgages for private homes. After the war Congress enhanced government support of home ownership by offering veterans mortgages through the Veterans Administration. The loans, a godsend for millions of families, also financed the phenomenon that became known as suburban sprawl.[53]

These were sweeping changes in American life. Another major change came from passage of the first Federal-Aid Highway Act in 1956, affirming the country's commitment to the automobile and to subsidizing motor vehicle transportation instead of railroads and other mass transit. Whether Congress intended to enhance real estate development outside cities is unclear, but the financial support offered for construction of interstate highways further encouraged the development of suburbia. Those who had the best jobs, whether as a rigger at Bethlehem Steel or a bank manager, could afford the new tract house and car to go with it, while those with lower incomes, frequently senior citizens and minorities, took over the smaller row homes and apartments in the city that the new suburbanites had vacated. Retail establishments gradually followed their customers from the urban core to the new malls of the suburbs or simply went out of business.

Poverty inevitably settled in center-city neighborhoods, which became afflicted with high crime, drugs, abandoned buildings, and poor schools. Retail in these neighborhoods catered to some needs of the residents: pawn shops, tattoo parlors, bodegas, check-cashing operations, and the like replaced the deli, clothing stores, music stores, and grocery stores.

How hard these seismic shifts hit a city sometimes depended on esoteric change with major consequences. In Pennsylvania a state law relating to city expansion touched off some of these shifts. Until 1968 the state's constitution allowed one municipality to annex a portion of another if voters of the annexing municipality and the voters of the portion to be annexed voted in favor of the action in a referendum. But that year an amendment to the state constitution set a higher bar: approval by a majority of all voters, even those who would not be affected, in the municipality with the portion up for annexation. The change brought annexation to a halt. Cities that had already annexed portions of the burgeoning suburbs around them faced the future in better shape than those restricted by prewar boundaries.

The history of a city's school district also dictated its progress in the latter part of the twentieth century. Before World War II and the immediate postwar years, public education in industrial centers like Bethlehem was of a far higher quality and offered more opportunity than in rural areas. Rural townships adjacent to cities were eager to become a part of the city's school district to gain access to the superior education the city school district offered. That changed in the 1960s as rural townships became suburban townships and as urban school districts began to face numerous challenges, while tax dollars flowed into the coffers of suburban districts.

Bethlehem and neighboring Allentown took opposite approaches. In the 1950s and '60s both school districts were excellent, with advanced science and mathematics programs as well as music and art, supported by the wealth of their industrial bases.

When the City of Allentown annexed a portion of South Whitehall Township to the western edge of the city, that portion was not simultaneously annexed into the school district. Today, west Allentown is the wealthiest area of the city, but a portion of it is in the Parkland School District, not the Allentown district. The city can use the excellence of the Parkland district to attract residents to a small section of town, but most of the city struggles with an urban school district that is not supported by taxes from some of the wealthiest Allentown residents.

In contrast in the early 1960s the Bethlehem School District agreed to merge neighboring Hanover Township and Bethlehem Township, which at the time were primarily farmland, into the city school district. Since then both townships have become wealthy suburbs and contribute substantially to the school district. Today the Allentown School District and the Bethlehem Area School District are, respectively, the fifth- and sixth-largest school districts in the state. Bethlehem has a mix of urban and suburban elementary schools and racially and economically mixed middle and high schools. The Allentown district is a predominantly minority district with a majority of students from low-income families.

Pennsylvania's archaic system of local government has spawned hyperlocal governance and acted as a barrier to regionalization, creating winner townships and loser cities across the commonwealth, not to mention long-term employment for a legion of lawyers and consultants. Within this environment the state's industrial cities fought a losing battle in the second half of the twentieth century.

SUBURBANIZATION IN BETHLEHEM

The roughly sixty thousand people of Bethlehem, home to mighty Bethlehem Steel, had every right to expect prosperity as they emerged from World War II, which they had helped win.[54] Although the war had brought my parents together, the powerful pull of opportunity was what determined my hometown.

My father was from Elsie, Michigan, home to dairy farms and known for lending its name to Elsie, the Borden cow. Albert Parks had graduated from Elsie High School in 1940 and was studying chemistry at the University of Michigan when the United States entered World War II. He joined the Army in 1942 and after basic training was shipped to Bethlehem to learn about cannons and their ammunition where they were being made and tested. He met Marilyn Fley at a USO dance that her mother was chaperoning. They were married on February 24, 1944, in Bethlehem when he was on a brief leave. Albert then was assigned to Mississippi, where the Army was forming the 227th Ordnance Ammunition Renovation Platoon. In November the platoon shipped out to Belgium, where they established a factory for renovating duds—the artillery, rifle, and small arms shells and grenades that were not functional. From then until the end of the war, his company renovated hundreds of thousands of shells and munitions. According to the records of the platoon, it suffered periodic explosions and fires during this dangerous work under difficult conditions.[55]

Albert Parks was discharged from the Army at Fort Indiantown Gap, Pennsylvania, in December 1945. He went to Bethlehem, stayed for Christmas with Marilyn's family, and then he and Marilyn headed for Michigan to begin their lives together. Because his family did not own a farm, my dad tried to find work, sometimes as a house painter or day laborer. But little work was available, and most of the locals who were not in farming made the one-hour commute to either Lansing or Flint to work in the Oldsmobile or Pontiac plants. But my father, who was suffering with the early stages of rheumatoid arthritis, could not break into that world. So he and my mother decided to go back to Bethlehem, which had better opportunities and better access to health care. I was born in late November 1948 at

St. Luke's Hospital, and we all lived with my mother's parents, which was not unusual in that time of scarce housing.

Eventually my parents, who could not afford a house in town, bought a lot from friends of my grandparents and built a "basement house" in suburban Hanover Township near the Allentown-Bethlehem-Easton Airport, joining millions nationwide who were spreading into the open land around urban centers. My parents' plan was to gradually add a house to the basement as finances permitted. As my dad's health continued to deteriorate, he accepted a job with my uncle Ed Stefko, to be the salesman for the Bayard Park subdivision in northeast Bethlehem, an area that had been farms before the war. We were his first customer when we purchased one of the tiny Levittown-style homes for $5,000, a princely sum at the time. It was our family home throughout my childhood (my parents sold the basement house).

In the 1950s Bethlehem felt like a boomtown. Bayard Park was a typical suburban development, with winding streets, single-family and duplex homes with driveways, front and back yards, and front porches. Landscaping was modest, families added garages as their finances allowed, and the school district worked frantically to build schools to deal with all the Jeffreys (always at least four in my grade-school classes), Susans, Lindas, Johns, Toms, and Sharons. Since Bayard Park was right next door to "the projects" (row houses owned by the public housing authority in developments called Marvine Village and Pembroke Village), we had Puerto Rican, and even a few African American, kids in our elementary school classes. We socialized in school, and some of those kids came to my house to play, but I was never allowed to visit kids who lived in the projects.

As Bayard Park was developed, a new commercial district evolved just three blocks from my house on Stefko Boulevard. The new shopping center had a grocery store, bank, five and dime, state liquor store, Laundromat, and women's clothing store. Although the family once had shopped in downtown Bethlehem, that ended when we moved to Bayard Park.

Suburban developments were sprouting in northeast and northwest Bethlehem (land annexed before 1968), away from the old downtowns: Liberty Park, Kaywin, Northdale Manor, and Clearview. Meanwhile growth exploded in Hanover Township, where larger and more expensive housing developments appealed to the middle managers at Bethlehem Steel as well as professionals in the community. Major arteries like Easton Avenue and Schoenersville Road grew their own strip malls, grocery stores, banks, and pharmacies.

Left behind were the blocks and blocks of mostly brick row houses in the center of Bethlehem on both sides of the river; they had small yards, hard-to-find on-street parking, and a crowded environment. Anyone who worked full time at the steel plant could afford a car and a tract house near parks, schools, and Little League fields. Those who could not were relegated to the older, more affordable housing. In less than twenty years Bethlehem's row housing stock on the south side and much of the north side became home to the poor. More ominous was that the populations of the older parts of town declined as entire families with young children migrated to the suburbs. Those who remained were neither numerous nor wealthy enough to support local businesses. Bethlehem, like many urban communities, inevitably slipped into decline. As builders were putting up suburban homes, Bethlehem's population grew from 66,000 in 1950 to 75,408 in 1960, but by 1980 the city's population, like that of other old industrial centers, had declined, to 70,400, according to the U.S. Census.

BLIGHT AND RENEWAL, AMERICAN STYLE

The cities that had emerged during the industrial revolution were not pleasant places to live, even for the wealthy. The poor were crammed into tenements or worse. Plumbing and sanitation were inadequate. Parks were small private spaces not meant for the masses. Smoke and soot spewed from industrial and residential chimneys. Something drastic had to be done.

This environment gave rise to urban planning, the idea of using a new partnership of government and the private sector to separate different uses of land, late in the nineteenth century.[56] In the United States sentimentality for old buildings was almost nonexistent. The overriding mandate was to rid cities of blight, a term that was adopted in the early years of the twentieth century for areas of indiscriminate growth now deemed undesirable. Blight was bad for a number of reasons. It harmed residents and drained urban resources. The rising costs of providing social services and police, combined with the loss of tax revenues as people left the city, placed an enormous burden on the government. Blight blocked the creation of a modern city and stunted an area's economic growth. Advocates saw vast potential in blighted areas because the land could be put to better use under the right circumstances. Finally, blight was deemed the precursor of dangerous and unproductive slums, which had to be stopped to maintain a productive city.[57]

The famous (some would say infamous) urban planner Robert Moses was the most avid early practitioner of urban renewal. His ardor to develop more urban parks later morphed into a push for more highways, bridges, and ultimately the redevelopment of entire areas of New York City, during a career that lasted from the 1920s to the 1970s.

In the 1930s political jurisdictions used eminent domain to acquire land for public use. In the 1940s the real estate industry, through the industry-supported Urban Land Institute, developed a plan for private developers to renew urban areas. A municipality could designate a "blighted area" for redevelopment according to a plan that the municipality had created and approved. A public agency, the redevelopment authority, would have powers to condemn the properties in the blighted area if the owners refused to sell. The authority then could accept bids from private developers for projects that would meet the requirements of the municipal redevelopment plan.[58] The idea was to take the land for public purposes but leave implementation to the private sector.

However, throughout this period constitutional scholars questioned these methods. The Fifth Amendment to the U.S. Constitution states "nor shall private property be taken for public use, without just compensation." The interpretation of the term *public use* was all important and became the subject of numerous court challenges.

By 1948 twenty-five states had passed urban renewal acts based on the Robert Moses model.[59] By the late 1940s state courts had accepted these state urban renewal laws. The real question was what the federal courts would do. In 1956 the U.S. Supreme Court concluded in *Berman v. Parker* that condemnation of properties in blighted areas in accordance with a redevelopment plan was constitutional, even though the property would be sold to a private developer and would not be used by the government.[60] Thus the court had defined *public use* as including private use of publicly taken property, opening the path for the massive "renewal" of hundreds of cities across the United States.

HISTORIC PRESERVATION

As a movement in the United States compared to that in Europe, historic preservation was a late bloomer. Perhaps that is because we are such a young country with not as much to preserve as the Europeans. Others would contend that it is not in our character to dote on the past but to move on and build something newer, better, and more appropriate to our ever-changing society.

Early efforts at preservation do exist, however. Two relate to our first president, George Washington. In 1850 the State of New York acquired and operated George Washington's headquarters in Newburgh as the first state-owned historic site in the country. The preservation of Washington's Mount Vernon, by a private organization, was begun in 1858. The first statewide preservation organization, now known as Preservation Virginia, was founded in 1889. Two southern cities, New Orleans and Charleston, South Carolina, commenced historic preservation programs as early as 1925. However, they were outliers. The National Trust for Historic Preservation, a nonprofit organization with a national mission, was not created until 1949. The first advanced-degree program in historic preservation was not established until 1964, at Columbia University.[61]

While local efforts were made to preserve sites like Independence Hall in Philadelphia, in the 1950s preservation was not considered a realistic option for addressing blight or renewing cities. In June 1961, with help from citizens of Bethlehem and their patrons at Bethlehem Steel, Pennsylvania passed the Historic District Act, which authorized municipalities to create historic districts to retain the character of the so-designated area.

However, most cities chose the heavily federally funded route of demolishing whole sections of town and "renewing" them along the lines of the suburbs. Urban malls, publicly funded sports and cultural facilities, and their supporting parking garages became the centerpieces of ambitious downtown plans. The majority of these projects failed to return downtowns to their former glory. One of the most notorious of these failures was Six Flags Auto World, a combination amusement park and museum in downtown Flint, Michigan, which in 1982 was "widely proclaimed the 'unemployment capital of America.'" Designed to revive the downtown in a spectacular way with an attraction that played on Americans' love of automobiles and amusement parks, the over-the-top domed Auto World opened on July 4, 1984, only to close six months later, an expensive symbol of desperate urban renewal.[62] It eventually was abandoned and demolished in 1997.

BETHLEHEM STEEL AND THE "NEW BETHLEHEM"

For the postwar leaders of Bethlehem Steel, the future looked rosy. Except for the compromise to allow unionized labor, mandated by the Roosevelt administration before the war began, the view from the boardroom was that the company had nowhere to go but up. Demand for cars, the construction of new roads and bridges, the continued eruption of skyscrapers in big cities, and the increase in global commerce positioned Bethlehem Steel to reach even more impressive heights than its wartime success. The paternalistic company decreed that Bethlehem needed to reflect its status as the hometown of one of the biggest companies in the world and decided to lead a renewal of the city. The degree to which the company was behind urban renewal for the next twenty years was not always apparent. In the eyes of Bethlehem Steel, the city was its fiefdom and it needed to watch over it. Compared to the company's annual income, the city's budget was a rounding error. When necessary the company used its resources to address what its home municipality needed. The department assigned to keep an eye on the city was the Department of General Services.

Overseeing urban renewal issues in Bethlehem from his perch in the Department of General Services was Ralph Grayson Schwarz, a Connecticut Yankee who had entered Lehigh University in 1942 but enlisted in the Army a year later. Schwarz returned to Lehigh in the fall of 1946 with a new perspective on the world. With the benefit of the GI Bill, he continued his major in engineering and added a minor in international relations. While a student at Lehigh, Schwarz befriended Laura Curtis Gross, wife of John Gross, a Bethlehem Steel vice president.[63]

Laura Gross, who had lost both her sons to the war, was pleased to take the veteran-student from Connecticut under her wing. She introduced him to the bigwigs at Bethlehem Steel, including Eugene Grace, the president and board chair. When Schwarz graduated from Lehigh in 1949, William Johnstone, the vice president who reigned over the Department of General Services, hired him. The department handled everything from buying coal mines to overseeing development plans for the Homer Research Center on Bethlehem's South Mountain to the postwar rebuilding of Saucon Valley Country Club to the acquisition of property and planning for what became the Burns Harbor Indiana plant, the last fully integrated steel plant to be built in the United States. The department also handled the City of Bethlehem. As the junior member in the office on Third Street, Schwarz was assigned to address urban renewal issues in Bethlehem. While he was breaking into his position, Schwarz obtained his master's degree in history from Lehigh; the field proved to be his life's passion.

Postwar Bethlehem was showing its age. Everything from the "nickel bridge," named for the fee to cross the Lehigh River at New Street, to the Moravian buildings on Church Street was rundown. The row homes and business district on the south side hummed with activity but were dirty and often shabby. The warren of homes, clubs, and industrial sites on Sand Island (in the Lehigh River between the retail districts) and along Monocacy Creek downtown (as the north side is called) would shock today's residents. Schwarz's engagement with downtown began in 1951 after the death of Annie Kemerer, a local antique and decorative arts collector. Kemerer, whose husband and son had both died in the 1920s, bequeathed her numerous decorative arts collections and considerable estate to the community for a museum. In the small power structure that existed in Bethlehem, the attorney for the estate, who had good connections at Bethlehem Steel, asked Bill Johnstone for advice about how to handle this opportunity for the community. The challenge was to find a permanent home and determine how to fit a museum into downtown Bethlehem; it would be the only museum in the city at that time.

Dealing with the Kemerer bequest started a complex chain of events that led to formation of the Moravian historic district in Bethlehem. Many of the district's eighteenth-century buildings were in rough shape. Moravian College for Women, which was located in Colonial Hall (comprised of what had been the Brethren's House and two adjacent buildings), was in bad shape financially. Moravian College and Theological Seminary, the men's institution ten blocks away, was not in much better condition. "Colonial Hall was covered in stucco, so that none of original stone structure was visible," Schwarz reminisced in an interview.[64] The city had no master plan, Lehigh University had no master plan, and the leaders of the Moravian community had no master plan, Schwarz said. With the resources of Bethlehem Steel and cooperation from a willing city government, Schwarz began to plan the future of Bethlehem.

In 1952 Schwarz used Bethlehem Steel's influence to create CURE (Citizens Urban Renewal Enterprise), a volunteer committee. Its purpose was to bring stakeholders together for the renewal of Bethlehem. The committee included representatives from Moravian College, Lehigh University, Central Moravian Church, the City of Bethlehem, and the Bethlehem Chamber of Commerce. Schwarz served as an adviser. Schwarz invited people from this group to sit on multiple boards of the nonprofits and public agencies created to meet the challenges of revitalizing Bethlehem.

In 1953 Schwarz retained urban renewal consultants from Pittsburgh who issued a how-to report that no doubt also was being presented to cities throughout the nation. Following the plan, the Bethlehem City Council created the redevelopment authority, a necessary player in the game of urban renewal. Its board members were carefully selected from the CURE membership.

Schwarz sought the best planners of this era and selected the New York landscape architecture firm of Clarke & Rapuano. The firm had conducted many projects in New York City for Robert Moses, including Bryant Park, the United Nations, the Conservancy Gardens in Central Park, and the Brooklyn Heights Promenade. Schwarz also brought in Russell Van Nest Black, a noted Philadelphia planner. With assorted other consultants, the team reviewed the downtowns retail districts on the north and south sides of the Lehigh River and issued a bevy of reports and plans.[65]

Schwarz was a historian, not a city planner or a historical preservationist, so he was free of preconceived notions. His approach was humanistic, tempered with an appreciation for history and for planning. He tackled his assignment with gusto and sought to reuse colonial-era buildings in the historic Moravian community, restoring them where possible while engaging their owners or other community stakeholders who could address their long-term use. At the same time he tackled the most important step in making the city appropriate for the headquarters of Bethlehem Steel—creating a new civic space that through its location, design, and scope would embrace a modernist future for the city. He worked with Clarke & Rapuano to begin taking the modest company town to a future as a cutting-edge, culturally vibrant city.

AN "INTERIM" REPORT

On May 1, 1956, the consultants hired by the city's redevelopment authority, with funds from Bethlehem Steel and suggestions from Schwarz and his colleagues, issued *An Interim Report on the City of Bethlehem*. Its checklist of projects for addressing the city's most pressing problems came out of meetings with people in the community. At the time these projects were ambitious, so much so that most residents considered them out of reach.

The report identified five priorities for the growth and economic and civic health of the community:

- Building a new civic center for local government, perhaps including a post office and state and/or federal government offices, in a central location
- Formally designating the "Old and Historic Bethlehem District" in the area of the colonial Moravian community
- Addressing parking issues in the north and south side retail districts
- Developing bridges and routes for through-traffic to support growth and ease vehicular movement in and at the edges of the city.

- Clearing and redeveloping slum or blighted areas, starting with the Monocacy Creek area in the downtown.[66]

Most members of the community viewed the report as a wish list for the far-off future and paid no attention to it. However, when the Steel wanted something to happen, it happened. What is stunning is the speed with which it happened.

One key was a change in government structure. Through the 1950s Bethlehem had a weak-mayor form of government—the mayor was merely the ceremonial head of the five-person city commission. Each commissioner headed a city department. No one person had centralized responsibility for overall city management, and, worse yet, Bethlehem had no centralized city hall. In 1957 the Pennsylvania legislature enacted a measure that allowed cities to change their government structure and include features that allowed central management by a strong mayor. In November 1959 Bethlehem voters approved a new city charter that encompassed a strong mayor and a city council.

Democrats, supported by the local unions, had ruled city hall since 1930 and had expected that they would continue to be in charge under the new government format. In the spring of 1961 Paul Jani, a city council member, ran in the Democratic primary against the incumbent mayor, Earl Schaffer, who had held that office since 1950. In a major upset Jani defeated Schaffer, creating a deep division among the Democrats. The Republicans, with support from Steel executives, were fielding a young businessman, H. Gordon Payrow, for mayor and a team for city council that included Bob Snyder from Moravian College. This team was part of a robust group of younger community leaders who had come up through the Jaycees (Junior Chamber of Commerce). The Republicans ran a strong campaign, going door to door, running ads in the local paper, and plastering the city with bumper stickers and billboards. The result was an astounding GOP sweep of all city offices except controller.

In that same election the voters of Bethlehem, Bethlehem Township, and Freemansburg overwhelmingly voted to create a unified school district. These were unimaginable changes for the people of Bethlehem.

Payrow got right to business. With a small planning staff and the assistance of the redevelopment authority, his predecessor had begun to acquire properties in the areas outlined by the consultants' report. Community leaders all agreed that the best site for city hall was on Church Street at its intersection with New Street in the oldest area of the city. The elevation of the location provided a beautiful view of the Lehigh River, South Mountain, Lehigh University, and Bethlehem Steel. The leaders whittled the ambitious Clarke & Rapuano plan down to space for the city's government needs and a public library to replace the inadequate space in the former Bethlehem Steel Band Hall on Market Street.

The discussion of the design for the new civic complex came down to a choice between a nondescript colonial-style complex of buildings or a modern complex. No serious consideration was given to mimicking the historic Moravian buildings. But the public hotly debated whether to put the contemporary building proposed by Bethlehem architects Lovelace and Spillman in the middle of the iconic colonial Germanic and Victorian architecture on Church Street. Those opposed to the modern design argued that the building would not meet the newly enacted historic district guidelines. However, the city government was exempt from those guidelines.

Ultimately the community concluded that the buildings on Church Street should be representative of the era in which they were built and therefore city hall should be modern. This also would allow visitors to study three centuries of architecture in a two-block walk.[67]

RESTORING MORAVIAN BETHLEHEM

On October 1, 1961, the *New York Herald Tribune* ran a story headlined, "What's Going on in Bethlehem?," an oddity considering that most New Yorkers probably did not even know where Bethlehem was. The article begins:

> The physical problem of Bethlehem, Pennsylvania is not unique. Like many another American city, particularly along the eastern seaboard, Bethlehem was faced with inner rot. Congestion, crime and obsolescence were all eat-

ing away at its core, and where there had once been a thriving downtown area that was a source of pride to its citizens,
industrial and residential slums were gradually taking over.
Depressing, but familiar.

What *was* unique in Bethlehem's plight was the community's proud historical and cultural tradition with many
surviving, but deteriorating, landmarks that spanned more
than two centuries.[68]

The story ran on the front page of the newspaper's Sunday supplement and included a rendering of the plans to return Bethlehem
to historic glory. An aerial photo from the early 1950s shows the
Monocacy Valley with assorted buildings in various degrees of dis-
repair and an auto junkyard, as well as industrial buildings on and
adjacent to Sand Island. The photo also shows the Church Street
complex of the Brethren's House, Old Main Dormitory, and the Victorian-era addition to the Brethren's House covered with stucco to
make them appear to be one building, Colonial Hall. Other photographs show the newly renovated Victorian Main Hall of Moravian
College and the herringbone-pattern doors of the soon-to-be renovated Brethren's House to demonstrate progress on the grand plan.
The article boldly states that Bethlehem intends to do it all.

Why did the *Herald Tribune* run an article about Bethlehem in
1961 that was essentially a report card for the work done in the
1950s to create a plan for historic preservation? The answer is Ralph
Schwarz. He recently had moved to New York from Bethlehem to
serve as assistant to the president of Whitney Communications. He
had met John Hay "Jock" Whitney, former ambassador to the United Kingdom, through social contacts at Bethlehem Steel. Whitney
owned the *Herald Tribune*, and Schwarz prevailed upon the paper to
cover the story of Bethlehem—and gave the reporter a copy of the
report issued by Clarke & Rapuano earlier that year. This report
included detailed renderings of a restored colonial industrial park
along the Monocacy.

While he was still in Bethlehem and trying to locate a home for
the Kemerer Museum, Schwarz had joined the board of Moravian
College and Theological Seminary as Bethlehem Steel's representative. Until that time the college had not been a priority for the com-

pany. Schwarz began working with Robert Snyder, a young administrator at the college who was a Moravian and a native of Lititz, Pennsylvania. Snyder was the right hand of Dr. Raymond Haupert, president of Moravian College and Theological Seminary.

In 1954, after two centuries of separate development, the college,
the Moravian Seminary, and Moravian College for Women united
to become Moravian College, the Lehigh Valley's first coeducational
postsecondary institution. The buildings on the south side of
Church Street at its intersection with Main had been the Women's
College and became the college's south campus.

In 1955 Schwarz, Snyder, and their colleagues arranged for the
Gemeinhaus, just east of Central Moravian Church, to be the new
home for the Moravian Church's museum, which it still is today. The
Kemerer Museum was temporarily moved into Old Main Hall, a portion of the former College for Women.

With these pieces in place Schwarz formed Historic Bethlehem,
Inc. (HBI), a nonprofit organization supporting the Kemerer Museum and historic preservation efforts for the colonial Moravian buildings. Schwarz realized that support from individuals would be essential to meet the goals he had set for the restorations and reconstruc-
tions in the historic area. "I made sure that the same people were on
the boards of the Kemerer Museum, Historic Bethlehem, and the redevelopment authority, so that it would be easier to get things done,"
he said.[69]

The role of the redevelopment authority in the grand scheme
for the colonial Moravian properties was to acquire the land along
Monocacy Creek from Union Boulevard to the creek's confluence
with the Lehigh River. As seen in the photograph that ran in the *Herald Tribune*, this acreage, all parkland today, was cluttered with industrial properties and other uses. A flood in 1955 made most of
the properties uninhabitable. By 1966 the city had acquired enough
properties that it could give HBI a one-hundred-year lease for the
portion that had been the Moravians' colonial industrial quarter, including the remnants of the original waterworks, tannery, miller's
house, pottery, smithy, dye house, oil mill, and the 1869 Lukenbach
Mill.

In 1961, when the *Herald Tribune* article was published, only a
small portion of the Kemerer Museum's objects were on exhibit in

its temporary home. The article includes photographs of the beautiful parlors on display. The Kemerer Museum of Decorative Arts ultimately was located at 427 North New Street in 1969, just a half-block north of where Schwarz's advisers had sited Bethlehem's new civic complex. When he left for New York, Schwarz had used Bethlehem Steel's influence and money to bring together people who restored and preserved the historic Moravian buildings, so they could tell their story and remain the heart of the city that the Moravians had founded.

In December 1961, after passage of Pennsylvania's Historic District Act, Bethlehem created the state's first formal historic district under the new law. Schwarz had left Bethlehem a few months earlier. He would continue his career with distinguished contributions to American history in Washington, D.C.; Indiana; California; Virginia; and Connecticut but would remain closely associated with Bethlehem.

GETTING THE DOWNTOWN PLAN FUNDED

Once Payrow had the design for the new civic center in hand, he had to go to the voters in 1964 for approval of a city bond issue to pay for the estimated $11 million project, which included four buildings: city hall, a public safety building, the Bethlehem Public Library, and the Rotunda (now called Town Hall), a saucer-shaped building in the middle of the plaza that would house city council chambers a place for public meetings with audience space for about two hundred. The referendum was a disaster. By then the mood of the city and the country had changed. John F. Kennedy had been assassinated; racial tension was on the rise; baby boomers were promoting sex, drugs, and rock 'n' roll; and working-class Democrats did not want their taxes to go up. The referendum was defeated.

Payrow and his team were defiant. They went back to the drawing board. With the approval of the city council, they created the Bethlehem City Center Authority, an entity that could buy and build buildings, establish a lease with the city, and issue tax-exempt bonds without voter approval. The city established an amount it felt it could afford for the thirty years of the bonds and based the cost of the project on that. When it looked like the Rotunda, which was central to the design, could not be included because of cost, Bethlehem Steel agreed to pay for it. When it looked like the library would be $500,000 short, Roland Adams, publisher of the *Bethlehem Globe Times*, put up $250,000 as a challenge gift, and the community raised the rest.

Construction of Bethlehem's City Center began in 1965, before H. Gordon Payrow was elected to a second term as mayor later that year. The building was dedicated on November 28, 1967, near the end of a two-year celebration of the 225th anniversary of the city's founding and the fiftieth year of its incorporation as a city. The dedication ceremony was held at 10:00 a.m. in the new City Center Plaza on a brisk day. Flags of the United States, Pennsylvania, and Bethlehem were raised on the three new flagpoles in the shadow of a sixty-foot sculpture, *Symbol of Progress*, by the Philadelphia artist Joseph Greenberg. The abstract sculpture, made of Bethlehem Steel's new Corten steel and designed to be sustainable with a rusted surface, resembles the poles of a teepee, with three lines coming together high above the roofline of the adjacent building, then branching off from each other as they reach toward the heavens. It represents the unity of the original three boroughs that formed the city of Bethlehem in 1917, fifty years before the sculpture's placement by an Army helicopter. With the Liberty High School Band bravely playing for the audience in unusually frigid weather, Payrow dedicated the complex to the people of Bethlehem; he made a point of introducing a young boy and girl and saying that this was for them and their future.[70]

That evening the Hotel Bethlehem catered a dinner for 1,250 guests in the parking garage beneath the plaza. With the garage doors covered and temporary heating installed, the city held back the bitter cold air as diners toasted with Governor Raymond Shafer. The Republican governor passionately promoted his own agenda, pledging the state was going to offer more expeditious support for urban renewal than the slow-moving bureaucracy in Washington.[71]

Even the Democrats who had opposed the project were swept up in the excitement. The Democratic president of city council declared, "This project is a symbol of unity of purpose and of achievement by all of the people in the City of Bethlehem."[72] During open house over the next several days, south siders who had vehemently opposed the project gleefully guided friends through their new city hall.

The new center opened only eleven years after the ambitious Clarke & Rapuano report, and the city had come surprisingly close to completing the consultants' checklist. City government was now housed in state-of-the-art facilities. The public library was first class, and the surrounding plaza, with a reflecting pool, gardens, and magnificent views, gave the visitor the impression that this was a city of substance and style.

What the report had called the "Old and Historic Bethlehem District" was now a reality with a state-approved program, guidelines for building improvements and alterations, and an area that included all the Victorian-era mansions; the last stretched all the way from First Street west of the Monocacy to Linden Street two blocks east of the proposal from Clarke & Rapuano. The Kemerer Museum would soon move into its new home on New Street just half a block from city hall; the Moravian Museum had moved into the oldest structure in the city, the five-story log Gemeinhaus. Moravian College's Freuhauff House (a single-family residence on Church Street that became the President's House) was restored, and the former Colonial Hall was restored to two buildings, Main Hall and the Brethren's House.

Historic Bethlehem, Inc., now managed the Bethlehem Colonial Industrial Quarter. Ralph Schwarz's vision of HBI as the nonprofit that would raise money for long-term support of the museum had blossomed into the organization responsible for fulfilling the vision of restoring or reconstructing more than a dozen colonial buildings on the site. The city had plans for a trail along the two miles of the Lehigh River and Canal within city limits; its centerpiece would be a park on Sand Island directly below city hall, where a Works Progress Administration–era public clay tennis court project was rehabilitated.[73]

REMOVING BLIGHT ON THE SOUTH SIDE

In 1968, the year before Payrow's second term ended, his administration released the city's 1967 annual report heralding the accomplishments of the administration and the renewal of the city.

Conspicuously absent was another redevelopment project designed to help Bethlehem Steel. The residents of an area of town called Northampton Heights lived next to the Bethlehem Steel plant, north of East Fourth Street. It consisted of five streets that had more than 250 houses and almost five hundred residents in 1964, when the city declared the community blighted.[74] As the redevelopment authority took people's homes by eminent domain, well-connected lawyers were getting high prices for homeowners. One of those lawyers was Justin D. Jirilanio, who also served as the Northampton County Democratic political boss. His power base, the south side, would lose voters, but all would be well compensated. The city turned the land over to Bethlehem Steel for its new basic oxygen furnace, which updated the plant's technology to make it more competitive in an increasingly difficult steel market. This takeover of an entire neighborhood was traumatic for the south side and a misbegotten attempt to make the plant competitive.

Redevelopment during the 1960s also supported the south side's other major institution, Lehigh University, which settled for a new neighbor in return for room for a much-needed expansion. A new nine-story tower went up at Fourth and New streets. The first floor was dedicated to retail, which aided the struggling retail district, but the upper floors were dedicated to housing for low-income seniors and people with disabilities, residents with little to spend in nearby stores. (The only building on that block that escaped redevelopment was owned by a state legislator who leased part of it to the state for a liquor store.) The other six blocks taken by the city were residential and were redeveloped by the then-landlocked university to expand its campus, including a new library that visually sealed off much of the hillside campus from the community below. Some south siders were angry about these development projects for many years.

These were pivotal years for my family as well. After my maternal grandfather died in 1956, my parents purchased his store, Lehigh Stationery, which had been at 14 West Fourth Street on the south side since my grandfather opened it in 1933. Lehigh students wandered in to purchase school supplies and the now extinct essential for engineers, slide rules. My parents catered to the office operations of local small businesses and industries. As the south side continued to decline, in 1965 my parents purchased a building adjacent to the

Broad Street bridge on the north side of town in an ill-fated effort to take advantage of what was left of the retail traffic in the north side downtown. I was a high school senior, and my friends helped my parents move the store during Christmas week, for their opening on January 2, 1966. My parents continued to eke out a living as both the neighboring businesses and the business offices of their industrial customers faded away.

CHAPTER 5
A BOLD NEW PLAN FOR DOWNTOWN

My parents' struggle with their business was symptomatic of what virtually all Rust Belt cities faced. Despite Bethlehem's accomplishments during the 1950s and early 1960s, the south side downtown continued to slide, with no new investment in retail businesses. The north side could best be described as in a state of slow decline. Gordon Payrow was running for a third term as mayor in 1969. He campaigned to keep the improvements coming, and at the top of the list was Main Street. He had reached out to allies at Bethlehem Steel and the chamber of commerce to once again hire Clarke & Rapuano to create a new plan for the downtown. The plan is dated December 1969, a month after Payrow won reelection.

From its first days in Bethlehem, Clarke & Rapuano knew that having a downtown meant the difference between having a viable city appropriate for the headquarters of a major corporation and suffering the decline, loss of population, and loss of identity that cities across the Rust Belt were experiencing. Mike Rapuano was not capable of thinking small. The plan his firm presented to the city was ambitious, to say the least. I suspect the report could have been released earlier, but it was held back until after the election because it called for tearing down much of the north side downtown and was certain to be controversial. The document also quickly dispatches one of Bethlehem's most challenging issues, having two downtowns, by opining that the south side retail district "cannot in this time and age endure."[75]

The plan, entitled *"Center City Bethlehem,"* sketches out a downtown worthy of Bethlehem Steel. Rapuano's team redesigned Bethlehem's Broad Street corridor, a six-block rectangular area that included Orr's, the town's only department store, and the dilapidated Sun Inn. The idea was to make downtown a center for retail, offices, culture, and conferences, and the plan included eight high-rises for offices, hotels, and apartments, an indoor mall anchored by two department stores, a transportation center, and a performing arts center with a plaza overlooking the Monocacy Valley. Broad Street's access to Route 378, the four lane controlled access highway from the Hill to Hill Bridge to US 22 that was also a product of the original Interim Report, would be redesigned, and high-rise apartments and neighborhood shopping would be developed on the other side of the Monocacy Valley, or what was left of it after a new interchange was built. The plan included parking structures for twenty-four hundred cars, to be created by a new parking authority.

The economic report supporting the plan urged speed in obtaining commitments from anchor department stores by touting Bethlehem's central location as an advantage that would attract shoppers from the eastern portion of the valley. The report also pays homage to the Hotel Bethlehem but suggests that even though regional occupancy rates were not high, a second hotel, combined with the use of the concert hall for meeting space, could attract conferences to the city. The report states, "Downtown contains some of the most valuable real estate within Bethlehem and private property owners and mortgage holders can ill-afford a path of inaction that would lead to an erosion of markets—and values." In other words, saving the downtown with such a radical plan was a necessity to stave off blight.

As I went off to law school in Philadelphia in the fall of 1970, the city dutifully began condemning and acquiring properties in the area designated for the new mall, office buildings, performing arts center, and parking facilities. As Bethlehem Steel moved into its new headquarters, Martin Tower on Eighth Avenue, a building that was not within walking distance of downtown, its executives were starting to understand the challenges the company was facing. Their appetite for grandiose civic plans was substantially diminished. While no one realized the depth of the Steel's problems at the time, it became clear that the company would not be a major player in developing the downtown. But perhaps its participation would not be necessary.

REESE D. JONES, "MAN OF THE DECADE"

At first Reese D. Jones seemed like the person who was going to transform Bethlehem into the modern metropolis the grandiose consultant reports envisioned.

He arrived in early 1967 as the new president of First National Bank and Trust Company of Bethlehem, the most prominent in the city with assets of more than $100 million. First National was considered rock solid, with conservative loan policies and substantial deposits from the residents of one of the commonwealth's wealthiest cities.

The son of a coal miner, Jones, then thirty-seven, had graduated from Wilkes College and received his master's degree in theoretical economics from the Wharton School of the University of Pennsylvania. He served an internship with the Federal Reserve Bank of Philadelphia before joining Studly, Shupert, an investment-banking firm.[76] These credentials and his leadership style brought him to Bethlehem and First National, a bank that traced its heritage to the Moravians. From the start Jones made it clear that he was going to grow the bank and assume leadership roles in the city.

Jones joined Central Moravian Church and became active in the chamber of commerce, Moravian College, Historic Bethlehem, and United Way. By 1969 he had renamed the bank First Valley Bank, making it the first old-line bank in the region to change its name in anticipation of the transformation of the industry. When the Clarke & Rapuano report was released, Jones embraced the concept of a new downtown.

Just as the earlier consultants' report had led to rapid development of the city center, the historic district, and Route 378, within a year of the latest plan's release Jones's bank had committed to build an eleven-story headquarters at Broad and New streets, to be designated One Bethlehem Plaza. The bank would be the main tenant of the tower, which would be immediately adjacent to the proposed Bethlehem Plaza Mall, a 100,000-square-foot indoor mall designed to bring downtown into retail competition with the suburbs. The two projects, and the existing Main Street businesses, would provide users for the new eight-hundred-space Walnut Street Garage. The Payrow administration condemned and demolished several blocks of downtown properties and created the Bethlehem Parking Authority to build the garage.

Jones's commitment to Bethlehem was personal. He actively participated in seeking a developer for the plaza mall and, failing to find one, created an equity partnership in which he invested and brought in nine other investors. The mall was financed through bonds issued by the Northampton County Industrial Development Authority, with First Valley Bank purchasing the lion's share of the debt, in effect taking a risky mortgage on property in which its president was part owner. Jones did attract a competitor, First National Bank of Allentown, to purchase some of the bonds and locate its first Bethlehem branch in the new mall.[77]

But Jones did not stop with the mall. As a member of Central Moravian, he had become its internal financial adviser, of the church that had been the original bank's parent. He encouraged the Moravian community to form the Moravian Development Corporation in 1971 to build a high-rise facility to take advantage of a federal program that would provide financing for housing for the elderly and disabled on land the redevelopment authority was taking on Main Street north of Broad Street. Jones was so eager to have high-rise buildings in downtown Bethlehem that he did not think about how its tenants, who by law had to be low income, would help develop a vibrant downtown, a mistake made by many Rust Belt cities. The first tower of Moravian House opened in November 1974, soon after the First Valley Bank Tower. Within a year Jones had convinced the Moravian Development Corporation to begin plans for a second tower.[78]

When my dad died in 1974, my parents were negotiating with the redevelopment authority, because the building they had bought in 1965 and moved their business into was part of the city's redevelopment plan. The beautiful four-story brick building was near the site proposed for the performing arts center.

My mother sold the building to the redevelopment authority and the business to two local entrepreneurs. She spent the rest of her working life as a clerk in a downtown jewelry store, finally free of the burdens of running a small business in a struggling downtown. The purchasers of the business moved it to another part of town because the redevelopment authority was eager to tear down the old building. The new owners went out of business within a year.

I had met Susan while I was a law student at the University of Pennsylvania, and we married after my graduation in 1973. One reason we chose to then settle to Bethlehem was that I was an only child; I felt the need to be near my parents because my father had been ill. In addition, Susan and I agreed we wanted to live in city smaller than Philadelphia or New York. After I passed the bar in the summer of 1973, I spent a year working for a local attorney. In 1974, I set out to practice law on my own, with my first office right off Main Street in Bethlehem's downtown.

While Jones was using his relentless energy to build a new downtown, he also was expanding the bank. At the time banks in Pennsylvania could have branches only in counties adjacent to the county of their home bank. Most of Bethlehem is within Northampton County, whose easternmost border is the Delaware River, which separates Pennsylvania from New Jersey. That left the ambitious Jones with expanding west into Lehigh County, home of Allentown; north to the Poconos; or south to Bucks County, a target of the Philadelphia banks. Given his roots in the coal region, Jones moved First Valley's corporate headquarters to Lansford, a small town in Carbon County to the north, although the region was already in decline. After making that leap, Jones began an acquisition campaign that by 1976 had given the bank twenty-six offices in four counties. The bank was valued at more than $500 million, placing it in the top 225 of the fourteen thousand banks in the United States.[79]

Jones continued to use his position and the bank's resources to try to attract developers to downtown Bethlehem. But he got competition in 1973, when the Pennsylvania Real Estate Investment Trust announced it was planning a massive mall that would open in 1976 just off Route 22 at Route 145, the main artery to downtown Allentown. The site is a ten-minute drive from downtown Bethlehem. Now Bethlehem had no hope of attracting department stores to its downtown. But Jones continued to relentlessly seek businesses and retail and to support the basic concepts of the Clarke & Rapuano plan. Jones even accepted a challenge from Mayor Gordon Mowrer, who had been elected in 1973 after Payrow declined to seek a fourth term, to use a $1.5 million state grant to raise the money to build the performing arts center proposed for downtown.[80]

On Friday, March 29, 1976, Jones flew to Florida for a short fishing vacation with a friend. Jones took with him materials he was going to use to pitch Bethlehem to another group of developers that was considering investing in Bethlehem's downtown. After a Saturday of fishing, beer, and sun, Jones retired to his hotel room to rest before dinner. When he complained of chest and stomach pains, the hotel called an ambulance. Jones died on the way to the hospital.[81]

More bad news awaited. Although the *Bethlehem Globe-Times* hailed Jones as "the man of the decade," and Mowrer called him "Bethlehem's Number 1 Citizen," Jones left the bank, and therefore Bethlehem, with problems. Reports issued by the Federal Deposit Insurance Corporation in early 1977 disclosed that it deemed $74 million of First Valley's $346 million in loans "adversely classified," meaning that their repayment was uncertain. First Valley suspended dividends and no longer could devote resources to revitalizing downtown as the bank fought to restore its profitability.[82]

It is impossible to speculate what would have happened had Reese Jones not died. He had almost single-handedly promoted a watered-down version of the Clarke & Rapuano plan. But with his death, First Valley's internal problems, and Bethlehem Steel's retrenchment, the private-sector resources for revitalizing Bethlehem's downtown were extremely limited. The city quickly realized that its grand plan for a new downtown was in limbo.

HISTORIC PRESERVATION REDUX

Gordon Mowrer was the scion of an old Bethlehem Moravian family. His family owned Mowrer's Dairy on Linden Street and established the Cup, an ice cream stand near the dairy that has become a Bethlehem institution, though long held by new owners. After Mowrer graduated from college in 1959, a general insurance agent hired him as his only salesperson. The Dickinson College grad met his wife, Mary Thaeler, on a blind date in Bethlehem the following year. The daughter of Moravian missionaries to Nicaragua was studying to be a nurse and planned to return to Central America to help fight malaria. While building his insurance business, Mowrer pursued a graduate degree at Lehigh. A psychology professor suggested that Mowrer's future was in politics, not in counseling. Mowrer agreed.

Mowrer first ran for mayor of Bethlehem in 1969. To the surprise of many local politicos, he won the Democratic primary, then lost to Gordon Payrow by 700 votes. Two years later Mowrer ran for city council and won. Then, after only two years on the council, he ran for mayor again in 1973. With tutelage from experienced politicians, Mowrer went door to door and visited the textile factories, where women sat at rows of sewing machines making blouses, braziers, dresses, and various other garments; he also waited outside the gates to the Steel during shift changes. He worked hard and won.

Mowrer's election led to a fundamental shift in thinking about what the city needed to do to save itself from decay, and what Mowrer embraced was the polar opposite of Payrow's approach.

In his book *The Comeback Kid* Mowrer describes how he and other community leaders visited many cities to see what they were doing. "When I came home to Bethlehem after these trips and I walked around the streets, it did not take very long for me to come up with a solution," Mowrer writes. "I said to myself, there's only one thing Bethlehem has to sell, and that is history!...Bethlehem is not a shopping center, it is not a modern brand new community, we are an old city that has charm and delight and we need to sell that."[83]

Mowrer hired a planning team that knew how to address revitalization by focusing on the existing assets of the community rather than trying to build a whole new downtown. The team sought out consultants who could come up with new concepts to support a revitalized center city without huge department stores. Bethlehem hired John D. Milner, a young architect with a passion for preservation who had founded his firm, National Heritage Corporation in West Chester, Pennsylvania, in 1968 as he began restoring historic buildings in Philadelphia and its suburbs.

The 1976 Milner report, *Bethlehem Main Street Restoration and Revitalization Study*, revealed what had been hiding in plain sight. Main Street is a collection of historic architecture that begins at der Platz, the colonial Moravian center of town in front of Central Moravian Church, and extends three blocks north to Broad Street, past buildings that constitute a collection of Victorian and early nineteenth-century architecture, some of which was hidden behind newer facades designed to support the businesses within. The street was wide, with no trees or plants, and was lighted by tall high-powered lights more appropriate for an interstate highway.

Mowrer's team also reached out to the Urban Land Institute for an updated evaluation of the second Clarke & Rapuano plan only seven years after its adoption and several million dollars' worth of acquisition and demolition. With financial support from Bethlehem Steel, ULI assembled a panel of experts in retail, lodging, traffic, parking, office space, high-rise residential projects, and tourism. The panel, individually and in teams, talked with more than one hundred citizens, businesspeople, government officials, union leaders, community representatives, and others.[84] The panel released its report in early April 1976, a month after Jones died and just before the Milner report was released. The two reports changed the course of redevelopment in Bethlehem.

The ULI report praised the restoration and preservation of the Moravian and Victorian structures on Church Street and the acquisition and creation of green space along the Monocacy Valley and the Lehigh River. "The historic area is a unique Pennsylvania asset which has not yet been fully promoted as an attraction to benefit the center of the city or the community," the ULI report noted. "The city center, while 'handsome,' is isolated from the downtown core and Main Street is a fine arrangement of buildings and businesses...but not tied to the Broad Street corridor."[85]

Its most biting comments were reserved for the components that either had been completed or were under construction. The office tower and mall are "optimistic, aggressive evidence of 20th Century development," but the mall was introverted, enclosed, and did not relate to the rest of the commercial district; however, it was already under construction. The high-rise building for senior citizens constituted an "insular environment." The report said downtown's greatest strength was its surrounding neighborhoods, which were not rundown. The report explained why a new hotel, convention center, and department store were not economically feasible. The Lehigh Valley Mall was about to open, and it permanently closed the door for another major retail center nearby.

The ULI experts supported several approaches either contrary to or omitted from the Clarke & Rapuano report and urged the city to

- Encourage more housing—Bethlehem had a low vacancy rate, and its housing prices demonstrated stability.
- Focus on attracting tourists and businesses that meet special high-end needs and forget about large suburban shopping centers.
- Restore the Sun Inn rather than tear it down.

The panel agreed on another interesting point: if the state was willing to put up $1.5 million and the city was willing to subsidize operation of the performing arts center, the proposed project could move forward. To boost tourism the panel recommended inauguration of a marketing program, tours, and a visitor center, as well as formation of a new nonprofit to coordinate the operating hours of historic and civic organizations.

One line in the report was near and dear to my heart. Ever since I had visited Europe, I had wanted to live in a city with sidewalk cafés. "Outdoor cafes, perhaps a quality dinner theater, [and] specialty food shops would also enhance life for residents as well as attract visitors," the report noted.[86] Now, forty years later, the cafes and many of the other recommendations are finally in place, but it was a long journey.

During the ULI panel's visit I had the opportunity to speak with some of its members. As a member of the chamber of commerce's tourism committee, and an outspoken advocate for tourism, I had been on some of the chamber's trips to other cities, including one to the Moravian section of Winston-Salem, North Carolina, called Old Salem. That visit was helpful in guiding our thoughts because like Bethlehem it was a colonial Moravian town.

After the reports were released, people in Bethlehem were relieved. Even though Bethlehem was not destined to be a major retail center, the city had a more modest path forward that was much more realistic. The problem was that several blocks along Broad Street were being torn down. How would these now vacant parcels relate to Main Street when it was transformed? (A portion of one block would be vacant for more than twenty-five years.)

Mowrer, with the support of the city council, commissioned the designs for Main Street's Victorian transformation. He secured the funding through the U.S. Economic Development Administration and federal community development block grants. But then he lost the Democratic primary for mayor in 1977. Nevertheless, the city broke ground for the Main Street improvements that December.[87]

While Mowrer was in office, the city completed the three high-rises for senior citizens, the First Valley Bank building, the Bethlehem Plaza Mall, and the Walnut Street Parking Garage. The mall struggled mightily to attract tenants, finally resorting to converting a portion of the windowless retail floor into a warren of small shops that rented for $1 per square foot, a paltry sum even in those days. Eventually a local technology company bought the entire building.[88]

Meanwhile on Main Street a force of nature was revving up the community to save the historic Moravian Sun Inn. Hughetta Bender was the widow of James P. Bender, a Bethlehem Steel executive. A native of Florida with a degree in bacteriology from Florida State University, Hughetta Bender was intelligent, extroverted, and passionate about the Sun Inn, which at that time had been so altered that it looked nothing like its colonial self. Its street level held shops while the upper level was home to a restaurant and a seedy lodging place. When Bender read that the building was to be sold and perhaps demolished to make way for new downtown development, she called a meeting to form a Sun Inn preservation association to "acquire the hotel and keep it from the bulldozer."[89]

This was right after Mowrer had been elected and was looking at the redevelopment plans with skepticism. With the direction of redevelopment in question, the Sun Inn remained in limbo until 1975. Bender attracted support from a community that already had seen the benefits of preservation and the risks of "tear down and rebuild." Her key adviser was Robert Margolis, a Bethlehem attorney and accountant. Restoring the inn to its eighteenth-century form would cost well more than $2 million. With the guidance of Margolis and the financial support of the community, Bender formed the nonprofit Sun Inn Preservation Association, which paid $140,000 for the Sun Inn. The young nonprofit also purchased the neighboring property on Main Street, which included a vacant lot, once used for parking, in the center of the block behind the inn. The group also acquired a building next to the parking lot on Broad Street. Those acquisitions made the association a major property holder in the key block connecting Main Street to the mall.

But as galvanizing as the purchase of, and preservation plans for, the Sun Inn were, what was going on in the steel industry at the time was more than worrisome. In 1975 Japanese steelmakers were more productive than their U.S. counterparts, a development that forced the layoff of nine thousand workers throughout Bethlehem Steel.[90]

In 1978 state representative J. Michael Schweder, son of a former Bethlehem fire commissioner, persuaded Governor Milton J. Shapp to transfer the money set aside for a performing arts center in Bethlehem (the request aligned with Mowrer's plans) and put it toward restoration of the Sun Inn and the 1869 Lukenbach Mill, which was still standing in the Colonial Industrial Quarter operated by Historic Bethlehem, Inc. Both projects moved forward and reopened to the public just a few years after the Main Street improvements were completed. As the lawyer for the Sun Inn Preservation Association during the restoration of the building, I had a front-row seat from which to watch the community support a leader who had stepped forward for a cause. Bender was smart, wise, and cunning but always in a genteel, southern way. For every occasion she would serve Virginia Gentleman bourbon. Then she would give a speech that always ended with a glowing smile, an open embrace, and the mantra "It's *your* Sun Inn." I credit her for my enduring affection for the Sun Inn and bourbon.

The public improvements to Main Street and along Broad Street to the Bethlehem Plaza Mall included wide slate sidewalks, parallel parking areas to replace the former angle parking, Victorian street lamps, planters and flowers, trees, furniture, trash receptacles, and the restoration of two Victorian-era public fountains. Owners restored the facades of their buildings. The change in Main Street between 1978 and 1982 was dramatic. Most owners restored their facades to their original materials as much as possible.

But all the success did not protect Bethlehem from the prevailing winds of the nation. Ronald Reagan became president in 1981, and shortly thereafter the Reagan recession hit the country. By 1982 national unemployment had reached 10.8 percent. The country was in an economic funk. A beautifully restored town with virtually no funds for marketing sat along the Monocacy patiently waiting to be discovered. Christmas patrons were the only thing standing between the shop owners and financial disaster.

The good news was that some of the scars of the condemnation and demolition of the previous ten years were gone. Two townhouse developments added new residents to downtown. A three-story office building went up on Broad Street, much smaller than what the grand plan had envisioned but a welcome addition. However, downtown remained like a smiling child with missing baby teeth: adorable and promising.

CHAPTER 6
DEINDUSTRIALIZATION

T he woes of Bethlehem's rejuvenated business district were directly traceable to not only the faltering economy but also deindustrialization, something every advanced economy has experienced. This sweeping change has been particularly dramatic in the United States, where the percentage of the non-farming workforce employed in manufacturing plummeted from 30 percent in 1950 to 10 percent in 2007.[91] The loss of manufacturing jobs has mirrored the rise of the service sector, which today employs more than 70 percent of the civilian labor force, most in jobs that did not exist even ten years ago. Many of those jobs require skills far different from those of industrial workers for most of the twentieth century.

The causes of deindustrialization are hotly debated, especially in political circles. Advances in technology have reduced the amount of labor needed to produce many manufactured goods, thus causing a reduction in employment. Manufacture of products that require intensive labor has moved to emerging economies with lower labor costs.

This seems academic from a distance. But between 1950 and 2000, for people living in Bethlehem, or any of the historic manufacturing cities of the country, it was a tragedy. In 1950 almost 60 percent of the civilian workforce in Bethlehem—27,328 people—were working in manufacturing.[92] By 2007 that number had dropped to 5,383, a decline of 80 percent. How the people of this community addressed this tectonic shift in their economy is a story of resilience and leadership.

The *Bethlehem Globe-Times Almanac* for 1947 offers a glimpse at a lost world. A section entitled "Industrial Bethlehem" is most revealing. The listing of sixty-six industries includes metals manufacturing such as Bethlehem Fabricators, Bethlehem Welding and Machine, and Steel City Chromium Plating. It also includes dozens of textile manufacturers like Chickadee Dress Company, Ed-Mar Hat Company, Josette Undergarment Company, Forte Neckwear, and Perfect Brassiere Company. By 2010 all but five were gone, including every one of the garment manufacturers.

Deindustrialization in the Lehigh Valley began with the garment manufacturers in the 1970s. The International Ladies' Garment Workers' Union represented most of the garment workers in the region. Once again, proximity to New York and the availability of female workers had made the region prominent in this field. However, as transportation and communication improved, new garment-manufacturing businesses located in the American South, where labor was less expensive and unions were nonexistent. To compete many manufacturers relocated their operations to states with lower costs. This movement prompted the powerful ILGWU to embark on its memorable "Look for the Union Label" campaign, which was promoted heavily on television in the late 1970s and early 1980s.

Soon even southern jobs were at risk as manufacturers found that they could employ workers in Asia and Latin America at a fraction of the cost of American workers and ship the goods economically on oceans protected by the U.S. Navy. Gradually all but specialty work, and work that had to be done in the United States for government-contracted clothing, was drifting overseas. Today the American consumer has a difficult task finding clothing made in the United States. The Lehigh Valley's remnant of this industry is Majestic Athletic in Easton, which has the exclusive right to Major League Baseball's uniforms and licensed souvenir caps, shirts, and jackets, and A&H Sportswear, a specialty swimsuit designer and manufacturer.

The grandiose plans for Bethlehem that the Steel supported had signaled to all that prosperity was here to stay. Just as the initial restoration of the Moravian area was advancing, Bethlehem Steel announced record profits. When *Business Week* reported the ten highest-paid business executives in the United States for 1957, seven were from Bethlehem Steel, which was churning out profit in record amounts. In 1959 Big Steel collectively decided that the spiral of increasing wages and benefits had to stop. The companies decided to stand firm in contract negotiations. The unions went on strike on July 15, and the industry left its customers without the products they required to do business. The strike, which became a national crisis, heavily affected the railroad, automobile, and construction industries. In a settlement negotiated by Vice President Richard M. Nixon, the unions won wage and benefit increases that made the steelworkers the best-paid industrial workers in the nation. However, during the six-month strike the industry's customers sought and purchased foreign steel for the first time. In 1959 steel imports rose to five million metric tons, a record. It was the beginning of the end. "That number would double in the next six years, as some customers never returned to buying domestic steel and others cut back on it even after the steelworkers returned to the mills," the *Morning Call* reported years later.[93]

Following Eugene Grace's belief that demand for steel in a growing country would continue to be almost unlimited, Bethlehem Steel proceeded with developing and building a new plant in Burns Harbor, Indiana, which opened in 1965. It would be the last integrated steel plant built in the United States. While it was under construction, the upstart Nucor was using electric furnaces to melt scrap metal. Bethlehem Steel executives scoffed at Nucor, which today is the leading steel producer in the United States.

In 1970 the Port Authority of New York and New Jersey was seeking bids for its World Trade Center project. Bethlehem Steel bid $117 million, beating U.S. Steel by $5 million.[94] Bethlehem thought it had won the contract. But the celebration was premature. The Port Authority rejected the bid, which was 50 percent higher than the agency's engineering estimates. The Port Authority also filed a price-rigging suit against Bethlehem Steel and U.S. Steel.[95]

The Port Authority ultimately accepted multiple bids totaling $83 million. Many bidders were using foreign steel. Bethlehem Steel never recovered its dominance in structural steel and closed its structural steel division in 1976.

Bethlehem Steel found itself in an environment of decreasing demand and increasing competition, both foreign and domestic. The burst of highway and bridge construction that began in the 1950s was petering out. With the gas crisis of 1973, automakers were finding ways to decrease the amount of heavy steel in their vehicles to get better gas mileage by using lighter materials, such as aluminum and plastics. And while construction of skyscrapers did not cease, the majority of buildings were now structures of one to three stories that required less structural steel. With the upstart Nucor and foreign steel companies offering steel at lower prices, the old-line steel companies were facing declining sales in a lean market. On top of that, the government was imposing tighter pollution standards on steel companies. American steel companies, with older plants, were at a disadvantage to foreign steel companies that had either rebuilt after the war or were located in countries with fewer regulations.

When the Steel joined forces with the United Steelworkers to convince the public that foreign steel, and foreign products made from foreign steel, were the cause of the Steel's problems and would cost American jobs, its challenges were visible to the community. In the mid-1970s a large steel beam prominently engraved with BUY AMERICAN was placed in front of the union hall next to Bethlehem's city hall. Company employees who arrived at work in a "rice burner" (a Toyota) were instructed to park at a distance from their workplace. None of this stemmed the decline. Between 1970 and 1980 the number of employees at the plant declined from sixteen thousand to twelve thousand.[96]

The day that got the attention of the entire community was September 30, 1977, Bethlehem's Black Friday. That day the company took the unprecedented step of laying off white-collar workers, distributing pink slips to twenty-five hundred white-collar employees throughout the company, including eight hundred in Bethlehem.[97] The community was shaken to its core. Everyone knew someone who had been laid off. People who had assumed that, despite the temporary challenges, Bethlehem Steel employees had jobs for life were distraught. Secretaries and clerks who were making much more money than the local wage for similar positions were suddenly jobless. Local professionals faced having to find work in their area or to uproot their families for a job elsewhere. Management hoped that this massive reduction of staff and shutting several facilities outside Bethlehem would stanch the red ink until conditions returned to normal and the company returned to prosperity. Many of those let go assumed they would be called back. No one was prepared for the new normal.

Conditions in the steel industry continued to worsen. In 1981 the Bethlehem plant laid off two thousand workers with little prospects for recall. The layoffs at company headquarters in Martin Tower continued through the early 1980s as management sought a way out of its deep financial hole. Bethlehem Steel continued to close plants, including its Lackawanna plant on Lake Erie near Buffalo. "Bethlehem Steel's total employment hit a peak of 115,000 in 1975. It stood at 83,800 ... in 1980. It was down to 48,500 by 1984," the author John Strohmeyer reports. The outplacement manager hired by the company estimated that 50 to 60 percent of the Bethlehem Steel employees who were laid off found jobs within ninety days, but nearly all had to settle for less money.[98]

To add to the misery, the United States entered a recession in late 1981 that lasted through early 1982. Pennsylvania's manufacturing economy usually enters a recession later and suffers longer than other areas because manufacturers assume demand will remain constant and don't pull back right away. When the overall economy recovers, manufacturing does not return to full capacity until customers feel confident enough to order new manufactured goods. This recession was particularly hard for the state. The fallout included the closing of most of the steelmaking facilities in the Monongahela Valley of western Pennsylvania in 1983. In Bethlehem the unemployment rate was a staggering 13 percent in 1982. From city hall to Harrisburg Pennsylvanians had little to celebrate and much to be concerned about as industries that had provided employment and tax revenues quickly disappeared.[99]

In this environment retail businesses were suffering too, but retail in the downtowns of the proud cities that had hosted the industrial giants was terminally ill. Shiny new malls or large chain stores, new chain supermarkets, and pharmacies provided most of what families with less to spend needed. Abandoned or boarded-up storefronts on Main Street sat next to row houses that had been converted to multifamily units that trapped low-income tenants in downtowns that either had no stores or only those that catered to low-income residents. Cities would grapple with these issues for decades. Bethlehem was one of them.

It is hard to describe to anyone who did not live through that period what a shock the new normal was. Everyone watched pennies, which affected not just retail but construction, car sales, vacation spending, and anything remotely considered a luxury as everyone waited for the next problem to appear. Between 1960 and 1980 Bethlehem's growth pattern reversed; it lost 7 percent of its population, which was modest compared to cities like Chester and Wilkes-Barre, which had lost more than half their residents by 1980. Worst of all was the brain drain as young, educated natives fled for greater opportunities elsewhere. Desperate times call for desperate measures. And these were desperate times for the country's gritty cities.

PART II
A NEW PARADIGM, 1982–2000

CHAPTER 7
TOURISM
AN ECONOMIC DEVELOPMENT FANTASY

In an earlier desperate time, the Great Depression year of 1937, Bethlehem's city leaders took the first step toward using tourism as a viable source of economic development. After persuading the U.S. Chamber of Commerce to declare Bethlehem "Christmas City USA," the city lit itself up for that year's Christmas season with a wooden star fifty feet tall covered with light bulbs atop South Mountain; a forty-foot Christmas tree, illuminated by floodlights and decked out with spinning aluminum squares that appeared to twinkle, in the center of the Hill-to-Hill Bridge; and twenty-two blocks of Christmas lights.

I grew up within this tradition and always associated tourism with civic pride. Christmas was a special time in Bethlehem. The lights, candles in the windows throughout town, the star on South Mountain (which in its current iteration is ninety feet high, powered by an LED system, and lit year-round as a symbol of the city), churches with manger scenes out front and a variety of special Christmas services, local Handel's *Messiah* sing-alongs, and school Christmas concerts combined to exude the joy of the season. December was the only time of year that tourists came to Bethlehem.

When I was young, I also yearned to travel beyond our family trips to the Poconos or the Jersey shore or to visit relatives in Michigan. I wanted to see the world. In the summer of 1970 after I graduated from Lehigh I got my first glimpse. A French professor and his sister were leading a tour of Europe for college students—ten weeks, eight countries, two Volkswagen buses, no frills. I decided at the last minute to join them, even though I would have to work for the first part of the summer and miss the first few weeks of the tour. The professor agreed that I could arrive for the last five weeks of the tour because they could squeeze one more person into a bus. My adventure of a lifetime began at John F. Kennedy International Airport; I was gripping a low-cost ticket on Icelandic Airlines from New York to Amsterdam. From Amsterdam I would have to find my way by train to Venice, where I would join the group. This was well before cell phones, the Internet, and translator apps. I had an Italian phrase book, six years of Spanish classes, and a great deal of optimism.

But at Kennedy I learned that the flight was overbooked. Icelandic gave me a voucher and wished me luck. Determined to get to Europe, I went from counter to counter. I got lucky, really lucky: Alitalia offered me the last seat on a plane to Rome—first class and at no extra charge. In a few short hours I was in a Sophia Loren movie. Wine was served, stewards in dinner jackets carved the roast beef, wealthy Italian passengers strolled around the cabin after dinner, and the pilot came out to offer us a tour of the flight deck. I was hooked.

Later, when I arrived in Venice, I strolled around the city of water and reflected light. It was July in an ancient city. The canals stank, cats and their droppings were everywhere, and finding your way around was impossible. I loved it. As I strolled into unknown territory on that hot July day, I found myself in a small sunlit piazza. The only other person around was a little boy kicking a soccer ball. To my surprise the boy was singing an American pop song, "Na Na Na Na Hey Hey Goodbye," but he was singing, "Na na na na hey hey ciao ciao." That was my epiphany about how American pop culture penetrates distant lands.

I was disappointed by the relatively small size of the Roman forum but was awestruck when I stood on the floor of the House of Commons, imagining Pitt, Disraeli, Churchill, and the history that those walls hold. Traveling through northern Spain, I learned that, thanks to my college professors, I spoke Spanish with a Chilean accent. But I must have spoken it well because they kept asking me if I was from Chile. Europe's sidewalk cafés were a revelation; I had my first-ever tortellini en brodo along the Tiber in Rome and, of course, coq au vin on the Left Bank in Paris. People were wonderful, despite my limited language skills. Even the Parisians were nice. And though I did not understand a word he said, the French tour guide at Napoleon's tomb spoke with such passion that I felt as though I understood it all.

But the art, architecture, and design left the greatest impression and the need for more. From the Uffizi and the Pitti Palace to the Prado and the Louvre, and the public sculpture and architecture all around, it was more than I could absorb in one visit. A little bar along the Arno River offered recorded Italian popular music as we drank and danced in a setting that was definitely not industrial. Then there were the Italian sports cars. The first time I saw a Lamborghini was in a traffic jam on the road to Rome. All of us got out of the VW bus and surrounded the car like the youthful tourists that we were.

Less than a year after I returned from Europe, I landed a summer job with U.S. Customs in Alburg, Vermont, fifty miles south of Montreal. I was twenty-two, had a customs badge and a '67 Mustang, and one of the greatest cities in North America was waiting to be discovered. I fell in love with Montreal that summer. The Place Jacques Cartier became my second home: outdoor cafés, music, eighteenth-century French architecture, and lots of young people. The historic area was just beginning its renaissance, and the site of Expo '67, Montreal's world's fair, was becoming a center for the arts. At the time one of my favorite albums was the Who's *Tommy*. I splurged on a ticket to see Les Grands Ballets Canadiens dance to the music of my favorite rock opera. The mix of rock and ballet was an artistic revelation.

When Susan and I were married in 1973, we wanted to honeymoon in Europe but could afford only a road trip to eastern Canada in our new Opel. New Brunswick and Nova Scotia were not as exciting as Montreal and Paris, but the natural beauty was well worth the trip. We visited local museums and shops and "discovered" the Beaverbrook Gallery in Fredericton, New Brunswick, where the main gallery boasts an enormous Salvador Dali painting. We became fascinated with modern art.

Our excursions came quickly after that: a Lehigh University–sponsored trip to Romania; a trip to Spain with my recently widowed mother, who had always wanted to go there; and in 1976 a trip to Germany and Austria with friends. The German trip included the famous Oktoberfest in Munich, the grandfather of all beer festivals.

Even with our best efforts we could not match the ribaldry of the Germans, but we did try.

It certainly was not clear to me then, but all this travel was leading me toward my life's work, instilling in me the belief that the cultural heritage of a place can be the key to its health and vitality and that music is a universal language.

But back home in Bethlehem in the mid-1970s, I had to hustle to find clients and persuade them that I was a reasonably competent lawyer. I sought various ways of getting involved in the community and was appointed to the Bethlehem Fine Arts Commission in 1974, even though I made it clear that I did not have an educational background in the arts. At some point in all this, during a presentation and discussion of business development in Bethlehem, I asked why we were not devoting more efforts to tourism. My reward was appointment to the tourism committee of the chamber of commerce.

Cultural tourism predates Marco Polo. However, cultural tourism as an industry that deserves the attention of, and promotion by, government is a relatively new idea, especially for cities in the United States. One reason is that its value is hard to measure because it affects lodging, recreation, retail, real estate, air passenger transportation, food and beverages, car rentals, and taxi services. Beyond that, civic attractions such as museums, cultural events, the performing arts, and sports also benefit from tourism. According to the World Travel and Tourism Council, the industry supports more than 6.5 million jobs in the United States and represents more than 8 percent of the country's gross domestic product. Most state and local governments offer financial inducements for businesses to locate in their community. Until recently this was not true of tourism, except in those areas where tourism is the dominant industry, such as Florida and Hawaii. It takes a leap of faith and a strong dose of naïveté to suggest developing tourism in a gritty city in the Rust Belt.

It is no surprise, then, that the idea was slow to catch interest in Bethlehem. Its Christmas tourism program crept along after World War II. The Bethlehem Post Office offered Christmas City, USA, cancellation on letters mailed there. In the 1960s the chamber partnered with the Moravian Museum to encourage group visits during the Christmas season. The program was oriented to bus tour promoters in the northeastern United States and Canada. Tour groups visited the Moravian Museum, shopped on Main Street, dined in the Hotel Bethlehem, and had nighttime tours of the light-bedecked city while a guide in colonial Moravian attire provided nuggets of history about the town and its Christmas customs. Eventually the Moravian Museum and Historic Bethlehem, Inc., joined the chamber to offer walking tours and bus tours for guests who arrived by car.

Sometimes change starts small. The idea of playing up tourism beyond the Christmas season was suggested by an observation from an astute member of the chamber of commerce's board. Jean Kessler, a former chamber employee who remembered well the popularity of the city's Christmas programs, joined the chamber's board in 1980 and was asked to head the tourism committee. She set about expanding the committee and giving structure to the tourism program at a difficult time for historic Main Street. Despite the restoration of the Sun Inn, the newly installed Victorian streetscape, and the enduring presence of the Moravian Book Shop, the street was not doing well. The effects of Bethlehem Steel's downward spiral and the growing popularity of the suburban malls continued to have an adverse impact on the small downtown. Bethlehem saw tourism, particularly the Christmas tourism program, as a partial remedy for the malaise. Virtually all retailers relied on Christmas sales for at least 20 percent of their annual revenue. Without the revenue from tourists, the small district would succumb to the fate of the South Side retail district, which had all but faded into oblivion.

Although times were tough, the Christmas tourism program grew and thrived throughout the 1970s and into the 1980s. The main attraction was and still is a Christmas visit to a city called Bethlehem. The program brought approximately 200 charter tours, about 10,000 people, to the town and Main Street. While most of the tours were day trips from nearby communities in Pennsylvania, New Jersey, Maryland, and New York, several were from Ohio, Ontario, Connecticut, and Virginia—bringing prized overnight visitors who stayed at local hotels and ate at local restaurants. Tourists also came to shop. Then, as now, the first and second Saturdays of December were the peak days of the season for local retailers.

Kessler's thought-provoking observation was prompted by a list the committee had made of events and activities in Bethlehem on a calendar. As she looked over the list, she noticed no activities during

August that might appeal to tourists. In 1982 Kessler, who had read a concept I had submitted for a German themed celebration, asked me to come up with an idea for an event in August that would fill that gap.

At the time, I was trying to devote less effort to civic affairs and more to developing my law practice. Our Victorian house, although lovely, is and was a true money pit. Fortunately, my law practice was doing well. I had acquired an office in nearby Nazareth and was managing two offices and a staff of three. I had just finished two years as chair of the county Democratic organization and four years on the Democratic State Committee; I was weary of politics and the drain on my time and money. I also was resolved to get serious about my law practice and reduce my commitments to community organizations.

However, sometimes passion overrules logic. I believed in my city and believed too that it could realize its potential with a little encouragement. With more conviction than common sense, I agreed to lead still another committee in 1982. This one would consider a concept for an event that would bring visitors to Bethlehem in August, a time of year when Main Street was empty and everyone was in the Poconos, at the Jersey shore, or somewhere else that was miles from Bethlehem.

CHAPTER 8
A SIGNATURE FESTIVAL

When I took on the challenge of setting up an event that would appeal to tourists in August, Bethlehem had only one event designated as a festival, the annual Bach Festival. Beyond that, the city had been edging toward larger public events in its newly renovated Bethlehem Historic District downtown. Spaces that did not exist in 1960 now were presentable and available. How to tie all this together was the challenge. Bethlehem's history offered both successful and not-so-successful examples of attempts at a signature attraction. That history would lead me in the right direction.

The festival of the Bach Choir of Bethlehem is the city's revered cultural institution. Founded in 1898 by J. Fred Wolle, a Moravian, the choir was the first in the United States to perform Bach's Mass in B Minor and the Christmas Oratorio. In 1905 the choir established annual performances as the Bach Festival. Although the choir began in Central Moravian Church, the main concert hall for the festival now is the more ornate Packer Memorial Church at Lehigh University. Held during two weekends in May, the festival always has attracted guests from around the country and the world to admire the work of the great composer as presented by the voices of the community and guest soloists.

The Bach Festival had demonstrated that people would travel to Bethlehem, even during the depths of the Depression and the years of grime and soot from a steel plant, to attend an event that offered something they did not have in their own community. The festival also is proof of the power in a community's musical heritage. In 1983, as the first August festival was in the planning stages, the Bach Festival hired a young artistic director and conductor, Greg Funfgeld, the music director of Bethlehem's First Presbyterian Church and a 1976 graduate of the Westminster Choir College. He was fluent in German, passionate about Bach, and visionary about what the revered Bach Choir could accomplish. He also was eager to expand the horizons of the choir beyond its May festival. Could this be a piece of the puzzle?

Studying the hits is one thing. Learning from less successful efforts was helpful too. In the 1960s Bethlehem created a fine arts commission as part of the national movement spawned by the establishment of the National Endowment for the Arts. The mission of Bethlehem's commission was to support the arts in the city, including the development and installation of public art. The city asked the commission to undertake a project on the east side of the new city hall complex and create a sculpture garden to further enhance the government center. The well-meaning mayor and council funded the commission with the annual stipend of $2,000. The Medicis would have been proud of the intent, if not the level, of support.

Undaunted by the meager budget, members of the commission embarked on a project to raise money to make the arts a prominent part of the civic landscape. In 1971 the Christmas City Fair premiered on July 17, the fifty-second anniversary of the official creation of the City of Bethlehem. The weekend event featured food from many of the churches and ethnic clubs in the community; booths for civic organizations like the Boy Scouts, YWCA, Jaycees, and Little League; an antique car display, puppet shows, artists, crafters, and two stages for musical performances by local bands and student groups. At first it was a hit. The profits came to more than $4,000. Work by a devoted group of volunteers yielded a happy community event that attracted thousands.

When I joined the fine arts commission in 1974, the development of the sculpture garden was its main focus. The fair provided the money to buy art to make the garden a place of civic pride. I vividly recall going to the studio of the noted sound sculptor Harry Bertoia in nearby Bally. We all had a grand time doing as Harry instructed, playing with his sculptures to induce whatever sound would come out. After several hours of enjoying art with childlike delight, we agreed to purchase one of his signature reed sculptures. These consisted of metallic reeds of the same size placed on a base. The stems of the reeds were designed to be flexible so that someone could move one or all at the same time to make different sounds. After this reed sculpture was placed in the garden, which has only modest pedestrian traffic, one of the reeds was bent, by either an enthusiastic patron or a vandal. A metal band now restricts the movement of the reeds, limiting damage and playfulness. It is still there today. Harry, God rest his soul, would not be pleased. And we learned a lesson about public art. Another purchase, *Crazy Otto*, was made of wood and within twenty years was so rotted that it had to be removed. Another lesson learned.

The Christmas City Fair, which was held in July from 1971 to 1997, was the first event in Bethlehem to take advantage of the space along the redeveloped Monocacy Creek basin. The area downhill from where the Hill to Hill Bridge joins Main Street at Central Moravian Church had been a warren of row homes and unsightly businesses during the postwar years. After Hurricane Diane in 1955, the dwellings were torn down. The city used redevelopment money to buy the remaining businesses, and the area became a large parking lot used by visitors to the Moravian Colonial Industrial Quarter on the east side of the Monocacy. Across the street from the parking lot was a new grassy square surrounded by streets and bisected on its western side by a railroad.

Mid-July in Bethlehem is historically the hottest time of the year. Steamy ninety-degree days are not uncommon between July 4 and mid-August. Given the variability of the weather, the Christmas fair, like many outdoor events, was not a reliable source of revenue. In some years the fair suffered losses, which caused the fine arts commission to experience great angst. As I was handed the assignment to create an event in August, emblazoned on my brain were the weather-related challenges of the Christmas City Fair. This was a problem I was determined to avoid, but at that point I did not truly comprehend that any outdoor event is subject to the elements.

In 1975 Bethlehem was preparing to celebrate the U.S. Bicentennial the following year, and our neighbor Anne McGeady was appointed coordinator of the celebration. McGeady had patience, intelligence, and a wonderful sense of humor, good qualities when working with volunteers and the public. My mother signed on as a volunteer, and I became a member of the Bicentennial Committee. I agreed to chair the Ethnic Weekends subcommittee, because I was eager to share the city's melting pot heritage. The Ukrainian, Jewish, Portuguese, and Greek communities had volunteered to present weekends featuring their cultures. As someone of Pennsylvania German heritage, I stepped into the obvious gap in the ethnic presentations. I would lead the charge for a celebration of German heritage.

The only place to start the quest for German culture in modern Bethlehem is the Beethoven Choruses. This German social group was organized by Catholic Germans affiliated with Holy Ghost Church. In the early 1960s the group had moved from Bethlehem to a rural area south of the city, where it bought fifteen acres and built a new social hall it named Beethoven Waldheim ("home in the woods"). I had been to the Waldheim several times and was aware that, in addition to being a place for German celebrations and social events, it was the home of two professionally led choirs, the Mannerchor and the Damenchor (men's choir and women's choir). I contacted the club and was told I should talk to Gus Skrivanek and his lively wife, Catherine. Skrivanek taught wood shop at the local vocational school and was a real son of the Fatherland.

I shared the idea of having a German night in Bethlehem as part of the Bicentennial. Skrivanek brought in members of the club and representatives of Holy Ghost Church. Bob Steinmetz, a friend of the Skrivaneks', traveled to Germany regularly. He had hosted a German exchange student who had become the leader of a small town band in Bavaria, the Stadtkapelle Berching. Virtually every small town in Bavaria and other German-speaking areas has a town brass band that plays marches, polkas, and oompah music.

In the 1970s Barnesville, which is about fifty miles northwest of Bethlehem, held a successful Bavarian festival in mid-July. Steinmetz had arranged for the Stadtkapelle Berching to perform there in July 1976. I immediately made Bob a one-man entertainment committee for our German night. The Beethoven Choruses and the Stadtkapelle Berching would be the entertainment, and the date was set for Saturday, July 10, to coincide with the band's visit to Barnesville.

The location I selected for the event was one that I walked past daily, Bethlehem's City Center Plaza. The designers of Bethlehem's City Center—four buildings and a vast plaza of pavers with a few areas of grass—intended it to be an esplanade overlooking the Lehigh River, the south side, and South Mountain with Lehigh University perched upon it and topped by the star of Bethlehem. The designers never thought through how Bethlehem could use the plaza. If it had been designed for passive use, it should have had some places to sit, relax, contemplate, enjoy a view, converse with others. In Europe such spaces offer restaurants and outdoor dining where people can enjoy the view. Planners also would have included a dramatic stairway from the steep south wall of the complex to make this bastion of democratic governance approachable by residents coming from the south side. Alas, the American architects simply created a plaza where the only seating is a ledge with a one-hundred-foot drop. And it was impossible to hold large civic functions there because it had no power sources, water supply, water drainage, or access to bathrooms. Its only use was formal ceremonies led from the city's unattractive portable stage, a large box trailer with a side that was raised to create an awning in front of the stage and protect those on stage from the elements.

Inexperience can be a blessing. If I had known all the limitations of the site, I would never have chosen it. None of the other ethnic celebrations was held at city hall. But this was a city celebration, and I felt it should be at the city's showplace, which then was only nine years old. On July 4, a week before German Night, the plaza was to be used for the major Bicentennial celebration for the whole city, which included an interfaith service followed by a parade. The celebration attracted several thousand people. Our goal had been to attract a few hundred.

When Saturday, July 10, arrived, fate gave us a beautiful warm summer day with lower humidity than usual. German Night had received small write-ups in the local papers, and several Catholic and Lutheran churches had promoted it. The plaza was decked out with Bavarian blue and white tablecloths, candles in wine bottles, attractive bunting, and a German flag that was temporarily replacing the city flag. The event was to run from 6:00 to 10:00 p.m., with concerts by the choirs followed by music by the Bavarian band and dancing. People started trickling in early, slowly filling the tables. By seven the trickle had turned into running water and then a deluge. I was too busy to count or enjoy the music. Food was running out, but so was the beer—an unthinkable catastrophe at a German party. At 8:30, in a panic, we set out for south side to hunt down an open distributor, get what beer we could, and throw it in the back of a borrowed pickup. We also found ice, an essential ingredient for serving beer on a summer night. By 9:15 we were back in the beer business, saving the night for the three thousand people who were dancing, singing, and roaming around the vast plaza. The band played on for more than an hour past the scheduled closing time, probably until we ran out of beer again. Our exhausted team basked in the glow of the smiles that radiated from our fellow Bethlehemites.

The event had struck a chord. Just as on St. Patrick's Day, when everyone is a little bit Irish, everyone was a little bit German that night. Six years later this midsummer event was a clear harbinger of what a new Bethlehem festival might be.

WALKING THE DOG

In addition to coping with the hoopla around the Bicentennial, in 1976 my pregnant wife and I made a commitment to the Bethlehem Historic District by becoming the owners of thirty-five hundred square feet of Victorian for our soon-to-be expanding family. We invited friends for an all-day wallpaper-stripping and painting party, which helped, but it was just the beginning. As a young couple in an old house in a neighborhood of older people, we felt like urban pioneers. Like others our age, many of whom would join us in the neighborhood in the next several years, we were rebelling against the suburbs and determined to be city folk. Walking in an interesting, friendly, and safe neighborhood has been one of the greatest rewards of this decision, counterbalancing the endless home improvements and maintenance an old house demands.

When Susan and I moved back to Bethlehem, our first apartment was a few blocks from my parents' home near Stefko Boulevard. After only a few months of marriage we went to the local animal shelter and adopted a spunky little terrier-beagle mix puppy. Each night we would dutifully put her in a box with some old socks, and the next morning we would wake up with her in our bed. We named her Gypsy. Three years and two apartments later, when we moved into the Church Street Victorian, walking Gypsy through historic Bethlehem became my daily meditation time. Except in the worst weather, we would amble past the Victorian homes, city hall, Bethlehem Public Library, the colonial Moravian buildings, Central Moravian Church, Hotel Bethlehem, Main Street, and the Sun Inn and its courtyard. On good weather days we would walk onto City Center Plaza and look over to the south side or just take in the cherry trees, a gift from our Japanese sister city, during the week in April when they blossomed. Sometimes we would wander along Monocacy Creek through the Colonial Industrial Quarter and on toward Old Brewery Tavern. Gypsy, never a totally obedient dog, was ever willing to walk the two to three miles daily. In the summer of 1982, I had a new assignment on which to meditate, and Gypsy was along for much of the my thinking about what would become Bethlehem's new festival.

Bethlehem's north side commercial district is the size of a small town's—three blocks of Main Street from Church to Broad streets and two blocks of Broad Street from Main to New streets—not that of a city of seventy thousand. It also offered only a few nooks for public events. As a result of the urban renewal projects of the 1970s, Broad Street between New and Guetter, just one block from Main Street, had been converted to an outdoor mall (Broad Street Mall) adjacent to the First Valley high-rise and the indoor Bethlehem Plaza Mall. Retail along the Broad Street Mall was modest, and the mall hardscape, an unnatural addition to a busy street, was not successful as a space for shopping or leisure. The outdoor mall adjoined what was supposed to be a miniature Rockefeller Center–style skating rink in front of the eleven-story First Valley Bank building. The rink's owner quickly abandoned it after learning it required staffing and maintaining the ice and entailed a great deal of potential liability. It stood empty, another sign of lack of forethought by the developers.

The Sun Inn Courtyard was run by a partnership of the city and the nonprofit Sun Inn Preservation Association. After the inn was restored, the city agreed to put public funds into an attractive courtyard, with the proviso that the city would control the land for thirty-five years and keep it open to the public. The space, which is surrounded by townhomes built in the early 1980s on one side and the backs of Victorian buildings and the Sun Inn on the other sides, is intimate and offers visitors a sense of discovery and urban tranquility.

Main Street invites visitors to look up and see the three centuries of architecture laid before them as though some thoughtful person had created a place for studying American architecture. Main Street looks as though it ends at the colonial Moravian Brethren's House, but the street actually makes a sharp right to go down the hill and cross the Monocacy, where it turns left and continues for another block to Lehigh Street. Three pathways and a street with sidewalks lead to the Monocacy Valley, where the Moravians had their colonial industries. Historic Bethlehem, Inc., fostered the restoration of four buildings on this site: the 1761 Tannery, 1762 Waterworks, Spring House, and the 1869 Lukenbach Mill. At the Main Street entrance to two pathways is the 1750 Smithy. The three pathways and the extension of Main Street encourage exploration of the Monocacy Valley from Main Street. The park system created along the Monocacy is easily accessible and barrier free for a contiguous event.

Behind the Brethren's House, which now houses Moravian College classrooms, and down a hill, the Monocacy winds its way to its confluence with the Lehigh River. A field, used by Moravian College as a student recreation area, was modified in 1977 with a gift from Bethlehem Steel. For its seventy-fifth anniversary that year, the company donated an outdoor music pavilion with restrooms and storage. The Steel had a good relationship with Moravian College and wanted to benefit the college as well as note the company's anniversary. The Community Arts Pavilion was erected in the summer of 1977, but when it was finished the fanfare was minimal because of the disruption caused by the Black Friday layoffs at Bethlehem Steel in September of that year. Ray Houston, a dedicated musician and city leader, made every effort to hold concerts there for a few years. Because no one had any money to publicize the performances or to hire other performers, and because the location is not really part of any neighborhood, concerts were poorly attended. The pavilion's main use became the annual two-day Live Bethlehem Christmas Pageant. Otherwise the facility was unused and unloved.

Gypsy and I walked repeatedly through an underused downtown in which the city had invested effort and money with paltry results. This blank canvas was waiting for someone to pick up a paint brush.

OPERATION BOOTSTRAP

The tourism committee had given me the task of coming up with an attraction for the month of August, but the challenge was much more complex and urgent, I realized. For most of the twentieth century the City of Bethlehem's brand was firmly bound to that of its eponymous major corporate citizen, Bethlehem Steel Corporation. As the Steel rose in power, might, and prominence, the city and its citizens benefited from all that meant, including prosperity and influence. What would our identity be after the Steel closed up shop?

Bethlehem, no longer would be the host city of a powerful industrial giant; rather, it was becoming the poster child for the tragedy of deindustrialization. In 1982 Bethlehem Steel's total workforce—not just in Bethlehem—was less than sixty-seven thousand, and the company reported the staggering loss of $1.5 billion, the first loss in what became a five-year string.[100] The city's future was looking bleak. In the emerging knowledge-based economy companies were finding that the talent business, health care, and education needed would be difficult to attract to the Lehigh Valley. Throughout the 1980s and 1990s materials for recruiting top talent to the region emphasized proximity to the arts, culture, and professional sports of New York and Philadelphia. Worse, in November 1982 Billy Joel released his song "Allentown," which became the theme song for deindustrialization. During his early days of performing Joel would come from New York to perform in Allentown and Bethlehem, and he was familiar with the towns and with the layoffs at Bethlehem Steel.

Four years earlier Temple University Press had released *Gritty Cities*.[101] Cities in the Northeast, including Bethlehem, studied the book intently. Although the authors were not negative about the cities they studied, they characterized many cities experiencing the loss of their industries as also losing their individual identity.

As Gypsy and I walked in the autumn of 1982, I realized a new event could do more than simply attract tourists in August. It could become a significant first step toward changing the narrative about the city. It would have to present Bethlehem as the historic, culturally vibrant city that it needed to be to survive. And with the city unable to offer financial assistance and no other visible source of funding, staging this event would require Bethlehem and its people to make do with what we had. These were the thoughts that ricocheted in my brain as I walked with Gypsy and contemplated a project I had come to think of as Operation Bootstrap.

According to the urban specialist Gregory Ashworth of the University of Groningen, Netherlands, "Place branding is the idea of discovering or creating some uniqueness, which differentiates one place from others in order to gain a competitive brand value." Ashworth adds that "such uniqueness is normally created through three efforts: personality association, flagship building (signature urban design and signature district) and hallmark events."[102] In other words, play up a famous citizen, construct some eye-catching buildings, and/or create a big event.

A clear-eyed assessment of Bethlehem's assets revealed no famous person with the celebrity status for building a community brand, but the city certainly had another of those key elements—the Moravian historic district, with its unique place in American history and architecture. We could work with that, I thought, to support a new signature event.

Given the history and significance of music in Bethlehem from the day it was founded, it was obvious to me that the key content of the event had to be music. The more difficult question was what kind. Most successful music festivals present a specific genre: classical, jazz, blues, folk, country. Because I had never been to a music festival, I had no idea who went to them or how to choose a specific genre. It seemed to me that the more diverse styles you could offer in one place at one time, the more people you could attract. While I grew up on sixties rock, I enjoyed many genres. After many conversations with friends, I decided we should start a multi-genre music festival that reflected the diversity of music popular in the community.

But simply having a music festival was not enough to distinguish our event from the many other music events. Bethlehem's roots are German, and at the time almost a quarter of the American population claimed some German heritage. Bethlehem has the largest collection of eighteenth-century Germanic buildings in the United States (more original buildings than Colonial Williamsburg), and German (not Pennsylvania Dutch) was the language of the community for its first hundred years. I reasoned that the festival needed a German flavor. The name Musikfest, German for music festival, came to me as Gypsy and I walked on a cold January morning in 1983.

Perhaps because the only real festivals I had attended were Munich's Oktoberfest, which lasts more than two weeks, and Milwaukee's Summerfest, which has an annual ten-day run during the July Fourth holiday, I thought that a festival on a single weekend would not have the heft we needed. For our new August event to give Main Street merchants a real boost, encourage tourism, and put the community on the map, I maintained that the event would have to incorporate two weekends and the weekdays between. I argued that this schedule would allow the festival to gain momentum over the nine days and provide a financial buffer if we encountered rain or blistering heat for a day or two during the event. Another major consideration was that once you spend the time, energy, and money to set up a temporary infrastructure and market the event, the cost for additional days is relatively small and the revenue opportunities are great (although you can reach a point of diminishing returns if you carry that logic too far).

After considerable discussion about having an event that would last nine days, the Tourism Task Force on Special Events agreed and chose August 18 to 26, 1984, for the new venture's premiere and enthusiastically agreed to christen it Musikfest. After discussing the many potential locations, including the Moravian College music complex at Main and Church streets, we made a list of music organizations, bands, and others who might contribute to the discussion. Each committee member was to contact one or more organizations and to come back with a report on their reactions and whether they might help us. I contacted the Beethoven Waldheim crew and Bob Steinmetz. More walks and talks led to an outline of a festival that built upon the plazas and parks strategically situated throughout the small north side downtown. The first iteration of the new festival was midwifed by many people representing historic and music institutions. It would change significantly.

The Bach Choir expressed interest, and its board president joined us. Bob Steinmetz had reached out to the Stadtkapelle Berching to begin talks about its becoming the resident German band. A special committee was created to mount a Viennese ball. We also drew up a preliminary budget. By the time the Tourism Task Force finished its report on holding an August event called Musikfest, and its blueprint for how to put it together, the group included representatives of key community organizations, the city, and some business organizations.[103]

Throughout May we tweaked the plan in preparation for presenting it to the chamber's board of directors in early June. The goal was to get the chamber's endorsement for Musikfest. The document reads like a manifesto for tourism. The argument supporting tourism incorporates Bethlehem's proximity to the New York and Philadelphia markets, Bethlehem's collection of colonial-era buildings and museums, and the city's unique cultural heritage. It notes the success of tourism in the Lancaster area, which focuses on Pennsylvania Germans. A nine-day Musikfest would feature "a broad spectrum of music, ranging from German, Folk, Classical, Rock and a variety of musical creations in between." It boldly proposed to attract 100,000 visitors to downtown Bethlehem over nine days.

While readers who have been to Musikfest will appreciate the modesty of our ambitions, and perhaps the lack of excitement, in this initial proposal, it is important to remember that this was Operation Bootstrap and highly conscious of the limited resources available. The plan included

- A Viennese ball on the Friday evening before the festival to raise money and create a gala atmosphere. Committee members were in contact with the German consul in New York to invite an official of the German government to attend, and they planned to reach out to Austria as well. The ball would use all the public spaces—the lobby and three event rooms—in the Hotel Bethlehem.
- An opening ceremony on the first Saturday at noon at City Center Plaza with public officials and diplomats in attendance.
- A one-block closing of Main Street, with the city bandstand in the middle of the street; food vendors, beer, and soft drink sales on the sides; and tables, chairs, and a dance area in the middle. This would be the Gemutlichkeit Café, which would feature the guest German band and regional polka bands nearly all day long and something more modern, perhaps even rock, for the last

show of the evening. The report includes details about types of food (German) and locations for sale of souvenirs.

- A beer garden in the Sun Inn Courtyard with a calliope for entertainment when a band was not playing on Main Street. (We thought a calliope would be a low-cost item until we tried to find one.)
- A second stage for performances in the skating rink area of the Broad Street Mall, with daily performances of rock, jazz, and other music.
- Special events throughout the festival at the Community Arts Pavilion, which is three blocks from the site for the bandstand on Main Street. The special events would include a performance of the romantic 1954 musical *The Student Prince*, about a university student in Heidelberg, by a local theatrical company; a German choral competition; an interdenominational (Protestant and Catholic) church service; a performance by a U.S. military band; Schuhplattlers (an Austrian folk dance); and a Moravian Love Feast, a worship service at which apple cider and Moravian sugar cake would be served.
- Candlelight concerts every evening from Monday through Friday at Peter Hall, a music performance space with beautiful stained-glass windows in Moravian College's music complex at the end of Church Street.

We also proposed two other special events: performances of the Bach Choir of Bethlehem at First Presbyterian Church, which is not in the downtown, and a canoe regatta on the Lehigh Canal.

We had a proposed budget of $100,000 with no money for marketing. We would set up a new nonprofit organization, Bethlehem Musikfest Association, to foster the development of the festival, qualify for tax deductible donations, and apply for a special occasion permit to serve beer and wine.

The plan concludes with a sober evaluation of the status of the downtown and the aspiration of the festival to turn it around. Citing the millions of dollars that had been invested in the downtown, it states: "As both the consultants and the community leaders have recognized, the future of downtowns like Bethlehem no longer lies in ordinary retail shops. The general shopping public has irretrievably fled to the suburban malls and it is not likely to return in the near future." Citing the attractiveness of Main Street and the downtown museums, the plan states,

> It is important for the leadership in this community to show...that tourism is a viable business and that with enough entrepreneurship in the downtown area, Bethlehem can begin to attract the kind of crowds that visit adjacent areas. Lancaster County is the fourth largest tourism destination in the United States....Bucks County attracts hundreds of thousands of tourists annually...and the Poconos...also attracts hundreds of thousands of visitors annually....With twenty percent of the population of the United States living within a three hundred mile radius of Bethlehem, it is an ideal site for a permanent tourism industry....What is necessary to make this event function is to get an immediate commitment from the Chamber of Commerce and from sufficient funding sources to guarantee at least $25,000 so that a full-time coordinator can be hired immediately.[104]

This was a big request. The chamber had never made grants to anyone for any reason. And the U.S. Chamber of Commerce was advising that tourism promotion was not an appropriate function for chambers of commerce. The national organization reasoned that, although state governments and city and regional tourism promotion agencies were devoting more resources to tourism, promoting tourism did not directly benefit large sectors of American commerce such as manufacturing. The very idea that arts and tourism could actually support the needs of a declining industrial community was simply unfathomable.

But the plan now had the support of nonprofits in the community, including the historic organizations and the Bach Choir, and the chamber's board was reluctant to be the naysayer. The board (except for two dissenters) voted to endorse the plan and to assist the committee with temporary support services to solicit funding. It did not offer any financial assistance.

This is the point at which a community representative on a task force would have thanked everyone for their participation, turned his papers over to the tourism committee chair, and gone back to his full-time profession. But I was a stubborn Pennsylvania Dutchman, young and determined that his city would realize its potential. I checked my social capital account, marched out the door, and embarked on a great adventure.

CHAPTER 9
FINANCING A VISION

As a lawyer who grew up in a family that owned a small business and who wound up counseling dozens of owners of small businesses in his professional practice, I was a keen observer of the successes and failures of entrepreneurs. New business ventures fail for three main reasons: poor leadership, a bad business plan, and undercapitalization. At this point Musikfest had unproven leadership, an uncertain business plan, and no capitalization. Musikfest never was supposed to make money, but the possibility of losing money was a major concern.

The budget we submitted with the plan to the chamber of commerce board included revenues from the Viennese ball (tickets to be sold in advance), some modest income from tickets for the Candlelight Concerts and the Bach Choir concerts; and money from the sale of food and beverages. The Tourism Task Force always intended to bring in concessionaires, whose contracts would specify that the festival would receive a percentage of their sales, and volunteers to sell beer and soft drinks, with the net income supporting the festival. All the other costs, including performer fees, were exceeding both sources of revenue, so the festival would have to make up the balance by enlisting sponsors and seeking the donation of goods and services. Although the only music festivals I had ever attended were Oktoberfest and Summerfest, I certainly had attended and watched on television both college and professional sports events. How hard could it be to enlist some of those sponsors for an event that would attract 100,000 people who would be grateful for the sponsor's support and become its customers? The revenue mix of concert ticket sales, food and beverage purchases, and sponsorships would become known as the three-legged stool upon which the success of the festival would depend.

BEER

The story of the regulation of beer in the United States is a sad tale about a society that has mixed feelings about alcohol and a checkered history of use, abuse, and control of alcohol. All I knew at the outset of my adventure was that the Commonwealth of Pennsylvania had some of the most restrictive regulations for the sale of alcoholic beverages. We Pennsylvanians had to buy wine and spirits at state-owned retail stores, known to all as "state stores," which are staffed by government union employees. We could purchase beer for home consumption only from a beer distributor or in limited quantities at a bar.

What I knew in early 1983 was that when I had chaired the Northampton County Democratic Committee, a long-time supporter was a nice guy by the name of Frank Banko. I had met him in Allentown at his beer wholesale facility, which covered the entire Lehigh Valley. What I did not know until later is that Banko owned a second Pennsylvania wholesale beer operation in the Scranton area, and several wholesale beer operations in South Jersey, which made him one of the largest beer wholesalers in the United States. I also knew that Banko was a native of Bethlehem and fond of our shared birthplace.

I had visited Banko in April to share with him the preliminary plans for a festival in Bethlehem. After confirming that we planned to sell beer at the festival, he mentored me in the workings of the beer distribution system and the people who made it work, information I sorely needed. He was a supporter of Democrats and Republicans alike, and his contacts in Harrisburg far exceeded mine.

Banko agreed to be our first major sponsor. Then we went to work. He suggested that I write a letter to the Stroh brewery in Fogelsville, at the western end of the Lehigh Valley. Detroit-based Stroh's had purchased a relatively new brewery that had been built west of Allentown by Schaeffer Beer, which had gone out of business early in the 1970s, when American breweries began to consolidate. Stroh's was hoping to use this brewery to expand its east coast markets but had not gotten involved in any local promotions. Banko was its wholesaler in his Pennsylvania locations. I wrote to Jim Finnan, Stroh's director of state government relations, at the Allentown brewery. Finnan had a deep, resonant voice that deserved to announce sports on the radio. He was affable, intelligent, and knew the ropes in Harrisburg.

Nothing is easy, and in Pennsylvania no one had done legally what I wanted to do. I needed a license for a nonprofit organization to sell and serve beer and wine for nine consecutive days at a few different locations in a small downtown and for the beer drinkers to be able to legally carry and consume it on public sidewalks and streets. For a state with volumes of statutes and regulations governing alcoholic beverage sales, this was like asking for a unicorn.

The Special Occasion Permit available to nonprofits organized for arts and cultural purposes in cities of the third class allowed only six nonconsecutive daily permits per year per organization.[105] Only the legislature could change it. We also had to get the Liquor Control Board to agree to issue one permit that would cover multiple sales and service locations. Finally, we had to seek permission from the city for festivalgoers to carry open cups of beer on public streets and sidewalks, which a local ordinance prohibited.

During the next several months Banko convinced the Stroh Brewing Company to become a sponsor of Musikfest and to promise a special appearance at the festival of the company's stylized Stroh Beer Car and Alex, a golden retriever–Irish setter mix who starred in Stroh television commercials at the time. All this assured that Musikfest would continue the long-term relationship of beer and music in Bethlehem that hailed to colonial days.

After a fairly arduous process that entailed several meetings in Harrisburg that both Banko and I attended, the Liquor Control Board agreed to give us a single special occasion permit that allowed multiple sales and service locations. The only tricky matter remaining was that issuance of the permit required a change in the law. A friend of mine, Paul McHale, had been elected to the Pennsylvania House of Representatives in 1982 from a portion of Bethlehem, and we got him involved early on. He agreed to introduce an amendment to the liquor code at the beginning of the 1984 legislative year, but he wasn't sure that it could pass before the scheduled August event. He told us to have contingency plans.

Another problem we faced was the beer delivery system. This is more complicated than it sounds. Beer must be cold. Period. Perfect beer-drinking weather is a clear day or evening with temperatures ranging from 65 to 85 degrees Fahrenheit. But beer must be served at 36 to 38 degrees. An electricity-powered beer-tapping system, called a cold plate, is available for outdoor use, but it cannot keep cold the quantities that we anticipated selling. Banko agreed to provide trailers specially adapted for serving beer. His fleet of trucks would bring us the trailers, which he kept in storage between events. The trailers had spigots along one side so that tappers could stand in a row and serve thirsty customers. The trucks could store kegs and the large quantities of ice necessary to keep them cold. Banko also provided his staff to make sure that the kegs were changed promptly and that ice was properly placed. All we had to do was pay for the beer.

When we drafted the budget in May 1983, we were guessing at the amounts of food and beverages we would need. What we now know is that holding a free festival is a bad business plan. (Surprise!) Tents, tables, chairs, sound systems, insurance, stages, marketing, equipment rental, sanitary facilities, cups, towels, signs, decorations, and the staff to run it are not free. The beer sponsorship and beer sales would partially address two legs of our three-legged stool. Securing sponsorships is critical because, regardless of the weather, that money is in place. Through sponsorship and sales, beer would be the economic foundation for the festival with an impossible business plan. Frank Banko did many good things for Bethlehem before he died in 2011 at the age of ninety-two, but one of the best things he did was give us the means to keep the festival solvent.

BANKING

After the chamber of commerce endorsed Musikfest in June 1983, I began to send letters seeking support for this new festival-and-tourism venture. The response was tepid. For some foundations and businesses, we had already missed the deadline for a 1984 grant. We received one affirmative response from B. Braun Medical, a subsidiary of a German company that had recently purchased a local company that made plastic syringes. I wish we had saved the $3,000 check, but we needed to deposit it. B Braun has its western hemisphere headquarters in Bethlehem and today employs more than two thousand local people in manufacturing, research, sales, and administrative positions. The company, under the leadership of Caroll Neubauer, the German attorney who has built the American operation into a successful medical device business, has supported Musikfest every year since its inception.

Some businesses simply did not respond. I called each person to whom I had sent a letter. I still wasn't getting anywhere. Despite support from Banko and Stroh's, by late July 1983, I knew that we were running out of time to plan and execute a festival a year hence. We certainly did not have the money in hand to hire a director, and making that job a volunteer position never would have worked.

I advised Jean Kessler, chair of the tourism committee, that we might have to postpone until 1985, which would mean Musikfest wasn't going to happen because it would be difficult to sustain credibility and interest. Jean urged me not to give up and suggested that I attend the chamber's annual summer outing, the Walla Gazoo, to see if I could drum up support. I am told that *walla gazoo* is a Native American term for happy times, although Google has never heard of it, except in connection with Bethlehem. The day includes a golf tournament, followed by a clam bake served with beer at a local park. Since I do not golf, I usually attended only the social hour and dinner. I had low expectations that I would find a pile of money at the Walla Gazoo, especially since the chamber board had such a lukewarm response to Musikfest. The good thing about low expectations is that they are easy to exceed. As I trolled the grounds for new acquaintances, I met Jack Trotter, the new marketing vice president of First National Bank of Allentown. Trotter grew up in Bethlehem, served in Vietnam, and had begun his marketing career outside the Lehigh Valley. He was glad to be back and was interested in Musikfest. We agreed to meet again.

Allentown and Bethlehem are two distinct communities, not to be confused with each other. Bethlehem's national bank had changed its name to First Valley Bank sixteen years earlier, a move that announced its regional intentions. The larger First National Bank of Allentown had not changed its name but had boldly placed a branch in downtown Bethlehem in the ill-fated Bethlehem Plaza Mall. The 1980s were a period of loosened banking regulations and the beginning of the era of big banks. It had not occurred to me that a bank would want to make a big investment in a festival.

Trotter was well aware of the ingrained parochialism in the Lehigh Valley, especially the rivalry between Allentown and Bethlehem. He knew that for the First National Bank to make headway with small businesses, professionals, and depositors in Bethlehem, it needed to make some gesture that would demonstrate its sincerity about becoming part of the community. Musikfest was that opportunity. Despite the problems at Bethlehem Steel—early in 1983 the United Steelworkers had agreed, for the first time ever, to cuts in wages and benefits of 9 percent during the next three years—the city still had many successful businesses, and First National Bank saw opportunities with those businesses.[106] By October we had ironed out a sponsorship agreement, a marketing plan, and even agreed that First National Bank would not be the exclusive bank sponsor of the festival, something that I feared would get us into trouble with Bethlehem's leaders.

Trotter committed much more than a cash sponsorship. He brought in Jamie Musselman, of Allentown-based Musselman Advertising, to manage the branding and marketing of the festival at the bank's expense. Musselman is the scion of a well-known Allentown family. Her father was an art teacher at William Allen High School for many years, as well as an artist and designer at the agency. Her mother, Bertie, helped run the agency and was active in the community. The agency was doing well under Jamie's leadership, with several graphic designers and a who's who client list. The marketing and design skills of Jamie Musselman and her team added a whole new dimension to the project. We now had more than our own bootstraps to work with.

Trotter also offered his skills in public relations, and in this he was supported by a young colleague at the bank, Jeff Gordon. Trotter and Gordon created a tantalizing public relations campaign that kept Musikfest front and center for the months before the festival and during it. He helped us develop strategies to entice local radio, television, and print to cover and sponsor Musikfest. Media participation in the first year was high and remains an important ingredient of the success of the festival.

Trotter and his wife, Bobbie, were enthralled with the concept of the Viennese ball. Both were former military personnel, and both loved formal events to which Jack, a Scotsman, could wear his kilt and formal highland garb and Bobbie her gown with tartan sash. They took on management of the Viennese ball and, with the help of Jamie Musselman and a committee, set out to make the ball an over-the-top event, the likes of which the Lehigh Valley had never seen.

With the Trotters and Musselman participating, the event took on a more regional tone. It did not go unnoticed that a group of thirtysomethings from different cities were working together. I am still not sure what *walla gazoo* means—or that it is even an actual term in any language—but for me it meant meeting a new friend and ally to birth Musikfest.

A MODIFIED PLAN

With two major sponsorships secured, confidence in the project grew, and Gypsy and I had plenty of time on our walks to think more about how Musikfest would work. We were reconsidering the layout for the festival because sponsors needed specific music locations and the city was concerned about our using the streets.

One thing I kept coming back to was the brilliance of Walt Disney, who took a relatively small piece of land and created the original Disneyland with Tomorrowland, Adventureland, Frontierland, and the others. Guests feel the excitement of exploring these themed areas of the park. That led me and my limited German to the concept of the *platz*, which means place in German and in Bethlehem originally was used as the designation for the town square. If we made each music site a platz, guests would have an opportunity to use German and to anticipate different music, food, and decorations at each location.

For the new plan we had to scratch the Gemutlichkeit Café on Main Street because the setup required closing the street to traffic for almost two weeks, an unthinkable economic burden for the merchants. We moved the polka programming to the parking lot next to Monocacy Creek, down the hill from the Hotel Bethlehem. A large tent would shield people from sun and rain, and it would have a stage, sound system, dance floor, tables, and chairs so that guests could buy and enjoy food and drinks, which would also support the festival financially. This would become Festplatz, the festival's most popular platz.

This move freed up the Sun Inn Courtyard, which would now be a "cabaret-style biergarten featuring food, beverage and choruses, folk and bluegrass music," according to the brochure for Musikfest '84. This intimate space, with its newly planted linden trees, would become Liederplatz, or Song Place.

Main Street would be closed to traffic in the evening so that festivalgoers could walk from Broad Street to Church Street and into the Monocacy Valley undisturbed by traffic. Because Main Street is a circulation artery, we didn't give it a new designation.

We had arranged for an exhibition of Martin guitars (C. F. Martin & Company is based in nearby Nazareth) and a craft show. The historical buildings in the Colonial Industrial Quarter, which is directly across the Monocacy from Festplatz, would be open. To those attractions we added a family-oriented performance space for music, puppet theater, and other family activities. We called it Familieplatz (later changed to the more correct Familienplatz).

At the ice skating rink on the Broad Street Mall, the entertainment and food for sale would celebrate the many ethnic groups that had settled in Bethlehem in the postcolonial era. The food and music of the Irish, Italian, Slovak, Windish, and others would be represented at Volksplatz, or People's Place.

We reserved the Community Arts Pavilion, the main stage, for performances by artists of the highest caliber. The name for this site became Kunstplatz, or Art Place. Most Germans would not understand this, as the word refers to visual art, not music. Although nearly everyone had trouble pronouncing it, everyone embraced this platz along with the others.[107]

Since German for "candlelight concerts" is the difficult-to-pronounce Kerzenlicht Konzerten, we decided to leave well enough alone for these nightly performances.

The new plan would offer guests continuous entertainment almost all day every day because music from the Sun Inn Courtyard would follow them as they walked from atop downtown Bethlehem's hill (the ice skating rink at the Bethlehem Plaza Mall) to Broad and Main. They would have an opportunity to window shop along Main

Street while strolling the two blocks to the Candlelight Concerts and then to the Colonial Industrial Quarter for exhibits and family entertainment at Familieplatz. Or they might choose to go instead to Festplatz for polka music, German food, and beer or to Kunstplatz, with its grassy lawn and headliner shows. It would be a world of music in six blocks, not to mention great exercise because of the elevation difference of 150 feet. If people came to the festival, they would surely discover the great shopping in downtown Bethlehem.

More sponsors signed on. First Valley Bank and Union Bank and Trust Company each sponsored a platz, with First National sponsoring Festplatz, which we expected to be the biggest attraction. Other sponsors quickly followed; these included Oaks Printing Company, whose president, Ken Oaks, donated the festival posters.

THE MAYOR OVERRULES HIS CABINET

When Gordon Payrow became the first full-time mayor under Bethlehem's new city charter, the professional department heads—the directors of the departments of water and sewer, public works, fire, police, and community development, as well as the city solicitor and business administrator—became members of the mayor's cabinet. One key member is the mayor's administrative assistant. Although that position has no formal power, the administrative assistant usually is the person who knows how things get done at city hall.

Barbara Caldwell, the administrative assistant to Mayor Paul Marcincin (1978–87), was involved in the discussions about Musikfest from June through November 1983. She was married to Douglas Caldwell, the dynamic young senior pastor of Central Moravian Church. Barbara Caldwell was from Nicaragua. Her mother had died when Barbara was a child, and her father wanted to send her out of the country for college because of the political unrest. At the behest of a Moravian missionary from Bethlehem, she enrolled at Moravian College. While there she met Douglas Caldwell, a North Carolina native who was studying for the ministry.

Barbara Caldwell was not a politician, but she was an engaged member of the community. She was in a position to tell the mayor what he needed to hear, not just what he wanted to hear. She took the phone calls from community members who wanted to talk about city issues. The top issues at the time were the decline of Bethlehem Steel and the accompanying loss of jobs, decline of the city's two downtowns, and low morale in the community.

Barbara Caldwell became a member of the tourism task force early in 1983. She kept the mayor well briefed on what we were doing and the support we were garnering from the community.

Before we made our plans for Musikfest public, Jack Trotter and I briefed the mayor, giving Marcincin a more in-depth picture of Musikfest and what it might mean to the city. We outlined the support that we had but also were frank about the support we would need from the city to get the festival going. We asked for full donation of city services during the first year, including garbage disposal, street cleaning, electrical wiring of festival locations downtown, and police, ambulance, and fire services. This could amount to a lot of money for a city in difficult financial straits. Our original estimate was $58,000, but that was simply a guess. We stressed that, unlike other festivals, this one would be held in Bethlehem's struggling downtown, where it had the possibility of attracting new patrons for the merchants, not to mention new businesses, investors, and even residents. But to pull it off, we needed support from city services. Marcincin was supportive but was incredulous that we expected to sustain the event for nine days. He strongly encouraged us to try a long weekend for the first year. I knew instinctively that, if we did that, we would face opposition, for whatever reason, to expanding the festival's length in future years. I insisted that the event had to be nine days to succeed.

Marcincin took our proposal to his cabinet. Jack Downing, the city's business administrator, said that supporting the festival would be crazy—it could bankrupt the city. He vehemently opposed the nine-day event. Only Barbara Caldwell spoke in favor, saying that the community needed something positive to happen and "we should give this idea a chance." She was the only cabinet member to vote in support of Musikfest. Nonetheless, Marcincin promptly announced that he would support the festival and that cabinet members should do what they could to assist in the planning. "The city needs something positive," the former civics teacher informed his advisers.

THE BIG ANNOUNCEMENT

With sponsorship agreements in hand, Trotter and I worked with Musselman and her team to develop a logo for Musikfest. My contribution was that the logo had to emphasize two things—music and beer. We also asked for a lyre, an instrument of the ancient Greeks and Romans that German choral groups had adopted, as we were planning a choral group competition. The creative team did not disappoint. The logo for Musikfest '84 included the festival name in Vivaldi script, placed on a musical score, with a lyre to the left and a beer stein to the right of the type. The face of the beer stein said STROH'S. It would be the only time a sponsor's name appeared in the logo.

We had the logo printed on a banner in time for a press conference on November 22, 1983, at the Hotel Bethlehem. Speaking at the press conference were Marcincin; Trotter and his boss, Jim Large, president of First National Bank; Bob McCarthy, vice president of company relations for Stroh's; and me. We discussed dates, music, and historic groups that had agreed to perform or offer special activities during the festival.

The community's response to the announcement was muted, but the news laid the foundation for reaching out to other businesses for support. We were going to have a festival. We had nine months to figure out what this festival was going to be and to iron out hundreds of details. We had the opportunity to make all the mistakes that can be made in a new venture. If we were lucky, no one would notice.

CHAPTER 10
FESTIVAL ENTREPRENEURSHIP

At its first meeting on January 19, 1984, seven months before the festival, the board of the fledgling Bethlehem Musikfest Association approved articles of incorporation and adopted the committee's plans for Musikfest. The board, which included representatives of sponsors, nonprofit organizations that were our partners, the city, and the county tourism agency, also adopted a preliminary budget of $270,000. The figure was based on attendance by fifty thousand people, each of whom would drink two beverages and eat some food. Those revenues, combined with donations of equipment and advertising and cash sponsorships totaling $75,000, would have to cover the $250,000 we expected to spend for performers, equipment, staff, and other operating expenses. We had come a long way since June, but we had a long way to go.

Business textbooks say that a twenty-one-member board is too large, but we needed a lot of members to ensure community participation and clear communication with key constituents.[108] I was the nonprofit's president and learned during that first year that to be an effective leader I had to make sure that the board was fully informed at all times. Musikfest soon became a hot topic in the media and the community, thanks to the aggressive public relations and marketing campaign run by Trotter, Gordon, and Musselman. We soon became victims of our own success, as rumors and controversy followed. The community had a new distraction from the bad news emanating from Martin Tower.

A STAFF OF ONE

During the planning I was adamant that we not move forward until we had the money to pay a full-time employee. I had been involved with nonprofits for many years and had witnessed mission failures because of understaffing. I knew that I would wind up doing some volunteer work for this event, but I did not want it to overwhelm me. I figured that one staff person could handle details while I focused on the organization, the board, and securing sponsorships.

As word of the music festival spread quietly through the community in the summer of 1983, Roland Kushner, who recently had earned an MBA at Lehigh University, was working in the school's Small Business Development Center. Kushner, a Canadian whose father was an American from Louisiana, was twenty-eight and in the process of settling in Bethlehem; before going back to school he had spent years on the road to attend folk, bluegrass, and assorted other music festivals throughout the United States and Canada. He had wandered the music world and would drive a cab back in Ottawa when he needed money. He had first visited Bethlehem in 1975 when he brought his 1939 Dreadnought Martin guitar to Nazareth for restoration. Kushner returned a year later to pick it up and stayed at the Bethlehem YMCA. While walking around town he passed a man carrying a guitar. He introduced himself, and the young man said he had just opened a coffeehouse on Fourth Street and invited Kushner to stop by. Dave Fry and his Godfrey Daniels Coffee House would become important to Musikfest.

By 1979 Kushner had become an agent for folk musicians and headed to the Philadelphia Folk Festival to see if he could get bookings for a client and to hear other artists at this well-established folk festival held on a farm in suburban Philadelphia. There he met Barbara Elm, a young woman from Bethlehem. It was love at first sight for people who shared a passion for folk music. They married in 1980 and moved to Ottawa. Soon a child was on the way, and they decided to move to Bethlehem, where Kushner, at his parents' urging, took the last three courses he needed for his bachelor of arts degree and went on to get his MBA at Lehigh as well.

At the Small Business Development Center he was advising small business and nonprofit clients on business and tax matters. He also wrote applications for tax exemptions as nonprofits for Godfrey Daniels Coffee House and *Sing Out* magazine (which had just moved from New York City). Kushner contacted me to propose that he research the types of music that we might want to present at the festival and perhaps act as a consultant for booking performers.

My first impression of Kushner was that he was confident bordering on cocky and highly intelligent. His large glasses reinforced a professorial demeanor, no doubt inherited from his parents, who were academics. However, for my purposes his knowledge of, and passion for, music were his most promising qualities. I had no connections to Bethlehem's lively folk scene. I told him the festival was not yet a sure thing and said we had no money to underwrite research.

Right after the formal announcement of the festival in November, we placed an ad in the local paper for a festival coordinator who would organize and run the downtown music festival. Kushner was in the process of moving from Nazareth to Bethlehem with his young family, so I assumed he had not noticed the ad. I called and offered him the job with modest pay and no guarantee of work after September 1, 1984. We were both young and interested in trying something that had not been done before. Kushner accepted the job and agreed to start work after the holidays.

In January Kushner became ensconced in the Brodhead building in second-floor office space donated by the Sun Inn's nonprofit parent. The place had a certain charm that those who have lived or worked in old buildings may understand. Heating from a cranky old system was unreliable. Air conditioning depended on a single window unit. The stairway from the Main Street entrance had twenty-eight steps that led from the entrance to the second floor; it had no elevator. But perhaps the most charming aspect was that the Ballet Guild of the Lehigh Valley rented the entire third floor (and still does). It was an ideal space, with wooden floors, no columns or interior walls, large windows, and an airy environment, albeit with the same heating and air-conditioning issues. The Ballet Guild's students were in school most of the day, but after 3:00 p.m. they came to class. We frequently worked into the evening, accompanied by the constant thumping of aspiring ballerinas over our heads. Nonetheless, the racket was a constant reminder of the work it takes to be successful in the arts.

With borrowed furniture, typewriter, and phone, by the third week of January 1984 we were deep in the process of designing a new music festival for a city that did not have much reason to celebrate. Indeed, by the time the year was out, total employment at Bethlehem Steel would be down to 51,360.[109]

WHAT'S A MUSIKFEST?

"I had a luxury when I was programming Musikfest," Kushner recalled. "I was programming an arts festival. My successors had to plan entertainment." I have been involved with the arts for more than forty years and find the differentiation between art and entertainment to be a vexing issue. My conclusion is that the quality of art and music is deeply personal, singular to each individual's aesthetic. Therefore, picking what to book for a show is not an exercise in objectivity but a reflection of the person making the choices. In my recent conversation with Kushner, he spoke of putting together the first four Musikfests with the goal of designing a well-rounded artistic presentation of diverse music.[110] I had the pleasure of working with his successors, who had the same philosophy but understood the constant challenge of meeting changing audience tastes.

By any rational standard, booking more than 320 hours of multiple genres of music for a nine-day festival is daunting for one person, and that one person also was responsible for the operational aspects of the festival. With a budget of $100,000 for the performers' fees and expenses, $20,000 of which was designated for the German band and $25,000 for the main stage shows, we had only $200 per show for all the other artists. While some local artists might accept $50 for a gig, anyone coming from out of town would need more. And anyone who had a reputation would need a great deal more. Popular polka bands can be expensive.

There were other challenges. Musicians who perform at outdoor festivals are accustomed to having to use outdoor lavatories, inadequate sound systems, and poor lighting, and they have learned to put up with raucous patrons and not being offered meals. Add our downtown location, closed streets, and limited parking, and our performers tend to experience high levels of anxiety. But what they were most anxious about was whether they would be paid. With the exception of a couple of the main stage shows, we paid no one in advance, so they had to hope that this festival, unlike many, would not go bust in its first year and leave them with a rubber check. This is the hard reality of being on the road, and it makes the job of a first-year festival programmer even more difficult.

Kushner assembled the first program platz by platz with advice from members of the community, including Dave Fry of Godfrey Daniels, Doug Roysdon, a local puppeteer, and contacts supplied by *Sing Out!* magazine, the Moravian College music department, the Beethoven Choruses, and ardent polka fans. Festplatz required the least thought because it would be all polka, all the time. We planned to open its big tent from noon to midnight every day. The Stadtkapelle Berching, like all German brass bands, was accustomed to playing for hours at a time. The band agreed to play three two-hour shows a day, with Monday and Tuesday off. Gus Skrivanek and Bob Steinmetz formed the core of a host committee responsible for picking up the band at John F. Kennedy International Airport, bringing its members to Bethlehem, getting them settled at the Moravian College dormitory just up the hill from Festplatz, and tending to their needs while they were in Bethlehem. This was more complicated than it sounds because it entailed renting a truck to pick up the instruments and return them to the airport, making sure the band had meals, and helping its musicians with whatever they needed to be comfortable in Bethlehem.

Kushner had to take a crash course in polka in an effort to engage the diverse polka fans in Bethlehem. Not everyone was satisfied with the result, as I learned from comments made to me during the festival, but for the most part people were so happy to have so much polka available at a free public event that they were kind in their criticisms. The bands had mostly Germanic names: Jolly Joe and the Bavarians; Steve Huber and the Happy Austrians; the Hosfeld German Band; Leroy Heffentrager German Band; the Alpiners; and so forth. Most bands were local, and many played outside the Lehigh Valley on a polka circuit that ran throughout the Northeast and Midwest. We learned that there was a big audience for Polish polka as well. Kushner had booked an up-and-comer for that audience.

A greater challenge was figuring out Kunstplatz at the Community Arts Pavilion. Here we had a real stage, with real dressing rooms and bathrooms and power for lights and sound, although not enough for a contemporary rock show. We decided that we would present shows at 2:30 p.m. both Saturdays and Sundays and at 4:00 p.m. on Friday. Evening shows would start at 7:30 every evening. Patrons would have to bring their own lawn chairs or blankets. In mid-February Kushner started a ritual that continues to this day, making a preliminary list of shows for the main stage. Entertainers and their managers distinguish venues according to their facilities: permanent facilities (arenas, amphitheaters, performing arts centers, clubs) and temporary events, including festivals and fairs. Although festivals have gained stature since the mid-1980s, historically entertainers have not held them in high regard. And venues must choose artists who are already touring their region during the time of the festival's event. Then the venue learns what the artist's appearance fee is. Further, the practice in the industry is to approach one artist at a time for a specific date. Breaking this rule causes loss of credibility with booking agencies, and they are a close-knit community. The venue must place an offer for a specific date at a specific fee and say how long the offer will be valid. The agent may reject the offer out of hand, hold the offer for discussion with the show's manager, or accept the offer immediately, which rarely happens unless an informal agreement preceded the formal offer. The festival booker then waits for the decision, unable to place simultaneous offers for that date. The cruel part of this dance is that early in the year, many entertainers do not know where they are going to do a summer tour or even if they will do one. So the agents hold offers, sometimes for months, and figure out how to route their clients to get the best financial and logistical deal for them.

On February 16, 1984, when Kushner handed me the first list of this kind, I did not know that this was the start of thirty-one years of midwinter anxiety and frustrations. The list groups performers in price ranges: under $5,000; $5,000–$8,000; $8,000–$10,000. The first notation below the list always warns, "Not all performers are available on all days." The list for that first year included Dave Brubeck, Ramsey Lewis, Dizzy Gillespie, Woody Herman, Bill Monroe, the Nitty Gritty Dirt Band, the cast of *Hee Haw*, Roy Orbison, and Tammy Wynette. The list was more aspirational than practical. We were an unknown event and summer bookings were well under way. In the end we offered the afternoon shows on Friday, Saturdays, and Sundays mostly to local groups: Stadtkapelle Berching (the band coming from Germany) with the Bethlehem American Legion Band; the Allentown Band; Parke Frankenfield and His Dixieland All-Stars; the Lehigh Valley Chamber Orchestra; and on the final Sunday, all the way from Philadelphia, the Polish American String Band, a Mummers show with all their fancy gear.

For the evening shows we opened with our biggest headliner, the pop star Don McLean of "American Pie" fame. His fee was a whopping $7,000. The other evening shows included, performances by local groups: the Allentown Symphony Pops; the Rob Stoneback Big Band; Lehigh Valley Chamber Orchestra; plays mounted by Touchstone Theatre; and the Beethoven Choruses; national acts: Johnson Mountain Boys (bluegrass), the Louis Armstrong All-Stars (alas, Armstrong had died in 1971); and the Musikfest Folk Festival, whose headliner was Claudia Schmidt, who appeared regularly on *A Prairie Home Companion*; and our international guests the Stadtkapelle Berching. Even by the standards of 1984, this was not a spectacular lineup, but it was a great lineup for our audience.

The other three stages were stocked with performers from eastern Pennsylvania and New Jersey, peppered with a few from New York and Maryland. Volksplatz would run from noon to 6:00 p.m., the first to close. Its theme was ethnic music, and we chose, from among many local options, the Beirut Band, St. Mary's Traditional Ukrainian Dancers; the Greek Daughters of Penelope; Ilona's Hungarian Orchestra; the Mackay Pipe Band; Portuguese American Folklore Group; Jan Lewan Polish Polka Band; Tatra Slovak Folk Group; and I Paesani, an Italian tarantella group. We booked all of them to encourage the members of their ethnic communities to come to Musikfest.

Familieplatz would be open from noon to 8:00 p.m. daily and was stocked with local institutions and performers such as Touchstone Theatre, the Mock Turtle Marionettes, Dave Fry, the puppeteer Duke Kraus, Harley the Clown, and an assortment of folksingers and storytellers. Liederplatz, with its charming location in the Sun Inn Courtyard, was to be an outdoor listening room offering a potpourri of folk, jazz, ethnic music, blues, and even some polka. Almost all the Liederplatz performers were from the region or had ties to the region. Liederplatz would be open from noon to 10:00 p.m. so that, with fair weather, people could enjoy music under the stars.

The Candlelight Concerts were the only ones that required admission tickets. Later we realized that we were competing with our own free concerts when we asked people to pay for an indoor show. Fortunately, the admission price was modest and the concert series was successful. The music was presented mainly by members of the Moravian College music department or people affiliated with its faculty. Their music ranged from classical guitar and a flute duo to German renaissance and baroque music to a solo classical piano concert and love songs by a solo tenor. The concerts, while not sellouts, definitely added depth to the programming, signaling that this was not just a beer festival.

After months of work the schedule was complete. The festival was a bit more contemporary than our original idea. It had folk, blues, jazz, and a tiny bit of rock 'n' roll, much of which was supplied by the polka bands, all of which played weddings and included popular music in their repertoire. Would this be the right mix to attract an audience?

BEVERAGES AND FOOD

Finding beverage partners was important to the financial success of the festival. We would be serving the beer of our sponsor, Stroh's, but under federal law it is illegal for one brewery to buy exclusive rights to an event or facility. Joining Stroh's on our beer taps were Miller, Miller Light, and Pennsylvania's own Rolling Rock.

For soft drinks we sought support from Coca-Cola, Pepsi Cola, Seven Up, and the locally popular A Treat. The Coca-Cola Bottling Company of the Lehigh Valley was aggressive in its community partnerships and as a result had a fleet of trailers that could be moved to special events. Richard Strain, the company's general manager, was the first soft drink supplier to express interest in a partnership. The trailers were equipped with fountains to dispense the Coke family of beverages as fountain drinks. All we would have to supply was ice, scoops, and volunteers. The Coca-Cola brand made the new festival seem official, a great American event. And, like our partnership with Banko Beverage, it has been an enduring relationship that supports the festival.

Food became the biggest issue. We understood that the variety and quality of food at a festival could heighten the experience. We were not operating a kids' ballgame or a local fair. If all people could get with their beer was hot dogs, the event would not resonate with the audience we wanted to draw. But where would we find vendors capable of producing the quality and variety we wanted for an event that had no track record?

The biggest challenge would be feeding people at Festplatz. With its twelve-hour daily schedule and the expectation that it would be the best-attended site, we needed a vendor that could produce German-style food in quantity and staff the place for nine days. We found the caterer a block from the site at Moravian College. M. W. Wood was a regional company that specialized in institutional food services, particularly for colleges. We found the company through Bob "Doc" Windolph, the dean at Moravian for most nonacademic things, including food service. We met first with the person in charge of Moravian's food service and then with executives at their headquarters in suburban Allentown. By June the company had agreed that, with permission from Moravian, it could base a catering service on the campus to support a large stand at Festplatz, offering wursts, Wienerschnitzel, sauerkraut, and potato salad, along with hot dogs, hamburgers, and chips. Joining M. W. Wood was a local vendor of funnel cakes. No festival in eastern Pennsylvania is complete without this Pennsylvania Dutch favorite, fried sweet dough covered with powdered sugar and optional gooey cherry topping.

Local restaurant operators undertook to provide food at the other sites. Rod and Diane Holt, a young couple who ran a restaurant at the Sun Inn, agreed to set up a stand selling Pennsylvania Dutch and American food at Liederplatz right next door to the Inn. They were joined by an ice cream vendor and Helga Pavelka, who owned the Viennese Pastry Shop on Main Street, purveyor of Old World pastries. John and Maria Katsaros, who owned a local Greek restaurant, would sell gyros and other Greek specialties alongside the Raspberry Street Eatery at Volksplatz. A free spirit who owned a local business known as the Handlebar signed on to offer pita sandwiches, yogurt, and salads at Familieplatz.

With these brave vendors we set out to meet the demands of 100,000 guests. Most vendors thought that number was awfully high, and the small vendors could not afford to order enough food to satisfy that many guests if they showed up. All of us were working with unknowns.

With the platzes determined, music and entertainment themes decided and bookings under way, food vendors engaged, and beer confirmed, we had the program for a festival. Now all we had to do was let the world know about it and staff the event so that we could show everyone a great time.

CHAPTER 11
THE SUMMER OF '84

Almost every year someone at Musikfest asks me, "Did you ever expect it to get so big?" The questioners do not realize that that was the goal. Musikfest had to be big to demonstrate that Bethlehem had the capacity to host a major event and change the narrative from gritty city to thriving cultural community.

The success of Musikfest '84 depended on attracting an almost entirely regional audience. We had no resources to do any respectable marketing beyond the Lehigh Valley, although we made a token effort to attract the charter bus tour market. If the festival were to succeed, the residents of the region would have to embrace it. Growth beyond the region would be incremental.

As I look back on the marketing for Musikfest '84, it seems primitive. Because these were the days before the Internet, personal computers, tablets, and cell phones, marketing was limited to print, radio, television, billboards, and word of mouth.

The marketing team met every few weeks in the Musselman offices in Allentown. After settling on a logo, we needed a poster that would tout the festival in all other marketing and convey the right image. Again, the direction was simple: beer, music, Bethlehem. Again, the team came through. The key element was a beer stein, its partially open pewter lid topped by a star of Bethlehem with musical notes on a score flowing out of the mug. On the stein is the image of a woman in colonial Moravian dress; she is holding a sheet of music, and a man next to her is dressed in Bavarian lederhosen and holds a tuba. In the background are an American flag and images of Bethlehem landmarks. Below the stein are the dates, August 18–26, 1984, and the location, Bethlehem, PA.

Even with the generous support of First National Bank, we were limited in how much advertising we could do because of the expense. The Lehigh Valley is a portion of the Philadelphia television market, the fourth largest in the country. Television advertising to reach people in the Lehigh Valley was prohibitively expensive. Radio was important because the event was a music festival. But even on local radio stations, advertising time cost way beyond what we could pay. In 1984 newspapers still were the most important source of information for area residents, and the area then had three local dailies, one in each city of the Lehigh Valley. But a traditional newspaper ad campaign would have eaten at least a third of our entire ad budget.

We needed exposure that we would not have to pay for, and the key to that was public relations. We already had some intimations that the media would follow the festival as a hot new story in an otherwise gloomy environment. If Musikfest succeeded, it would do a lot to counter the conventional wisdom that the Lehigh Valley in general, and Bethlehem in particular, were in decline. If it failed, it would reinforce the image of decline. We conceived of a dramatic and multifaceted public relations campaign:

- Musikfest provided printed information to sponsors, the city, and the nonprofits, which in turn reprinted it in internal publications for their employees and members. The city included information about Musikfest in the water bills it sent out.
- We convinced the regional gas company, UGI, to insert information about Musikfest in its July cycle of monthly bills.
- Beginning in May Musikfest sent out weekly press releases about the lineup, foods, special events, and even off-site parking. These often generated calls from reporters seeking more information and sometimes requests to interview performers. The announcement that Alex the Stroh dog would visit the festival got a great deal of attention.
- We worked with Stroh's to create promotional signs for placement in bars and beer distributors.
- We printed and distributed table tent cards promoting the event in restaurants and bars a month before Musikfest.
- We met with the editorial boards of the newspapers to ask for their endorsement. All responded favorably.

- Several Musikfest board members sat for radio interviews to generate excitement about the festival.
- We solicited coverage from regional German publications and a national magazine focused on German events.
- We rented twenty-five billboards at a reduced price, and Banko Beverage and Coca-Cola Bottling Company agreed to make some of their trucks rolling billboards for the festival.

Once the plan kicked in, Jack, Jeff Gordon, and I promoted the new festival to anyone and everyone. I had been involved in regional political campaigns before, so I understood that repetition is critical to sell a candidate or a product. With the able guidance of the professionals, Musikfest was as well known as a first-year event could be. But until the festival started, we had no way to know whether it would resonate with the community. We had done all we could with the resources available, and that would have to be good enough.

Between June and August tension began to mount. In June a city council member announced at a council meeting that the mayor had told him that Musikfest was going to cost the city $58,000 in services, including police services. The council chair remarked that this was unprecedented, setting off a controversy about whether a city in dire straits should be investing so much money in such a risky venture. Under pressure from the council we agreed to pay $15,000 for the off-duty police who would be the visible part of our security team. The city agreed to cover $43,000 for setting up, cleaning up, and on-duty police coverage. The local papers covered the controversy, and after it was over the editor of the *Bethlehem Globe Times*, John Strohmeyer, wrote an editorial praising the city's support, demonstrating that he understood what we were attempting to do and what it could mean for Bethlehem:

> A recent report tells the grim story that unemployment in Northampton County was 13.1 percent last year, significantly higher than state and national levels. Two days after that report appeared, Bethlehem Steel confirmed that it was trimming 30 employees in its engineering department, the latest in a distressing string of layoffs that have spanned several years [by the end of 1985, the Steel would employ

only 5,661 at the local plant].[111] ...Bethlehem is an economically troubled community located mostly in a county that has taken the effects of the recession squarely on the jaw. ...Musikfest, unlike other attempts to spawn outside interest in Bethlehem, will take advantage of one of the region's strengths—a musical heritage that, for Bethlehem, goes back 240 years to the first Moravian settlers. ...The City's approval of the request is a fitting response to the enthusiastic support given the venture by a wide range of businesses, private institutions, performers and local individuals. ...The community has joined to take on an ambitious and exciting project and city participation is a proper show of support.[112]

The headline was "City Services for Musikfest '84 Are Investment in the Future." Strohmeyer could not have known how right he was, but his prescience endeared him to me forever.

VOLUNTEERS

Volunteerism, like the nonprofit corporation, is an American tradition. The pioneers who settled remote areas had to rely on each other to address the hardships of daily life. Freed of the constraints of the landholding interests in Europe and their governance, the pioneers and their descendants created new ways of addressing community and social issues. Americans of all ethnic and racial backgrounds, although not always recognized, donate time, talent, and treasure to causes in which we believe. As a native of Bethlehem, I had observed both the formal and informal ways that people volunteer to help others and the community. As a volunteer I hoped that the community would take a leap with me to make this festival a success.

In early March, Marlene Gilley climbed the twenty-eight steps to the tiny Musikfest office and introduced herself to Kushner. Gilley, a resident of the affluent Saucon Valley suburb of Bethlehem, had read a recent newspaper article about Kushner and his herculean task. Like him, she was a native Canadian with a strong interest in music, jazz in her case. She was curious to know whether Kushner was serious about booking jazz and stopped by to see if he needed advice from a singer and ardent fan of the genre. Gilley was coming off a twenty-five-year gig of raising four children with her husband, Joe. By the early 1980s the last two were in college, and she was looking for some new experiences. Raising four kids had prepared her for the all-hands-on-deck nature of a start-up festival. Kushner recognized that he and Gilley had had a great deal in common and invited her to do "a little" volunteer work. She instantly became the unpaid full-time "other duties as assigned" staff member. Joe Gilley learned to fend for himself at dinner as Marlene joined us for nine-hour days that became fifteen- to seventeen-hour days as the festival approached. Her positive attitude and her extroverted personality were a perfect complement to others on our team. She supervised volunteers; helped Kushner with operational details, contracts, and calls; worked with the Musselman team to develop and stock the souvenirs; and ultimately took on the challenge of getting advertisers for the souvenir program book. Roland, Marlene, and Jeff became a team that shared the little triumphs and defeats along the way, experienced the deep anxiety about whether the festival would actually be successful, and encouraged each other in difficult times. Our meetings on the concrete landing overlooking the Sun Inn Courtyard created a bond that lasts to this day.

With periodic calls for volunteers, we soon had a core group of people willing to make phone calls, stuff envelopes, and do the nuts-and-bolts work we needed to try to manage the office. Kushner had assembled a team of musicians and music fans who had wandered in the door and assigned them tasks for organizing a stage or becoming stage managers. Another team put together the first-ever Musikfest program book while yet another organized the ball, now titled "A Night in Old Vienna."

First National Bank asked tellers to volunteer to count money and tickets in trailers; they would miss the festival but secure the revenue. A teller named Kay Moran decided she wanted to do it. She was the senior teller at the Bethlehem branch, and as such she became the head of the new green team. Kay and Regis Sopko, First National Bank's chief of security, became our go-to team for the cash and ticket system of the festival. Early on we decided to have patrons buy tickets and exchange them for food and drinks. Volunteers would run the ticket booths, but the Green Team would take in the cash and audit the cash boxes. The ticket system was best because it centralized cash in a secure location rather than having it in the booths of food vendors and the volunteers selling beer and soft drinks. We were relying on receiving 10 percent of food revenues, and with cash sales we would have had no way to verify that we were getting our share. The Green Team gave us confidence and assured that the vendors got paid in a timely way.

As the festival approached, we knew we would need three hundred to four hundred volunteers, especially for the ticket booths, Coca-Cola trailers, beer stands, merchandise stands, and the Clean Team, to empty garbage cans, pick up trash, and keep the festival tidy. We were hoping that dozens of volunteers could come out during the week before the festival to set up tables, chairs, signs, banners, decorations, and so forth. We also needed them for specialty functions, including stagehands and a supply team. The only paid people were affiliated with companies under contract, usually local individuals, to operate the sound systems at the stages. Because the staff of one and the volunteer leaders could not be everywhere, we created site supervisor and assistant site supervisor positions for each site.

More than four hundred people volunteered during Musikfest '84. Many organizations, like the Jaycees and the Rotary Club, and some businesses, like the sponsoring banks, solicited volunteers from their ranks. Thus began a tradition for some groups to get together each year at Musikfest. Pouring beer is one of their favorite jobs.

For site supervisors I relied on a network of people I knew who could run a special event—an election. Of the twenty site supervisors for Musikfest '84, ten were members of the Democratic committee or elected officials. Most of the rest were friends I begged to participate. Some were humoring me, not really sure whether this event was going to fly. Neither were we.

THE FINAL PUSH

July and August 1984 remain a blur. Roland, Marlene, and Jeff divided the workload. Marlene became our second salaried employee.

With the help of dozens of volunteers, our one office typewriter, three phones, and lots of checklists, we did what had to be done. We ordered food and beverage tickets. When we realized we did not have enough chairs and tables for the Festplatz tent, we called the school district and begged for cafeteria tables and chairs from the high school. When we found we needed still more chairs, we called Wally Long's Long Funeral Home and borrowed more chairs. We asked a friendly architect to design ticket booths and the carpenters union to build them. To get the best deal on shirts for the volunteers, we called the ILGWU and learned how. We got permission from Bethlehem Steel to use the Martin Tower parking lot at night and on weekends because the downtown lots could not hold all the cars we expected. The owners of the Lehigh Shopping Center gave us permission to use the large parking area adjacent to a vacant department store. We arranged for Trans Bridge Bus lines to carry patrons from the distant lots to the festival. We arranged for or obtained ice chests, corkscrews, bottle openers, cups for beer service, cash boxes for ticket sales, parking lots for volunteers and transportation to and from the lots, a volunteer training manual and training sessions, fire extinguishers for the tents and booths, and carpeting for the stage floors. We also borrowed music stands from Moravian College and the school district, installed fencing to keep the railroad tracks off-limits, called the railroad to find out when trains would come through, got a direct phone number for the National Weather Service, and got radios for the site supervisors (clunky old walkie-talkies).

From July through the festival and cleanup we worked sixteen to eighteen hours a day. We reinforced each other. I remember mostly the "we're in this together" good humor of Marlene and Roland. We had to laugh because the only alternative was a complete breakdown. We disagreed at times. I soon learned that Canadians can be quite stubborn when they think something is important. Regardless, we always moved on in the spirit of making Musikfest a success. We got bits of encouragement from outside. Marlene took over the advertising for the souvenir program book in May and had enough sponsors by July. Even the state legislature cooperated by passing the Musikfest Special Occasion Permit law in mid-July, assuring that we could have beer in the streets for all nine days. Of course the tightly written law was only for 1984, which meant we would have to revisit the issue if Musikfest became an annual event, but we left that problem for another day.

One of my most vivid memories is about using an early computer to make schedules. I was the proud owner of a Compaq computer. It weighed more than twenty pounds, could accept one floppy disc, and had the capacity of a fluke worm. We had not made any real arrangements for scheduling the hundreds of people who had agreed to volunteer for us. At two o'clock one August morning I was in my den at home, frantically creating individual sheets for scheduling volunteers for beer or soft drink service, ticket booths, cleanup, and site supervisors. At times I thought I was losing my sanity.

We kept fending off fatigue by playing Whack-A-Mole—dealing with issues as they popped up. The week before the festival someone wrote an encouraging editorial that commended our efforts but concluded by asking, "Will anyone come?" The author hoped people would, but when Roland, Marlene, and I read it, we felt like we were teetering on the edge of a cliff.

The Stadtkapelle Berching arrived on Thursday, August 16, at JFK. In 1984 no one had security worries about the large cases containing the instruments of a twenty-five-member brass band. Bob Steinmetz, Gus Skrivanek, and our host committee met the band with a bus and a truck and escorted the musicians to their temporary home at the Moravian College Old Main dormitory, a turn-of-the-century building with no air conditioning. The Germans were not accustomed to the August heat of a Pennsylvania summer, but they soon would be. I met briefly with Hans Stadler to go over the plans for the opening ceremonies, which would be followed by a small parade to Festplatz, where the band would perform. They were tired but excited, just like me.

At 6:00 p.m. on Friday, August 17, Roland and I were setting up the last row of chairs in the Sun Inn Courtyard. The volunteers had gone home, and we were expected at the Night in Old Vienna Ball. Too tired to speak, we rushed to our homes, got cleaned up, changed into our rented tuxedos, and reappeared less than forty-five minutes later at the Hotel Bethlehem for the preview event. We were both running on pure adrenaline and much too tired to be nervous.

MUSIKFEST 1984
North Side Downtown

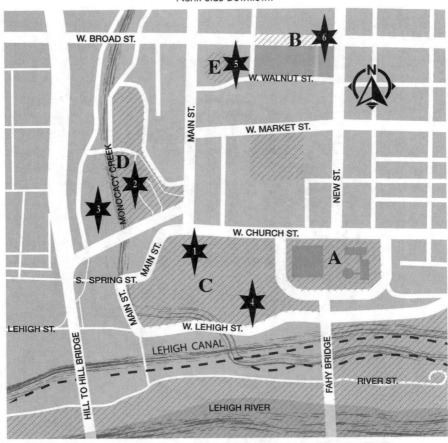

VENUES
1. Candlelight Concerts
2. Familieplatz
3. Festplatz
4. Kunstplatz
5. Liederplatz
6. Volksplatz

PARKS, PLAZAS, HISTORIC SITES
A. Bethlehem City Center Plaza
B. Broad Street Mall
C. Moravian College
D. Moravian Colonial Industrial Quarter
E. Sun Inn Courtyard

CHAPTER 12
MUSIKFEST UNVEILED

When Susan and I got to the Hotel Bethlehem, the place was jumping. Boosted by a marketing effort that promised an extravagant event with international flavor, A Night in Old Vienna had sold out weeks in advance, with more than five hundred people paying $60 for each ticket. The organizing committee, which had outdone itself to provide a sample of the festival to come, had signed the twenty-three-piece Lehigh Valley Chamber Orchestra to play waltzes and fox trots in the ballroom; had Steve Huber and the Happy Austrians performing polkas, waltzes, and pop music in the Continental Room; and arranged for Ilona's Strolling Violins (the violinists from her orchestra) to serenade people in the Candlelight Room (the terrace). Greeting arriving guests—and entertaining locals who had brought their lawn chairs to watch the festivities from the sidewalk—was a brass quartet, the first sidewalk show of Musikfest.

Musikfest also marked a new lease on life for the Hotel Bethlehem, a key character in the saga of Bethlehem. Built in 1922 by Bethlehem Steel, the ten-story hotel had replaced the old Eagle Hotel, which had been built on the site of the first house in Bethlehem. Although almost everything else in Bethlehem Steel's history is heavily documented, no records explain why the company chose to invest in a hotel on the north side of town instead of near its offices. But a look at the nearby Victorian homes and colonial buildings offers a clue: the company did not want its guests to have to contend with the earthy establishments that catered to their employees on the south side.

The hotel was built two years after completion of the modern Hill-to-Hill Bridge, the southern side of which was two short blocks from Charles Schwab's home. On the northern side of the river, the bridge forked east to Main Street and the hotel and west near

Prospect Avenue, so that Eugene Grace and the other executives who lived on "Bonus Hill" in west Bethlehem could easily travel to work on the south side and to the hotel by taking a roundabout at the north end of the bridge. The three ramps of the bridge connected the three former boroughs—Bethlehem, South Bethlehem, and West Bethlehem—that had become one city in 1917. The deeper message of the bridge and the hotel was that the Bethlehem Steel Corporation, which underwrote most of bridge's construction, was the economic powerhouse that drove the city.

But by 1984 the hotel was a dowager. For the Steel it was an obligation from another era and a low priority for scarce capital. The hotel's eight floors of rooms had become threadbare, no longer first class. The public rooms included the old Pioneer Tap Room on the first floor, with a direct exit to Main Street. This intimate room was a favorite watering hole for local businesspeople. (The room was eliminated in the renovations of 1999 to allow for an open lobby with the bar and its patrons as part of the atmosphere.) Murals depicting the history of Bethlehem lined the room, giving patrons a sense of the hotel's role in local history. (The murals were moved to the Continental Room during the renovations.)

The hotel's grand entrance is on Main Street, under a marquee in the center of a series of two-story Palladian windows that lend grandeur to the front and south facades. Cut-glass chandeliers, overstuffed furniture, and a piano graced the small lobby; the reception desk is next to the elevator bank. To the left of the two elevators is the first-floor Continental Room, which is quite large and suitable for banquets and weddings. Across the lobby are white marble stairs that lead to the terrace, the hotel's most attractive room, which has windows on three sides that provide a panoramic view of Central Moravian Church and the colonial and Victorian buildings of Moravian College, as well as the Hill to Hill Bridge and South Mountain with its star of Bethlehem.

The two-story Grand Ballroom on the mezzanine level lives up to its name, with cut-glass chandeliers and its own balcony on two sides to accommodate onlookers or extra dining tables for events. It is not the Waldorf Astoria, but it also is not the Holiday Inn. It is a sentimental spot for me because we held our wedding reception there in August 1973.

Donald Trautlein, the Price Waterhouse accountant who became the president of Bethlehem Steel in 1980, was in the process of shedding nonessential business assets, including the hotel, in an effort to return the company to profitability. The buyer would be responsible for renovating the hotel and bringing it up to code. The biggest issue was that it did not have life safety systems, including sprinklers. The hotel needed a savvy entrepreneur to figure out how to renovate it, bring it up to code, and make a profit just as competitors were developing motels throughout the region and business from Bethlehem Steel was diminishing.

Enter Robert and Dee Decker, who owned a successful roofing business. They were eager to try to save the Hotel Bethlehem and believed an upscale hotel had a place in the local market. They bought the hotel only months before Musikfest. A Night in Old Vienna would be the hotel's first big community event under their stewardship. Change was happening all over Bethlehem.

The tone for the evening and the festival was set by the receiving line and the opening ceremonies. Jack and Bobbie Trotter were determined to give the ball a patriotic, military flavor. Like everything else, the ceremony was over the top. Among those in the receiving line were Mayor Marcincin; the Austrian cultural affairs consul, in from New York; the honorary consul general of the Federal Republic of Germany, in from Philadelphia; F. Otto Haas (whom I later found out was one of the principals of the major Philadelphia pharmaceutical company Rohm & Haas); the Reverend Douglas Caldwell of Central Moravian Church and his wife, Barbara; U.S. Representative Don Ritter; the Trotters; Susan; and me. Jack Trotter was in his finest formal kilt, and Bobbie was similarly attired in a ball gown with Trotter tartan sash.

The ceremonies began with Marines from the air base in Willow Grove escorting dignitaries to the front of the room. Then the Mackay Pipe Band marched in, followed by the Army Recruiting Command Color Guard. The ceremony included the national anthems of the United States, Germany, and Austria performed by the Chamber Orchestra and comments from several dignitaries. Here we were, dressed in our formal finest, surrounded by lush music, lavish floral decorations, and an international feast to celebrate an event that was yet to be.[113]

When the Stadtkapelle Berching arrived at the ball around 9:00 p.m., guests were thrilled to be the first to greet our honored musicians, who had dressed in their colorful Bavarian costumes.

Susan and I left at midnight, shortly after the formal part of the ball ended, while others stayed for drinks and a bit of celebrating. Formal wear and formal events are not my favorite, but A Night in Old Vienna was the best formal event I had ever attended.

DAY ONE

Weather is a universal variable for virtually every business, but it is front and center for outdoor events. And bad weather can sink an event. In eastern Pennsylvania the hottest month is July. By mid-August the risk of humid 90-degree days is lower. Rain always is a risk, but thunderstorms are less frequent in late August than during the rest of the summer. As early as January we asked the local office of the National Weather Service for a forecast for the festival's nine days. It responded that the average daily high is in the upper 80s with lows in the mid-60s. Better yet, the chance of precipitation was 10 to 20 percent, low for our region.

When I woke up at dawn on Saturday, August 18, 1984, the sun was shining, a good sign. The newspaper reported a Canadian high during the next several days. With two Canadians helping to run the event, a weather pattern from Canada seemed like a good sign.

After a quick shower and coffee, I donned what was to be my garb for the next nine days, shorts and an official Musikfest golf shirt, yellow for supervisors, plus a name badge. Carrying my sports jacket, dress shirt, tie, and slacks in a garment bag, I rushed out the door and got to the office by seven. Throughout the morning we managed information for the constant flow of vendors and volunteers seeking direction on festival operations and supported the volunteers answering our two phone lines. The anticipation was palpable. By 10:30 I had changed into my sports jacket, tie, and slacks to be ready for the show.

The interesting thing about traditions is that those who create them are seldom aware of what they are doing at the time. All of us hoped that Musikfest would become a tradition and a signature event for the community. What we did not anticipate were the specific aspects of the festival that would become perennial favorites. Today festivalgoers, or festers, carry infants through the festival in backpacks, just as their parents did. Children dance the polka with their grandparents, just as their parents did. And families share waffles and ice cream as their annual Musikfest treat. One tradition that we inaugurated quite deliberately was having the Moravian Trombone Choir, the oldest music organization in Bethlehem, herald the arrival of the festival from the steeple of Central Moravian Church, just as it has rung in special religious occasions since the church was built in 1806.

At 11:00 a.m. opening ceremonies began at City Center Plaza, with the speakers addressing the assemblage from the portico of the public library. The sun was bright and the families of the Stadtkapelle Berching and of members of the host committee made up much of the audience. Representatives of our primary sponsors, the honorary German consul from Philadelphia, the cultural affairs consul of Austria, Mayor Marcincin, and I said a few words. I brashly announced that the festival was the beginning of a new tourism industry in Bethlehem. Perhaps the most important contribution to the ceremony came from Douglas Caldwell, the senior pastor at Central Moravian Church who invoked the Almighty to support the farmers with rains overnight and sunshine during the day for the next nine days. "Music is a universal language understood by all," declared Helmut Feil, the Austrian representative. "The organizers of Musikfest have touched on a great idea."

The Stadtkapelle Berching bravely performed "The Star-Spangled Banner," the German national anthem, and the Austrian national anthem as flags of the three countries flew from the City Center's three flagpoles. A folk singer performed "Get Together," the Chet Powers song popularized by the Youngbloods; the song seemed appropriate because of Bethlehem's difficult times.

With formalities completed, we lined up behind the Stroh Beer Car and the Stadtkapelle Berching to march down the Church Street hill, past Central Moravian—where the trombone choir was serenading us—to Festplatz. At the entrance we stopped under the shade of the Hill-to-Hill Bridge and ceremonially tapped the first keg. The honor went to Mayor Marcincin, who then was joined by Northampton County Executive Gene Hartzell, the mayor of neighboring Allentown, and other notables. Volunteers distributed complimentary cups of beer to people gathered around the Stroh car, and I climbed on the running board and toasted our sponsors, wishing everyone a "happy Musikfest." After a quick sip I shouted, "The ticket booths are open!" a cry I would repeat at the end of the opening ceremonies for many years to come. As I greeted and thanked the various dignitaries who had attended the kickoff, my eye was repeatedly drawn to the large tent fifty feet away. It looked like people were in the tent and, better yet, people had lined up at the food area, and we had just opened. Would this really work?

Meanwhile, back at the office, the windows were open to Liederplatz, and the gentle sounds of folksingers Mary Faith Rhoads and John Pearse wafted through the air. Roland looked over at Marlene and said, "Mrs. Gilley, I believe we have a festival." Marlene looked out the door, saw people gathered at the tables and chairs in the courtyard, and responded, "Indeed we do."

Attendance can become an obsession for people who run events. I would walk to all five platzes five, six, or seven times each day, just to see how many people were there, how the vendors were doing, and to thank the volunteers. With the different sites on a hill with a healthy walking distance between them, I never worried about gaining weight during Musikfest. One thing I learned was that vendors are seldom happy unless they are too busy to talk, and then they smile. The more they smiled, the happier I was.

As I walked into Festplatz after the beer tapping, still in jacket and tie, I saw many happy faces. Lots of people were sitting at tables, many were eating or drinking, a few dozen folks were on the dance floor twirling to the polka, and youngsters were learning the dance from their elders. People were smiling at being under a tent by Monocacy Creek in downtown Bethlehem on a beautiful August day. Better yet, I did not know most of the people.

Only one pedestrian bridge crosses Monocacy Creek between the parking lot that we used for Festplatz and the Colonial Industrial Quarter with its restored waterworks, grist mill, and tannery. In 1984 the bridge was a narrow wooden affair designed for modest traffic, with room for one pedestrian in each direction; it wasn't built for strollers, wheelchairs, and dozens of people at a time. The first time I noticed its limitations was when I crossed the bridge to see how the adjoining Familieplatz was going. Traffic on the bridge was causing congestion at both ends. The second thing that I noticed was that perhaps we had goofed by locating this low-key family entertainment site so close to loud polka music. The sound bleed was a nuisance. But that did not seem to matter to the dozens of families camped out in front of the tiny stage tent next to the tannery. Little tots were running around on the grass adjacent to the clear flowing creek with its native brown trout, a bucolic setting in the middle of a steel town. Several people were walking through the Martin guitar exhibit, and the colonial crafters were busy explaining their weaving and spinning techniques to engaged observers. As I climbed the hill to Main Street, I passed a few people traveling in the opposite direction. The street did not appear crowded, but it definitely was carrying more auto and pedestrian traffic than on a typical Saturday in August. As I walked, I saw that the horse-drawn wagon we had arranged to provide rides was already full of parents and children as it moved slowly past the Victorian buildings.

I also saw a last-minute addition to the festival. A few months before Musikfest, one of the most iconic businesses on the street closed. Tom Bass was a high-end men's and women's fashion store. For as long as anyone could remember, it was where the local elite preferred to buy clothing. But it had succumbed to the recession and was the only boarded-up building on Main Street, a sad reminder of the times and definitely not the impression we wanted to make. A young graphic artist, Michael Sayre, came up with an idea—why not invite local artists to create murals on the plywood? On my way up the street, Jim Davis, executive director of the chamber of commerce and a well-known local sketch artist, was doing one of his caricatures. It was me!

I finally reached the office, where Marlene and I traded information about the first ninety minutes of the festival. The Sun Inn Courtyard had quite a good crowd, and after a few hiccups early on, things were going smoothly. One of the biggest issues was the radios. We had borrowed walkie-talkies from a local company, one for each site, plus a few more for staging, security, and our supply team. Many had never used a walkie-talkie. Someone would sit on or otherwise inadvertently press the talk button without realizing it. Everyone would hear their conversation, which also blocked other transmissions for long periods. People tended to use the battery-operated devices like a telephone, having extended conversations rather than responding quickly and signing off. By late afternoon many of the devices were running out of juice, and we had to circulate with spare batteries. Other than that, the opening hours were remarkable—nothing awful happened and people were coming.

After changing into shorts, sneakers, and my Musikfest shirt, I wandered out into Liederplatz, then walked to Volksplatz, where a sizable audience had gathered for Jan Lewan, the Polish polka prince. Roland had engaged the polka community to learn which shows would yield the best investment of our scarce funds. Lewan, a native of Poland who lived in Hazelton, Pennsylvania, was already a hit on the polka circuit. Known for his flashy costumes, blond hair, and spirited music, he was a star in the making. As he took the small stage, the larger-than-expected audience found places to dance and cheer on the defunct skating rink and the adjacent street-turned-mall. People were having a party in front of the eleven-story First Valley Bank and for a short time were not worrying about what was in their account.

Then I headed back through Liederplatz and down Main Street. That was when I noticed the fruits of our thirteen months of labor in the fields of Harrisburg politics. Happy patrons were doing something that probably had not been done legally in Bethlehem since colonial times—walking down Main Street carrying cups of beer. And they could not quite believe that they really were permitted to do this. Many people knew each other, so they stopped to chat, beer in hand, catching up on old times and commenting on how they had not been to downtown for quite a while.

I headed through the passage between the colonial-era Brethren's House and the Victorian Old Main Dormitory to the large field that was now Kunstplatz. For the first time in its seven-year history, the Community Arts Pavilion was decked out for real concerts. Special lighting was hanging from the trusses in the ceiling, large speakers were set up on the sides of the stage, and—something new in my vocabulary—the sound position was set up in the field a hundred feet back from the stage. The bright yellow banner with blue print announcing Musikfest '84 hung proudly over the stage.

A crowd had gathered on the sunny lawn for the first concert at Kunstplatz. The host Bethlehem American Legion Band, conducted by the dedicated Ray Huston—the only band at Musikfest to have performed previously at the Community Arts Pavilion—played traditional American marches and tunes from the American songbook. Next up was our guest band from Germany, with its first formal concert in the United States. The program that afternoon also included traditional Bavarian music.

We had set out only two hundred folding chairs because we had suggested that people bring their own blankets or folding chairs. Curiosity in parts of the community was high, and members of the Beethoven Choruses and Holy Ghost Church brought family and friends to this show. It was a warm day, the stage faced straight into the afternoon sun, and the audience had no shade. But the show went on. Both bands doffed their uniform jackets and rolled up their sleeves. Afterward, some in the audience lingered to meet and greet the musicians, who had played for more than two hours. The Germans retreated to Old Main Hall for a snack and a quick change before they took the stage at Festplatz at 6:00 p.m. They were real troupers, and this would be a grueling day for them after marching at noon, a concert at 3:30, and shows at Festplatz from 6:00 to 7:30 and 10:00 to midnight.

As the audience for the afternoon concert cleared, blankets promptly appeared for the evening show, placed by locals who were quick to adapt to the need to reserve a space at the free concert. Our volunteer stagehands were busily removing the chairs and music stands from the stage to prepare for the evening's feature act, Don McLean. We had decided to present the biggest show at Kunstplatz on the first night of the festival instead of holding it for a grand finale. The logic was to attract as many people as we could for the first day of festival so that they would want to come back during the next eight days. We hoped that this show was going to be our big one.

I continued my journey around the festival. As I returned to Festplatz, I heard the song that would become the unofficial anthem of Musikfest for many years to come, the "Chicken Dance." No one is certain when the song was played for the first time at Musikfest, but everyone knows that it became a staple of Festplatz. The "Chicken Dance" is believed to have originated in Germany as the "Vogel

Tanz" (bird dance). Sometime in the 1960s it migrated to the United States and became popular with polka and wedding bands. The simple motions of flapping your folded arms as wings, shaking your tail feathers (hips), and clapping, then repeating the routine several times before turning to the person next to you and swinging your partner around in each direction require little coordination or rhythm so almost anyone at any age can do it. Indeed, I was watching multiple generations do the dance on our wooden floor in front of the stage as well as in the aisles. The wee ones who could not stand were chicken-dancers-in-training in the arms of their parents. Every band repeated the song at least once an hour, and as a tradition it sometimes outpaced even the German drinking song "Ein Prosit" as something every visitor to Musikfest had to do.

The first volunteer shift change took place between 5:30 and 6:00. The arriving volunteers had committed to working at Festplatz until midnight. A six-hour shift is a lot to ask of a volunteer, but that was what we needed. By the middle of the shift change more and more people were arriving, not knowing what to expect but eager to see what was going on. Ticket booths now had lines, and the M. W. Wood crew was meeting a food demand greater than it had anticipated. The wursts were disappearing off the charcoal grills as soon as they were cooked. And lines were forming at the beer tent! People were relaxed, enjoying the outing, and striking up conversations with people who were friends of friends or even distant relatives. No one was annoyed by having to wait for their beer.

As evening settled in, the pace picked up. Available seating in the fifteen hundred chairs in the Festplatz tent gradually became scarce. Many in the daytime crowd had left, but others had settled in for the duration. At 6:00 p.m. Volksplatz became the first platz to close for the day, while Liederplatz was filled with upbeat shows by Les Papillions, two women singing gospel and pop songs, and Ilona's Hungarian Orchestra. The families stayed until 8:00 p.m. for shows by a local puppet theater and a clown and his son at Familieplatz. At Kunstplatz an audience we estimated at three thousand had gathered to hear folk-pop artist Don McLean at our big show. Our only ticketed venue, the Candlelight Concert at Moravian College's beautiful but difficult-to-find Peter Hall, had attracted more than a hundred peo-

ple for a harp duet playing airs and graces, and jigs and reels, traditional Irish music.

By 9:00 p.m. I had made my second stop of the day at the security
trailer where the Green Team was headquartered. I would be their
pest for the entire festival. While having an audience was great, we
needed revenue. My frequent visits prompted Kay Moran, the head
of the team, to keep a running total of cash receipts. If she got too
busy to do that, I considered it even better news. Others have told
me that I was pretty manic about revenue. And for good reason. We
were more than $100,000 over budget. We were going to have to
make a considerable amount on food and beverage sales to break
even. Everything was on the line.

One of the wonderful things that the Deckers did for us was to
give us a ninth-floor suite at the Hotel Bethlehem. Jack Trotter and
Jeff Gordon used the room as a media center, where they could
dispense festival credentials to reporters and hand out information
about the festival. It was also stocked with soft drinks, and tucked
away from reporters' eyes was a special refrigerator for beer.

We had agreed that at 9:30 each night we would gather to discuss
the day and what information we wanted to release to the media.
The main conversation was about daily attendance. To be as accu-
rate as possible, I called or visited each platz during the afternoon
and evening to gather attendance numbers. We actually tried to
count heads and to allow for people who were between platzes or
not visible, and we counted attendees at Kunstplatz to the best of
our ability. When people ask me now how we determine attendance,
I say that we count feet and divide by two. The truth is that while the
military has probably come up with a way to count people in large
crowds from a satellite photo, when you have a free event in a downtown with shops, restaurants, parking garages, and indoor concert
spaces, along with tents, sidewalks, streets, alleys, and assorted parking areas, putting a number on attendance is pure guesswork.

The nightly meetings also became the time to critique, regroup,
plan for the next day, and, much like a political campaign, to try to
figure out how we were doing. Much to our amazement, we were
doing well on that first Saturday. After much debate we agreed that
approximately fifteen thousand people had attended the first day of
Musikfest '84. Not bad for a new event.

After checking in at the office, I headed back down to Festplatz and found the place was jumping. We started joking that this was just another Saturday night in downtown Bethlehem. I was exuberant, but exhaustion was slowly creeping in. At 11:30 my friend Jim Stocklas, the site supervisor, suggested that because the audience was having such a good time, why not keep the site open until 1:00 a.m.? And he pointed out that we could sell more beer that way. I checked with Hans Stadler, the German bandleader, and he said it was no problem, though I can't believe that their exhaustion was any less than mine. However, Bavarian fests require bands to have a considerable amount of endurance. Jim confirmed that he had enough volunteers to run the beer tent so I agreed to the extension.

We shut down promptly at 1:00 a.m. with maybe a hundred people left in the audience and a valuable lesson: stick to the schedule. I thanked the band profusely, joined my colleagues in the office, then made it home and into bed by 2:30. We had survived and thrived the first day. Could we be on a roll?

CHAPTER 13
"A SUCCESS BEYOND ANYONE'S WILDEST DREAMS"

When I awoke on Sunday, I rushed out to the porch to get the newspaper, much like a Broadway producer who wants to see what the critics have written. Lo and behold, the front page had a photograph of the tiny pedestrian bridge filled with people under a headline of "Jamming into Musikfest." The story proclaimed that fifteen thousand people had attended and had a great time listening to music, tasting German foods, dancing, and drinking beer. The article provided quite an inducement for Sunday readers to come to Bethlehem. And they did.

Sunday's crowd was bigger, bringing out the curious and some repeat guests. People discovered the Red Trolley, which for fifty cents gave a docent-narrated tour of the town, carried a festivalgoer throughout the festive downtown, and eliminated the need to climb the hill from the Monocacy to Main Street. The Belgian draft horses were an attraction for city folk. Everyone wanted to visit the platzes. Even the Portoplatzes were an attraction, though few lingered. One evening we heard from a woman who had accidentally dropped her keys into the portable toilet. She wanted to know whether we could get them out. The request went to Regis Sopko, our head of security, who responded, "I'll do a lot of things for Musikfest but not that." We advised the woman to contact the company that cleans the units to see if they could reclaim the keys.

Official Musikfest T-shirts became all the rage. We had to reorder them on Wednesday. The twenty-two-ounce plastic beer mugs and the thirty-two-ounce beer pitchers sold out as well, and we could not reorder them. By midweek unofficial souvenirs were showing up in stores on Main Street. One of the favorites was a T-shirt that asked, "My Platz or Yours?" Most people did not invest in the souvenir program book, choosing to wander through the festival to happen upon whatever it was offering at the moment. The newspapers printed a schedule each day, which made the book less necessary.

Strollers and wheelchairs on crowded sidewalks and pathways became an issue that good-natured attendees dealt with in the most considerate manner. The profusion of these devices, and infants in backpacks and pouches, demonstrated the multigenerational appeal of the festival. But they also started traditions that were not good for a free festival. Baby carriages, strollers, and all sorts of backpacks provided ways to bring in food and drinks, thus cutting into the revenue Musikfest was counting on. Most people who did this convinced themselves that they were being frugal, but they did not understand that, without their financial support, the event would not survive. Because we did not serve food and drinks at three of the platzes, and had encouraged people to bringing food and beverages to Kunstplatz that first year, we had in some ways brought the problem on ourselves. When I saw a local judge and his wife sharing a bottle of wine they had brought to a Kunstplatz concert, I realized that in the future we had great revenue opportunities at this site, if we had a future.

The participation of so many volunteers proclaimed that this was a community event, not a commercial venture, a significant contribution to the success of Musikfest '84. Some volunteers were grieving at the loss of their jobs, some were retired, and others came on days or evenings when they didn't have to work. Many volunteered with a friend, spouse, sibling, or child. A few organizations volunteered as a group. The volunteers displayed pride in their community as they greeted guests from out of town as well as friends from other parts of the Lehigh Valley. They went out of their way to help and to share information about their city, which now was a place that others wanted to visit. One volunteer later wrote in a letter to the editor, "I am literally bursting with pride at what we in Bethlehem CAN do if we put our hearts into it." Volunteers demonstrated their pride by picking up litter, cleaning out trash cans, and wiping off tables. The city was in Sunday-best mode throughout the festival.

By evening on that first Sunday, we were beaming. Bethlehem had not seen this many people downtown in many years. We estimated that twenty thousand people had attended that day, and we speculated whether crowd sizes would drop off during the week. Monday through Wednesday would be the riskiest period. People in the Lehigh Valley did not usually go out on those evenings, let alone during the day. We prepared for the worst and again were pleasantly surprised.

The weather on Monday mirrored the weekend—sunny, warm, and not too humid. As I grabbed the paper from the front porch, I scanned it for festival stories. The news article was favorable, but the editorial was even better. Under the headline "Musikfest '84: Great Attraction," the *Morning Call* complimented the concept, the city, the sponsors, the organizers, and the event's international flavor. It even pronounced the event not just a Bethlehem event but "a Lehigh Valley event deserving Lehigh Valley area support." The editorial in the Allentown-based paper concluded: "Musikfest '84 is an attraction not to be missed. If you haven't taken it in thus far, there's lots of time to make up for the fact. And if you have [attended], chances are you will want to return."

On Monday I took a few hours off to catch up with my life and stop in at my law office, so I got to the Musikfest office later in the morning. Marlene and Roland were nervously working away, all of us ignoring the elephant in the room, the fear that Musikfest would be unable to sustain its opening weekend popularity. The acid test was going to be how attendance held up Monday through Wednesday. We were looking for any hints of how this day would work out. Getting the answer to the other nerve-wracking question, we were doing financially, would have to wait until later. All our deposits from the sales of tickets and souvenirs were in the night vault at First National Bank and would be counted throughout the day. I would have to wait until Tuesday to get the number. In the meantime the food vendors were dropping off bags of tickets they had counted and expected checks for their 90 percent share of the total. We also had bags of tickets from beer, wine, and soft drink sales. Down the hall from us a small group of volunteers was counting the tickets in the Sun Inn boardroom under the supervision of Anne McGeady. As noon rolled around, a few people began to trickle into Liederplatz. Soon we heard the blues riff of the guitarist Mike Dugan emanating from the platz below. As we peeked out the door, we saw he had a nice little audience. People who worked downtown had decided to take their lunch break at Musikfest, and some people from the community had joined them. The real test would be Festplatz. Roland and I walked down Main Street to grab lunch and see how it looked.

Monday and Tuesday were days off for the Stadtkapelle Berching. We knew the band members would have to work hard, that they had traveled far, and that they could not play for nine days straight. They were going to get to enjoy some Lehigh Valley hospitality during their days off. We treated them and their thirty-two guests to a picnic at the Beethoven Waldheim, followed by swimming and games at a city park one day and a day at a local amusement park the next. We understood that without our star attraction on those two days, we risked losing attendance. So when we entered Festplatz on Monday, it was with some trepidation. The Leroy Heffentrager German Band was playing a waltz, and a few dozen dancers were on the floor, including some in German folk costumes. The tables in the center of the tent were neatly set with tablecloths, some with small vases holding wildflowers. It was a reasonable start to what we expected to be our slowest day.

Attendance grew throughout the day, even at Familieplatz, where presumably employed parents found an inexpensive vacation for the whole family. Festplatz swelled after 5:00 p.m. when people left work, and the Allentown Symphony Pops concert at Kunstplatz well exceeded our expectations. We estimated ten thousand attendees for Monday.

One of the surprises was how few complaints we received. One was well taken. Sometime during the middle of the week my law partner's mother, Gertie Fox, came to see what was going on. Gertie was legendary because she was an avid protector of Monocacy Creek from pollution and overdevelopment. It is the only creek that supports native brown trout and flows through a city the size of Bethlehem, and she was determined to keep it pristine. I was surprised to find a phone message from her at my law office. When I called her back, she said in her polite but firm grandmotherly way that the trough that caught the wasted beer at the pouring station had a line that emptied it into the Monocacy. I made a lame joke about wanting to share the joy of beer with the trout, but she was not amused. We fixed the problem.

Reporters spoke with merchants on Main Street who were effusively positive about the festival. They had never experienced so many people on Main Street and in their stores during August. These eclectic entrepreneurs stayed open until 10:00 or 10:30 p.m. to accommodate Musikfest patrons. Many opened on Sundays during the festival, something they never had done before. The exception was the Moravian Book Shop, the oldest book store in America, which is owned by the Moravian Church. It held to its motto of "Never on Sunday" for nearly twenty more years. Festivalgoers from nearby suburbs reported that they were visiting downtown Bethlehem for the first time in years. Trotter and Gordon had developed surveys that volunteers were using to solicit comments from patrons. These surveys revealed that we had exceeded our goal in a special way. Our word-of-mouth promotion had reached as far as the Philadelphia area and other parts of eastern Pennsylvania and New Jersey. We had attracted people from outside the area in our first year! On Tuesday attendance ticked up to fourteen thousand, and we learned that weekend receipts had been good.

The Stadtkapelle Berching returned on Wednesday, and its cult of fans grew. The tuba player was the tall, muscular ninety-year-old Ludwig Bayerschmidt. When he set his instrument on the floor, it was as tall as he when he was seated. He was a fan favorite.

On Wednesday and Thursday we reported daily attendance of seventeen thousand each day. The "Chicken Dance" was played more often and the beer kept flowing. On Thursday morning we had a new experience: rain. But the morning downpour subsided by 10:00 a.m. and skies cleared for still another sunny day. The weather report for the weekend looked favorable. By Thursday evening we knew we had a hit, even though the financial forecast was still uncertain. Our part-time bookkeeper was writing out checks, which I was signing, but the account balance was a mystery. We were always two days behind in receiving deposit information because of the large number of deposits and the amount of cash that had to be counted. We received a daily statement of the amount of beer delivered but had no previous year's records to compare with our receipts, and our part-time bookkeeper simply could not keep up with the volume of activity. The stress was enormous.

The topic of our nightly assessment on Thursday was what to do next. The public and the press already had declared Musikfest a success. Everyone was happy except the guy who had to worry about paying the bills. I was still pestering the Green Team and trying to figure out whether we would end in the black, pink, or doomsday red. Even with those concerns, we had decided to confirm what we had already printed in the program book—yes, there would be a Musikfest '85: August 17 to 25. Mark your calendar. Somehow that announcement did not seem sufficient. We needed something more celebratory to commemorate what we had accomplished. That was when someone uttered the word *parade*.

I never have been a fan of parades. Sitting on a sidewalk or curb, lugging heavy furniture, jostling with others for a view of a celebrity or a clown never has appealed to me. And being one of the people everyone was looking at had even less appeal. However, the cost (free) of this conclusion to Operation Bootstrap did have charm. Because candles have a specific significance for the Christmas City, we decided to have a simple candlelight parade. We would invite the public to bring candles. We would use the horse-drawn wagon and the trolley for the volunteer leaders, and we would assemble some bands. The Polish American String Band, one of the famous mummer bands from Philadelphia, was our major act for Sunday afternoon at Kunstplatz. We would invite the band to stay a little later and be part of the celebration. The parade would begin at the Broad Street Mall (Volksplatz) and end at Festplatz, where everyone could have a celebratory beer and go home. Roland and I agreed to work on this on Saturday and Sunday. The confirmation of the 1985 festival and the plan for the closing night parade appeared in the newspapers on Friday. It was the only notice we sent out.

Friday continued our streak of beautiful summer days. Crowds arrived earlier in the afternoon and stayed later. The Festplatz tent became the belly of the beast, with a steady oompah beat and the "Chicken Dance." More people showed up in German, Polish, and Ukrainian costumes. A local favorite, Parke Frankenfield's Dixieland All-Stars, drew an older audience to Kunstplatz. At Liederplatz the Happy Boombadears brought their fans to a raucous dinnertime show. This group demonstrated the strength of local programming. The boomba, a sort of instrument holder, is a local creation that originated in the Pennsylvania Dutch community of nearby western Lehigh County. Whoever makes a boomba and brings it along may participate. A boomba includes a one-inch-thick hardwood dowel, three to four feet in length, with a heavy spring and rubber cap at the bottom like a pogo stick. The types of percussion instruments attached to the boomba include, but are not limited to, tambourine, cow bell, wood block, Swiss bells, symbols, and sometimes a bicycle horn. The Boombadear uses his hand to bounce the pole (which clashes the symbols), tap the tambourine, and/or to squeeze the bicycle horn, alternating with the drumstick to elicit sounds from the wood block and cow bell. Imagine twenty of these players singing to an accordion while creating the percussion together. Quite a show!

The food vendors had geared up for a big weekend, and they were not to be disappointed. Festplatz was completely full from 5:00 p.m. until closing, frequently with crowds gathered on the periphery. We reported that twenty-four thousand people were at the festival and that we had now exceeded the 100,000 guests whom we had hoped to attract. The weekend weather looked promising.

The last weekend of Musikfest '84 was idyllic. The weather was sunny and warm, with a slight September chill sneaking in after dark. As music from Liederplatz bled into Main Street, people were dancing in the street. People had called relatives and friends to join them for the last weekend of this new event. It was an affordable alternative to staying home and watching television or going to the movies. I had to say this was going better than expected, and, true to the concept, the nine straight days gave the event time to catch on.

Saturday night's big concert was by the Louis Armstrong All-Stars, featuring musicians who had performed with Armstrong, Bessie Smith, Cab Calloway, Harry Belafonte, Count Basie, and Duke Ellington. While the Greatest Generation and their parents (the grandparents of the boomers) were showing up at Festplatz, this was their big night at Kunstplatz. The audience was bigger than the one for Don McLean and equally enthusiastic. Later that evening we had the only rain that fell during festival hours for the entire event. Clouds were covering the stars that evening, and the threat of rain was in the air. At precisely 11:45, after beer service had ended for the evening, the skies opened up and soaked everyone with a downpour. People outside the Festplatz tent moved under it or rushed for other cover.

A CANDLELIGHT PARADE

On Sunday morning I donned my uniform for the day, the authentic lederhosen that I had purchased in Germany with knee-high socks and a classic white Bavarian shirt with horn-style buttons. It was time to be theatrical. The storm had cleared and the morning was sunny, promising great weather for the day. The atmosphere in the office was guarded relaxation. All of us were tired, but our work would continue after the festival ended. Cleaning up was going to take even more adrenaline than we had already used. Everyone was determined to enjoy this last day.

Roland had been busy assembling the parade. The horse-drawn wagon and the trolley would carry the board, staff, mayor, and other assorted dignitaries. The parade would now include the Stadtkapelle Berching, which would rush up from its 7:30 show to be the last band in the parade; the Polish American String Band; and the Mackay Pipe Band, a Scottish-themed group from Lansdale, Pennsylvania, that was performing at Volksplatz that afternoon. We arranged to buy as many candles as we could find at local stores to hand out to people who did not bring their own. We asked a few key volunteers to lead the parade carrying the yellow banner that had been quickly touched up to say Musikfest '85 with the new dates. The rest was go with the flow. It was not clear what was going to happen when we got to Festplatz, except that that the mayor and I would make a few quick remarks and everyone could drink, dance, or disband.

I remember that Sunday as a blur of thanking volunteers and sponsors, and being congratulated and thanked by people I knew and many I did not. I stumbled across my mother and her friends later in the day as they were enjoying the celebration. At Kunstplatz the Polish American String Band shed the head gear and jackets of their beautiful costumes because of the sweltering sun. At the end of their show the band members did what mummers do best—they marched. Volunteers led them from Kunstplatz to Festplatz, where the German band was on stage. The gaudy costumes, unusual instruments, and strange music of the mummers were a shock for the Germans. It was as though a group from outer space had suddenly appeared. To me it was a quintessential moment of what Musikfest was and could be, an opportunity for cultural discovery for every visitor.

The Bach Choir's Musikfest performance also was scheduled for Sunday at First Presbyterian Church, more than twenty blocks from the festival. Unfortunately, ticket sales did not cover the costs, adding to our financial worries. However, the choir's participation was important to the overall image and success of the event.

At dusk the Stadtkapelle Berching and the Beethoven Choruses took the stage at Kunstplatz for the festival finale and to say goodbye to the German band. The crowd of more than two thousand was enthusiastically appreciative. I introduced the band and the choruses and thanked them for all that they had done, some of which I said in fractured German. It was an emotional moment that took us back to our first partnership in 1976 for the Bicentennial. After listening to part of the concert, I headed back to the office to help organize the parade.

Marlene and some volunteers had invited all the board members, key volunteers, the mayor and city council, Banko, and members of the state legislature to the parade. Assigning people to the trolley, the wagon, or to walk would be a last-minute decision. Mayor Marcincin rode at the front of the wagon with the driver. Anne McGeady, Marlene, and I, as well as Susan, seven-year old Jonathan, and several board members, were in the back of the wagon. Roland organized the bands and walked along. Before we knew it, we were heading down Broad Street. As we turned the corner to Main, we saw a sea of candles all along the street. As the banner proclaiming Musikfest '85 came into view, the crowd cheered and raised candles. That journey down Main Street made the whole two-year process worthwhile. The cheers wiped away our lingering concerns about paying the bills and the challenges of making this an annual event. For this night we simply could celebrate the resilience of our community, a town worth seeing and worth saving.

The Mackay Pipe Band marched on into Festplatz, followed by the politicians and volunteers. My family and I squeezed through the crowd inside the tent, which at this point was blocking all the aisles, the fire department's worst nightmare. Mayor Marcincin took the stage and I followed, holding Jonathan in my arms and dragging Susan. The mayor reveled in the success of the event, thanking all who had made it possible and extolling the virtues of the city. He then dubbed me "Mr. Musikfest." The crowd was shouting, "Jeff, Jeff!" Just as the mayor was introducing me, the sound died and the lights flickered. Once again beer had played an important role—a patron had spilled some on an electrical box, which caused a power surge. I managed to croak out a few words above the din, thanking everyone and urging them to come to Musikfest '85. Hardly anyone heard me, but they cheered anyway. We left the stage and worked our way through the crowd. My family headed home but I stayed. My good friend Jim Stocklas had decided to start a festival tradition, the after party. With contributions from food vendors and spigots left open in the beer truck at Festplatz, word got around to the tired but exuberant crew of volunteers. Stunned and thrilled with the success of the event and the spirit exhibited by the community, we savored the accomplishment together.

The first year of Musikfest was a classic community success story. No one had a right to expect success from a new music festival in a city on its knees. Operation Bootstrap required that hundreds of people get in the same boat and row in the same direction under the same leadership for a long time to accomplish a specific goal. We had mixed local performers with nationally famous artists, talented local amateurs with professionals, and a wide array of musical genres from polka bands to blues, classical to pop. This was an unheard-of mixture of musical styles, but it had worked.

AFTERGLOW AND AFTERMATH

After all the numbers were crunched, we announced hard figures for attendance during the nine days of Musikfest: 182,000, nearly double our original goal. As we bade farewell to the Stadtkapelle Berching, then tended to the details of cleaning up, praise was pouring in. The *Bethlehem Globe Times* noted that "Musikfest '84 made downtown Bethlehem look more like New Hope," the nearby Delaware River artist colony that attracts large crowds on summer weekends. In a second editorial the writer noted the festival demonstrated that "tourism can be a year-round source of employment and economic development" and that successful promotion would rely on the city's heritage.

The *Morning Call* stated, "Let's face it. Musikfest '84 was a success beyond anyone's wildest dreams—even those of Attorney Jeffrey Parks, who conceived the notion and is most singularly responsible for bringing it about." Appropriately, the writer goes on to credit Roland, the volunteers, sponsors, the city, and the audience. It concludes: "This will be, in the vernacular, a tough act to follow. It's hard to conceive how they can improve on this year's event. But then it's hard to conceive how they staged this first-ever Musikfest so brilliantly."

At my law office letters and phone calls were pouring in. Some came from businesspeople who had responded to my pleas for help. Many were from members of the community. My favorite call was from Walt Dealtrey, the owner of Service Tire Truck Centers. He congratulated me on Musikfest, saying, "Someone forgot to tell Jeff Parks that he could not do that in Bethlehem." I have never forgotten those words. Rather than stifling new ideas, community elders had said yes, maybe we need to embrace change and see where it leads.

Cleanup took a week. Tables, chairs, stages, sound equipment, tents, and miscellaneous items were picked up by or returned to their owners. Booths were put storage. Sidewalks and streets were cleaned. The city returned to normal.

My biggest challenge was dealing with the accounting for the festival. We did not have the resources for a full-time bookkeeper, let alone an audit. We did the best we could with Anne McGeady, our volunteer treasurer, and a part-time bookkeeper, the amazing Ruth Paul, who had started with us in July and stayed with the growing nonprofit for the next five years. As the information trickled in from the bank, and the bills started accumulating, the picture became clearer. One of my new friends was an accountant named Bob Oster of the Allentown accounting firm Concannon, Gallagher, Miller & Co. I reached out to him for help. I already was hearing rumblings from board members and city hall that we needed a formal accounting for the festival. As we kept paying bills and trying to figure out if we had enough money to keep Roland paid and his health insurance current, Oster reviewed the books. Once he saw the bags of uncounted beer tickets, the piles of loose food and beverage tickets left over from the ticket booths, and the difficulty of matching some bank deposits to their source, he knew he had a challenge.

Another issue was how we were going to staff Musikfest moving forward. I knew I had to have a role, but I could not afford to spend 40 or 50 percent of my work time as a volunteer. The board and I agreed that I should accept $25,000 per year as the part-time president, which would include management, fund-raising, government relations, board relations, and acting as primary liaison for public relations and marketing. We all realized that I would be cramming a law practice and a full-time job together, but I was young.

At the same time reporters kept asking for the financial report. None of us had any problem with making this information public as soon as we had it verified. It would have been foolish to offer information that we would later have to correct. The board discussed stricter oversight issues, and we hired Bob Oster's team to thoroughly vet the festival's finances before we released any statistics.

The coverage that had been so supportive turned negative. An indignant *Globe Times* editorial on October 5, less than six weeks after the festival, huffed, "Musikfest has yet to come up with a financial statement....What possible reason could the directors have for not saying how much money they made, what they are doing with the money, and how much they plan to pay for leadership for next year's festival?"

By the October 16 meeting of our board, we had the report from the accountants. The firm had worked with us to ascertain in-kind contributions from the companies that had supported us. To our amazement Musikfest '84 had generated $690,453 in income, which included $147,156 worth of in-kind support, $89,594 in cash sponsorships, and $4,800 in government grants. Total expenses for Musikfest '84, including a bill from the City for $18,000, were $669,557, leaving a positive balance of $20,896. Not much, but enough to say we broke even.

The revenues generated by festival operations included $326,496 from the sale of food and beverage tickets, more than three times what we had budgeted. The expenses for concessions (food and beverage) totaled $213,522, giving us a net profit of almost $113,000. We had a blueprint for future success—sell beer. Ein Prosit! Other revenues included souvenir sales and $7,115 from Candlelight Concert ticket sales, which also exceeded expectations.

The total value of the advertising that promoted Musikfest in the local media (radio, cable television, newspapers, and magazines) was $158,000. Trotter had succeeded in having much of the media donated, and what was not donated was paid for by First National Bank of Allentown in addition to its cash sponsorship and the donated time of Trotter, Gordon, Sopko (security), Moran (Green Team), and dozens of other staff members.

On October 19 we made public my employment for the 1985 festival. Shortly thereafter we released the accountants' report. At a city council finance committee meeting in November, I reviewed festival finances in preparation for a discussion of the city's support for 1985. One council member grilled me on the numbers that we had released. It seems that he had calculated the ounces in a half-keg of beer, divided that by the ounces in a cup, multiplied that figure by what we were charging, and then multiplied that result by 1,100 kegs of beer and came up with a larger figure than we had reported. He implied that something was wrong. It was a difficult moment, but I bit my lip and explained that inexperienced volunteers had a high volume of spillage in this first-time event and vowed to address this with better training next year. In fact some volunteers had helped themselves to a cup or two and shared it with their friends. It seems that beer, like cash, is a fungible commodity and even more difficult to track.

While some in the community grumbled about a part-time salary of $25,000, the glow of the successful festival and what it meant for the city carried us through as we began to make announcements about Musikfest '85. In November we revealed that Die Algunder, a band from the Tyrol, would be our guest band. That gave people something concrete to anticipate. It helped assuage the bad news that kept coming from Bethlehem Steel's Martin Tower.

Thirty years later, with full benefit of hindsight, it is possible to summarize why Musikfest was so successful in 1984:

• Bethlehem has strong cultural institutions, a critical source of social capital.

- All members of the community felt the uncertainty generated by the condition of Bethlehem Steel. The festival generated more social capital by bringing together people from many parts of the community who never would have interacted otherwise.
- Business participation was not just transactional. As Frank Banko said, "Anything for Bethlehem." That was the spirit in which businesses and volunteers participated.
- Musikfest capitalized on the work done by community leaders in the three decades before the festival, not to mention two centuries of community cohesion before that. Moravian Bethlehem is a charming place. Musikfest capitalized on that in the nick of time.
- Musikfest had clear, consistent leadership that stated a mission and delivered what it promised. Jack Trotter, Jamie Musselman, Roland Kushner, Mayor Marcincin, Frank Banko, and many others made a commitment. Without their help the results would have been far different.
- The weather was good. It would be disingenuous not to credit such divine intervention. Each year since, I have eagerly awaited a report of a Canadian high, but it's never been seen again.

I do have to say that the program for the festival was comfort food for a distressed community. For the Greatest Generation and their parents, who had lived through the Depression, Musikfest offered polka, big band, swing, and jazz. For boomers there was folk music, pop, and some rock 'n' roll. And for everyone there was classical music, a cherished tradition in Bethlehem. All this was performed by mostly local artists and musicians.

As it turned out, the business plan was not good for realizing a profit, but it worked as a community development plan. Capitalization was just enough to prevent first-year failure. And the collective leadership that promoted the concept proved sufficient to carry the day.

When other communities ask me today about a theme for a new community festival, I stress that, to be successful, the festival must reflect the community. That was as true for Musikfest '84 as it is for Musikfest 2018.

MUSIKFEST 1999
North Side Downtown

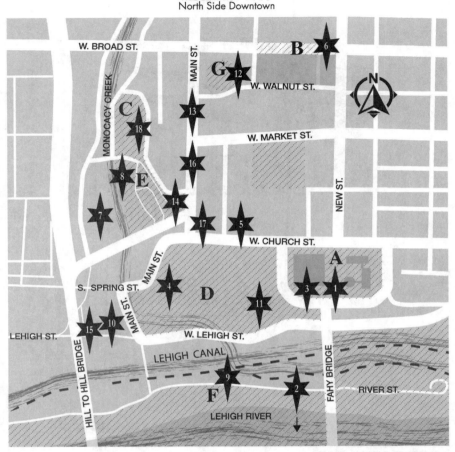

VENUES
1. Americaplatz
2. Asa Packer Concert Series
3. Blumenplatz
4. Candlelight Concerts
5. Chamber Series
6. Familienplatz
7. Festplatz
8. Handwerkplatz
9. Ice House Sand Island
10. Kinderplatz
11. PP&L Kunstplatz
12. Liederplatz
13. Main Street Musikfest
14. Muralplatz
15. Musikfest Bandstand
16. Street Performers
17. Vesper Concerts
18. Volksplatz

PARKS, PLAZAS, HISTORIC SITES
A. Bethlehem City Center Plaza
B. Broad Street Mall
C. Johnston Park
D. Moravian College Priscilla Payne Hurd Campus
E. Moravian Colonial Industrial Quarter
F. Sand Island
G. Sun Inn Courtyard

CHAPTER 14
GROWING ROOTS

M usikfest became an August fixture, but between 1984 and 2003 the relentless forces of deindustrialization and suburbanization still had their way with Bethlehem. The town's only department store, Orr's, closed along with the department stores in downtown Allentown and Easton. The Deckers' heroic effort to save the Hotel Bethlehem ended in bankruptcy and the loss of Bob Decker's profitable roofing business. The Bethlehem Steel plant closed in November 1995, leaving eighteen hundred acres of industrial property vacant; Bethlehem Steel filed for bankruptcy and its assets were sold, leaving the twenty-one-story Martin Tower vacant and with no prospect for reuse. Most of the remaining industrial businesses in Bethlehem vanished.

During that same period Musikfest became the largest free music festival in the United States, with thirteen stages and more than five hundred performances. Bethlehem Musikfest Association developed a second festival to anchor the Christmas holiday season, purchased a cluster of properties at a strategic location on the south side, and created a community arts center. It also began after-school enrichment programs for low-income students and in late December 2002 changed its name to ArtsQuest, the brainstorm of board member Ron Unger. The young arts organization became the biggest in Pennsylvania outside Philadelphia and Pittsburgh, serving more than one million people a year with an annual budget of $9 million.

Throughout this critical period ArtsQuest programs were a key factor in the decision of investors to risk purchasing property or locating a small business in Bethlehem's downtowns. Musikfest provided a second Christmas for businesses savvy enough to use the festival to market their wares. ArtsQuest's Christkindlmarkt Bethlehem, begun in the early 1993 and held adjacent to Monocacy

Creek right across from the Colonial Industrial Quarter, bolstered the Christmas season (see chapter 16), providing a strong attraction for retail visitors. ArtsQuest's investment in a new arts center on the south side marked the start of an effort to bring a defunct retail district back to life. ArtsQuest's programs also became a staple in recruiting new businesses and skilled employees to the region. In 2010 the mayor of Allentown told me that renewing his city's downtown was proving difficult. Bethlehem is different, he said, because of ArtsQuest.

The Kingston Trio song "Desert Pete" is about a man traveling through the desert who has run out of water. He finds a bottle of water left in a safe place so travelers could prime an old pump, and a note of instructions from the pump's owner, Desert Pete. Prime it, and water will flow from it prodigiously, Pete assured the traveler. Should the traveler drink the bottle of water or should he believe Pete and use it to prime the pump?

Bethlehem was a desert bereft of resources in the latter part of the twentieth century. Asking the community to invest in the arts while manufacturing was abandoning the city required residents to respond with trust and faith. The miracle of Musikfest was not just that it succeeded but that it offered encouragement to the community to take other risks it might not have taken if the festival had failed. While few people connected the arts, economic development, and jobs that would support a family, Musikfest had made people feel better about their community and its chances for success. As the businessman and former city council member Walt Dealtrey said, "Musikfest was community therapy."

It would be wonderful if I could say that we had a grand plan to use the arts for economic development with Musikfest as the first step and all that followed was part of the plan. However, our initial vision was more modest—a major festival to support a failing downtown and change the narrative for the community. But for the next thirty years arts programs and facilities expanded, and artists flowed into Bethlehem to participate in these programs. This required continuous priming of the pump. In 2002 the Bethlehem Musikfest Association became ArtsQuest to better reflect its diverse arts programs. The crisis in the community offered an opportunity for a rebirth through the arts. ArtsQuest became the midwife and Musikfest was our first child.

VOLUNTEERS

Without volunteers Musikfest and all that followed would not have been possible. From filling seats on the board to emptying barrels with trash, volunteers have been engaged in the evolution of Musikfest and all the other programs. A committee managed every single aspect of the festival in conjunction with a staff member, an arrangement that continues today. Committees handle food and beverage selection, site design, operations, supply, sponsorship, flowers, program, and security, staff the Green Team, and even manage the volunteers. Volunteers are involved in every step of putting on Musikfest and cleaning up afterward.

Volunteers, like highly paid executives, are not afraid to take the initiative, solve problems, and make decisions. Many work six- to eight-hour shifts for the entire nine days for $5 worth of food and beverage tickets and a golf shirt, now a T-shirt (two if they work four or more shifts). Others work for the week of setup and the week of cleanup so that they may enjoy the festival. They are my heroes, and I thank everyone who ever has given his or her most valuable commodity, time, to make this community event a success.

Like everyone else who has been involved in Musikfest, I have made many friends during the festival, and I have been amazed by how much individuals have been willing to take on. Let me introduce you to a few of the thousands of people who have made amazing contributions to the success of Musikfest.

Pat Holetz was an executive assistant at Bethlehem Steel when she became a volunteer in 1984. By 1985 she had become the "Chicken Lady," an unpaid goodwill ambassador for Musikfest. In a specially made chicken costume, she danced the chicken dance with generations of families for almost twenty years at Festplatz, bringing a smile to young and old alike and becoming the most photographed icon of the festival.

Joan Sheldrake was a retired teacher with a quick wit who became the festival's first "base radio" operator, making quick management decisions and advising volunteers about how to solve problems. She was the pioneer of what is now a major operation for each festival, with high-end technology and procedures.

The Gray Team, four members of the Greatest Generation, worked together for almost fifteen years to build stages, stairs, and dressing room mirrors; repair ticket booths and other stuff that broke; and fix our offices. Maurice "Mo" Latrenta, Stanley Paul, Erv Nothstein, and Tom Ridyard, all veterans, will always stand out as representatives of the generosity of spirit that made Musikfest possible.

Bob Behney and Bob "Doc" Windolph, known affectionately as "the Bobs" have worked together at Liederplatz since 1986 and vow to continue as long as their health allows. They don't see each other much outside the festival, but each year they reunite with their festival family, as do many other volunteers.

Tony and Judy Sabino, met while volunteering at Musikfest in 1989. One year later they were engaged at Musikfest. They married and had two sons. They have volunteered together every year since they met at the festival, and now they are joined by their adult sons, John and Paul, each with more than ten years' experience as a volunteer. They are truly a Musikfest family.

Rosa Velasquez moved to the Lehigh Valley soon after the first Musikfest. She fell in love with Bethlehem and its culture. She started volunteering for Musikfest in 2010. Now her adult children, Carolina, Cesar, and Cristian, also volunteer. All four members of the Velasquez family have graduated from the ArtsQuest Ambassador volunteer leadership program.

Since Musikfest started, well more than twenty thousand people from all parts of the community, all ages, and all ethnicities have served beer and soft drinks, sold tickets, gathered trash, counted money, delivered supplies, managed stages, helped performers, answered phones, carded beer patrons, and performed hundreds of other tasks to support Musikfest. Some volunteer with friends, family, social groups, or coworkers. Others, like the Bobs, volunteer individually and find kinship with other volunteers. The visibility of so many volunteers at the festival, with their "color of the year" shirts and friendly attitude, differentiates Musikfest from a commercial event by emphasizing that residents of the community and sometimes friends from far outside the community support it. The value of the volunteer support goes way beyond the time that they generously donate by generating incredible amounts of goodwill for the patrons and the community.

As the demographics of the country have changed, so have ArtsQuest's volunteers. Today more than half are introduced to volunteering through their companies, which offer groups of employees to volunteer at Musikfest. Dozens of companies participate and usually have special shirts printed for their Musikfest volunteers that identify the company. The business community has found Musikfest to be a great team-building opportunity that gets positive response from the employees, while the company demonstrates its support for the community.

Volunteers participate in every aspect of the cultural programs offered by ArtsQuest. They also ensure that ArtsQuest is responding to the cultural needs of the community. Faced with a community in crisis, volunteers have taken an active role and channeled their collective talents to create a culturally robust city.

FUNDING A FREE FESTIVAL

While Musikfest was a success from the start, the financial status of the organization was tenuous. However, we knew that the event would have to grow in stature and size if it was going to achieve its mission of rebranding the community and contributing to its economic development. In developing an economic equation that would propel the festival's growth, we were blessed with the legion of volunteers whose participation allowed us to keep paid staff to a minimum. With this base of support the original three-legged stool of food and beverage sales, sponsorships, and concert ticket sales continued to provide sufficient revenue. As the festival grew, we based many decisions on whether and how we could support new programs, and every calculation assumed increased attendance, at least for the first ten years.

Food and Drinks

Because the most heavily promoted theme of the first Musikfest was the German-Austrian heritage of the community, the foods offered by vendors reflected traditional fare from these countries, including the eastern European countries that had been part of the Austro-Hungarian Empire and were therefore staples for many immigrants to south Bethlehem. The season and the cuisine went best with beer.

As the festival grew, so did the competition to become a food vendor at Musikfest. The food and beverage committee selected the vendors each year and awarded only one-year contracts. Many local restaurant owners sought a coveted slot. The committee realized that the festival had to appeal to foodies and used variety, quality, and the ability to serve patrons as the criteria for choosing vendors. Musikfest quickly became known as much for its food as the music.[114]

Pennsylvania's wine industry, begun in the late 1970s with support from Penn State's College of Agricultural Services, was starting to get a foothold in the Lehigh Valley. In the fall of 1984 Susan and I visited Franklin Hill Vineyard with our son. A young couple had purchased land on a rural hillside and had found sufficient capital to plant hearty wine grapes. Two years later they were producing a modest amount of wine. It was a clear fall day, one of the prettiest times of the year in the region, and the grapes had been harvested. I met with Elaine Pivinski Flatt, whose two children were about my son's age. I told her about Musikfest and asked if she could provide special bottles of wine made for the 1985 edition of the festival. My thinking was that locally produced wine would enhance the quality of the experience, even though the hearty grapes grown in Pennsylvania at that time produced a wine sweeter than the then-popular merlots and pinot noirs of California.

Elaine describes her reaction as a bit taken aback, but thinking we could have a music festival in Bethlehem was not crazier than starting a vineyard in Pennsylvania. So it was settled: we would sell specially labeled red and white wines by the bottle at Musikfest '85. We had no idea how much wine we would need.[115] While wine sales have never approached the level of beer sales the beverage added a new dimension to festival offerings. Every year since then we have served wine at Musikfest.

Today, food and beverage sales at Musikfest continue to be a major source of financial support for what remains a free event. Audiences and vendors' sales have grown, so Musikfest now receives

30 percent of food sale revenues. The annual mugs are also a steady source of income. The original was a yellow plastic twenty-two-ounce mug with a handle and the Musikfest logo in blue. Purchasing the mug provided the buyer with twenty-two ounces of beer for the price of sixteen ounces, a true bargain. It was our biggest-selling souvenir item and the most profitable. The tradition has endured. Each year Musikfest offers a new mug with a design from the festival's poster. Today's mugs are better engineered to keep the beer cold and have lids to reduce spillage. They remain the top-selling souvenir. Better yet, they are manufactured in western Pennsylvania and reduce waste by replacing disposable cups.

Sponsorship

When we started Musikfest, we had few viable alternatives for financial support. City funding was not an option, except for in-kind support. Since that first festival we have worked closely with the business community. We became known as a good investment for businesses, although they put money into Musikfest for a variety of reasons. This is true of any kind of philanthropy, but it is a basic tenet that it took me a while to learn.

The main reason most businesses sponsor anything is marketing. These relationships tend to be transactional. A business will give money, product, and/or in-kind services in return for acknowledgment in a way that showcases the business, its product, or services to the public. From the first year we made sure these agreements were in writing and stated the expectations of both parties in full. Did the business plan to have an on-site presence at the festival? Would it buy an ad in the souvenir program book? Would festivalgoers be able to sample its product? Could the sponsor hand out brochures or provide samples of products? Was the sponsorship exclusive or could its competitors also become sponsors?

These contracts played out in different ways. Stroh was the principal sponsor but by law could not be the exclusive beer. Coca-Cola Bottling Company of the Lehigh Valley, on the other hand, was the exclusive soft drink provider. First National Bank of Allentown agreed not to be the exclusive bank sponsor because other banks would probably want to participate in the festival. The compromise was that First National's colors—yellow and blue—would be the festival's colors.

In 1988 Don Hunt, an executive of Service Electric Cable TV, approached us about a novel partnership. John Walson, Service Electric's founder, owned an appliance store in Mahanoy City, Pennsylvania, near Pottsville. His stock included televisions, which he could not sell because the broadcast signal did not reach to the valley where his customers lived. Frustrated, he placed an antenna on a nearby mountaintop and ran a cable into the town. TV sales soared and he found a way to generate recurring revenue by hooking his customers up to his cable system. Walson was a pioneer of cable television.

Don Hunt's idea was to sponsor Musikfest to see if he could convince people to switch their cable television allegiance to Service Electric by soliciting them personally at Musikfest and offering them an incentive. It worked. Service Electric was pleased with the number of new customers it signed. Hunt, who saw the power of this local festival, then wanted to expand the partnership by making Service Electric the exclusive cable system for broadcasting Musikfest. This was the beginning of a great partnership that continues to this day. Today Service Electric provides hundreds of hours of live programming from Musikfest on two cable channels every year and supplies festival operations with Internet access that supports the festival's communications and credit card systems. This partnership is a model for benefiting the community, the festival, and the sponsor.

Many companies contribute to Musikfest as part of their commitment to the community and their employees in general. This was the motivation for the initial support by B Braun as well as from other regional companies such as Air Products, a Fortune 500 company based in nearby Trexlertown that sells gases to industry; Mack Trucks, which manufactures trucks in Macungie; and Lutron, an electronics company based in Coopersburg.

For other regional businesses, supporting Musikfest makes sense because of the festival's programming. C. F. Martin & Company, based in Nazareth, makes the finest guitars in the world. Its involvement with the festival and the artists who perform there supports its brand. Crayola, the crayons manufacturer based in Easton, is a great local corporate citizen and supplies its products to the children's area for the legions of kids who flock to Musikfest. Dozens of other local companies contribute in-kind support to Musikfest, from fire extinguishers for the tents to first aid services. Without this support the event might not be possible.

Since the beginning of Musikfest, event marketing by consumer products companies has become increasingly popular. Companies hire event marketing specialists to develop exhibits that support the marketing of their product to people attending special events (such as state and county fairs) and festivals. At large events like Musikfest, the marketers induce event patrons to enjoy an experience that markets the car, food or beverage, electronic games, or other product they are promoting. Since the event marketer pays for the space it occupies, it is not strictly a sponsor of the event, but it is a form of business support. The marketers are seeking access to the audience, and the festival is using the rental fees they pay to sustain the event. Since many of the event marketers give out free stuff, they actually attract patrons. Every year sponsorship and mobile marketing (as event marketing now is called) are a major source of support for the free festival.

Concert Tickets

For the concert industry the primary source of revenue is admission tickets. Because we created a free music festival, we didn't have this source of revenue, except for a select few shows. In 1984 we charged admission only for the Candlelight Concerts and the Bach Choir, both of which were at indoor venues. As the festival grew, a variety of indoor locations in the downtown, as well as Packer Memorial Church and Zoellner Arts Center at Lehigh University, were used for concerts, some with an admission charge.[116]

However, as the appetite for bigger shows at Musikfest's main stage (Kunstplatz) continued to grow, the cost of the artists and renting the stage, sound system, lights, and backline (instruments provided to the bands; only big-name bands carry their own, and even they often require augmentation) increased. We had no choice but to charge admission for the bigger shows, starting in 1985. That year we charged $2, not a princely sum, for chairs at the front of the venue. We set up a few hundred chairs that first year and left plenty of room for blankets and lawn chairs. By 1989, when the Kunstplatz lineup included Johnny Rivers, the Association, Nancy Wilson, and the famous Celtic band Clancy Brothers, we also inaugurated a new premium seating section with front-row seats for sponsors and their guests. We got some backlash and heard talk of elitism, but most people accepted the policy.

In 1992 we raised the fee by $3 to $5, depending on the cost of the show, and we increased the number of chairs. By 1999, the last year Kunstplatz hosted the main stage, we were setting up five thousand chairs, which covered much of the field but left some room for blankets and lawn chairs. That year seating prices varied from $10 for the country singer Mark Chesnutt to $32 for the crooner Tony Bennett.

In 2000 we moved the main concert venue to RiverPlace on Sand Island and no longer offered free admission to anyone. We started booking bigger shows and never looked back. Like much of the concert industry, Musikfest nets little from these concerts because the artists' fees and the cost of putting on the shows often exceed ticket revenue. The business model makes financial sense only with revenue from sponsorships and the sale of food and drinks. For most big urban venues parking is another source of revenue. Musikfest did not get a percentage of what the parking authority made at the parking garage—more than $75,000 during Musikfest—or of the $35 tickets for parking violations during a special event (which also brought in $75,000 or more).

WHAT'S NEW?

From the day Musikfest opened, it's been a newsworthy event. It changed perceptions about the arts, the city, and the people of the community. Expectations for continued success were high. During every one of my thirty-two years as festival president, friends, sponsors, patrons, and reporters would begin asking me each February, "What's new for Musikfest this year?" The expectation was that we were cooking up something even more exciting than the previous year's edition. While some said they miss the early years of the festival, many more begged to know what new features were going make Musikfest even more dynamic each year. Our goal was to both please our regular patrons and to keep the festival fresh for an ever-growing audience from around the world.

Platzes and Programs

From 1985 to 1999 Musikfest grew in physical size and with new programs. Usually the growth involved a new platz or an indoor location. Without a great deal of financial reserves, we had to carefully calculate each element of growth to be sure we did not break the budget, and we always tried to arrange a sponsorship, the best kind of insurance against financial disaster. "Operation Bootstrap" continued to use facilities that already existed in the small downtown. The community almost expected a new platz or program every year. Some were great successes and others were tweaked or discarded.

Americaplatz, 1985, Bethlehem City Center Plaza.
The platz that we eliminated from the original plan for Musikfest was the first we added after we knew Musikfest would work. Although German Night in 1976 had taught us the limitations of City Center Plaza, the open plaza, view of South Mountain, and proximity to Main Street made it the logical place to expand the festival. Although August daytime temperatures made it too hot, it became a favorite evening venue with its American music and food. It was always the best place to watch the fireworks.

Muralplatz, grounds of the colonial pottery.
Inviting local artists to create murals on the plywood covering the defunct Tom Bass clothing store on Main Street was an innovative approach to ridding Musikfest of an eyesore. We institutionalized mural painting on the opposite side of Main Street in 1985 with mounted and framed four by eight foot sheets of plywood that featured a different local artist at work every day. It became a popular stop on the walk from Main Street to the Monocacy Valley. It was discontinued in the early 2000s.

Vesper Concerts, 1985, Central Moravian Church; Chamber Concerts, 1989, Moravian Old Chapel.
By working with the Reverend Douglas Caldwell, we were able to add religious and classical music within the beautiful interiors of

these historic buildings. Festival patrons still enjoy these well-attended series.

Musikfest Chorus, 1985–91.

Greg Funfgeld, director of the Bach Choir, created a chorus, mostly of Bach Choir members, to present a variety of classical choral works. The series was first held at Christ United Church of Christ in downtown nearer the festival then moved to the Asa Packer series in 1987.

Kinderplatz, 1986, Broad Street Mall.

This site originally was a chalk-drawing space to supplement family activities at Musikfest. It changed in concept and location several times before its last appearance in 2016. For a time it included a stage dedicated to children's performers. Children's programming is now integrated with other programs throughout the festival.

Street Performers, 1986, Main Street.

We began this program as the merchants became more positive about Musikfest and agreed to allow the closing of Main Street on weekday evenings and all day on weekends. It has expanded with each edition, particularly in recent years with world-class street theater. This program appeals to all ages.

Asa Packer Series, 1987–2010.

To incorporate the south side in Musikfest, we created programming at Lehigh's Packer Memorial Church. The Bach Choir and Musikfest Chorus, each presenting concerts, moved to the church in 1987 when they initiated this series. The series moved again, to Lehigh's Zoellner Arts Center, when it was completed in 1998, and the program of the Asa Packer Series changed from large choral concerts to an assortment of jazz, classical music, and intimate special rock shows. The series was discontinued in 2011 when Musikfest expanded into SteelStacks.

New Volksplatz and Familienplatz, 1988.

Musikfest expanded into Johnston Park along the east side of the

Monocacy Creek, north of the Colonial Industrial Quarter, in 1988 by moving Volksplatz from the Broad Street Mall. The same year we moved Familienplatz from the Colonial Industrial Quarter to the Broad Street Mall, where it was isolated from the sound bleed of Festplatz and was adjacent to Kinderplatz.

Bandstand, 1990–2000, Main and Spring Streets.
This grassy lot near Festplatz was a great opportunity to expand Musikfest. Itbecame site the home of the Bandstand, which was an ugly portable stage. Programming included American standards and rock.

Candlelight Concerts, 1990, Foy Hall, Moravian College.
After several years in the small and difficult-to find-Peter Hall, the series moved to the four hundred–seat Foy Hall, the college's prime music concert venue. The programming expanded to nationally recognized classical, jazz, folk, and New Age shows. This series was discontinued in 2011 when SteelStacks opened.

Handwerkplatz, 1993, Colonial Industrial Quarter.
The difficulty of booking artisans who specialize in producing crafts with colonial-era techniques led to the creation of Handwerkplatz, which became a craft show within Musikfest. Spaces for this show are in high demand and remain a festival favorite.

Foreign Relations

From its inception Musikfest had a reputation as an international event. Our challenge was how to maintain the sense of novelty with our German relationships. For the first decade of the festival, I would, at my own expense, cart my family off to Europe for vacation and interview bands. Later, Gus Skrivanek and Bob Steinmetz, my partners for the 1976 German Day, would run tours to Europe, visit towns where the bands came from, and audition them for future fests. The goal was to find bands that had experience performing at festivals. Skrivanek and Steinmetz formed the host committee responsible for making sure the bands were comfortable at their accommodations, knew their schedule, and appeared at the festival when they were supposed to. Skrivanek and Steinmetz also took care of moving and storing instruments and planning outings for the bands and their family and friends who accompanied them. August is a major holiday month in Europe, and almost all the bands took a tour of the United States after their appearance in Bethlehem. Some went to Florida for Disney World, but many went north to Niagara Falls, a wonder of the world that we Americans take for granted.

Each year we would announce with fanfare the German band coming the next year, complete with a picture of the band at their town hall or another scenic location. We always referred to the band as a German band, even though the group might be from Austria or Italy's South Tyrol. Saying that the German band was from Italy invited much curiosity in 1985 when Die Algunder band arrived. Many of its musicians were single men, and they were eager to make an impression in America. Apparently, our local women were eager to meet Italian men, and the festival gained a reputation for international matchmaking long before Match.com.

All the bands were well behaved, but some seemed determined to reinforce the hard-drinking reputation of Germans. We'd find some men lost on the streets of Bethlehem in the wee hours. The police handled these situations with good grace and humor, returning the musicians to their temporary residences with a hearty Ein Prosit.

The first two bands, Stadtkapelle Berching and Algunder Bohmische, were the featured bands at the festival three times each. All the others visited only once. The musicians met local people and established lifelong friendships. As wonderful as this program was, it became increasingly expensive as airfares increased in the new century and security rules became stringent. We also found that tastes were changing. The polka fans wanted more American bands with more diverse popular music programming. The last German town band to play at Musikfest performed in 2003, for the twentieth-anniversary festival.

Fireworks, Preview Night, Artrain, Parades

We did not have fireworks at the first Musikfest, because we did not realize how inexpensive they are on any day but the Fourth of July. We had wised up by Musikfest '85 and ordered fireworks to be staged from Sand Island, where they could be seen from much of the festival and from all over the city and neighboring communities. As the folks at Disney have proved, fireworks encourage an audience to stay at the park longer and spend more. We were hoping that people attending the fireworks would spend more on the last night of Musikfest, with the food and beverage tickets expiring the next day.

For Musikfest '85 our fireworks budget was $7,000, which would have paid for a fine main stage show, but we hoped fireworks would be a wise investment. This theory was severely tested when it rained throughout the day and evening of the last day of Musikfest '85. At some point I naively asked, "Can you shoot fireworks in the rain?" Of course, but would anyone be watching? We had no choice but to shoot the fireworks that Sunday night. I will never forget standing in the rain with a few festival patrons in ponchos and watching $7,000 worth of beautiful fireworks. Our big gamble was literally going down the drain. I was not sure if the water on my face was rain or tears.

But there's a happy ending. Musikfest has survived and thrived, and its fireworks have gained a reputation as the best in the Lehigh Valley. Shot from Sand Island, they are visible from Musikfest, South Mountain, and higher elevations in north Bethlehem and east Allentown. More than 100,000 people watch Musikfest fireworks, according to one estimate.

On Friday, August 13, 1993, which we designated Preview Night for the community, Musikfest held a parade to celebrate the tenth anniversary of the festival and the beginning of a new sister city partnership with Schwabisch Gmund, Germany. The parade, which featured Stadtkapelle Berching, included office holders from Bethlehem and Schwabisch Gmund and the Chicken Lady. That first preview night included only Americaplatz, but the event, sans parade, gradually expanded to include Festplatz and the Bandstand, and finally became part of the official programming for Musikfest '98 (not just a preview night). Two years later the entire festival, except the children's area, opened the Friday evening before the opening ceremonies. The evolution of Preview Night coincided with the decline of the Musikfest ball, which for the first ten years was the festival kickoff. We tried to hold it a few times in various locations, including Saucon Valley Country Club, but its time had passed.

An affordable cultural feature that helped enhance Musikfest's program was Artrain. I first heard about Artrain at the annual conference of the International Festivals Association (now IFEA). Artrain was established in 1971 by the Michigan Council for the Arts with a goal of fostering arts organizations and providing access to outstanding art exhibitions for residents of villages, towns, and cities across Michigan. As its website says, it is "a train converted into a museum that house[s] world-class art exhibitions." It was so successful in Michigan that the National Endowment for the Arts funded its eight-state Rocky Mountain tour. In 1975 Artrain became a nonprofit offering art exhibits throughout the country. Artrain was designed to help build local community arts organizations, and it certainly helped us.

Bethlehem is graced with a plethora of train tracks, most of which run through the city's two downtowns along the Lehigh River. The track of the former Central Railroad of New Jersey extends into the Musikfest grounds at the southern end of Main Street. Why not extend the festival to the railroad track? We had intentions of eventually supporting a visual arts program of some kind, and Artrain was perfect for helping us understand what engaging the community with the visual arts entails. Artrain first visited Bethlehem for Musikfest '93, scheduled as part of our tenth anniversary celebration. The exhibit's title was "The Romance of Transportation: Vehicle and Voyage in North American Art." More than thirty-five thousand festival attendees saw the exhibits, making Musikfest one of the train's more successful stops. Artrain helped us prepare for our next project, the Banana Factory Arts Center. We hosted the train twice more, in 1999 and in 2005, and each time it added a great dimension to Musikfest.

As I said, I never have been a big fan of parades. They usually are uncomfortable for anyone not in the front row, are vulnerable to weather, and, most of all, require tight organization. Musikfest was exceptionally well organized, but parades were not our expertise. We reserved them for special occasions like the tenth anniversary and usually relied on the visiting German band and other performers to join the parade. Sometimes a friend would donate a historic car to add luster, and occasionally a governor or senator would participate. But except for the first year's candlelight procession, Musikfest parades were lackluster affairs that did not add much. One exception was a New Orleans-style funeral march on Main Street on a night Queen Ida and her Bon Temps Zydeco Band were playing at Kunstplatz and we happened to also have a blues band that agreed to march along and play appropriate music. Mike Zovko, a sponsor and board member, obtained a coffin from a local funeral director. He assembled a group of volunteers with umbrellas and costumes. Thanks to the 1973 James Bond movie *Live and Let Die*, most people had an idea of what a New Orleans funeral parade looks like. The ersatz funeral attracted a great deal of attention, and the Queen Ida show was well attended.

These are some of the tactics and promotions that we used to expand Musikfest and to provide something new and reliably interesting for patrons. The greatest thing about a downtown festival is its flexible concept, which is conducive to adding street performers, pop-up or festival-long art exhibits, fireworks displays, artists in residence, and even mobile marketers, who now offer experiences that range from the latest PlayStation games to a digital tour of Texas. People attend Musikfest for the whole experience, not just the main stage show. They are excited to discover musicians they have never heard, street performers they have never experienced, art they have never seen, and people they have never met, all while surrounded by parks, buildings, shops, restaurants, and museums with much more to offer.

But starting and growing a festival in a downtown was not without obstacles, some of which were fierce.

CHAPTER 15
GROWING PAINS

Once Musikfest had demonstrated its value, the dark forces of self-interest and uninformed opinion came from every direction. The Bethlehem Musikfest Association remained true to its mission to support the economic development of Bethlehem's downtown but different interest groups chose to interpret this mission in various ways. The level of conflict that we experienced, particularly in the first five years, is the primary reason music festivals are held in fields, indoor venues, or parks, not on streets and plazas adjacent to businesses.

THE BATTLE FOR MAIN STREET

In 1984 downtown had few restaurants. The Hotel Bethlehem and the Sun Inn were the two fine dining establishments, and Orr's Department Store had a lunch counter and small dining area. Downtown had furniture stores, a carpet store, and multiple clothing and shoe stores but no stand-alone restaurants or outdoor cafés. Our intent was to bring prospective customers to the doorsteps of the businesses and encourage festivalgoers to come back after the festival. However, although the chamber of commerce and its Downtown Bethlehem Association were involved in the planning, we did not put much thought into preparing the merchants for how to capitalize on the festival audience. That was a mistake.

When the crowds did come, merchants had strong differences of opinion about whether those throngs were good for business. Opinions ranged from an unqualified yes to "I lost business." Had everyone waited a few weeks to see whether they had gained new customers, they might not have disagreed, but they didn't wait and soon the lines were drawn. A few merchants became the festival's biggest boosters. One, Neville Gardner, who had just opened a shop to complement his mail-order Celtic specialty company, credits Musikfest as a key factor in the early success of his business, Donegal Square.

However, several other merchants experienced a decline in business and turned against the festival. In the public conversation in the year after that first festival, we invited merchants to consider ways in which they could entice festival patrons to become their long-term customers. Some merchants who had suffered a drop in sales remained opposed to the festival; these were mostly store owners who relied heavily on back-to-school sales and complained that their regular customers could not get to the stores because of festival crowds. Trying to change the conversation to a discussion about how to make customers out of people who otherwise never came downtown was a Sisyphean task. My parents had owned a small business so I understood. Just keeping a shop open after regular hours and on Sundays was a mountain too high for an already overworked business owner who also would have to pay sales staff to work those extra hours.

In early 1985 we aggravated the problem by asking the city to close Main Street while the festival was open. Opposition from those who had professional offices on the street was quick and fierce. Their clients would not want to make appointments for that week, and the professionals would suffer financial harm as a result. We worked with them and the city to reach a compromise that Main Street would be closed after 5:00 p.m. on weekdays and from noon to 11:00 p.m. on Saturdays and Sundays. (Today, being able to walk to the festival is a prized benefit of having an office in the Moravian Historic District, as it was renamed in 2016.)

In an effort to direct the merchants toward being constructive, the Downtown Bethlehem Association agreed to coordinate sidewalk sales during Musikfest. The outcome was predictable: people attending a festival did not want to purchase a lamp or shoes, let alone furniture. They were more interested in eating, drinking, and having new experiences.

The issue simmered as merchants looked for an easy way to capitalize on Musikfest. While some merchants were holding sidewalk sales in 1985, one entrepreneur used the sidewalk in front of his building to create "Chickenplatz"—he set up a portable grill and sold chicken dinners. Although he was not in the restaurant business, he understood the opportunity. Soon he was joined by the Hotel Bethlehem and Orr's Department Store, both of which had year-round liquor licenses that allowed them to extend sales to their sidewalks. The rest of Main Street took notice.

Mayor Marcincin's city solicitor issued an opinion that noted that while the city had an interest in the public right-of-way on city sidewalks, the owner of a building had legal ownership of the sidewalk and could lease it to a third party during Musikfest, provided that the business maintained a six-foot right-of-way.

Based on the solicitor's opinion, in 1985 the city issued permits for temporary vendors, as it does throughout the year, but required vendors for the festival to locate in areas approved by Musikfest. In 1986 the city, with our encouragement, decided not to issue permits for sidewalk food sales to any merchant who did not engage in that business year-round. This would have eliminated Chickenplatz. The merchant threatened to sue. The city backed down. Mayhem ensued.

In an effort to give an artistic twist to an increasingly tawdry Main Street, we brought in street performers (also known as buskers) in 1986; Main Street was now closed to traffic on weekday evenings after 5:00 p.m. and all day on weekends. The performances, which have gotten better each year, have become a feature of the festival. (In recent years street theater artists from Europe have enhanced the international reputation of the festival.) But despite our artistic efforts to soften the gaudiness created by the food and sales booths lining the street, the situation worsened.

By Musikfest '87 Main Street looked like a shantytown. Food vendors ruled much of the sidewalk. At one corner a building owner created a plywood lean-to with colored Christmas lights. Others were worse. The whole idea of promoting the beautiful Victorian ambiance of the street was lost in a sea of tacky temporary food booths. While there was plenty of blame to go around—the Musikfest association was guilty of failing to persuade building owners of the festival's long-term benefits—the threat to the festival was so dire that when Mayor Ken Smith began his term in 1988, he agreed to tackle the issue.

With much public discussion the city council approved an ordinance that required anyone setting up a temporary stand before a special event to file for a permit at least forty-five days in advance, submit a design of the stand, and state what it would sell. The measure also required a $100 application fee, eliminating the most marginal vendors, and prohibited the sale of alcoholic beverages by vendors who did not have a permanent liquor license. Musikfest had sought to simply eliminate sidewalk vendors during the festival. I argued that any stand in front of a restored building denigrated the experience the city and Musikfest had worked so hard to create. However, the city recognized the tough times faced by merchants and building owners and decided that allowing them to use the sidewalk was a way to extend to them an important financial benefit of the festival.

The ordinance remains in place but did not resolve the issue of Main Street's appearance. In 1988 the street looked better than it had, but problems still lingered five years later. In the end time solved the problem. As building ownership and tenants changed through the years, the newcomers acquired a better understanding of how to present a business at Musikfest. And the proliferation of restaurants and seasonal sidewalk cafés has greatly reduced the number of vendors on the sidewalks during Musikfest. Most, but not all, are licensees of Musikfest; they use the sidewalks in partnership with building owners. They and Musikfest receive a percentage of sales.

As Main Street continued its painful evolution, Musikfest often gave building owners an advantage. Buyers of Main Street properties factored revenue from renting their sidewalks into their budgets for paying mortgage and operating expenses. New businesses relied on the exposure and sales from the festival. In 1993 Orr's Department Store closed. It would be almost five years before Lou Pektor, a local stockbroker-turned-real-estate-developer, purchased the complex, which was originally three buildings, and converted it into Main Street Commons. When the complex reopened in 1998, one of its tenants was Bethlehem Brew Works, among the first craft breweries in the region. Just half a block away, Rod and Diane Holt, who had pioneered downtown Bethlehem restaurants at the Sun Inn, opened the Apollo Grill on Broad Street. The two restaurants became the anchor for Bethlehem's restaurant row.

Just as the restaurant renaissance was beginning, in January 1998 Dee and Bobby Decker were forced to close the Hotel Bethlehem. The hotel was in bankruptcy, and for most of that year its future was in doubt. A plan to convert the hotel into a senior living facility surfaced, alarming the community. Finally, a Lehigh alumnus, Bruce Haines, a former U.S. Steel executive, and Bill Trotter, an Air Products executive, assembled nine investors to purchase and renovate the hotel. The hotel reopened in September 1999, to the delight of the community. With public rooms restored to their 1920s grandeur, Moravian tiles uncovered in the floor of the Terrace Room (the former Candlelight Room), and historic murals well displayed in the Continental Room, the hotel reclaimed its place as a community treasure.

The new owners of the hotel were not sure how to handle Musikfest at first. Although their rooms were fully occupied during the festival, their initial reaction to the many other festival patrons was to post security and keep them out. That approach has changed in the years since. With its sidewalk café and its beautiful Tap Room in the open lobby, the hotel has fully embraced Musikfest, when it offers special menus indoors and out, mug refills on Main Street, and outdoor entertainment at night. Most recently the hotel has had a platz, with a festival stage abutting the building. Musikfest has been part of the resurrection of this community institution, which now does a robust business.

Pennsylvania has been liberalizing its antiquated liquor laws since 1984. Musikfest has been a learning experience for the state and its other communities. Bethlehem and the state police have been rigorous in enforcing liquor and criminal laws to ensure that Musikfest is a safe experience. However, the relaxation of liquor laws and the proliferation of restaurants and bars have created serious competition for Musikfest. Bars fill Musikfest mugs, frequently at prices below what Musikfest charges. Given this friendly competition, the best Musikfest can do is sell more mugs—and the festival has the official mug market cornered.

Teenagers posed another growing pain. In 1985 a local radio station placed its promotional van in front of the Hotel Bethlehem and blared rock music at night, attracting teens. Before any of us knew what was happening, hundreds were gathering nightly on Main Street. The throngs grew. The street became the biggest source of festival arrests because of teen fights, illegal alcohol, and public drunkenness, usually from alcohol purchased outside Musikfest. The festival is known for strictly checking young people's identification and enforcing the rules. For a long time we had to station fifteen to twenty-two officers on Main Street to assure patrons that teens would not disrupt the festival. We dubbed this phenomenon "puberty platz."

Puberty platz was a constant source of annoyance for festival organizers and of unsolicited advice from the community. We always were polite, but we tried everything legal to curb the teens' shenanigans. We surveyed the kids in the crowd to see why they were at the festival and what kind of music we might provide to entice them to another area. Year after year the growing teen audience responded that they were on Main Street to flirt with members of the opposite sex. In a classic case of unanticipated consequences, we were hosting an adolescent meet-up space. We tried deterrents and distractions. We put polka bands and classical music on Main Street. The teens moved to another part of Main Street. We put rock, rap, and hip-hop music on stages. The kids stayed on the street. The Lehigh Valley has few places where teens can congregate, and Musikfest filled that need for ten summer nights. Initially puberty platz was all white kids from Bethlehem. Gradually it attracted students from other school districts. And gradually the mix of the crowd changed with the increasing diversity of the community. Yet the number of arrests during the festival was not high—the worst year saw forty to fifty arrests of teens or of adults who were hanging out with teens. The presence of the young people, however, was enough to scare some patrons away from Main Street at night.

Musikfest and the city now bring in more temporary lighting, a mounted police patrol, and book hip music for the two stages on the street. Teams of high school students help the festival with some of the programming, and teens seem to be more disbursed among the platzes. Mark Duluzio, the police commissioner in Mayor Robert Donchez's administration, now issues a humorous annual list on social media, "How to Get Arrested at Musikfest." It includes "If you are considering doing something you would not do in front of your mother, don't." Everyone at the festival knows what kind of behavior is expected. In 2016 Musikfest had the fewest arrests since the 1980s–sixteen.

The effort to tame puberty platz gave rise to a tradition of its own, the sweep, now a nightly event that draws an audience. Starting promptly at 11:15 p.m., two police cars, four to eight mounted police, and several officers on foot come up the hill from Festplatz, round the corner at Central Moravian Church, and continue past the Hotel Bethlehem all the way to the Brew Works. The message from the bullhorn in the lead police vehicle never changes: "Musikfest is over for the evening. Please get off the street."

CITY GOVERNMENT

Whenever a municipal government provides a benefit for a private organization, including a nonprofit, that preferential treatment is rightly subjected to public scrutiny. We always viewed our organization as an unofficial economic development and cultural arm of city government. We could be entrepreneurial in raising funds, such as from business sponsors, that a government simply could not. But because the festival was not an official part of city government, we had no assurance we would receive the level of support many cities now routinely extend to publicly supported festivals.

During the first Musikfest the city agreed to contribute all city services the festival needed except police and fire services. The use of city services was broad and necessary. The electrical bureau installed power for the platzes, and city employees helped pick up trash and clean the streets daily, spruced up the parks before the festival, and attended to multiple other tasks. Most of the property we were using for the festival, including the streets, was city property, and Musikfest has formally rented that property from the city since the first festival.

What we feared most in the early years—and it's a fear that never really goes away—was that one major storm would ruin the festival and wipe out its cash reserves. We liked to think that the city would rescue us if something dramatic happened, but that would have created a political storm, even if the city had the money to help, which it did not. After five years of full city support for Musikfest, which was showing a profit, the city asked the festival for reimbursement. In the end Musikfest agreed to pay a fixed amount for city services. The difference between that amount and the actual costs to the city is the city's donation. I was not a fan because the city counted use of trucks and machinery at a rate equal to what it would have cost the festival to rent them, and the city charged the festival for city workers assigned to festival-related duties even though they were salaried. As the festival shifted the majority of the platzes to properties not owned by the city, this changed. Musikfest now uses private contractors for much of the work that used to be done by city workers and has reduced these costs. In turn, the city has continuously reduced staff because of constant concerns about its budget.

FREEDOM OF EXPRESSION PLATZ

All publicly owned property is subject to the U.S. Constitution, including the First Amendment. Over the years we have encountered issues with unions that want to demonstrate against their employers who have a promotional booth at the festival, candidates for public office who want to work the crowd, people who want to hand out literature for a candidate or political position, and individuals who wish to proselytize their religious beliefs. Because so much of the festival was on public property, and a portion of it is still on public property, and our leases specifically require that we not deny access to any member of the public, we have to accommodate free speech. So we created Freedom of Expression Platz. Although you will not find it on any festival map, the police and festival staff are quite familiar with it. It is on the Main Street bridge over Monocacy Creek. Here Musikfest patrons might be handed a pamphlet or hear someone speaking loudly about his or her beliefs.

ECONOMIC IMPACT

Because Musikfest was billed from the beginning as an economic development program, the organization had a real burden to demonstrate that it was deserving of the in-kind support it received from the city, even though the value of those services became an increasingly smaller percentage of Musikfest's budget. Although privately owned sports teams that generate vast profit for their owners rely on lavish, taxpayer-funded stadiums and arenas, the arts are usually left to grovel for the crumbs of public support. And to justify that support arts organizations and their supporters are urged to produce expensive studies showing how much economic return they bring to the community. Just as arts programs in most public schools are jettisoned way before the football program, so the arts are second-class citizens in terms of government largess.

During the first ten years criticisms and controversy surrounded Musikfest. The regional economy gradually improved, but Bethlehem Steel continued its decline and the resulting angst pervaded the city. The suburbs were growing economically, but the city faced such major challenges that they were beginning to threaten basic services. Public officials and residents quick to criticize at budget meetings scrutinized every penny not spent on basic services.

In 1988 we commissioned our first economic impact study by Cate Cameron, an assistant professor of anthropology at Cedar Crest College, and her husband, John Gatewood, a professor of anthropology at Lehigh University, in partnership with Kamran Afshar, a professor of economics at Moravian College. Cameron and Gatewood devised a survey that was taken on each day of Musikfest '88. It was the first to identify where our guests were from and how much they were spending. Afshar took that information and calculated the economic impact and financial benefit to the city and Bethlehem merchants. We were surprised to find out that in our fifth year, 39 percent of festivalgoers lived more than thirty miles away. The regional income from Musikfest attendees, including what they spent at Musikfest and at hotels, restaurants, and shops, was approximately $6.5 million, which included $2 million in "new money" for the Lehigh Valley (money spent by visitors from outside the valley). Economic impact studies always use a multiplier factor for new money. Afshar used a relatively conservative multiplier and came up with an economic impact of $10 million generated by the festival. He calculated that for every dollar spent in connection with the festival, the City of Bethlehem receives four to five cents in tax income.

We repeated the study in 1993. This time we found that 41 percent of attendees came from outside the region, with 10 percent coming from more than a hundred miles away. Afshar estimated the economic impact at $22.3 million. We proudly shared this information with the community.

In 1997 we laid out all the figures for the public. We listed all the expenses the city calculated it had incurred as a result of Musikfest. Then we listed the revenues that the city received from the festival. We found that the city earned $74,800 more than it had spent to support the festival. Bethlehem was making a profit on Musikfest. This simple information excused us from doing any further economic impact studies. When Americans for the Arts, the nonprofit founded in 1960 to advance the arts and arts education, produced a formula for arts organizations to calculate economic impact in 2010, we used it to report Musikfest's gross economic impact, which as of 2016 was about $60 million.

FLOODS

Floods are a pestilence of biblical proportions. With a festival along a creek, and a river not far away, Musikfest is always one big tropical storm away from a flood. The first one came in the middle of the night. On Monday, August 16, 1993, rain pounded Musikfest. After the festival closed for the evening, vendors leaving downtown noticed that the creek was rising. Our staff warned food vendors, crafters, and even our suppliers of sound equipment to remove as much of their inventory and equipment as possible because of the flood threat. Sometime around two in the morning, a flash flood cresting three feet above the creek drenched all of Volksplatz and Handwerkplatz, hitting food vendors and artisans. Many vendors had removed inventory but all left equipment behind, some of which was ruined or floated away. City crews arrived at 3:00 a.m., followed by Musikfest staff and volunteers. They brought wood chips in to soak up the moisture, removed debris, brought back the sound equipment, and the platzes were up and running by 2:30 p.m. on Tuesday. The next time, eighteen years later, was not as easy.

On Saturday, August 13, 2011, the Lehigh Valley recorded 3.68 inches of rain, with more predicted for Sunday. Once again the

Monocacy rose to critical levels. At 9:00 p.m. Musikfest ordered the evacuation of Handwerkplatz and warned vendors to remove all food products, sale items, and loose equipment. It was a slow, painful process because the ground was already soaked and access to the site was limited. The creek gradually rose above the bank, and by later that night the area was completely flooded, far worse than in 1993. Once again damage was limited to equipment and some supplies, but we had to close the site for the final Sunday of Musikfest because the ground was such a mess and more rain was probable. We were already struggling that year because it was the first at our new south side campus. It looked like we were going to lose $750,000 that year.[117] (The loss turned out to be more than $1 million.) I made a plea for financial help to a community still suffering from the Great Recession. We did receive more than $30,000 from the community, but the sympathy was not universal. A local barber put an old toilet on his front lawn with a sign on the open seat that said DO-NATIONS FOR JEFF PARKS. I could just feel the love.

Fortunately, even with all the challenges and obstacles, the overwhelming sentiment of the community was that Musikfest is an important expression of the community's well-being. That consensus gave us the courage to move forward with additional arts strategies for urban development.

CHAPTER 16
KEEPING CHRISTMAS IN THE CHRISTMAS CITY

As the region's industrial base continued to erode, many in the community were willing to listen to alternative strategies from an organization that had demonstrated success. For the first five years of Musikfest, we were busy addressing the many challenges involved in developing the festival, its board, and relationships with a broad base of stakeholders. I began my paid position in fall 1984 and focused my energies on ensuring that Musikfest would become a cultural tradition and a force for revitalization.

In the spring of 1987, as we headed into the fourth installment of Musikfest, I gave notice that I would be resigning from my paid position with Musikfest after that year's festival. I joined Bill Platt, the former district attorney of Lehigh County, in developing business in the Lehigh Valley for a Pittsburgh-based firm. I had no interest in making a career of managing a music festival, although I still believed that the festival had opportunities for developing the future of Bethlehem. In September I returned to the Musikfest board as president but as a volunteer. Back when I was a volunteer, I had the freedom to think beyond the festival and enjoyed the excitement of a new business endeavor. Tom Kwiatek, a Bethlehem native, was manager of a nonprofit health care agency and was eager to take on Musikfest. He became executive director of the Bethlehem Musikfest Association and faced a significant learning curve because Roland Kushner also had decided to leave the organization to pursue an academic career..

CONFIDENCE AND HUBRIS

The line between confidence and hubris is a fine one. For any individual or organization to be successful, confidence is essential or failure is certain. Success, such as we had experienced at Musikfest, breeds more confidence. Musikfest became the organization to watch. It also became the organization to join. We were fortunate to attract dedicated community leaders to our board, which was one of the few that welcomed women as members and leaders. I continued to receive press coverage and awards, including one for leadership in economic development that I truly cherished. The label of visionary was one that I had mixed feelings about, but I continued to offer my opinions (some would say pontifications) about tourism development. With a touch of hubris our organization saw itself as leading the community into a new, challenging era and continued to dream of expanding its role. By our fifth year we had outgrown our office and desperately needed more storage for the paraphernalia it takes to run a festival.

But most of all we were a music festival without a permanent music facility. Somewhere along the way the Boyd Theatre on the Broad Street Mall became our great white whale. Before we had even begun to address the office and storage issues, with the consent of the owners we commissioned a study of the Boyd. It was built in 1921 as a vaudeville and movie house and now the last operating single-screen downtown movie theater in the Lehigh Valley. All the others in Bethlehem had been torn down, done in by new five-screen houses in Allentown, Easton, and Whitehall. The Boyd, with a stage, stage house, orchestra pit, and fifteen hundred seats, seemed like a good bet to become a permanent, year-round cultural attraction for the community.

The challenges involved in developing the Boyd as a contemporary arts center were funding, competition, and timing. The competition was impressive. The Allentown Symphony Association had the Lyric Theater, a nineteenth-century vaudeville house that accommodated concerts but also was leased to community groups for shows. The number of seats was similar to the Boyd's. In Easton the State Theatre, built in 1910 as Neumeyer's Vaudeville House, had been extensively renovated in 1926, with beautiful frescoes inspired by Spanish and Italian themes. The theater was renovated again in the 1980s but was still having difficulty operating as a performing arts center. Although its future was uncertain, the State too was about the same size as the Boyd. At the same time Lehigh University was considering building a performing arts center on campus.

By 1991 we had come up with an operating plan for the Boyd that was oriented to the charter tour market. Through the Christmas program Bethlehem had maintained a good relationship with charter tour companies in the northeastern United States. We believed we could parlay this kind of tourism into visits during other seasons, with a passion play during Lent and musical theater at other times of the year. During Musikfest and off times, we would present live music at the Boyd.

The recession of 1990–91 saved us from this plan. While we continued to negotiate with the owners of the Boyd, they eventually decided not to sell for the price we were willing to pay. Mayor Ken Smith and his business administrator, Bob Wilkins, discussed with us the possibility of floating a $2 million bond to support the Boyd project. But the recession and the continuing decline of Bethlehem Steel—which at that point employed only 4,340 people locally and fewer that thirty thousand companywide—made everyone hesitant about taking on any major projects, and the city had to reduce its ambitions.[118] The project probably would not have been successful. Performing arts centers of this size in small and large cities throughout the country continue to struggle to stay afloat. Their business plans rely on touring Broadway shows to be profitable, and for us Broadway is only seventy-five miles away. Charter tours are a declining market because they hold little attraction for baby boomers. We were fortunate because, had we acquired the Boyd, we would have been saddled not with a white whale but a white elephant. It would be another twenty years before we finally got our performing arts center.

But Musikfest still needed an office for an expanding staff. In 1990 a small building on the Broad Street Mall became available. We acquired the building because it was adjacent to one of the Musikfest sites downtown, which made it ideal for operating the festival and giving the organization a year-round presence downtown.

By 1992, I could see new opportunities for advancing arts strategies for economic development as Bethlehem continued to evolve. The city still had not hit bottom, although the Lehigh Valley region as whole was experiencing physical and economic growth as the home to successful companies like Air Products, B. Braun Medical, Binney & Smith (Crayola), Just Born, F L Smidth (a global engineering company), Lutron (designers of dimmers and other lighting controls), and Follett Corporation (manufacturers of ice machines for the food service industry). Working with the board of the Bethlehem Musikfest Association, I arranged to return to work for the organization, with the specific goals of initiating a new festival, Christkindlmarkt Bethlehem, and exploring avenues for a new arts facility to help revitalize the community. Within five years we would have both a new festival and a new arts center but not the one we thought we would.

CHRISTKINDLMARKT BETHLEHEM

During a family trip in 1984 we visited Rothenburg ob der Tauber, a small walled medieval city that remained just as it was in the 1600s after being sacked by Catholic forces during the Thirty Years' War. With a town square surrounded by authentic medieval buildings, churches, narrow streets, restaurants, shops, and a park overlooking the Tauber valley, Rothenburg is the jewel of the Romantic Road, a chain of medieval cities in central Bavaria. After staying with members of the Stadtkapelle Berching band in their beautiful walled town just a few hours from Rothenburg, we were strolling through Rothenburg when we noticed a large shop called Christkindlmarkt Kathe Wohlfahrt across from the town hall. It seemed to be attracting a lot of tourists, so we followed.

It was an experience akin to Disney, only in an authentic medieval building. It also demonstrated retail genius. This all-year Christmas market is still one of the most attractive retail experiences anywhere. Visitors, shopping basket in hand, are directed to a one-way path through a wonderland of all things Christmas. They are invited to explore German Christmas traditions of *rauchers* (wooden figurines that "smoke" incense), nutcrackers, and pyramids (wood-carved structures that rotate slowly as heat from small candles rises to

wooden paddles); hand-carved wooden manger scenes, music boxes, clocks, and hanging ornaments made of wood, glass, or tin; holiday linens, dolls, and decorations of all kinds. All this is displayed in
a wonderland of Christmas trees and exquisite lighting.

I was smitten. I walked up to a salesperson and asked to see the
owner. In only a few minutes I was escorted upstairs to a room
that Martin Luther might have recognized. The conference room,
with bottle-glass windows, slanting floor, and aesthetically appropriate table and chairs, was tiny. When a six-foot-five young German
ducked through the door, he introduced himself as the son of the
owner. A long-term, long-distance friendship began that day and has
lasted through the many years since. Harald Wohlfahrt was born in
the early 1950s as Germany was recovering from war. His father had
worked with the U.S. Army and with IBM. The Wohlfahrt family
had lived in Minnesota for several years during Harald's childhood.
Harald speaks perfect American English and always is alert to a business opportunity. His father had started the family business by doing
favors for friends in the American military, purchasing music boxes
for them for Christmas presents. As the business grew, the family decided that Rothenburg would be the best location for the business as
the town was already a popular German and American tourist destination.

I learned that the Wohlfahrts had established several stores in
Germany, primarily in locations where Germans and Americans
spend recreational time. During the Cold War many Americans were
stationed permanently in Germany. The company also had a presence in many of the holiday Christkindlmarkts throughout German-
speaking countries. These events, sometimes called Weihnachtsmarkt, are common in most towns and cities throughout Germany,
Austria, the Italian South Tyrol, and French Alsace. They are held
outdoors in town squares or other public spaces. The tradition started in medieval times when itinerant vendors would bring special
foods, clothing, and household goods to the town square to sell as
Christmas gifts. Today the markets in most towns start on December
1 and continue every day until December 23 or Christmas Eve. The
towns rent the stalls in the square, some of which sell food. Wursts
are a must, but the food can include everything from smoked fish on
a stick to all sorts of cookies and candies. The markets sell the tradi-

tional *Gluhwein*, a sweet warmed red wine loaded with sugar, cloves, and oranges. The wine is sold warm in small ceramic cups that can be purchased as a souvenir.

Since the mid-1980s Christkindlmarkts have become major tourist attractions, with bus tours and river cruises stopping at the best of them. Even cosseted Americans wander through ancient town squares in the wintry shadows of gothic cathedrals to shop for holiday treasures. These markets range from small town affairs with twenty to thirty stalls to the elegant major markets in cities like Stuttgart, Strasbourg, and Munich. The market in Salzburg is so accustomed to Americans that the signs are only in English.

By the late 1980s Bethlehem's Christmas tourism program was beginning to diminish. We were facing increased competition from other cities, like Wheeling, West Virginia, which had established an amazing lighting program, and the Sight and Sound religious theater near Lancaster, not to mention New York. Motor coach tours to places like Bethlehem were declining as boomers' parents stopped traveling and boomers drove themselves to destinations. We needed an attraction that would amp the desire to visit Bethlehem during the holidays. We had borrowed from our German friends for Musikfest, so why not have a Christkindlmarkt? I introduced the concept to the board of Bethlehem Musikfest Association in 1990, and by 1991 the board had agreed to start our own Christkindlmarkt in 1992. However, Musikfest '91 was not as financially successful as we had hoped, and we wanted to be on a strong financial footing in anticipation of losing money on a new enterprise. We postponed the event until 1993.

We did not even consider holding an outdoor event. Perhaps this was a mistake. Philadelphia and Chicago have outdoor Christmas markets. However, we were convinced that we would have to have tents, and they would have to be heated. For the first year we set up a series of tents at Musikfest's Festplatz, which is just down the hill from Main Street. To try to ensure that patrons of Christkindlmarkt also would visit the permanent downtown businesses, we ran a trolley to take people up the hill to Main Street.

I had hoped that our Christkindlmarkt would feature Kathe Wohlfahrt, but the famous European retailer was not ready to staff and stock an American event. Wohlfahrt had established an outpost

in Minnesota to service mail-order business and was focused on cat-
alog sales for his American customers. We forged ahead without
him. Our Christkindlmarkt opened with one large tent that contained sixty-two pipe-and-drape stalls for retail vendors, including
those selling specialty foods, small special holiday gift items, clothing and children's gifts, and the juried offerings of artists and artisans. At the rear of the tent was a large Christmas tree and a performance stage with tables and chairs between the stage and four food
vendors. German specialties like schnitzel with German potato salad, and pork loin with sauerkraut, were part of the fare. To add au-
thenticity we brought in two Germans from Schwabisch Gmund, a
contemporary jewelry artist and a traditional woodcarver. A smaller tent next to the main tent was called Dreamland; this children's
area included a shopping area for kids (Kindermarkt), a puppet theater with bench seating, a big gingerbread house, and a hill in front
of a woodland scene upon which sat St. Nicholas. In the first few
years we had an extra tent near the entrance with a petting zoo for
children. This proved to be a daunting task between the vagaries of
weather and the need to care for the animals. For the first five years
First Valley Bank sponsored Christkindlmarkt, which helped reduce
the financial risk.

The first Christkindlmarkt opened on Black Friday, November
26, 1993, a crisp sunny day. We had done a good job of marketing
the event. A huge line waited to get in, far beyond what we expected.
Seven thousand people crammed into the tents on the first day.
They were not impressed. The community was expecting a mini-
Musikfest in an area that took up just a fraction of the Musikfest
grounds. We charged an entry fee of $2 to shop, a concept that
seemed absurd to many. The presence of a genuine locally manufactured Allen organ, musicians, high school and church choirs singing
holiday music, and a petting zoo were no reason to charge admission, many thought. Of course, the cost of the tents, heat, electrical setup, and so forth was not obvious to the patrons. The first day
was the busiest of that season, which ran for three weekends, Thursday through Sunday, excluding Thanksgiving Day. Fifty-five thousand people attended the first year's event, which was not bad. Many
loved the market. People who had been to Germany commented favorably on the similarities between our market and the German mar-

kets. When the dust settled, we lost $60,000. However, the business community deemed the market a success. Sales were up for the merchants on Main Street, which they widely attributed to the market. Tourism activity was up for the year. The food vendors, crafters, and retailers at the market reported profitable sales. We went back to the drawing board to tweak the event.

For its first four years Christkindlmarkt lost money, more than $150,000, a considerable amount, and it came out of Musikfest's revenues. Although a dedicated group of volunteers continued to improve the event, today's Christkindlmarkt, unlike Musikfest, is similar to the first year's. The challenge for the volunteers and the organization was to improve key elements: handmade arts and crafts, specialty gifts, and food and drinks, and to pay more attention to decoration and atmosphere. As the volunteer and staff team visited craft shows, sought out unique retail vendors, and added decorations, Christkindlmarkt gathered a core group of dedicated fans. In 1998 Harald Wohlfahrt was ready to experiment with an American Christkindlmarkt. His team treated our market like the ones in Germany. They created a specially designed store within our tent, with giant toy soldiers at the entry, display stands with Plexiglas windows through which to view the merchandise, a central service area with counters, and storage space under the displays. Sales well exceeded Wohlfahrt's expectations as the company learned what merchandise would sell well in the American market. During the next fifteen years, it gingerly entered a few other American Christkindlmarkts and remains a fixture in Bethlehem's market.

In 2011 we moved Christkindlmarkt to SteelStacks, our new arts and culture campus. With better parking attendance soared. The retail business community feared losing business with the move, even though the trolley system was expanded to run between SteelStacks and the Bethlehem Historic District. The Downtown Bethlehem Association started a new Weihnachtsmarkt, a street market, in the Sun Inn Courtyard. That smaller market also has been successful, and both markets are contributing to a continuing increase in the number of holiday guests.

With the continued marketing of Bethlehem as a Christmas destination, visitors from out of the area increased. The event gathered an audience that saw no problem with paying admission for a spe-

cialty art, craft, and holiday show, and those who attend are reward-
ed with more than a hundred artists and artisans, fifty specialty retail
booths, a charming St. Nick, Austrian and German foods, live holiday music from local musicians, and an outdoor plaza next to Bethlehem's iconic blast furnaces, with glass-blowing demonstrations by
ArtsQuest's Glass Studio, wreaths and table decorations from cut
pines, and more shopping outdoors, just like the German markets.
And since the event moved to SteelStacks, it features the best ameni-
ty of all: indoor restrooms. Today Christkindlmarkt even has a bar
with specialty holiday drinks. The bar includes a wide-screen television so that football fans can watch their favorite sport while the rest
of the family shops, an American twist on a German tradition.

Since 1993 Christkindlmarkt has contributed to regional economic development by attracting more holiday visitors, enhancing
retail and restaurant sales, increasing overnight hotel stays in what
would otherwise be a slow season, and supporting the marketing of
Bethlehem as Christmas City.

Since 1998 a profitable Christkindlmarkt also has supported
many free arts and cultural programs offered by Musikfest's parent
organization. The biggest factor affecting annual revenues is, as for
Musikfest, the weather. A major snowstorm during the first or second weekend of December makes all the difference between a year
that is profitable and one that is not.

Even while Christkindlmarkt was losing money in its first five
years and deindustrialization continued to its inevitable conclusion,
we pressed on with the goal of establishing a permanent arts center
as yet another way to revive the community.

CHAPTER 17
THE BANANA FACTORY ARTS CENTER

Inspiration is a funny thing. I got the idea for Musikfest while walking Gypsy and thinking about Oktoberfest. And I found a model for a new arts center after two visits, ten years apart, to Alexandria, Virginia, where I saw changes that bowled me over.

The first visit came in 1980, during the ill-fated reelection campaign of President Jimmy Carter, after I was invited to a reception for local Democratic leaders in the East Room of the White House. Aware that this could be my only opportunity to enter the White House as a guest of a sitting president, I attended. One of my law school classmates was living in downtown Alexandria, just across the river from the District, so I asked him to put me up for the evening. We decided to go to dinner. My friend warned me that Alexandria's shabby downtown had only two decent restaurants, so we picked one. I remember thinking that the city reminded me of Bethlehem, down on its luck. I also learned during that visit of a project under way along Alexandria's waterfront at the base of its main drag, King Street. The Torpedo Factory Arts Center was in its initial phase of renovation by artists occupying studio space and renovating the building themselves. When I returned to downtown Alexandria in the early 1990s during a family visit, I saw a whole new city. Long before creative place making became a theory of urban revitalization, the Art League and the City of Alexandria had collaborated on a waterfront plan that converted the former torpedo factory into a major center for working artists, as well as a city museum and archeological center. Expensive townhomes with water views, parks, and recreational areas bordered the Torpedo Factory along the river, and King Street, that dingy avenue of the 1970s, had become a bustling thoroughfare with shops, restaurants, a new hotel, art galleries, and lots of life.

When the Boyd Theatre project was falling apart, I thought often of the Torpedo Factory and its impact on Alexandria. It was not a music project, but it was an arts project that revived a city. Would a similar concept work in Bethlehem? New York City was the art and design center for wealthy residents of eastern Pennsylvania and New Jersey. Nothing, however dramatic, would change that. But perhaps a more locally relevant model would work. I began to think about how to stretch a music festival organization into a visual arts institution.

A SILK MILL ON SAND ISLAND

Sand Island is really a peninsula at the confluence of Monocacy Creek and the Lehigh River. It became an island when the Lehigh Canal was dug. The island became home to such businesses as lumber companies, coal for home heating, a graphite mill, an ice house, and a boardinghouse. However, as industry moved out and floods ravaged the island, businesses faded away. By 1995 Bethlehem had made the canal towpath a linear park along the Lehigh, and the city had acquired the former ice house. Only three businesses remained, an old silk mill at the far western end of the island, the Asbury Graphite plant, and Fritch Fuel, a home heating business that had once delivered coal to residences. Fritch uses the old stone boardinghouse for its offices, and the silos that once held coal support a large billboard on Hill to Hill Bridge. Early in 1995 the owners of the graphite company and the silk mill approached the city about purchasing their properties, which would have been difficult to sell to other commercial entities because they are in a flood plain. For those of us at Musikfest, this was an opportunity to consider a new arts center and perhaps expansion of Musikfest to the island.

The 1886 Cutter Silk Mill on the western end of Sand Island was a solidly built four-story brick structure with heavy yellow pine beams, wooden floors, and a primitive elevator. At its peak in the late 1800s, it employed five hundred people. By 1993 the family that owned it was renting part of the building for storage but not doing much maintenance. The building had high ceilings, large windows, and open floors, with a light monitor on top and a small power plant beside it. Best of all, it was between the Lehigh River and the Lehigh

Canal. All the windows had a water view, which reminded me of the Torpedo Factory.

In our constant quest for affordable storage space close to the festival, Musikfest had rented a small portion of the building. Internally we developed a preliminary plan for use of this property. The opportunities included much-needed storage space for the organization and for our offices. Like the old torpedo factory, the large building could be adapted to accommodate artists' studios; gallery space; education space for visual arts, dance, and music; and dedicated space for nonprofit arts education organizations that we might partner with. We also envisioned costume and set design and storage, a food service area with a patio on the waterfront, and a modest outdoor performance area. We set up meetings with arts organizations, youth organizations, and educational institutions to see if there was any synergy for creating a community arts center.

We had some constraints. In the early 1990s the Bethlehem Musikfest Association had only $370,000 in reserve funds. Thanks to a grant from the local Laros Foundation, we were able to commission architects to determine whether the building could be converted into an arts center and at what cost. The architects came in with an estimate of $5 million to renovate the building for the uses we envisioned but with many caveats. Even though we were replacing the roof, all electrical wiring and equipment, heating, plumbing, and so forth, we had to be prepared to face some unknowns in the structure that could appear during renovation. Working with our local U.S. representative, we sought a grant of $3 million from the federal government. We also reached out to the state, which was in the middle of still another financial crisis. And we approached an area resident we believed might help us. By the end of 1995 we had solid no's from everyone. It also was a bad year for Musikfest. We lost $220,000 that year, leaving only $150,000 in the bank. The project died. But the concept of a community arts center had resonated through the arts community. If not at the Silk Mill, perhaps it would happen elsewhere.

In January 1994, as we were exploring the feasibility of using the old silk mill for an arts center, Bethlehem Steel announced the inevitable: the Bethlehem plant would end steel production in November 1995. Suddenly a lot of property became available on the south side. Frankly the end of steelmaking was too much to process, and we did not immediately think that any of the plant would be available for development, let alone for an arts center. We pursued the silk mill until it no longer made sense, at about the time the steel mill closed. By then city hall needed us to consider a project in the challenged retail district of the south side that might spur development in the shadow of the ghostly blast furnaces.

LINNY FOWLER

Sometimes, in the peculiar way that social entrepreneurship advances, one person changes the game. In this story that person was Marlene O. "Linny" Fowler.

Linny Fowler was the daughter of Harold Oberkotter, who became chief executive officer of UPS (1973-1980). She was majoring in biology at Skidmore College when she met Beall Fowler at a dance at Lehigh University. They soon married and had four children. Beall Fowler became a professor of physics at Lehigh, and the couple moved to the Bethlehem suburb of Lower Saucon Township, settling into a quiet life of raising their children and attending faculty events. During those years Linny Fowler created stained glass, working in a private studio in her home. When her children were grown and out of the house, she began to pursue her passions, which included the arts, children, and addressing the needs of low-income families.

In 1992 the Fowlers acquired a large stone house in Bethlehem's Moravian historic district just two blocks from our house. Pat Kesling, who became Musikfest's director of development in 1994, had met Linny Fowler when Kesling was features editor and social columnist of the *Globe Times*. They became friends and Kesling introduced Fowler to the committee that was working on the silk mill arts center. During meetings she joined the representatives of the Latino community in support of free programs for young people. She also strongly supported having the arts in schools, preschools, and summer programs. She was fond of saying, "No child can fail at art. Whatever he makes is an original."

Fowler quickly became a friend, mentor, and supporter of the arts center concept. As we continued to explore best practices, she and

I visited Pittsburgh to see some of the arts institutions supporting the revitalization of that city. We visited the Mattress Factory, a contemporary art exhibit space in an evolving part of the city; an arts center with community education facilities; and Manchester Craftsmen's Guild, a multifaceted nonprofit that teaches job skills and includes a music studio with educational programs. But at the Andy Warhol Museum I saw Linny Fowler the artist. Her observations of color and design reinforced my understanding that artists see things in a different way and why they are important to our society.

D. THEODOREDIS & SONS

When I was in high school I drove the delivery van for my parents' stationery store. One of their customers, located only a few blocks from the store, was the D. Theodoredis & Sons banana company across Second Street from the six-acre Bethlehem Steel building where steel was fabricated. I delivered to the Theororedis office, which was toward the rear of the building in a relatively new addition. It also contained the docks where the bananas arriving from the Port of Newark were unloaded and put into "banana lockers," where they were refrigerated until they were shipped out to grocery stores throughout the Northeast. Emmanuel "Em" Theodoredis had an office with windows looking out on the docks. The wall behind his desk was covered with tropical wallpaper, including banana trees. As we Pennsylvania Dutch say, it wondered me how he made a living selling bananas in Bethlehem.

In the 1980s Em Theodoredis retired to Florida after transferring the business to his two sons, Roger and Stanley. They ultimately sold the business to United Fruit Company's Chiquita Banana, which built a modern facility in suburban Bethlehem Township. The Theororedis building on the south side included three structures, built in 1900, 1928, and 1960 and totaling forty-four thousand square feet. The property included a parking lot that held sixty-five cars but was separated from the buildings by a little-used public street. The upper floors of the oldest building had been used for storage and therefore were unfinished. The upper floors of the 1928 building had most recently been used as a blouse mill that had gone out of business in the early 1990s. The property was at a strategic location, at the entrance to Third Street from Route 378, a four-lane highway from Route 22. In 1995 the family was eager to sell the property, and city hall wanted the property to be a showcase that would encourage other development on the south side. As the silk mill project was falling apart and the steel plant was closing, Mayor Ken Smith met with me and encouraged the Musikfest Association to look at the Theodoredis property.

The property's access was good and the parking lot was a plus, even though we had to cross an alley to get to it. The proximity to south side neighborhoods was excellent for serving low-income families. The property is between the two bridges that cross the river from the sites where Musikfest was held and thus a good location for our storage needs. But the interior was a huge challenge. The cinderblock walls that enclosed refrigerated banana bins meant the first floor of the two three-story buildings was a warren of small spaces.

We later heard many stories about employees' having to dodge large spiders and snakes to work in the building. Tearing out the bins was going to be a major expense. Above the first floor the two buildings were not connected at all. The 1928 building had one freight elevator that could be converted into a passenger elevator, but it was at the far end of the building from the parking lot. The silk mill's asking price was $125,000, and the asking price for the Theodoredis property was $550,000. And there was the small matter of not having any substantial source of capital.

With the city's intervention and the disclosure of the identity of the party interested in purchasing the property, the Theodoredis family agreed to drop the price to $250,000. Thinking Musikfest would use it for storage space until we could raise the money to renovate, the board agreed to purchase the property. We now had the building, which was christened the Banana Factory, inspired by the Torpedo Factory and the Mattress Factory.

ORGANIZATIONAL RESTRUCTURING

As we were developing the Banana Factory, we restructured the organization to engage more volunteer leaders who could choose the organization's programs for their focus. We created three councils, one each for Musikfest, Christkindlmarkt, and the Banana Factory.

Each council had volunteer leaders who assisted with the development, management, and operation of those three main programs. The board of trustees, on which sat representatives of the councils, became responsible for overall management and finances of the organization. This restructuring allowed us to have more than fifty volunteer leaders engaged in the organization. It was a great way to make use of the volunteers' expertise.

As all this change was developing, some in the organization believed we were straying too far from our original mission, Musikfest and event production. Some board members and Tom Kwiatek, who had become executive vice president responsible for sponsorships and for managing Musikfest and Christkindlmarkt, felt strongly that the Banana Factory should be separated from the Musikfest organization, which should focus on operating events. As a result Kwiatek, who was largely responsible for the expansion of Musikfest between 1987 and 1997, left to pursue his passion for managing special events. He became executive director of the Lehigh Valley Automobile Dealers Association, where he organizes the annual regional car show.

A CAPITAL CAMPAIGN

Building or renovating a building is a perilous activity for a small nonprofit. And our nonprofit executives had little or no experience in renovation and construction but had to complete the project within a limited budget and produce results that would satisfy diverse constituents. We also were under scrutiny by the media and the community. The Banana Factory was one of the biggest investments in the declining—but recently rebranded—SouthSide in many years. Our job was to meet the programming needs that we had established and telegraph the message that Bethlehem would have a postindustrial life. It was a lofty goal.

The original estimate for renovating the building was $2.3 million, later expanded to a more realistic $2.7 million. We had eight hundred members of a support group called the Musikfest Verein (meaning club in German) to call upon, as well as our sponsors and the business community. We also brought credibility because of our success with Musikfest and Christkindlmarkt. We had strong support from Mayor Smith. For almost two years we were dragging people through a building in various states of demolition and construction to persuade them that this was going to be a vibrant arts center and a keystone to the redevelopment of the SouthSide. Both the mayor and I would profess that the Banana Factory was part of a plan for revitalizing the SouthSide with a focus on the arts. There was no real plan because, unlike today, cultural districts in small cities were unheard of. The project would have been much easier to advance if it had indeed been a part of an overall plan.

As we pieced together support, Linny Fowler became our primary advocate and our angel donor. Her vision of serving the children of the SouthSide, and offering access to the arts for all, regardless of abilities or financial circumstances, was the guiding philosophy of the Banana Factory. With commitments of $5,000 to $100,000 from dozens of individuals and businesses, as well as foundations such as the Laros Foundation and the Kresge Foundation, and modest but important participation from Northampton and Lehigh counties and the Commonwealth of Pennsylvania, we gradually neared our goal. Fowler gave the largest amount, more than $1 million. Without her support we would have been in debt for many years. One of the most important things I learned was that she wanted her name attached to her gifts so that others would know she supported a cause and join in. Some donors prefer to be anonymous, which is understandable in today's world. But leading by example is a way to foster confidence in a project. While some prospective donors may have thought that because Linny Fowler was supporting the project, we did not need any other support, those who were more astute knew that the project would be successful because of her gift and therefore their gift would support a successful project.

Demolition at the Banana Factory started in the fall of 1996, less than a year after Bethlehem Steel stopped making steel in its hometown and at about the time the company announced it would sell three divisions in Bethlehem and its shipyard at Sparrows Point in Baltimore.[119] Construction of the Banana Factory was completed in December 1997. We moved our offices from Broad Street Mall to our new arts center between Christmas and New Year's Eve. We had planted a stake on the SouthSide and would soon start to create a little excitement for residents who badly needed some good news.

PLANNING

Once we decided that the Theodoredis property was going to be our arts center, the question then became what that meant. A key issue was whom we were planning to serve and whether they would come to this location. As we were considering our potential constituency beyond our immediate neighbors, we held focus groups to see who would be interested in coming to the SouthSide for art lessons, First Fridays, shopping, and special events. The Banana Factory was right at the exit from Hill to Hill Bridge, Route 378, across the street from the successful Comfort Suites, the lodging closest to Lehigh. A few businesses preceded the Banana Factory by settling in old buildings in the next block over on Third Street. More than a dozen restaurants, mostly serving residents or the Lehigh community, were on Third and Fourth streets. But the area still had a lot of vacant storefronts. Right behind the proposed arts center was the six-acre building formerly used by Bethlehem Steel that was now partly leased to a structural steel company. West of that was the abandoned Union Station, which had not seen passenger traffic since 1975. Worse yet, by Hill to Hill Bridge ramp lay the remains of large coal bins, which still held chunks of coal and once were part of a now-defunct fuel delivery company.

Stories of the sprouting of hip districts on former industrial sites were legion in the 1990s. The Williamsburg section of Brooklyn was becoming the star of New York City, Philadelphia's South Street was booming along with the neighboring Queen Village, and even Cleveland had the Flats. Many in the Lehigh Valley were eager for a district that offered the diversity, restaurants, arts, and entertainment that big cities were developing. Musikfest's investment in a large arts center on the SouthSide gave hope that the Lehigh Valley might be part of this national trend. Our stakeholders said loudly and clearly that they would come to this location and were excited about it.

While the building seemed large, once we listed everyone's desires, we realized it was not going to be big enough. After converting the 1960s-era loading docks to warehouse and storage space for Musikfest and Christkindlmarkt, using the third floor of one of the buildings to provide offices for the growing staff and volunteer needs of the organization, we wound up with twenty-three art studios of four hundred to eight hundred square feet each; space for Pennsylvania Youth Theatre's programs (two dance studios, two drama studios, a vocal studio, offices, costume shop, and storage for costumes and props), a small gallery, a gift shop, a community room that doubled as exhibit space and classroom space, a general arts classroom, and a tiny kitchen. The storage was insufficient to hold all of what we had acquired for our festivals. Frank Banko, who also ran a transportation company, donated eight tractor trailers for us to use to store Musikfest and Christkindlmarkt booths, decorations, and other material. Twenty years later ArtsQuest is still using those trailers.

While many in the community were inspired by the thought of using the arts to revitalize the SouthSide, one institution saw an opportunity to reach out to the Latino population and establish a new program. Don Foellner, the director of the Bethlehem Area Vocational Technical School, asked us to consider leasing space in the new building to establish the Academy of Video and Media Arts at the Banana Factory, advanced thinking at a time of rapid technology development. The kinds of upgrades the building would need to support this were far beyond what we could afford. We agreed that if Vo Tech would help us set up the technology for after-school programs and classes, we would welcome the partnership. Foellner did and overcame bus transportation issues and other obstacles to get the program established. With a Latino instructor the program succeeded and stayed in the Banana Factory for almost ten years before moving to larger facilities and newer technology on the Vo Tech campus.

As we firmed up the plans for the Banana Factory, internal disagreements emerged. Some wanted only full-time professional artists in the building, which would have eliminated most of the artists in the region. Some wanted to institute a policy that studios were only incubator space and artists had to leave after a stated period of time. This was determined to be impractical at the start because we were not sure what the demand would be and what the quality of the artists would be. We agreed that the artist population needed to represent as many media as possible and that we should encourage the in-house artist community to engage in collaborative projects. We discussed selecting art for the small gallery, and people voiced concerns about the quality of the art represented in the building. We were going to learn much about how art is judged during the next few years. I continued my policy of trying to avoid any discussion about the quality of art, something so subjective that it is a constant source of debate.

GOING BANANAS

The Banana Factory opened in January 1998 with a reception and open house. All but one of the artists' studios was occupied; the artists represented a diversity of cultures and media, including printing, sculpture, painting, ceramics, photography, fiber, drawing, and print making.

The artists soon sorted themselves out. Several left within the first year, finding that it was not for them. The purpose of the project was not to create low-rent studios so that artists could ignore each other and the greater community. The goal was for artists to interact with each other and the community.

Having the Pennsylvania Youth Theatre in the building created a vibrancy that would have been otherwise absent. After school, on Saturdays, and during the summer months, the PYT students and their parents filled the building with a buzz of excitement. We learned too late that we should have provided space for waiting parents. Parents have to wait in the halls, sitting on uncomfortable benches, the floor, or in the car while their children learn to dance and sing.

Diane LaBelle is an architect with a strong interest in community development and the arts. Just a few months after the building opened, she took charge of the visual arts and education programs for the Banana Factory. During the next several years she set the course for the institution, establishing several key community programs. One was B-Smart (now ArtSmart) for underserved middle school students; this program offers after-school instruction in the visual arts. Another, with initial support from Fowler, is the Holy Infancy Arts Program created for the K-8 Holy Infancy Roman Catholic School four blocks from the arts center. Each semester the students walk to the Banana Factory for art instruction. In partnership with the regional state employment agency, LaBelle also created BananaWorks, a now-discontinued summer program that taught job skills to teenagers who had never had a job. The program covered such basics as showing up on time, following directions, working as part of a team, and working with a client. Each year the program partnered with a nonprofit or a government agency to create a piece of public art for public housing facilities, hospitals, and the local airport, among others.

The Banana Factory has become known as a place that offers access to the visual arts for all members of the community throughout the year. The galleries are open and free every day. Exhibit space now includes the hallways of the building. On the first Friday of every month except August, the Banana Factory anchors the First Friday program on the SouthSide. First Fridays usually are the kick-off for a gallery show, and the artist or artists attend. At the Banana Factory all resident artists are asked to be in their studios to greet guests and to sell their art.

In the fall of 1998 the Banana Factory began offering public courses for adults and children, and by summer 1999 it had summer camps. The Banana Factory quickly became an anchor for SouthSide development. In at least one instance it was too attractive.

EXPANDING THE BANANA FACTORY

The Valley Auto Parts store fronted on Third Street with a two-bay repair garage bordering the Banana Factory along the alley called Plymouth Street. The three-building complex included an old auto sales showroom, a two-story brick house, and what can best be described as a lean-to, a garage that had a roof attached to the south wall of the Banana Factory and the north wall of the other two buildings. Attached to the roof of the complex was one of the last billboards on the SouthSide, and the billboard was not attractive. As we were developing the Banana Factory, I approached John Vargo, the owner, to see if he was interested in selling the building. He said no, that he planned to be there for a long time. I then asked that he work with us to close Plymouth Street because we were concerned that our main entrance was right on the alley and it created a hazard for our patrons, especially children. The city required that all property owners adjacent to the street agree to a closing. If he would agree, we would grant him access to his garage through our parking lot and more parking for his customers. He declined.

Less than six months after we opened the building, we learned that Vargo was negotiating to sell the building. In a bizarre twist of fate, two real estate entrepreneurs from New Zealand had decided to explore opportunities in the United States and, uncertain where to go, they put a map of the country on a wall and threw a dart at it. It landed on Bethlehem. When they came to town, they saw a university full of students, a new arts center, a hotel, and a busy street and decided that Valley Auto Parts would make a great college bar. They offered Vargo $450,000 for the property, more than twice what it had been worth a year earlier. A bar would not have been the best choice as a neighbor for a cultural facility used by children so we offered to buy the property. After several communications Vargo agreed to sell to us for $451,000. We had not yet paid off the mortgage for the Banana Factory, and we certainly had insufficient savings to even put down a deposit. Once again Linny Fowler came to our rescue. She agreed to advance half the purchase price if we could finance the balance. We bought the property later that year, and all of the sudden we had a whole new project.

We did not begin planning for the expansion of the Banana Factory until 2000. We did succeed in getting the city to vacate Plymouth Street, which meant that we now owned it. We embarked on the Vision 2000 capital campaign to raise $1.3 million to pay off the debt for the Banana Factory and underwrite renovations to incorporate the annex. With more help from Linny Fowler, we were able to break ground in October 2001, a month before Bethlehem Steel filed for bankruptcy, and dedicated the Fowler Center for Art and Education, the three buildings that constituted the original Banana Factory, on April 4, 2002. It was an uplifting moment for a community that was now in uncharted territory.

The renovations and additions created a large gallery donated by Binney & Smith, the parent company of Crayola crayons, in the former auto showroom on Third Street. The front windows, combined with a skylight that we found after purchasing the building, made it an interesting room for displaying art and for holding events. We moved the gift shop to a space adjacent to the gallery that could be entered from the parking lot. The former garage space became an all-purpose classroom.

Although I had opposed using all of the auto showroom for a gallery, this was a wise choice. The Crayola Gallery is the major exhibit space for the Banana Factory, capable of accommodating three-dimensional as well as two-dimensional art shows. It also has proved to be a popular place for rentals, primarily for wedding receptions. Using an art gallery for receptions and dinners was controversial within the artist community for many years. Now we make this clear to exhibitors and explain that the rentals generate money for maintaining the gallery.

We hired landscape architects to design the parking lot and the area that had been Plymouth Street. The design included plantings, space for sculpture, seating, a bicycle rack, and outdoor activities while still leaving space for more than fifty cars. We commissioned the local sculptor Karl Miklaus to create original pieces for the plaza, which have contributed to the sense of creativity at the center. Years later a former Banana Factory artist approached us with a less formal colorful floral sculpture that we placed near the main entrance from the parking lot. First-time visitors may not know immediately what a Banana Factory is, but from its exterior they can tell that it is a place that encourages design, art, and creativity.

Diane LaBelle was so good at leading the Banana Factory that she was hired away, first to work for a charter school but eventually to work in Reading for a new, much bigger version of the Banana Factory, GoggleWorks. The former manufacturing plant for military goggles, four times larger than the Banana Factory, was being developed as a key to revival of that city's downtown. LaBelle had the experience and skills to pull it off. We deeply regretted losing her, but we wished her success. It's always good to be a model for successful projects.

Her replacement was Janice Lipzin, a native of Miami Beach who had grown up in a household of classical musicians and learned to play the flute, which she had thought would be her career. In high school she found a camera and her passion. She moved to New York to pursue her education, then pursued her passion for photography, and eventually wound up working for Magnum, the cooperative owned by some of the world's best photographers. She met Paul

Kodiak, a playwright who became the love of her life. When they were ready to start a family, they moved out of New York to the Lehigh Valley. She was teaching photography at the Art Institute of Philadelphia when the Banana Factory directorship became open. By September 2003 she was adding her touch to the arts center.

In 2004 Olympus America, the digital photography and medical equipment company, announced it would be moving its headquarters from Long Island to Center Valley, just outside Bethlehem. Dave Willard, the community relations person for the company, approached me on behalf of Mark Gumz, the company president, who lived in nearby Saucon Valley. Olympus wanted to be the principal sponsor of Musikfest to demonstrate that it now was part of the community. We had no sooner concluded an agreement for a three-year sponsorship of Musikfest, 2005–2007, than Lipzin began to share her wish for a digital photography program. Willard took the concept to Mark Gumz, and after a meeting at the Banana Factory, Lipzin announced that the arts center would become the site of the new Olympus Digital Imaging Center, a fifteen-computer-station–classroom for teaching digital photography, to be used for tuition-based classes and for after-school classes for B-Smart and other programs for low-income children. The relationship with Olympus has made it possible to offer after-school photography classes to elementary school students in low-income neighborhoods and dozens of other opportunities for gallery shows and photography experiences.

In 2009 Lipzin created our organization's first exclusively visual arts festival, the InVision Photography Festival. It is held the first weekend of November and includes a college student photography competition with awards, portfolio review opportunities for amateur photographers, lectures by famous photographers, panel discussions, and a great party. For its first year Lipzin pulled together forty galleries in the region to exhibit photography during November to celebrate the medium. InVision is the organization's signature visual arts event.

During a visit to Venice, Italy, I became fascinated with hot glass as an art medium. Watching mere mortals dip pipes into two-thousand-degree molten material, then use their own breath, wooden tools, and gravity to create objects of ethereal beauty fascinates and terrifies me. When Lipzin became director of the Banana Factory, I asked her to see if she could figure out how to incorporate this art form. She found a local resident, Jim Harmon, who is an accomplished hot glass artist. We also found financial resources to retain Jim to design a glass studio in the warehouse of the Banana Factory and to help us prepare an operating budget. A glass studio requires a great deal of equipment, including a furnace, which usually is built on site. It also requires lots of electricity and natural gas. Once we had a capital budget, we sought support. It turned out that one of our new neighbors in the historic district, Bruce Lawrence, was a manufacturer of equipment used for flameworking, the little brother of blown glass. Flameworking uses an instrument that looks like a high school Bunsen burner to melt small quantities of glass for jewelry, ornaments, and the like. The idea of having a hot glass education facility in town appealed to him, and he contributed the major gift that made the glass studio possible. By the fall of 2006 the Glass Studio at the Banana Factory was up and running, bringing fire back to the SouthSide. Glass has become one of ArtsQuest's most popular programs, with its own coterie of long-term students, apprentices, and volunteers.

IMPACT OF THE BANANA FACTORY

As with many projects related to the arts, it is difficult to quantify the impact of the Banana Factory. In the minds of local residents, the Banana Factory changed the neighborhood's narrative. Suddenly going to a First Friday gallery crawl, followed by a drink or dinner there, was cool. It would be fair to say that the project encouraged other development. After we announced the project, the locally popular Lehigh Pizza purchased the building between the arts center and the Fahy (New Street) Bridge for its new home, and the city created a small public parking lot. The Sayre Mansion Inn, at the top of the hill above the Banana Factory, was a troubled project until taken over in 2002 by the current owners, who now operate a successful high-end bed and breakfast there. The developer Louis Pektor purchased the dilapidated Union Station and converted it into a medical facility for St. Luke's Hospital. In 2005 an investment group led by Pektor purchased the six-acre steel fabrication building across Second Street from the Banana Factory. He acknowledged that its renovation was sparked by the arts center, and in partnership with the parking authority he converted the property into a four-hundred-car parking garage, a four-hundred-seat restaurant, and 188 condominium units. The units sold well; only twenty-five had not been sold when the recession hit in 2008. While its decision was not directly related to the Banana Factory, the medical testing company OraSure Technologies became a tenant of the city's second technology center a block from the new condominiums. OraSure eventually purchased that building and added a second structure across the street for manufacturing and offices.

The Banana Factory certainly has achieved the goals of adding to the cultural amenities of the region and providing access to the arts for all. In addition to the galleries and classes, local art organizations of painters, photographers, and others use the Banana Factory for meetings, exhibits, and events. In 2013 a low-to moderate-income housing developer from Lancaster, Pennsylvania, Housing Development Corporation MidAtlantic, chose the SouthSide as the site for developing its first housing project oriented to artists. The forty-six-unit complex opened in 2015, with nineteen units leased to artists, several of whom moved from outside the area. This is bricks-and-mortar evidence that Bethlehem enjoys a reputation as a desirable location for practicing artists.

Over the years ArtsQuest has had many inquiries from other communities that want a Banana Factory to kick-start a struggling portion of their community. My admonition always is to secure support for operating expenses before seeking building capital. The Banana Factory is supported by an endowment and the gifts of individuals and businesses as well as government and foundation grants, in addition to two major festivals. Many arts facilities are undercapitalized, without sources of continuing support, and they fail. I also warn about the expectation of profit. The Banana Factory never has reported one, nor will it. It is a mission-based enterprise that serves a diverse community with many different programs. The community has embraced the Banana Factory, which is what makes it a success.

MUSIKFEST 2000
North Side Downtown

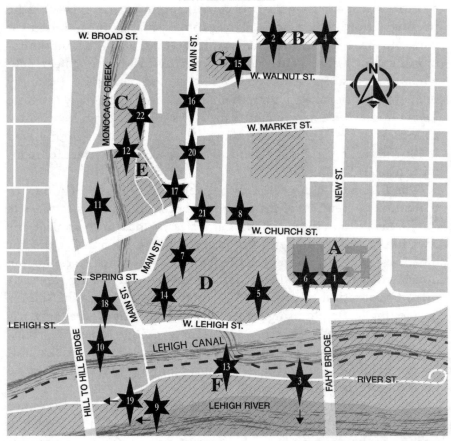

VENUES
1. Americaplatz
2. Artwalk
3. AT&T Wireless Asa Packer Performing Arts Series
4. Banana Cabaret
5. Bandstand
6. Blumenplatz
7. Candlelight Concerts
8. Chamber Series
9. Dankeplatz
10. Expo

11. Festplatz
12. Handwerkplatz
13. Ice House Sand Island
14. Kinderplatz
15. Liederplatz
16. Main Street Musikfest
17. Muralplatz
18. Plaza Tropical
19. PPL Riverplace
20. Street Performers
21. Vesper Concerts
22. Volksplatz

PARKS, PLAZAS, HISTORIC SITES
A. Bethlehem City Center Plaza
B. Broad Street Mall
C. Johnston Park
D. Moravian College Priscilla Payne Hurd Campus
E. Moravian Colonial Industrial Quarter
F. Sand Island
G. Sun Inn Courtyard

CHAPTER 18
THE MILLENNIUM

A s the new century approached, the big question was whether our computers would go crazy at the stroke of midnight. In Bethlehem things were ticking up. Unemployment had dropped from nearly 6 percent in 1990 to just above 3 percent, perhaps because many former steelworkers had removed themselves from the labor market. A sense of revival had infused Third and Fourth streets as new merchants and eateries joined the Banana Factory neighborhood. On the north side the Hotel Bethlehem was welcoming guests once more, and Fegley's Brew Works anchored the other end of Main Street. Musikfest was about to expand its space and programming. Yet the heart of the former Bethlehem Steel plant, anchored by the hulking blast furnaces, stood silent and brooding over the SouthSide with no progress yet on how best to use or dispose of the industrial giant's remains.

RIVERPLACE

Within a year after we turned our attention from the old silk mill on Sand Island to the Theodoredis property, the mill burned down. The city acquired that property as well as the Asbury Graphite property. The five acres on which the huge silk mill had sat were now vacant, as was the graphite plant property closer to Main Street. For Musikfest opportunity was knocking. We began working with Mayor Don Cunningham, who had taken office in 1998, to use Sand Island for Musikfest. Cunningham was eager to extend the riverfront recreational opportunities of these once industrial properties. He retained consultants to study uses for Sand Island. They recommended the five acres become a public park, with a boat launch and grassy area between the canal and the river for public recreation. The former Asbury Graphite site would become a paved parking area for the island. At our request lighting and power for the new park were designed to handle a large stage and backstage area with most of the lawn dedicated to seating for concerts during Musikfest. We established an audience limit of sixty-five hundred, with food and beverage stands to line the stone roadway on the river side of the site, with a hospitality area near the entrance. RiverPlace would be the new home for our main stage, but its name, Kunstplatz, would be eliminated. Located four blocks from Festplatz, with a pretty walk along the riverfront, this site would allow us to book bigger shows and eliminate problems that had arisen because we still allowed free admission to people who brought lawn chairs or blankets. As the shows at Kunstplatz had grown in stature and popularity, we realized we had to fill most of the lawn with seating to cover the cost of the shows, so the free area was confined to the back of the site, which was not the most desirable situation.

RiverPlace was far from perfect, but it served us well for eleven Musikfests, between 2000 and 2010; however, we faced a number of challenges.

I'll start with the geese. The site lies between two bodies of water, the canal and the river, and the Canada geese stayed in the water, except when they needed to eat and poop, which they did on the grass. It was a problem we faced from that first year on, after patrons placed their paper plates with freshly purchased festival food on the ground under their chairs, only to find the bottom of the plate dressed with goose droppings. After a few years we learned to place fencing along the canal and the riverside a month before the festival, time enough for any droppings to be washed away naturally. The geese did their business elsewhere for that month.

Another problem was the configuration of RiverPlace, which is long and narrow, less than 120 feet wide at most places. Within that space we had to have utilities, food vendors, beer trucks, port-o-potties and chairs for five thousand of people plus room for the chairs or blankets of as many as fifteen hundred people who would purchase lawn-seating tickets to sit six hundred feet from the stage, which is as bad as being in the nosebleed section of an arena.

To complicate our lives further, the Norfolk Southern railroad track ran right along the site before making a sharp turn to cross the river at the main entrance to the site. An average of thirty-five trains a day form in the Allentown yards just west of RiverPlace, then head east to New York across a railroad bridge. Of course we naively asked the railroad whether it could stop the trains for a couple of hours in the evening during Musikfest, which got a hearty roar of collective laughter from the folks at the railroad. The trains became a regular feature of a Musikfest RiverPlace concert, frequently drawing comments from the stage.

And to top it all off, below the railroad trestle was a street that served as the main entrance to our main stage, and it had poor drainage. When it rained during a show, the roadway, which had been dug out so eighteen-wheelers could pass beneath the trestle, would fill with as much as two feet of water. As concert goers leaving a show reached this point, they would realize that they had no option but to walk through the water.

The most memorable incident at the site happened at Musikfest '05 with the show by the Steve Miller Band. It was the last night of the festival, with a storm predicted. Despite my urging, the band would not take the stage early, even though we could see that the storm was coming. The band began to play at 8:25, and by 9:05 we had the first rains of the worst storm we ever had at Musikfest. The smart people in the audience left when the lightning started to flash. I was on the radio with our stage manager, telling him to stop the show. Our manager spoke with the band's road manager, who said, "If he gets off the stage he's not going back on," to which I replied, "That's just fine with me." The show stopped at 9:15, with true fans (and crazy people) booing through the thunder and lightning. As people were rushing toward the gully under the trestle, it filled with two feet of water. A couple of hooligans got up on top of the trestle and were throwing things in the water and on the fans. A major donor rushed back to the tent to tell me what was happening. I radioed Walt Keiper, the vice president of ArtsQuest, who brought a police officer with him to climb up the stone-covered hill to chase the idiots off the trestle. When they saw the law on its way, the young men ran south, across the trestle over the river. Keiper and the officer were in hot pursuit when the track suddenly was illuminated by a large light from a train that had just rounded the bend toward the trestle. The train, pulling at least a hundred cars, could not have stopped in the short distance between it and the pursuers. Keiper and the officer turned around and jumped off the track to the bank between the trestle support and the river. We never heard from the young idiots, but we assume that they outran the train to the south side of the river. This was far too much excitement for any festival manager.

PLAZA TROPICAL

As we were planning the Banana Factory, our conversations with members of the growing Latino community made it clear that they wanted to be more engaged in the wider community and in Musikfest. This fit with our goal of inclusiveness in all that we do. Women, people with disabilities, and people of color have long served as board members. Latinos were growing in population and influence, increasingly represented in business and the professions locally.

But although people of color had long performed at our festivals—including Dizzy Gillespie, Ray Charles, the Neville Brothers, Queen Ida and her Bon Temps Zydeco Band, Donna Summer, Patti Labelle, and LL Cool J—we had never presented a Latino show on our main stage.

We asked the Latino community for suggestions. One of thing I learned during this process is that saying there is a Latino culture is akin to saying there is a European culture. People broadly classified as Latinos live on three continents, speak varying dialects of two languages, and have widely divergent tastes in music, not to mention the divergence of music preferences among age groups. We received several suggestions from the community and proceeded to see who we could book for Musikfest '98. We managed to sign Celia Cruz, the Cuban singer who had been a favorite throughout the Americas; she was known for salsa, the musical style also popular in Puerto Rico, where most of the Latinos who live in Bethlehem are from. The Lehigh Valley also has many residents whose families hail from the Dominican Republic, where bachata reigns.

The Celia Cruz concert was a learning experience for us. Those were the pre-Internet days, so we were selling tickets by phone and at our offices in Bethlehem. Latinos preferred to buy tickets in cash at a local bodega or music store. We had support from the Spanish newspaper and radio station, but getting the word out was difficult. The need to deliver tickets to bodegas and pick up cash was also new for us. The concert was not a sellout but attracted a respectable audience of nearly two thousand. Cruz, then seventy-three, was a real pro, and it was a good first experience.

Because we were remodeling Musikfest for 2000 by adding River-Place, we were breaking the tradition of calling each venue a platz. Why not add a plaza? Someone suggested that we dub one venue Plaza Caribe and primarily present music popular in the Caribbean, especially salsa and bachata, as opposed to tango, Tex-Mex, samba, or any of the many other genres of Latin music. Community representatives suggested broadening the name to Plaza Tropical so it wouldn't be limited to Caribbean styles. Musikfest's first plaza for Latin music would be located on the grassy block just across the street from Festplatz, a strategic location between the traditional festival sites and the new RiverPlace. We moved the children's activities closer to RiverPlace, on the macadam parking lot at the entrance to Sand Island, which we had formerly used for Dankeplatz . which held the tents sponsors used for catered events during the festival. And we moved Dankeplatz, to the new parking lot right before the trestle entrance to RiverPlace. The beauty of an event with no fixed facilities is the ability to create new experiences each year.

Our staff energetically began the search for vendors of Latin and Caribbean food. Holy Infancy Church in south Bethlehem asked to become a vendor. As the Catholic church for the Portuguese- and Spanish-speaking community, Holy Infancy had volunteers willing to spend weeks preparing specialty foods. For the next fifteen years the church was only the second nonprofit vendor at Musikfest, which proved to be the church's biggest fund-raising event of the year.

I suppose it was inevitable, but after we announced Plaza Tropical, we got some backlash. Some people asked why we hadn't located Plaza Tropical on the SouthSide, where many of the Latinos lived. We had considered the SouthSide but then firmly concluded that the Latin music plaza should be part of the historic main area of the festival, not segregated. As it turned out, the entire festival that year, from the tip of Sand Island to the Sun Inn Courtyard, was a wild success. Anglos liked exploring Latin music and some Latinos took to the chicken dance. Plaza Tropical became one of the great food centers of the festival, and everyone enjoyed drinking cerveza.

I give full credit to our board of trustees for continuing to address the economic and community development mission of the organization. Many boards would have resisted by saying that we were jeopardizing Musikfest by changing its successful formula. RiverPlace, for all its challenges, gave us the ability to present bigger shows, which gave the festival greater credibility. Plaza Tropical sent the unmistakable message that everyone in the community is welcome at Musikfest. Today about 15 percent of the organization's volunteers identify as Latino, and Musikfest is quite a diverse event.

HOSPITALITY

Like many who live in the Lehigh Valley, Susan Drexinger was born here but left to pursue her education and gain experience in her chosen field. She earned a degree in hotel management, the broad category that includes hotels, restaurants, and catering. After working in Washington, D.C., and a few exotic places, she moved home to settle down with her new husband. Like Steve Jobs, she sold me something I didn't even know I needed, when she arrived in my office one day in February 2003 to make her case for hospitality opportunities for our organization. Broadly defined, hospitality is the business of event planning and facility rental. This includes food and beverage catering as well as ancillary services like decorating, valet parking, and audiovisual equipment. This was not a concept that was familiar to us. No one on staff was actively pursuing this potentially lucrative area. At the time we were taking orders and passing them on to the external company that managed the food service at Musikfest's Dankeplatz, and in the Banana Factory's Crayola Gallery for rentals throughout the year.

At the time of my first meeting with Drexinger, we needed better organization of charter tour reception services in Bethlehem. This was another business with which Drexinger had experience. We soon realized that we did need a professional hospitality team, with Drexinger as director of hospitality.

For the rest of the decade Susan Drexinger inspired development of catering and hospitality. For the holiday season we developed much-needed new attractions for tourists such as concerts by the von Trapps, the great grandchildren of Maria von Trapp, during the first two weeks of December; a theatrical interpretation of the early history of Bethlehem at Central Moravian Church; and use of the Banana Factory as a welcome center for charter tours coming to Bethlehem for the Christmas season. Drexinger pointed out that we were taking visitors to the unattractive basement of a bank building to welcome them to our town when we could be inviting them to a beautiful arts center with a tasteful gallery exhibit and gift shop. All charter tours need a rest stop when they arrive at their destination, so why not include coffee, snacks, gifts, and a visit to the art gallery? She was right on all counts.

Drexinger also recognized the potential of the Banana Factory's Crayola Gallery and the Banko Community Room, an all-purpose room that serves as a supplemental gallery, classroom, and meeting room. Every arts center includes space for catering, and most newer ones have some form of bar and restaurant. With a full-time promoter on board, these spaces became a source of revenue for the Banana Factory. Drexinger's experience in food service, room settings, decoration, lighting, and customer satisfaction made these spaces special for weddings, bar and bat mitzvahs, special birthdays, anniversaries, and other family and corporate events.

With regard to Musikfest Drexinger pointed out that Dankeplatz often went unused. Because Musikfest ran for only ten days, we should be selling the time that was not being used to SMURFs, which is the tourism business acronym for social, military, union, recreational, and fraternity groups. Soon we had class reunions, church groups, and community organizations renting Dankeplatz. Then we opened new hospitality spaces: RiverPlace Garden, RiverPlace Deck, and Americaplatz Diner.

Hospitality became a reliable source of additional revenue for the organization, which quickly gained a reputation for it. Susan Drexinger taught us that her motto is check, check, and check again, to make sure that our client is having a great event.

One of the most interesting exchanges we had was on a morning in late November when a bus group was scheduled to arrive. When she opened the gallery for the guests, Drexinger noticed something new in the exhibit by the Banana Factory's artists. She came to my office with an expression on her face I had never seen before—or since. "What are you going to do about the penis?" she asked. Knowing Drexinger, and seeing the expression on her face, this was not a matter of levity or prurience. We had a problem. Keeping a straight face, I responded, "I'm sorry, I don't know what you are talking about." "Then you'd better come to the gallery," she said in a voice that was as commanding as she could get with her boss. One of our artists, the sculptor Scott Atiyeh, had finished a piece that he had been working on for a long time. He had painted it at the last minute and had brought it into the gallery the previous evening to make sure that it was in the annual show. The piece was a six-foot-high fiendish-looking anatomically correct male gargoyle in a seated position, wings to the rear, that Atiyeh had painted black and given red claws and incisors. And right there was his male member, fully erect. Nothing says welcome to the Christmas City like a tumescent pagan gargoyle.

For those interested in creating an arts center, here is a tip: never tell artists what subject matter they are permitted to portray. From the artist's perspective that is censorship. Nevertheless, I realized that we had a problem. I could not remove the piece without causing backlash from the artists. Nor could I invite the Saint Emily's Bible Study Group into the gallery with that piece in it. Our temporary solution was to drape a black tablecloth over the lower part of the sculpture. Susan agreed that throughout the Christmas season, after the bus groups had left, she would have the cloth removed every day. This led to a year-long conversation by the Banana Factory Council about nudity in art and in public spaces in the Banana Factory. James Nallo, a businessman, board member, and forward thinker, brought the artists, the education community, and others with strong opinions together to address the issue.

The decision was that nudity would be permitted in the gallery but not in any hallways or other locations accessible to the general public, including the hundreds of young students who used the building every day. When nudity was displayed in the gallery, we would post a cautionary sign at the entrance advising adults that the exhibit included nudity so that they could choose to enter or not, with or without their children.

THE ARTSQUEST FOUNDATION

In December 2002, just before the Bethlehem Musikfest Association formally changed its name to ArtsQuest to better reflect all that the organization was doing, Linny Fowler told us that she wanted to create a $1 million endowment for the Banana Factory. This was an unsolicited gift and we were ecstatic. The board, on advice of counsel, decided to establish the ArtsQuest Foundation, an independent nonprofit organization whose sole mission is to support ArtsQuest and its programs. Fowler served on both boards until her death in 2013. The endowment continues to support the Banana Factory.

As the decade wore on, we embraced Internet data collection, communicating with our many stakeholders by email and moving to online ticket sales. We had good relationships with the business community and the trust of public agencies. Although we continued to add staff as needed, we still had hundreds of volunteers who remained key to the success of the organization. We would need all these attributes and more to address the opportunity and challenges that awaited us in the heart of the old steel plant.

At the beginning of the new millennium ArtsQuest was doing well, but Allentown, Bethlehem, and Easton continued to struggle, surrounded by a region that was one of the few places in Pennsylvania that was growing in both population and economic prosperity. As in many areas of the country, our cities were home to traditional cultural, educational, and health-care institutions, while wealthy and middle-class residents, mall and shopping areas, business parks, and newer industries were based in the surrounding suburbs. The good news was that the region had gotten its act together. But the steel plant was closed and vacant, and deindustrialization had hit bottom with the bankruptcy declaration of Bethlehem Steel in 2001. By 2003 Martin Tower was a vacant fossil, the plant was a neglected ruin, and the city's problems were by no means solved. Would the city manage to become a viable partner in a region that was experiencing prosperity, or would it succumb to the fate of similar cities and simply fall into a downward spiral?

CHAPTER 19
THE LEHIGH VALLEY EMERGES

Bethlehem native Bert Daday was instrumental in creating a Lehigh Valley region that allowed Bethlehem the opportunity to avoid the downward spiral of other Rust Belt cities. Much like the title character in *Shrek,* Daday was a lovable curmudgeon. He was gruff, direct, and pushy but not in a bullying sort of way, unless someone maligned his beloved Notre Dame.

He had been handpicked for the herculean task by the president of Pennsylvania Power & Light, the regional electric utility, which had a vested interest in economic growth that spread beyond the limits of the three rival cities, Allentown, Bethlehem, and Easton. That rivalry was one of long standing. When I was a child, the only business in the region that used Lehigh Valley in its name was a dairy. And the cities were especially competitive around economic development. In the 1980s PP&L was acutely aware of the decline of Bethlehem Steel, which was one of its biggest customers, and realized that it needed to actively engage in bringing the region together in a way that the fractious local government structure could not.

In the 1950s Daday, a native of Bethlehem's south side, left a supervisory position at Bethlehem Steel to become assistant director, then director, of the Bethlehem Area Community Chest, where he stayed until 1972. During his tenure he helped establish three agencies that would have regional impact: the Lehigh Valley Community Council, a coordinating agency for regional social welfare programs; the Community Action Committee of the Lehigh Valley, an antipoverty agency; and the Lehigh Valley Business Conference on Health Care. In 1972 PP&L (now PPL) recruited Daday to serve as its first community relations officer. For the next twenty years he worked on community affairs and answered directly to the PP&L

president. If anyone could lay claim to midwifing the modern Lehigh Valley, it would be Bert Daday.

LEHIGH VALLEY PARTNERSHIP

In 1985, with the support of PP&L's then CEO, Bob Campbell, Daday assembled the Lehigh Valley Partnership to use private-sector resources to respond to the needs of the region. Because he recruited top executives of the major private-sector employers in the Lehigh Valley, the partnership became the place where the biggest business stakeholders addressed regional issues. One of the first issues the partnership took up was education. Workforce development was, and continues to be, a major challenge. The partnership established the Lehigh Valley Business/Education Partnership, under the leadership of Ed Donley, the retired CEO of Air Products. This organization is charged with addressing employers' workforce development needs through communication and partnerships with high schools, vocational schools, community colleges, and colleges.

Transportation was another major issue regionally. Interstate 78, the valley's major east-west highway, was completed in 1989, but development was dependent on further improvements to highways, railroads, and air transportation. With the help of the partnership in 1993 Daday gained a seat on the Pennsylvania Transportation Commission, where he represented the Lehigh Valley for eighteen years. He succeeded in pushing through several major roadway improvements as the Lehigh Valley, with its strategic location within a day's drive of one-third of the U.S. population, became a major center for logistics (warehousing and intermodal distribution centers—rail to truck—for national companies like Walgreens). With its modern air, rail, and highway transportation facilities, the region was in position to assume a role in the new world of Internet retail delivery, manufacturing in proximity to distribution facilities, and even as an inland port for the new giant container ships. Daday also served on the Lehigh-Northampton Airport Authority Board. In 1994 he convinced the board to change the name of the airport from Allentown-Bethlehem-Easton to Lehigh Valley International Airport, although the official designation still is ABE.

The partnership worked behind the scenes to develop regional strategies when Pennsylvania's archaic local government system failed. The region consists of two counties that contain twenty-one smaller jurisdictions—cities, boroughs, and townships—so gaining cooperation on economic development issues was challenging. The counties had created a regional bus system, a regional airport, and a regional planning commission, but each retained its own economic development programs, as did each of the three cities. The partnership realized that a centralized marketing and development agency would be more effective for economic development of the region. Such a centralized agency would need access to Harrisburg and its resources, as well as both counties. In 1995 Daday worked with Elmer Gates, former CEO and part owner of the Bethlehem-based Fuller Company, which built cement plants around the world, to raise $900,000 for the first year of the nonprofit Lehigh Valley Economic Development Corporation. Then they worked to raise $7.9 million more during the following five years. They even convinced the two counties to reduce their economic development operations and focus their efforts through the LVEDC.

Daday knew that relying solely on the business community to fund the LVEDC was not sustainable long term. He also could see what other regions were spending to get the attention of businesses. He knew that the Lehigh Valley had many advantages in terms of location, infrastructure, transportation, water, and workforce, but marketing those assets aggressively would be expensive. Daday worked with the region's Harrisburg delegation to solve the problem. Pennsylvania law permits counties to set up a regional hotel tax, with the revenue going partly to the county but mostly to regional travel promotion agencies. The Philadelphia and Lancaster regions had done this quite effectively.

The Lehigh Valley Convention and Visitors Bureau was established in 1984, but its budget was inadequate. With the weight of the Lehigh Valley Partnership behind them, Daday and Gates threw a lifeline to the convention bureau, with a catch: Daday and Gates would convince the state legislature to approve a 3.5 percent tax on overnight room sales in the two counties, with 1 percent of the proceeds going to the economic development corporation, slightly more to the tourism bureau, and the balance to the county in which the hotel is located. All parties agreed and the tax took effect in October 2000. The region finally had a reliable funding source for tourism marketing and for regional economic development efforts. Both the tourism bureau (now renamed Discover Lehigh Valley) and LVEDC are vital to the success of the Lehigh Valley.

The Lehigh Valley Partnership also led the way toward consolidating the disparate operations of the Red Cross, United Way, and local chambers of commerce, all of which came under the umbrellas of regional organizations by the early 2000s. Some, like the Lehigh Valley Chamber of Commerce, retained offices and local boards in the cities and towns of the region, while most simply unified in one regional office. Daday played a part in all of it. The Lehigh Valley repositioned itself as an attractive place for twenty-first-century businesses through the efforts of strong leaders who saw beyond municipal boundaries and petty interests.

LEHIGH VALLEY INDUSTRIAL PARK

Daday and PP&L were not the only ones in the Lehigh Valley who recognized that the Lehigh Valley could not survive on Bethlehem Steel alone, nor were they the first. Back in early 1959 a group of business leaders recognized that someone needed to develop an industrial park to attract businesses to the region. The group included a banker, the owner of an insurance agency, a vice president of PP&L, an accountant, an attorney, and Frank Marcon, who owned a construction business and was serving as president of the Bethlehem Chamber of Commerce, on whose board all these men sat. They created the nonprofit Lehigh Valley Industrial Park (LVIP) in May 1959.

The leaders had identified four farm tracts along U.S. Route 22 near the ABE airport. To purchase the 226 acres they raised $250,000 in personal notes from eighteen individuals, and the National Bank of Bethlehem financed the balance of the $572,000 purchase price. The new nonprofit went on to issue debentures to repay the bank and to begin developing the land. The City of Bethlehem committed to building the streets, curbs, water lines, and sanitary and storm sewerage in the park; LVIP agreed to repay the city for these infrastructure costs as lots were sold. After a few lots were sold,

LVIP officials realized that there was a market for "spec" buildings, but no one in the region was building industrial buildings on spec. The leaders created another nonprofit, the Bethlehem RISK Corporation, raised $25,000 from 250 investors, and built the first spec building, which National Cash Register promptly rented with an option to purchase after twenty years. When Bethlehem RISK officials sought $25,000 more from investors, interest in the bonds was so high that they had to stage a lottery to allot the shares. No one was investing with an expectation of profit, but when Bethlehem RISK was liquidated because the private sector had stepped into the industrial spec market, each $100 share was worth $600.

The board started getting inquiries for lots with rail access. In 1963 LVIP purchased 150 acres of farmland from PP&L on the north side of the airport property. The land had access to a rail line but was in a neighboring township. It took until 1968 for the several municipalities and the airport to reach an agreement to provide all necessary utilities for the park. Sales of lots in LVIP II, as this project was called, were so brisk that in 1973 LVIP went on to purchase 318 acres south and west of the airport from Bethlehem Steel. LVIP III was in development through the 1970s when Liberty Property Trust, the company established by Philadelphia's renowned developer Willard G. Rouse III, started to develop industrial properties in the parks on spec.[120] The portfolio of Liberty Property Trust continues to expand today in the Lehigh Valley, one of the organization's primary markets.

As LVIP was running out of land around the airport and demand continued to grow, the nonprofit created LVIP IV and LVIP V off U.S. 22 north of Bethlehem in the late 1980s and early 1990s. When a segment of Route 33, a four-lane highway that connects I-80 to I-78, was completed between U.S. 22 and I-78 in the mid-1990s, LVIP acquired 178 acres in Bethlehem Township at one of the new interchanges. Lots in LVIP VI sold quickly, thanks to its strategic location.

As LVIP celebrated its fiftieth anniversary in 2009, the nonprofit could boast ownership of a system of twenty-five hundred acres with 460 businesses that provide twenty-two thousand jobs and more than $10 million in annual local tax revenue. LVIP has been a bright spot in the region since its economic woes began in 1960. LVIP played a major role in the growth of the region before the demise of Bethlehem Steel and was about to play an even greater role in addressing the void left by the closure of the steel plant.

BEN FRANKLIN TECHNOLOGY PARTNERS

The first general purpose electronic computer was created at the University of Pennsylvania in 1946. But by 1980 Pennsylvania had lost whatever edge it had in technology to the orbits of MIT-Harvard and Stanford–Silicon Valley. While centers of excellence still existed around Penn, Carnegie Mellon, and Penn State, the state as a whole was not a leader in the technology revolution, as it had been in the industrial revolution. This was readily apparent to Dick Thornburgh, a Republican from Pittsburgh who became governor in 1979, because his home town, and virtually all of western Pennsylvania, was in crisis as a result of deindustrialization. The governor's team realized that the state desperately needed development and the growth that private-sector technology businesses would bring. By 1981 they had developed a plan to create nonprofit organizations near academic centers of excellence but not as part of the universities. The nonprofits would receive state funding but also would be free to seek outside funding to support the development of businesses and jobs in the technology sector throughout the state. The goals were to provide seed money and venture capital to start and grow innovative tech firms, including by working with, and encouraging, the creation of regional venture capital funds; providing fledgling firms with business expertise, including product development, marketing, fund-raising, accounting, operations, and human resources; and fostering networks to bring ideas and talent to the state.

As Thornburgh and his team were hatching the technology innovation project in 1982, word of it reached Don Stabler, a major land developer in Pennsylvania and a Lehigh alumnus. He tipped off Lehigh, which handed the ball to Mike Bolton, who had started in Lehigh's Development Office in 1972. His first assignment had been to visit major universities such as MIT, Duke, Carnegie Mellon, and Stanford to assess the practices that had spelled success for these schools in their partnerships with businesses. Bolton came back from that survey with information crucial to what Lehigh did subsequently. To spawn new enterprises, Bolton learned, the universities had partnerships that made startup capital available to innovative new businesses, as well as incubator space where entrepreneurs could have their offices in an environment conducive to innovation and collaboration. He also observed that it was important for the university to adopt a more collaborative attitude about use of intellectual property developed at Lehigh, to encourage its practical application in the business sector. For the next several years Bolton honed his development skills by encouraging academic and research programs with industry and obtaining funding special university-based programs like the Small Business Development Center, Martindale Center for the Study of Private Enterprise, Rauch Center for Business Communications and the Iacocca Institute, as well as strengthening general financial support from foundations, businesses, and alumni.

When Stabler got word to Lehigh about Thornburgh's tech innovation project, Bolton was in a good position to encourage the university's participation in the project. Bolton and Joseph Goldstein, Lehigh's assistant vice president of research, began meeting with Walt Plosila and other representatives of the state commerce department to discuss what the state was looking for and what Lehigh might offer. As the state project advanced, it took the name Ben Franklin Technology Partnership after the most famous Pennsylvanian, who was also a well-documented innovator. Thornburgh proposed legislation to create the Ben Franklin program with funding of $1 million per year, to be divided into three grants of up to $350,000 each. It was clear that the state was planning to establish partnerships in Pittsburgh, Philadelphia, and State College. With the help of Stabler, Bolton and his team convinced the state commerce department that institutions elsewhere in the state should also be able to apply. The 1982 enabling legislation was changed to allow for four annual grants of up to $250,000 each. Lehigh and eight other institutions submitted applications. Lehigh's, a plan for northeastern Pennsylvania, was the first chosen. Three other grants were made to start partnerships in Philadelphia (southeastern Pennsylvania); State College (central and northwestern Pennsylvania); and Pittsburgh (southwestern Pennsylvania).

Lehigh's president chose Bolton to run Lehigh's program. Within a year Ben Franklin Technology Partners of Northeastern Pennsylvania had established its first incubator at Lehigh's campus. Today Ben Franklin has more than fifty incubators throughout the state and is believed to have the largest system of state-funded incubators in the country. The program has helped hundreds of businesses and has created more than 140,000 jobs, most of which pay far above the state's average salary. The Lehigh-based regional program supports business development in twenty-one counties, including the Scranton–Wilkes Barre, Lehigh Valley, Reading, Pocono Mountains, and Williamsport-Lewisburg areas.

One of Ben Franklin's most successful projects is the Bethlehem-based OraSure. In its early years the inventor Sam Niedbala created a quick saliva test for AIDS. The company most recently has received a U.S. government contract to develop an oral test for the Zika virus.

Bolton encouraged the creation of the Manufacturers Resource Center (MRC). Through the MRC Lehigh University and other partners—including Penn State, the National Institute of Standards and Technology, and the Pennsylvania Department of Economic and Community Development—provide manufacturers with training, coaching, and certifications in a variety of areas. Since the center was established in the early 1990s, the Lehigh Valley has seen a renaissance in manufacturing.

Ben Franklin, Manufacturers Resource Center, and the Small Business Development Center are central to why the Lehigh Valley has managed to transition from a history of heavy industry to a more diverse economy that has retained and attracted significant modern manufacturing that requires employees with far different skills.

As a result of the regional cooperation in attracting businesses and assisting emerging new businesses, as well as the Lehigh Valley's proximity to major markets in the northeastern United States and the talents of the workforce, manufacturing has continued to be a significant employer in the region, contributing to its economic success. Unlike the manufacturers of the industrial revolution, the new companies do not need to be near the river or even the railroad for power or transportation. Most new manufacturers and other successful businesses are outside city limits and close to the highways, leaving to the cities the challenge of deciding what their role is in the new economy.

And the cities had nowhere to go but up. By 2000 Allentown had lost all its department stores, had almost no first-class office space, and its school district was in crisis. Bethlehem's small north side downtown had become stable but was not growing. And Bethlehem's SouthSide was paralyzed, waiting for someone to figure out what to do with eighteen hundred acres of former steel plant.

Can a Rust Belt city pivot and participate in the success of a region, or must it figure out how to survive within its restricted boundaries and as a repository of poverty, crime, and traditional nonprofit institutions? At the turn of the twenty-first century this was the question the community was trying to address. Bert Daday, who died in November 2015, lived to see his native city rebound, though not in the way any of us had anticipated.

PART III
TRANSFORMATION
STEELSTACKS AND THE REDEVELOPMENT OF
THE BETHLEHEM STEEL PLANT, 1992–2016

CHAPTER 20
THE LAST WILL AND TESTAMENT OF BETHLEHEM STEEL

In the midst of its death throes, beset by overseas competition and declining demand for its product, Bethlehem Steel had picked a leader who did the right thing for a community traumatized and diminished by the company's demise. His efforts set the stage for Bethlehem to return to its role as an economically thriving community.

His name is Curtis "Hank" Barnette. He grew up on a family farm in St. Albans, West Virginia, and attended the West Virginia University, where he met the woman who would become his wife, Joanne Harner. She too grew up on a farm in the Mountain State. After a stint as a Fullbright scholar in England and in the Army as an intelligence officer in Germany, he studied law at Yale, and the Barnette family settled in New Haven, where he taught at Yale and was associated with a local law firm. In 1967 Barnette left what he expected to be a comfortable life as a litigation attorney and teacher in New Haven to accept what he and Joanne felt might be a greater opportunity at Bethlehem Steel.

Within eight years Barnette had become the company's general counsel and centralized the legal services in a single law department, a forward-thinking move at a time when each department in large corporations often had its own legal team. He was made a member of the board of directors in 1986. He is soft-spoken, and his voice contains a hint of Appalachian twang; he exudes a homespun, Abe Lincoln–style manner that made him a trusted adviser at board meetings. In 1992 he was elected board chair and CEO, the first and only lawyer in the history of the company to rise to that rank.

During those dark years, as the leadership had to close one after another of the company's operations and lay off thousands, Barnette understood what that decline was doing to the communities in which it had plants. Bethlehem Steel's home town hosted the eighteen-hundred-acre plant, corporate international headquarters (Martin Tower), information technology facilities, the Homer research complex atop South Mountain (once the home of engineers and scientists who advanced the science of steel products like the weathering steel called Corten and state-of-the-art engineering techniques for using steel), and dozens of other properties scattered around the community. Barnette emphasizes that a key principle of Bethlehem Steel was good corporate citizenship and that meant preparing communities for what was to come. When I interviewed him for this book, Barnette recited the steps necessary to revitalize the home town plant site and other similar sites: a development plan for the former steel plant; mitigation of environmental concerns; zoning to implement the plan; infrastructure to support it; and a plan to sell the real estate. Barnette directed the process, giving it priority and funding.[121]

PENNSYLVANIA'S ACT 2: AN ENVIRONMENTAL WAY FORWARD

Perhaps the greatest issue in planning a future for any industrial site is environmental contamination. If the industry has polluted the ground and any groundwater, it and any future owner are liable for the cleanup under federal law. Barnette and his team worked with Pennsylvania governor Tom Ridge and the state legislature to develop a law that would make it easier to redevelop industrial land. In 1995 the legislature approved the Land Recycling and Environmental Remediation Standards Act, known as Act 2. The law creates a realistic framework for setting cleanup standards, provides special incentives for developing abandoned sites, releases responsible parties from liability when cleanup standards are met, sets deadlines for action by the state Department of Environmental Resources, and provides funding for environmental studies and cleanups.[122] Once the process is complete, the state, in coordination with the federal Environmental Protection Agency, issues a closing letter that assures the purchaser of a property that, subject to certain restrictions, it may use the property without liability for previous use of the property.

According to Barnette, before this law was adopted, the only reasonable alternative for a business closing an industrial site was to clear the structures, plant grass, and surround it with a fence, not something he wanted to happen to property that accounted for 20 percent of the acreage within the city of Bethlehem.

Pennsylvania's land recycling program has served as a model for other states. The program received a 1997 Ford Foundation Innovations in American Government Award, an honor administered by the John F. Kennedy School of Government at Harvard and the Council for Excellence in Government.[123] With passage of the act Barnette and his team had a process for moving forward with plans for the former Bethlehem plant.

THE LARGEST BROWNFIELD DEVELOPMENT IN THE UNITED STATES

Unlike the families of most Bethlehem Steel executives, the Barnettes chose to live in Bethlehem, specifically the west Bethlehem neighborhood known as Bonus Hill, a name it acquired in the 1920s when it became the neighborhood preferred by steel executives of that era. But by 1940 most of the executives had moved their families south of Bethlehem to be near Saucon Valley Country Club. As a resident of the city Barnette was aware of the historic significance of the plant's steelmaking section, that included the blast furnaces adjacent to the business district and neighborhoods on the city's south side, where workers had lived for decades. The former plant is shaped like a quotation mark, with the steelmaking section the downstroke in the heart of the city and the rest, where the steel was made into beams, cables, and many other products, ballooning out to the southeast, where few residential areas abutted it. Barnette wanted to preserve the historic steelmaking core that included the blast furnaces, Number 2 Machine Shop, Gas Blowing Engine Building, the Hoover-Mason Trestle, and the Steel General Office Building, which preceded Martin Tower as the corporate headquarters.

Even before the legislature passed Act 2, Barnette had assembled a team that would help determine the best use for the steel property, including preservation of the historic core. The team included Steven Donches, vice president of public affairs; Tim Lewis, the division president; Charles Martin, the plant engineer and others. Advisers from outside the company included Robert Weis and Jeanette Dunlap, former Disney Imagineers who had formed their own Florida-based consulting group, Design Island; Lee Butz, president of Alvin H. Butz, Inc., the largest construction manager in the Lehigh Valley; David Scott Parker, a Connecticut-based architect whose focus was historic preservation and who had been doing work for Historic Bethlehem, Inc.; Robert Barron of Enterprise Development Corporation; and Ralph Schwarz, historian and museum developer, who began his career with Bethlehem Steel, then left in 1960 to begin an impressive career that included advising the Holocaust Museum in New York, working with the Ford Foundation to design its headquarters building in New York, and assisting Richard Meier in development of the Getty Museum in Los Angeles; and others.

This team created the dual concept plan for redeveloping the steel plant: Bethlehem Works and the Bethlehem Commerce Center. They envisioned the former as a museum-entertainment-tourism district of 126 acres (including the historic core) in the heart of the city. They saw the latter as a sixteen-hundred-acre industrial park next to the Bethlehem interchange of Interstate 78, the highway that connects the Lehigh Valley to New York City. The opening of I-78 in 1989 had dramatically increased the Lehigh Valley's access to New York–area markets and made the Bethlehem Steel property prime for development.[124] Barnette's vision was that an industrial park with access to the major markets of the northeastern United States and the comparatively low tax environment of Pennsylvania had the right ingredients for replacing many of the jobs lost when the steel plant closed.

BETHLEHEM WORKS

Ralph Schwarz had begun working as a consultant to Historic Bethlehem, Inc. in 1992 and played a crucial role in unifying four small historic organizations, two of which he had been instrumental in creating. Historic Bethlehem, the Kemmerer Museum of Decorative Arts, the Moravian Museum, and Burnside Plantation became the new Historic Bethlehem Partnership. Schwarz recognized the historic core of the Bethlehem Steel plant had potential as a site for a museum that would tell the story of Bethlehem Steel and its importance in building the bridges and skylines of twentieth-century America, as well as the ships and munitions that helped win both world wars. Schwarz envisioned using the western forty acres of the plant, including the blast furnaces, for an iron and steel museum celebrating Bethlehem Steel, and using adjacent land for retail, entertainment, and recreational purposes. Schwarz briefed Barnette on these ideas, and he agreed to a more formal discussion.

On June 24, 1994, Schwarz met with Barnette, Donches, and Andy Weller, Bethlehem Steel's treasurer. Schwarz pitched an ambitious project. Acknowledging that building a traditional museum would cost too much, he proposed the "marriage of high tech theme park technology" and "high quality, serious, industrial museology" to preserve key buildings and tell the story of Bethlehem Steel. The group told him to explore the possibilities.[125]

Schwarz was aware that the Walt Disney Company was planning a project in Manassas, Virginia, that would loosely interpret the history of the country in a theme park within driving distance of the heavily populated northeast corridor. In June 1994 a battle was raging about the propriety of Disney's building a theme park next to the hallowed ground of a Civil War battle site. In the face of heavy opposition, Disney pulled out of the project that September. Schwarz sought to convert Disney's exit into an opportunity for Bethlehem.

By March 1995 Schwarz had convinced Weis and Dunlap, the two former Disney Imagineers, to plan a combination museum–amusement park at the historic core of the steel plant. By June they had a plan they called Bethlehem Works. The centerpiece would be a Disney-like experience, engaging visitors with the excitement, danger, noise, and heat of steelmaking. It would include sports facilities, entertainment and retail centers, movie theaters, a hotel and conference center, expansion of the Discovery Science Center (a science education center formerly housed in a steel company office building on Third Street, which is occupied today by Northampton Community College), artisans' workshops, and manufacturing facilities for popular brand-name retail item that would give visitors an opportunity to watch how these items are made.[126] Weis and Dunlap presented their ideas to Peter Rummell, chair of Walt Disney Imagineering. He was impressed but said that Disney's participation was unlikely though he suggested they prepare a market analysis as the next step. The analysis, which found that the project could draw 3.8 million visitors a year, was completed in late 1995.[127] The Bethlehem Steel team and the Disney representatives continued to discuss the project, but in the end the Disney team turned it down.[128]

It was suggested that the Steel approach the Smithsonian, and this had the support of Senator Daniel Patrick Moynihan of New York. He was a friend of the steel industry and Bethlehem had a plant in Lackawanna, New York. He was also the senior Regent of the Smithsonian. The institution had more objects than it could ever exhibit, including many industrial artifacts. A conversation with representatives of the Smithsonian in early 1996 led to a discussion about the need for a museum that would tell the history of industry in the United States.[129] This was timely because the Smithsonian was already discussing how to make its collections more accessible to the public. In September 1996 the Smithsonian created Smithsonian Affiliations, a national outreach program that does not fund projects but develops partnerships with museums and educational organizations to share collections, exhibitions, and research expertise.[130]

Smithsonian representatives were impressed with the space available at the Bethlehem site, something that the museum lacked in Washington. The conversation evolved quickly into a discussion of a national museum of industrial history, with the historians encouraging a traditional museum and some of the team in Bethlehem continuing to argue for a concept that combined museum and technology (think amusement ride). In their rush to show progress, Bethlehem Steel Corporation and the Smithsonian Institution signed a memorandum of understanding in January 1997 with announcements of the relationship at events in Washington and Bethlehem on February 28, 1997. The memo included the requirement that Bethlehem Steel create an independent, nonprofit national museum of industrial history, which would become the first affiliate of the Smithsonian, which in turn committed to loan the new museum the 1876 Industrial Exhibit from the Philadelphia Centennial Exhibition, a cumbersome group of industrial equipment from the era.

According to the announcement, the museum would occupy the 275,000-square-foot Number 2 Machine Shop, a structure built in 1888 to make armor plates for the U.S. Navy. When it was built, the shop was the biggest building under roof in the country. The industrial museum would be the anchor for development of Bethlehem Works, with other attractions such as the Iron and Steel Experience, a high-tech journey through the blast furnaces complete with heat and lighting effects. Portions of Bethlehem Works would be designated for such recreational amenities as a skating rink and swimming pool, plus hotels, restaurants, and retail stores as well as parking.

Everyone was eager to see the project move forward. In April 1997 the new National Museum of Industrial History announced that a "preview center" would be established in the building known as the Electrical Repair Shop. The building had a good location, on Third Street adjacent to the Discovery Center (a science education facility), which was attempting to develop an Imax theater. The preview center was expected to cost $8.25 million and open in December 1998. The museum of industrial history, with an initial estimated cost of $80 million, would take "a while" longer. The preview center never opened. A far smaller version of the National Museum of Industrial History would finally open on the first floor of the Electrical Repair Shop in 2016, after a public and protracted failure to garner sufficient financial support for the concept. The museum would not be the anchor for Bethlehem Works. The high-tech Iron and Steel Experience was abandoned along the way.

THE GREAT ZONING BATTLE

Barnette's team knew that, whatever the company ultimately decided to do, the project would need a new zoning designation that would permit a wide range of development. In 1995, the year the home plant was to close, the company had proposed that the City of Bethlehem create an industrial redevelopment district that would allow virtually any kind of development except garbage dumps and adult bookstores on 160 acres that included the historic core of the plant, soon to be identified as Bethlehem Works plus some adjacent properties. (The sixteen hundred acres of the proposed Bethlehem Commerce Center was to be zoned for an industrial park, which encountered no opposition.) The Bethlehem Works zoning proposal brought immediate and vehement opposition. The decline of Bethlehem Steel had destroyed residents' trust in the great corporate benefactor, and few believed that the company cared about what it left behind. The company said that the purpose of the zoning change was to promote economic revitalization. But as the ordinance wound its way through the planning commission and city council, outraged citizens fought it. Accusations of conflict of interest flew, some referencing contributions from steel executives to Mayor Kenneth Smith's political campaigns. The retirement plans of a member of the city council and the chair of the planning commission, both retired steel employees, held steel stock, which protesters said created a conflict of interest.[131](The lawyers disagreed.) The deep grief and resentment that the community was suffering because the plant was closing made people profoundly skeptical that Bethlehem Steel was trying to help the city.

The final city council vote on the new zoning category came on the evening of April 2, 1996. Thirty-five people addressed the council, fifteen in favor of the measure and twenty against. Perhaps surprisingly, those looking to the future won the day. By a 5–2 vote the council approved the new zoning district, which Mayor Smith promptly signed into law. (The dissenters were future mayors Don Cunningham and Robert Donchez.)[132]

Of the many obstacles in the way of redevelopment of the steel plant, the one most stressful for Hank Barnette was that zoning vote.[133] On the day of the vote U.S. Representative Paul McHale had endorsed the position of Donchez and Cunningham, further undermining the company's efforts.

Both sides had made good points, but Barnette's plan was the only logical way to move forward. However, opponents saw Bethlehem Steel as a dying entity that might not control the outcome, even if its intentions were good. Barbara Flanagan, a writer who sat on the planning commission, expressed the worst of all fears: "If progress halts, the company will sell the property to developers who will take advantage of the new zoning and build whatever they want next to whatever they want. That could happen in the blink of an eye. Then we will be stuck asking why we didn't write in some controls to make sure we didn't end up with a zinc smelter next to a food-processing plant."[134] During the next ten years the community held its breath until the disposition of the property was decided.

THE BETHLEHEM WORKS TIF

The final deal struck before Barnette retired as chair of Bethlehem Steel in April 2000 was creation of a tax increment financing (TIF) district for Bethlehem Works, a designation used to advance public money through bond financing to redevelop blighted areas with the expectation that bonds will be repaid by new real estate tax revenues generated by the improved property. The Bethlehem Works project needed the financing to pay for streets, water, sewerage, lighting, parking, and other infrastructure on the 126 acres containing the most historic part of the plant.[135] Usually private developers or companies that benefit from the TIF back the funds advanced by TIFs through a bond. In some cases a municipality backs the funds because the private sector has already committed to a development project, and the municipality knows it will recoup the infrastructure costs it advances. In this case Bethlehem Steel wanted the city to advance the infrastructure costs without any commitment by the company to develop Bethlehem Works. Bethlehem Steel argued that without the infrastructure, the company could not sell the property. Bethlehem Steel simply was no longer in a position to either advance the expenses or back the debt.

Mayor Don Cunningham, who had voted against the new zoning district in 1995, was changing his mind about the plans for the plant site when he became mayor of Bethlehem in January 1998. The thirty-two-year-old was facing immediate threats to his city's welfare. The day after his inaugural ball at the Hotel Bethlehem, Bob Decker had called to tell Cunningham that the hotel was closing and entering bankruptcy. Decker had kept it open only for the inauguration. To make matters worse, in Cunningham's first year in office, Bethlehem Steel stopped all remaining production at the plant, shut down the coke works, and filed for tax refunds on properties that were now nonproductive. "Talk about stress. The pressure was intense," Cunningham told me.[136] Because of the potential of Bethlehem Works, he became its cautious ally. Ultimately he pledged money from the city's precious block grants from the U.S. Department of Housing and Urban Development (HUD) to move the project forward. As it turned out the city didn't have to use the federal money, but at the time Cunningham's decision was highly risky. "I knew if we did nothing, nothing would happen," Cunningham said.

When Hank Barnette retired, he had accomplished most of what he had set out to achieve for the city, if not for the company. With the help of Governor Tom Ridge and others, Act 2 had made redevelopment of the site possible without the prohibitive expense of covering eighteen hundred acres with two feet of topsoil. Despite extensive opposition, the Bethlehem Works property now had zoning that would permit its redevelopment. The Steel had presented the city with plans for Bethlehem Works and the Bethlehem Commerce Center, an industrial park that covered the area of the plant outside Bethlehem Works. Both land uses carried the promise of bringing jobs back to the community. And the Steel's lobbyists and transportation consultants had convinced the state that Route 412, which connected I-78 and the Bethlehem Commerce Center to Bethlehem Works, needed to become a four-lane boulevard to smooth traffic flow between the interstate and the massive proposed development.

These steps were the key to successfully developing the former Bethlehem Steel plant, for which Barnette's team and those who worked with them deserve the undying gratitude of the community. No one could save Bethlehem Steel, and after Barnette retired, the end came quickly. But the fresh start for the property did not.

BANKRUPTCY

On November 15, 2001, Bethlehem Steel filed for bankruptcy, an end that was anticlimactic. Martin Tower was mostly vacant. The company had sold its research center property to Lehigh University. A parcel of Bethlehem Works had been sold for an ice-skating facility, but otherwise Bethlehem Works was locked up behind chain-link fencing, as was most of the rest of the former steel plant.

Early in the new century great uncertainty remained about what would happen to all of the Steel's property. In November 2002 the "vulture investor" Wilbur Ross, who would later become Donald Trump's secretary of commerce, and his partner Rodney Mott, creators of the International Steel Group (ISG), purchased the remaining assets of Bethlehem Steel, including Martin Tower and the entire former Bethlehem plant. The transaction meant disaster for many:

Those employees who had moved to the company's Baltimore facility to work long enough to be eligible for a pension were cut off with nothing. Some were a day short. Thousands receiving pensions had to collect whatever they could from the Federal Pension Benefit Guaranty Board, which reduced pensions according to its regulations. Health care benefits ended. Hundreds of families no longer had an income. Deindustrialization had hit them with a final powerful burst of misery.

Despite the progress the region had made in the previous twenty years as one of the bright spots in the Northeast, the City of Bethlehem was stuck with an eighteen-hundred-acre hole and a lot of industrial ruins.

CHAPTER 21
A CHANGE OF PLAN

In 2002 ArtsQuest was completing the second phase of the Banana Factory with the new gallery facing Third Street, additional classrooms, and the gift shop. We were almost alone in investing in the SouthSide at the time. The six-acre building behind the Banana factory where steel was fabricated was gradually losing tenants.

No decision had been made about redeveloping Bethlehem Steel's eighteen hundred acres. We saw the uncertainty about the property as a potential opportunity and developed a plan for a small but important part of the acreage. In early 2003 we presented it first to the ArtsQuest Long Range Planning Committee. The Riverside Arts Park Plan called for a thirty-five-acre park at the historic core of the steel property. It would include walking paths, elevations for views of the river, places for sculpture, three outdoor performing arts venues, activity areas, a café or restaurant, a roller-blading path, and an indoor concert venue with seating for five thousand.[137]

That year ArtsQuest celebrated its twentieth Musikfest. The organization had become one of the most experienced event organizations in the country. Musikfest and Christkindlmarkt were supporting the community and its brand. The Banana Factory was an established arts anchor for the SouthSide, contributing to the emerging new restaurant and retail cluster in the area. Paul Harryn, a well-known regional artist, established his studio two blocks east of the Banana Factory, across the street from an Asian bistro, a hip optician, and an architect's office. A second art gallery, the Bookstore (a speakeasy-style restaurant with 1920s music and drinks), and Italian and Mexican restaurants joined the Indian, Thai, and several other existing restaurants on the emerging scene.

For years we had studied other successful festivals by sending staff to the International Festivals and Events Association conferences and by visiting other festivals. The gold standard was the one that I had originally used as the model for ours, Summerfest in Milwaukee. Summerfest had started as a small event in 1967, but by the time I first visited it in 1978 it was a major event with multiple stages. In 1987 Summerfest opened the twenty-three-thousand-seat Marcus Amphitheater so that it could continue to attract top performers. We aspired to have a similar venue that would put Musikfest and the region on the major festival-concert tour map. In 2002 we did a survey of amphitheaters within a three-hundred-mile radius of the Lehigh Valley. It concluded that amphitheaters were expensive, had varying degrees of success, and required a population center of at least one million to be successful. Even the Marcus Amphitheater struggled to book shows because of competing venues in the nearby Chicago area. Because we were between New York and Philadelphia, both with large venues, we realized we would struggle to book shows.

This research was what led us to propose a more modest five-thousand-seat indoor venue that also could be used for non-concert activities such as conventions. As it turns out, few shows can fill large amphitheaters or even five thousand seats in the era of digital music and a much greater diversity of artists and genres.

Putting the venue in a park that also could be used for Musikfest was important. We had always hoped to find a location for part of Musikfest on the south side so that the benefits of the festival could spread to this part of town to support community and economic development. Until the steel plant became vacant, the densely built south side simply had no space large enough that made sense for a platz.

The possibility of offering other festivals throughout the year, as Milwaukee was doing, also was in our thinking because we believed that operating festivals was the organization's strong suit and would meet civic and cultural needs. A study of the south side done for the city by Sasaki Associates of Boston found that what residents wanted most was "a strong open space network with a hierarchy of regional, Southside and local open spaces."[138] An arts park would be a step in the right direction.

EXPLORING PARTNERSHIPS

With these ideas, and a vacant and available steel mill, its future still in limbo in spring 2003, the ArtsQuest Long Range Planning Committee and staff reached out to twenty-three nonprofit organizations in the Lehigh Valley to assess their interest in what we were thinking. Would the organization be interested in having a presence at a regional arts center? Might the organization want to move there? Those were the key questions we asked every college, nonprofit art gallery and art museum, music-presenting organization, theater and dance company, and nonprofit media organizations, PBS 39 and the NPR affiliate WDIY. Once we knew who was interested, we scheduled two meetings for the fall, one to outline opportunities, issues, and levels of interest and a second to review a draft concept plan to determine who would want to advance to the next steps. The robust discussions were the only time in memory that so many arts organizations had gathered to assess the state of the arts in the region.

By the end of the summer of 2003, we had the outline for a project, a large group of interested partners, and a list of funding possibilities. ArtsQuest and the city asked our state legislators to endorse the application of the arts park in Bethlehem for a grant from the Pennsylvania Redevelopment Assistance Capital Program (RACP), funding that was used for urban revitalization projects. None of the dozens of people now engaged in the process was fazed by planning for property that we did not own. What we needed was an exemplar of such a park. What better place to go than the deindustrialized heartland of Germany?

BRAINSTORMING BETHLEHEM WORKS

Organizations that participated in explorations of how to put the steel plant property to good use:

Media

- Lehigh Valley PBS
- WDIY (public radio)

Music

- ArtsQuest
- Godfrey Daniels (folk music venue)
- Young People's Philharmonic

Dance and Theater

- Hispanic American League of Artists
- Lehigh Valley Charter High School for the Performing Arts
- Pennsylvania Youth Ballet
- Pennsylvania Youth Theatre
- Touchstone Theatre

Colleges (with various arts disciplines)

- Desales University
- Kutztown University
- Lehigh University (Zoellner Arts Center)
- Moravian College
- Northampton Community College
- Penn State—Lehigh Valley

BACK TO GERMANY

The plan for the arts park drafted in early 2003 was heavily influenced by Granville Island, a former industrial site in Vancouver, British Columbia, that had been redeveloped as a vibrant public market surrounded by upscale residences, theaters, shops, and restaurants. Although I am a native of Bethlehem and appreciate historic preservation, and the National Trust for Historic Preservation had proclaimed the Bethlehem Steel site one of the ten most endangered historic sites in the United States, I saw nothing remotely attractive about the industrial relics on the south side. I understood the history of the plant and the company, but I failed to see any beauty in the rust. I had assumed that, like Granville Island, most, if not all, of the industrial ruins would be removed as we turned Bethlehem into a thriving postindustrial city.

Monika Buchheit saved my reputation as a visionary. She was responsible for managing the sister city relationships of Schwabisch Gmund, Germany. Because I was responsible for creating its sister city relationship with Bethlehem, she and I spoke or emailed from time to time. At some point I mentioned our interest in trying to do something at the old steel plant in Bethlehem. Buchheit asked if I would like to tour the Ruhr Valley, where Germans were working to preserve and reuse former steel mills and coal mines. I had already borrowed concepts from Germany, including an urban music festival and a holiday market, so why not go for a third big idea? Buchheit was happy to set up the tour.

In September 2003 a group of the arts park plotters left Bethlehem with me for Germany: Donna Taggart, chair of ArtsQuest's board and an experienced public development manager; the developer Frank Gillespie and his wife, Lisa; and Angelika Thiel, a native of Germany who was development director for the Pennsylvania Youth Theatre. We would be joined by Timothy Fallon, who sat on the board of the local public television station, PBS 39. Our four-day visit would change how all of us regarded our steel plant.

Germans have a much different perspective on industrialization. Before 1870 there was no single country called Germany, only a German language. The largest German-speaking country was Austria. The rest of German-speaking Europe was a group of independent cities, principalities, church-related states, and kingdoms that had been part of the Holy Roman Empire and led by the Austrian Hapsburgs until German unification in January 1871. "The Germans had a national rail network as early as 1840—fully three decades before Germany actually consolidated politically.... Industrialization *unified* the Germans as a country and a people to a degree unheard of elsewhere, before or since," writes Peter Zeihan, an expert in geopolitics.[139]

More than fifty years before Asa Packer's railroad and ironworks were in operation in Bethlehem, industrialization was fully under way in Germany's Ruhr Valley, which was dotted with coal mines and ironworks.[140] In the late twentieth century the decline of the coal and steel industry in the Ruhr Valley was a few years ahead of the American downward spiral. Germany was shifting from coal to petroleum and lost nearly half the jobs in the region between 1965 and 1998. Recognizing the problem and the need to rethink use of the region, the German state of North Rhineland Westphalia created the International Building Exhibition Emscher Park in 1989 to work with local government and the private sector. The Emscher is a fifty-two-mile tributary of the Rhine that runs north of and parallel to the Ruhr. By the 1960s it was a filthy repository of industrial and municipal refuse, a sad legacy of the industrial era.

What struck us as we toured the results of the ten-year planning and implementation process was that the state government had recognized the problems and established an approach that allowed state, national, and European Union agencies to focus on redeveloping the region. This was not something that we had seen or heard of anywhere in the United States.

Because the Emscher is not navigable, between 1906 and 1914 a canal had been built along the route of the river to join the Rhine to the central German river system. The canal moved coal and steel from the Ruhr Valley, and the Emscher was the repository for industrial and municipal waste. We first toured the small region from Duisburg, where the canal meets the Rhine, to Dortmund, the major city at the eastern end of the region. It was jaw dropping to see the many adaptive reuses and new buildings both in the towns and in the former steel plants and coal mining facilities. In Essen, after a presentation by a representative of Emscher Park, we toured Zeche Zollverein, which had been declared a UNESCO World Heritage Site in 2001. The major architectural feature of the site is the Zeche Zollverein Coal Mine, a complex of Bauhaus buildings built in the 1920s during the brief economic boom between the two world wars.[141]

While the preservation of the historic buildings and operating equipment of the coal mine was interesting, we were most impressed with plans for reusing much of the site; those plans included a visitor center, hotel, design center sponsored by the state, an art and design school, conference center, buildings to be reused by creative businesses, and space for events, art installations, and performances. Like Bethlehem and its steel plant, Essen had grown around the mine. Modern highways and rail systems were designed to serve the mines. Redevelopment plans included cultural events such as a triennial music and art celebration. Essen is a city of more than a half-million residents, which makes it the ninth-largest city in Germany. This plan was appropriate for a city of this size. We dined in a modern restaurant located in the compression house of an old coal mine. The contrast of the cement walls and in-place mining equipment with the contemporary lighting, furniture, art, and floral decorations was stunning.

We also were amazed by the Inner Harbor at Duisburg, where industrial buildings had been converted to museums and gyms with rock-climbing walls, beautiful hiking and biking trails meandered along the crystal-clear Emscher, mounds of slag (the waste product of steelmaking) had become monuments to the audacity of creative renewal, new homes were under construction along waterways, and former coal-mining buildings were becoming offices with specially treated floors to keep coal gases from seeping into the buildings. But we had come to see the steel plants and we were not disappointed. Landschaftspark (Landscape Park) Duisburg Nord grew out of popular sentiment to save this former steel plant. The resources of Emscher Park allowed the community to dream. The first thing that struck us was the railcars designed to carry ingot molds were still strewn about the site, rusting in place. New paving, lighting, signs, landscaping, and banners made the rust seem part of the environment. The park included whimsical features like a large concrete tube made of old industrial materials and placed on an incline as a sliding board with a pitch black interior. The tube invited the public to play with industrial remnants. The park has pathways that wind through old concrete foundations where visitors can observe how nature is gradually overcoming the concrete and metal debris. The park offers the visitor a sense of discovery. From the diving school in the former gasometer—a four-story circular building filled with water in which divers can explore an artificial reef formed by two cars and an airplane wreck—to the night club in the old Blower House complex, this place showed us how the old can be rethought and become new. And it was just like our steel plant.

Landschaftspark was a revelation. A casting house, where molten iron had once run thirty feet aboveground to railroad cars below, had been converted into an outdoor concert venue. The stage was the casting house itself with seating that slopes up and away from the stage, affording the audience an incredible view of the stage and the blast furnace looming behind it.

That evening we came back to see the nightly show. The designers of Landschaftspark understood the importance of the blast furnaces as an industrial artifact and a piece of installation art that the creativity of a lighting artist had enhanced. To top it all off, Visitors are permitted to climb the four-feet-wide stairway that rises more than eight stories to the top of the blast furnace, where a small platform affords a view of greater Duisburg. As we were climbing up, and others were climbing down, the only lighting came from ambient light. The pathway took us through dark portions of the furnace. The lawyer in me was amazed. We could never do this in the United States without safety features that would compromise the experience or, worse yet, without demanding signed releases from every visitor.

On our way back to Frankfurt, we stopped in the Saar Valley near the French border to see another World Culture Heritage Site, Volklinger Hutte. The presentation here was more like a museum of iron and steel, with both indoor and outdoor art and photography exhibits throughout the tour area. Volklinger Hutte uses a welcome center, a self-guided tour route, excellent signage, and well-designed, universally accessible walkways and elevators to tell the story of the steel mill, a company, the people who worked there, and the country they built. In both steel plants the Germans had chosen to leave areas where visitors could see nature gradually taking back what humans had converted to industry, a cautionary nod to the fragility of humans.

We boarded the plane to return home as converts to the idea of preserving enough of the steel plant to tell the story of Bethlehem Steel. We had learned of ways to use the old for new generations so that they could experience the industrial workplace in ways that their ancestors would have never envisioned. Many thanks, Frau Buchheit. The arts park plan had a new model and soon would have a new name.

STEELSTACKS

By December 2003 we were still operating on our own, trying to come up with a concept that might work at the vacant plant. We had surveyed the organizations that had been part of the exploratory process that year to see who wanted to have facilities in the new park. Our wish list included a multifunctional theater with a thousand seats; a four-hundred-seat theater; a theater designed for experimental performances; two television studios; a multimedia center; radio studios; offices and classrooms for several partners; dance and drama studios; metal, wood, and glass art classroom space; a large sculpture gallery; an outdoor plaza with a stage; and a visitor center. Each of the performance venues would be designed for television cameras so a digital regional arts channel could carry live or prerecorded productions to homes throughout eastern Pennsylvania. The estimate for this part of the project, excluding parking and the park itself, was $50 million.

Based on this guesstimate and with support from Mayor James Delgrosso, local legislators put an ambitious placeholder on the state Redevelopment Capital Assistance Program for a $25 million grant for the park, although such a sum was unlikely to be funded. Like the industrial museum planners of the mid-1990s, we were dreaming big. Our dreams were tempered in November 2003 when the National Endowment for the Arts rejected our application for a grant to fund a design competition for the arts park. We later learned that the NEA staff liked the concept but thought moving forward was senseless because we had no rights to the land for which we were developing a plan. Good point. Despite the uncertainty about disposition of the property, through 2003 and the first half of 2004 we kept planning and working with our state legislators. In the meantime, with a little help from my son, Jonathan, we decided on a name for our project—SteelStacks.[142]

CHAPTER 22
AND THE NEW OWNERS ARE...

T hroughout 2003 and into 2004 many rumors circulated about the sale of the steel plant while ArtsQuest and members of the community were dreaming of its possibilities. The principals of International Steel Group (ISG), which in 2002 had purchased the remaining assets of Bethlehem Steel, including Martin Tower and the entire former Bethlehem plant, made it clear that they wanted to sell the property, the sooner the better. The challenges of selling the plant property were substantial, including the lack of Act 2 remediation of the vast majority of the acreage designated for the Bethlehem Commerce Center. Buyers had good reason to be wary.

In the end Bethlehem's forty-five-year-old nonprofit, Lehigh Valley Industrial Park (LVIP), put together the deal to develop the Bethlehem Commerce Center under the volunteer leadership of Jeffrey Feather, an entrepreneur who was a native of the Lehigh Valley.

In 1970 Feather and four colleagues from his years at IBM had created Pentamation, a firm designed to meet the computer technology needs of the health-care industry, school districts, and local governments. The Lafayette graduate said that when he and his associates left IBM, they had one committed client, St. Luke's Hospital, and an investor who had promised the new enterprise $250,000 in seed money. The investor backed out and Feather went to Reese Jones at First Valley Bank for a loan. Jones gave them a line of credit for the full $250,000. Pentamation grew to 750 employees with offices in six states and eventually was sold to SunGard, a Pennsylvania-based multinational.

Flash forward to 1996. After a tennis game at Saucon Valley Country Club, Walt Dealtrey, then chair of the LVIP board, asked Feather if he would consider joining the board. Feather's business success had made him a great candidate for the volunteer board of an organization dedicated to creating jobs through industrial park development. Feather became its treasurer and worked with Dealtrey; Grover Stainbrook, the executive vice president; and the architect Robert Spillman, himself a long-time board member, to secure property for LVIP VI. Feather became board chair in June 2001, and Kerry Wrobel, a development professional who had honed his skills with the Bethlehem Economic Development Corporation, was named LVIP president.

Feather recalls that from his first days on the board, he and Dealtrey would ask Bethlehem Steel whether LVIP could develop the Bethlehem Steel plant property. They were repeatedly rebuffed. However, after Bethlehem Steel filed for bankruptcy protection, the new owner, ISG, asked LVIP to develop the sixteen-hundred-acre Bethlehem Commerce Center, which the consultants had suggested for an industrial park. Feather and Wrobel negotiated with ISG on behalf of LVIP. ISG asked LVIP to buy all sixteen hundred acres of the Commerce Center, then sell Los Angeles based Majestic Realty the 450 acres it had been negotiating to acquire from Bethlehem Steel before the bankruptcy. And ISG had a few conditions: LVIP would have to manage the mandated cleanup of the massive site, build a new intermodal rail-to-truck facility on the former coke plant site, and build a road, Commerce Center Boulevard, from near the intersection of I-78 and Route 412 to the property that Majestic was buying. (The Majestic purchase included the existing intermodal facility, but Majestic wanted to use the land for other purposes, and the facility was too valuable to the region to not replace it.) [143]

All this was a tall order for a modest nonprofit. The team at LVIP investigated what they would have to do to complete all the work. In early May 2003 LVIP and ISG announced they had reached a tentative agreement, and within a year LVIP had lined up the financing to complete the sale. Northampton County would supply a grant of $13 million toward construction of Commerce Center Boulevard. The state provided $20 million for site development. In May 2004 LVIP took possession of the real estate. Within a month LVIP had sold the first industrial lot to US Cold Storage. The recovery of jobs and real estate taxes lost during the previous twenty years had begun.

MICHAEL PERRUCCI, BETHLEHEM WORKS

Mike Perrucci, a first-generation Italian American born in Philips-burg, New Jersey, became a lawyer, then a politician, and ultimately a law partner of former New Jersey governor Jim Florio. Perrucci became a well-respected trial attorney and an equity partner in law firms practicing throughout New Jersey and as affiliates of New York firms.

In 2003 Perrucci took a break from the law, tired of the constant pressure of litigation. He rented an apartment on Main Street in Bethlehem, where he had attended Moravian College, and was "just hanging out." During this respite he followed the story of Wilbur Ross's takeover of Bethlehem Steel through ISG. Perrucci realized that while ISG wanted the pieces of Bethlehem Steel that remained in operation, the bankruptcy judge was forcing it to also take the property in Bethlehem. Perrucci contacted Pennsylvania governor Ed Rendell and learned that while the property had some environ-mental issues, the governor and local leaders wanted the property on the market as soon as possible. Perrucci called Richard Fischbein, his former New York partner who had once represented Ross, and asked Fischbein to be an equal partner in purchasing the entire for-mer steel plant.

Fischbein set up a lunch with Ross in New York and asked about buying all the land that Majestic was not buying. Perrucci recalls that Fischbein called him after the lunch and said, "We're in. It's a deal. Wilbur is flying to Korea to make a deal. I'm going on vaca-tion. When we all get back we'll get the paperwork. Wilbur said not to worry about the price, we'll figure that out when we get back."[144] Every lawyer knows that there is no such thing as an oral contract for real estate, and Perrucci was wary about a handshake deal with no price. While Fischbein was in the south of France for several weeks, Perrucci was hearing rumors that ISG was making a deal with anoth-er buyer. Then Bethlehem mayor James Delgrosso announced that the parcel designated for the Bethlehem Commerce Center had been sold to LVIP.

Fischbein called Ross and learned that he had neglected to tell his ISG real estate team in Cleveland that he and Fischbein had a deal. As a consolation prize, Ross offered to sell the 126-acre Bethlehem

Works property to Fischbein and his partners. This was the property that the consultants had suggested for a museum-entertainment-tourism district (see chapter 19) and that ArtsQuest was hoping to use for SteelStacks. Perrucci was not happy. He and Fischbein knew that developing the Bethlehem Works site would be expensive and that taking ownership of the blast furnaces could entail unforeseen complications, if only because they are so enormous. At Fischbein's suggestion he and Perrucci brought in a partner, Newmark, a New York real estate management firm. The new partnership signed an agreement to purchase the property in May 2004. The principals anticipated gradual development of the property during the next twenty years, including converting the thirteen-story, 1930s-era Bethlehem Steel office building into apartments or condominiums. This building had housed the Steel's offices before construction of Martin Tower. The Perrucci-led partnership had no idea that their opportunities were about to expand exponentially even before they closed on the property on September 17. Neither did anyone else in the community.

MAYOR JOHN B. CALLAHAN

John Callahan is a Bethlehem native of Irish descent. He is ambitious, industrious, gregarious, congenial, and a bit cocky. When he was thirty-two he ran for Bethlehem City Council and won. Two years later, when Mayor Don Cunningham resigned in 2003 to take a cabinet position with newly elected governor Ed Rendell, Callahan announced his candidacy for mayor. The city council had appointed Jim Delgrosso, the council president and the anointed candidate of the Democratic establishment, to serve as interim mayor until the election that November. No one was supposed to challenge Delgrosso in the primary. Callahan defied the party, ran, beat Delgrosso in the primary, and then went on to win the office and embrace his new job with passion even though the salary was half what he had been making in the private sector.

By the time he was sworn in, Callahan had become eager to take on the challenge of the vacant steel plant and understood that his main role was cheerleader and facilitator. As he frequently said, neither the city nor the mayor could redevelop the site, but the city

could open doors, remove barriers, and use its bully pulpit to encourage investment. In April 2004 the newly elected Callahan received a call from a contact at the U.S. Conference of Mayors. Did
he want to present the Bethlehem Works project at the Mayors' Institute on City Design (MICD), scheduled for two weeks hence in
Charleston, South Carolina? A presenter had backed out at the last
minute, and MCID was interested in Bethlehem's unique situation.
The MICD is a partnership of the National Endowment for the Arts,
the American Architectural Foundation, and the U.S. Conference of
Mayors.

At MICD Callahan met Charleston mayor Joseph Riley, who had
gained national recognition for his leadership of that city's revival.
Callahan presented the challenge of redeveloping the steel site to an
experienced team and shared what he knew about Bethlehem Works.
He asked for advice from the experienced group of architects, designers, mayors, and arts experts in the room. The most impressive
piece of advice was "Do not tear down the blast furnaces. They are
a landmark." Two years later we arranged for Callahan to visit Landschaftspark and Volklinger Hutte. SteelStacks had a cheerleader and
a partner who would lead the charge for the development of the
Bethlehem Works site with SteelStacks as part of it. The big questions was where we could find the funding for such a major project
in a small city. That was when opportunity knocked and Callahan
led the charge to open the door.

CHAPTER 23
GAMBLING ON THE FUTURE

For years the Pennsylvania Legislature had discussed the possibility of establishing slot-machine casinos in the state to help with its chronic shortage of revenue. On July 1, 2004, only months after ISG sold the Bethlehem Steel land to LVIP and Perrucci, Fischbein, and Newmark, the legislature surprised everyone by finally adopting a slots gaming law, which Governor Ed Rendell promptly signed on July 5.

Act 71, the Pennsylvania Race Horse Development and Gaming Act, is widely recognized as having successfully launched the gaming industry in the state, which today ranks second only to Nevada in gaming revenues. The new law permitted fourteen licenses for slots parlors, seven of which were to be issued to racetracks and two to resort hotels, leaving five as stand-alones, two of which had to be in Philadelphia and one in Pittsburgh. That left two undesignated. Given the Lehigh Valley's proximity to New Jersey and New York City, everyone agreed that we were destined to get one. Where would it go and which gaming company would develop it? Which Lehigh Valley city would hit the jackpot of host fees, real estate taxes, jobs, and employment taxes?

LAS VEGAS SANDS COMES TO THE CHRISTMAS CITY

Mike Perrucci and his partners were so focused on developing what they now called BethWorks that building a casino was not in their thinking. During the summer of 2004 they announced their purchase of the BethWorks property. They started to think about casinos only after a Bethlehem developer asked to meet with them. The developer and a representative of a casino company showed up in black silk shirts and gold jewelry, according to Perrucci. The pair claimed that, thanks to their political ties, "the deal is in" for obtaining a slots license. They wanted the Perrucci group to sell them twenty-five acres at the eastern end of the BethWorks site for the handsome sum of $250,000 per acre. The new owners would recoup their purchase price and then some by flipping a quarter of the property in a few months. And of course the value of the remaining property would be enhanced with a casino adjacent to it. When another local developer arrived for the meeting and declared, "I smell money in the room," the Perrucci group was not impressed. They made no deal that day but other opportunities soon followed.

Through another business contact, Perrucci soon heard from William Weidner, president of Las Vegas Sands. Meanwhile, one of Perrucci's partners, Barry Gosin of Newmark, was negotiating on behalf of a client for retail space at the Sands properties in Las Vegas. Weidner played it coy, saying that the BethWorks site was one of several they were looking at in Pennsylvania. But Perrucci and his partners recognized the opportunity they had before them. They knew they were in the bull's-eye of tourism and that the site came with an incredible American story. Even better, Bethlehem was host to more than a million visitors each year for Musikfest, Celtic Fest (an annual event in downtown Bethlehem that includes Highland games, crafts, food, and, of course, beer), Christkindlmarkt, and the city's historic sites, events, and colleges. Plus, it's close to New York, which would give a casino easy access to out-of-state revenue.[145]

Within a few months the BethWorks partners had reached an agreement with Las Vegas Sands to develop a casino on the eastern end of the BethWorks site, less than a mile from the Bethlehem exit of I-78. To get the license they would need a plan that would impress the state gaming board.

AN UNLIKELY PARTNERSHIP

A few years earlier Susan and I had toured Australia, taking in beautiful scenery, diverse wildlife, and the Great Barrier Reef. But as a student of urban development, I also was amazed at what the Aussies had done in their inner cities. Sydney gets much of the acclaim, as well it should, for the beauty of the harbor with its iconic opera house and bridge. But Melbourne was more relevant to what we could do in Bethlehem.

One morning during our stay in Melbourne, I walked beyond the historic city center and across the bridge over the Yarra River, where I discovered the South Bank Promenade. I found an architecturally distinguished building that was the Melbourne home of the Australian Broadcasting Company. Across the street was a beautiful new performing arts center. Along the walkway were shops, waterside restaurants with outdoor dining, apartments and condominiums, and a large hotel and casino. After we got home, I learned that the South Bank had been an industrial area that was redeveloped in the early 1990s. The economic anchor was the casino. Gaming is ubiquitous in Australia—in the smallest towns and the largest cities, with few barriers for entry. In all our travels in Europe, Asia, and North America, I had never seen a casino used as an anchor for urban revitalization. It struck me as a brilliant proposition, but I never dreamed that conservative Pennsylvania would come around to casino gaming just a few years later. Seeing the Australian approach prepared me for what was to come.

By 2005, as Perrucci was reaching out to community organizations, he steered ArtsQuest to Gosin by saying that his partners were interested in working with us. Our first meeting was challenging because we had our original plan for a forty-acre cultural park, which was way beyond what the partners were willing to give. However, they said they did want to work with us. I suggested that we could work with less acreage but would like to concentrate on the space around the blast furnaces. They agreed, so we identified the Beth-Works lots (previously laid out by Bethlehem Steel) south and west of the blast furnaces for the location of the SteelStacks Arts and Culture Campus at BethWorks.

At about the same time I shared the concept of SteelStacks with two key donors who had made Musikfest and the Banana Factory possible, Frank Banko and Linny Fowler. Both responded with generous donations totaling $450,000, which allowed us to move forward on the project. That meant consultants, architects, and the freedom to explore the project without having to curtail ArtsQuest programs. It is fair to say that without their early support, the project would have fizzled and died.

One priority was to make sure we had people with the right skills to put the project together. One of my weaknesses is detail work, and this project meant keeping an eye on a lot of details. We needed a detail person. Ron Unger, the board member who came up with the name ArtsQuest, is just such a person. He has a creative streak and is experienced in banking and commercial lending, which would be important to our success. By October, just in time to help ArtsQuest choose an architect, Ron stepped into his new job as director of advancement for ArtsQuest.

Meanwhile, the Sands had been working proactively with Perrucci to develop community support for the proposed casino. Mayor Callahan was on board immediately. All of us recognized that the Las Vegas Sands had a unique pedigree in the gaming industry. The company was credited with leading the effort to make Las Vegas a more family-friendly destination for conventions, conferences, and vacations. The Sands people reiterated that they were interested in creating a destination that would provide their company with revenue streams from hotels, food and beverage sales, and retail to supplement its gaming income. And we were reassured that Las Vegas Sands's vision for the property emphasized respect for the site's history. During my first meeting with Andy Abboud, the government relations officer for the Sands, he said, "We are active in four markets: Las Vegas, Macao, Singapore, and Bethlehem." I replied, "I've never heard those four cities in the same sentence."

By July 2005 the Sands had agreed to be a sponsor of Musikfest '05 and of the Banana Factory's annual fund-raising event. At Musikfest the Sands erected a tent that offered information about its plans and tried to gain community support. We knew our partnership was not without risk. We were diving head first into the most controversial community issue in decades. But like the mayor we understood that no other business had stepped forward to be the anchor for BethWorks, nor was one likely to do so.

Both the casino itself and ArtsQuest's decision to partner with the Sands proved to be controversial. People wrote letters to the editor. Musikfest patrons wrote letters to ArtsQuest. One afternoon during Musikfest, a woman came up to me and said this was her last visit to Musikfest. I said I was sorry to hear that and asked her why. She pointed to the Sands's tent and said, "Because of that. It will bring drugs and prostitution." Did she go to Atlantic City to use the slots? I asked. Yes. Did she use drugs or prostitutes while she was there? "Of course not." I asked her why this casino would be different. She gave me a scowl and walked away.

When the Sands rolled out the plan for BethWorks, SteelStacks was prominent, with buildings grouped around the blast furnaces. The Sands BethWorks team assured us they would donate the land, and they followed that up by negotiating and signing a letter of intent. We had a major in-kind gift, assuming the Sands got the license.

Meanwhile, Perrucci was making countless presentations before church groups, nonprofit organizations, neighborhood groups, and anyone else who invited him. He did not avoid controversy and embraced the opportunity to correct wrong information and assuage misgivings. When John Morganelli, the district attorney, expressed concern about the potential for crime around the casino, Perrucci brought in security experts from Sands to address the issue. Under the state gaming board's rules, state police are always stationed at Pennsylvania's casinos, watching out for the state's share of the take as well as for the safety of the patrons. Casino security teams are visible at all times, and city police are called in as needed to deal with criminal acts.

During this time Perrucci learned that another casino was interested in making an offer for former Bethlehem Steel land now owned by Lehigh Valley Industrial Park adjacent to the I-78 exit. That location would have easier access than the BethWorks site but contribute little to the revitalization of the downtown. Perrucci approached Jeff Feather and the LVIP board. He asked that LVIP not sell the land to another casino and offered to match any offer. Once again, the leadership of LVIP based its decision on what was best for the community, not what would generate the greatest profit. They understood that the Sands BethWorks was a Hail Mary for the SouthSide and the city. LVIP told the community it had no intention of selling the land to a gaming company.

THE HOME STRETCH

The Pennsylvania Gaming Control Board set hearings for April and May 2006 to consider applications for slots licenses. As everyone had anticipated, the most intense competition—six applicants—was for the two stand-alone licenses. In addition to the Sands, Tropicana was pitching a location in Allentown near the new Coca-Cola Park, a baseball park. The consensus was that the Lehigh Valley would get a casino. Two groups, Mount Airy Lodge and Pocono Manor, were competing for a license in the traditional Pocono Mountains tourist area, which is just north of the Lehigh Valley. Two other competitors were from Gettysburg, where defenders of the historic sanctity of the community were opposed to the casino, and Limerick, home to a major outlet mall in the Philadelphia suburbs.

I attended the Sands hearing as a community supporter and to verify its partnership with ArtsQuest. Each applicant submitted massive plans, documents, and, where they could, evidence of community support. To shore up support locally, Sands and local political leaders signed an agreement, which the state legislature incorporated in a statute, that divided the host fee—the revenue going to the community in which the casino is located—among Allentown, Bethlehem, and Easton, and Lehigh and Northampton counties. Even so, as the host city Bethlehem would get more than 50 percent of the host fee.

That June, Sands BethWorks held a reception in the state capitol where it displayed a huge model of the BethWorks site. By then ArtsQuest had lined up more than fifty letters of support for the Sands project from our stakeholders, including many businesses. We also had worked with Perrucci to obtain endorsements from the regional Lehigh Valley Convention and Visitors Bureau and the Lehigh Valley Chamber of Commerce.

The Sands had one issue it would have to resolve before the gaming board's public vote on December 20 to award the licenses. When the City of Bethlehem created the zoning district in which the casino was to be located, the law stated that any legal use not specifically excluded in the ordinance would be permissible. Back then a casino was not a legal use in Pennsylvania, so the city council would have to amend the ordinance. Perrucci, the Sands, and residents on all sides of the issue began lobbying the city council.

Bethlehem's city council has seven members elected at large. Gordon Mowrer, who had become a Moravian minister, was a member in 2006. But the Moravian Conference had passed a motion opposing the casino, and Mowrer had decided to abide by the wishes of his church. Joseph F. Leeson Jr., a former city solicitor (now a federal judge) who was on the council, opposed the casino on the ground that gaming losses would devastate families. Leading council member support for the casino was J. Michael Schweder, a former state representative who had become a vice president of AT&T. Schweder appeared to have solid support from council members Karen Dolan, Magdalena Szabo, and Jean Belinski; the last two were long-time south side residents. The vote of Robert Donchez was in doubt until the Sands signed a nonbinding letter of intent supporting historic preservation of much of the site and promising to incorporate the steel mill in the design of the casino and seek employees from the community. Most council members voting to amend the ordinance pointed to the financial condition of the city. With debt higher than Allentown's, revenues still not back to 1995 levels, and employee retirement benefits increasing, the city needed new sources of revenue. The project was expected to bring $1 billion in improvements to the site. During the council meeting Schweder, the council president, said that he had "learned over the years and lots of debates that a project never ends up being as good as was presented, and it is never as bad as the opponents think it is."[146] But even if the project brought in half the estimated amount of revenue, Bethlehem would be in better shape. Council amended the ordinance, 5–2.

On December 20 a group of us were sitting in the conference room at the Banana Factory to watch a live broadcast of the gaming board's vote on licenses. With great joy we popped a bottle of champagne as Sands BethWorks LLC was announced as one of the recipients of the coveted stand-alone casino licenses. That was the easy part.

CHAPTER 24
DESIGNING A TWENTY-FIRST-CENTURY PERFORMING ARTS CENTER

The hard part was actually planning the SteelStacks project. The first architect we consulted was Barry Pell of the Bethlehem firm Spillman Farmer, which eight years earlier had designed the Banana Factory for ArtsQuest. Pell, a senior member of the firm, and a member of the board of the Pennsylvania Youth Ballet, agreed to do a study to determine whether the programs we wanted would fit on the parcels that Sands BethWorks had agreed to donate.

In early 2005 the nonprofits participating in the project were ArtsQuest, PBS 39, the Hispanic American League of Artists, Pennsylvania Youth Theatre, and Pennsylvania Youth Ballet. The last three organizations had little experience with fund-raising, and the annual budgets of each were less than $500,000. The youth theater and art league were already tenants of the Banana Factory. Our vision for a modern performing arts center incorporated art cinema, a café featuring musicians, a theater for the youth groups, rehearsal and education space, two television studios, and office and support space. A second building, the festival hall, would be a large music performance venue seating four to five thousand.

Pell determined that we could fit everything we wanted into the acreage available, assuming the building could have four stories. Our priority was the performing arts center–public broadcasting station–education center, but the big festival hall stayed in the plan. Our next step was to award the contract for designing the building. Here we took a serious misstep. We had learned in Germany that the blast furnaces were the most significant structures on the site. Like all architecture, they are art. Once illuminated by lighting artists, the furnaces would become round-the-clock artistic expressions.

Because we had never worked with nationally recognized architects before, we retained an adviser and invited some of the most noted architects in the country to come for interviews. We were dazzled. We said we did not want a design that would deflect attention from the blast furnaces. That demonstrated our lack of understanding about how the world of architecture works. Famous architects design buildings that stand out. So we spent more than $100,000 during 2006 and 2007 working with two New York architecture firms and struggled to figure out which programs we could afford to include and a design that would meet our programming and budgetary needs.

By spring 2008 we realized it would be impossible to meet the needs of all the partners and still have an affordable project. The PBS team decided to have a separate building. The station and the performing arts center would be connected to allow for broadcast of shows in the performing arts center but function separately. As the projections of construction costs evolved and fund-raising did not yield what we had hoped, we had to abandon the idea of a theater for youth programs, as well as education space and offices for those programs. Both programs and their offices would have to remain at the Banana Factory arts center and use rental space for theater and dance productions.

Eventually we realized that the architects with whom we were working, while excellent, did not understand our arts community. We also could not afford them. So we came full circle and brought Spillman Farmer back into the project, with Joseph Biondo as the lead architect. The PBS team chose architects with experience in television station design, with Spillman Farmer acting as the on-site architects.

THE DESIGN PROCESS

We settled on the ArtsQuest Center as the name for our new performing arts center. Until then we had not promoted our organizational name, choosing to promote our programs instead, just as General Mills promoted its cereals, not its corporate name. But because we were seeking financial support for a capital campaign, and ultimately for our various programs, we decided that ArtsQuest needed to be a brand, with the ArtsQuest Center at SteelStacks its signature building. We based the design and functions of the center on our understanding of the cultural programs the Lehigh Valley community was lacking and the desire for a place flexible enough to accommodate diverse cultural programs. Looking through that prism is the easiest way to understand the design.

MUSIKFEST CAFÉ

Musikfest had taught us that the Lehigh Valley is a vibrant place for music fans and musicians. But the region lacked a quality space for presenting shows that could not fill a thousand seats or more (the size of the region's three existing performing arts centers). Lehigh Valley venues for rock, jazz, blues, funk, pop, world music, folk, and other genres were small and not always appealing. Our original concept was similar to the World Café Live in Philadelphia, a privately owned club-restaurant that is a partner of public radio station WXPN and its syndicated show, *World Cafe*. This sophisticated space accommodates diverse styles of music.

One of our architects took us to venues in New York City to help us decide what we wanted. While we continued to push the World Café Live example, we were most impressed by Dizzy's Club Coca-Cola, an intimate jazz club in a high rise on Columbus Circle and part of Jazz at Lincoln Center. Dizzy's has a small stage in front of windows that look out on Central Park. The brand is New York jazz. We had the blast furnaces and wanted our stage to be backed by glass looking out on the illuminated blast furnaces. The brand would be pure Bethlehem, steel and music.

The Musikfest Café would be the jewel of the building. Biondo's team did not disappoint. It designed a four-story building; the café occupies the top two stories. In early 2009, only a few months before we were to start construction, Biondo and I had a really heated discussion. He had hired an acoustic engineer who proclaimed that the café's stage had to be at the east end of the room, perpendicular to the windows, for optimum acoustic performance.

My response was, "Figure out how to get the acoustics right with the stage in front of the windows. That's the whole purpose of having this site." With this direction, Biondo and the acoustician designed sound-absorbing materials for the cement walls and the ceiling. The stage is in the center of the windows and equipped with a top-of-the-line sound system. Shows in this venue are a delight, with extraordinary acoustics, lighting, sight lines and breathtaking views of the blast furnaces.

The Musikfest Café is designed to be flexible. The balcony (on the fourth floor) extends about halfway into the room and is suspended so that no columns block the views of patrons at the stage level on the third floor. It has no permanent stage. The stage can be multiple sizes, depending on the show. The only permanent features in the room are bars at the east and west ends and a bar on the west end of the balcony. The room is designed for multiple seating arrangements. The usual arrangement seats 480 at tables and chairs. This format accommodates table service for food and beverages for all patrons. But the café can be reconfigured to accommodate 650 to 750, with rows of seats on the main floor and tables and chairs on the balcony level. This arrangement is used for presenting the most expensive shows. The standing-room-only array for rock and pop music for younger audiences has only a few stools at the bar on the main floor but does have tables and chairs on the balcony and can accommodate as many as a thousand.

The main kitchen for the building also is on the third floor. Designed to support meal service for as many as seven hundred people, it is as flexible as the café and caters public events, fund-raisers for nonprofits, lectures, corporate meetings, and social events.

THE BEALL AND LINNY FOWLER BLAST FURNACE ROOM

The second floor of the performing arts center, like the café, is designed to be multifunctional. The Fowler Blast Furnace Room has glass walls on three sides, including the internal wall that looks out on the first floor, the adjacent open-space loft, the campus, and the blast furnaces. The room is equipped for intimate music concerts but can also be used for dance, theatrical performances, lectures, and spoken-word events with theater seating for three hundred. The room also can be used for dinners and catered events, with as many as 175 guests seated at tables. The loft contains the only space in the building for two-dimensional art exhibits and may be used for receptions for events (usually a dinner or business event) in the Blast Furnace Room.

FRANK BANKO ALEHOUSE CINEMAS

The two-screen art cinema was always meant to be a signature feature of SteelStacks. We originally envisioned fifty seats in one theater, one hundred in the other, but as we were developing the business plan, we learned that film distributors would not look with favor on such small theaters. We wound up splurging on one hundred seats for one screen and two hundred seats for the other in an art cinema that probably would not show a first-run action blockbuster (the average theater in a multiplex has more than 130 seats and fewer than 250).[147] Our experience told us that, even with fixed luxury seats and a bar just outside the doors, making it the first cinema in the region that served beer or other alcoholic beverages, we would need flexibility. Each theater has space for a small stage between the front row and the screen and a lighting grid in the ceiling. We were not sure what these theaters might be used for, but we figured the flexibility was likely to prove valuable.

The first floor of the building was designed to include retail walk-up food service and a bar, dining, and performance space looking out on the blast furnaces, a small gift shop, and a multifunctional space called the Connect Zone that would focus on technology-based programs. The Creativity Commons, also on the first floor, is for community-based music programming, including ethnic cultural programs by college students and performances by local musicians and high school music groups. We also envisioned staging free Saturday morning programming there for families with children aged three to eight.

SANDS DECK

A large outdoor deck on the third floor was the brainchild of Joe Biondo in his initial design presentation who promoted the importance of public space in the building. My immediate response was that it was a luxury that we could not afford, but I could see it had potential, given its view of the blast furnaces and its position next to the main kitchen. The deck, which highlighted a marquis entry to the building as well as offering a hospitality revenue opportunity stayed in the plans and is another nod to Bethlehem Steel. The deck is cantilevered from the roof so that it has no support from below, which means no columns clutter the busy entryway to the building. Because the deck runs the entire width of the building, it was assembled from multiple pieces of steel that had to be bolted together in midair, a first for the builder.

THE ART OF THE ARCHITECTS

Joe Biondo's reverence for the site was evident. He understood that the building could not compete with the blast furnaces. The firm designed a building that made extensive use of steel beams, which are visible inside and out. In a demonstration of how well it knew the community, the firm's presentation showed the beams painted orange. After I ranted about my dislike of the color, they advised that it was the same color as the Golden Gate Bridge. Our building would incorporate the hue as a bow to Bethlehem Steel's enormous stamp on the iconic structures of the United States. I relented.

The design team also inserted a spiral staircase above the main entry foyer to take visitors from the second to the fourth floor. Again, my reaction was that it was too expensive and had no way to pay for itself. Biondo reasoned that the broad stairway afforded a memorable experience for patrons entering and leaving a big show at the Musikfest Café in a building with only two passenger elevators. He was right.

Another element of the design is precast concrete walls with the rough side on the exterior to add to the industrial feel of the site. A final nod to Bethlehem Steel was the giant bolts for lifting and handling the pre-manufactured wall panels are on full display. These usually are hidden and treated to prevent rust, but at the arts center they are visible and untreated, another echo of the industrial history the building is designed to evoke.

THE MARKET

In 1995, way before casinos, Sue Yee, a friend and former Musikfest board member, called me to encourage Musikfest to set up a website on the Internet. Sue's parents, Lee and Stella Yee, pioneers in the cable television industry, established Twin County Cable Television. They had sold the company to RCN, and Sue was involved in her own technology business. She agreed to walk us through the process of getting a URL and establishing a website. In the beginning that meant putting a brochure on the Internet and letting people find it. But by late 2006, as we were preparing our marketing plan for Steel-Stacks, we had more than 100,000 names and email addresses in our database, most from Musikfest. We could use the data to deduce what kind of music potential patrons liked, valuable information for opening a new concert venue.

After examining our database, we decided to target the region within a forty-mile radius. That took us east into central New Jersey, a sea of suburban and exurban residents, and south almost to the Pennsylvania Turnpike, which runs through the northern suburbs of Philadelphia. The area also extends west and north, but the demographics of those markets were less robust than the more affluent suburban communities. The target area included 2.7 million residents, more than the metropolitan population of Pittsburgh or Portland, Oregon. With Internet marketing, our location was no longer a disadvantage. We were free to think big. We could tout the building as a regional cultural center. With a casino going up just a half-mile away, marketing to the same region and then some, we had reason to believe that we could capture this market.

LIVE MUSIC

When we were ready to hire a performing arts director for the facility, we hired Patrick Brogan, a native of Allentown who had been an intern with ArtsQuest while he was a student majoring in event management at Temple University's School of Hospitality and Tourism.

After he graduated from Temple, Brogan worked at the 2004 Olympics in Athens, then settled in Philadelphia to become director of the Philadelphia Film Festival and the Philadelphia Gay and Lesbian Film Festival—big tasks for a recent college graduate. During that time we asked him to manage the main stage for Musikfest, a job that also requires maturity. In 2006 he accepted my invitation to come to the organization full time as director of performing arts. He would be responsible for booking all concerts for the organization, including those for Musikfest, Christkindlmarkt, and eventually SteelStacks and the events to be held there.

Brogan's inherent drive to succeed, break records, and compete against the big guys is a joy to behold, especially in the tight spot of trying to compete for big shows for ten days in August in the greater Philadelphia market. Brogan also is competent and honorable. His reputation as a reasonable person who treats performers well has spread throughout the national music community. Brogan also became the internal adviser for SteelStacks's music and film programs.

The business plan for concerts at the Musikfest Café and the Fowler Blast Furnace Room came directly from the textbooks for concert promotion. Ticket sales from 60 percent of the house must cover the cost of the artists, any additional contract costs (housing, meals, travel), marketing, booking staff, and any other direct concert costs. We were going to rely on sponsorships and food and beverage sales to cover the costs of the performing arts staff and operating the building. Using this basic formula and the seating capacity of the café, Brogan settled on his budget for booking shows—acts with fees from $3,000 to $15,000. These were acts that had not appeared in the Lehigh Valley because it had no permanent venue for them. The plan was to try to present shows three or four evenings a week in the café, with special programs at least once a week in the Fowler Blast Furnace Room.

The business plan for the Creativity Commons and the outdoor Town Square in front of the building was simple. Find sponsors for this free space, and book local artists for shows on Thursday through Saturday evenings, plus family shows on Saturday mornings and concerts by school groups on Sunday afternoons.

Brogan established relationships with the art cinemas in Doylestown and on Philadelphia's Main Line. They generously shared information, and then we devised a plan based on fewer attendees than the Main Line and with below-average pricing. Ticket sales account for 100 percent of the revenue earned by the ArtsQuest cinemas, with 40 to 60 percent of the box office going to the film distributor. The balance pays for the projectionist, equipment, and building expenses related to the theaters.

In early 2010, while the building was under construction, we once again surveyed the community to see what we might be missing on the regional arts scene. We were surprised when one art form stood out—comedy. Until then comedy was not on our radar screen, nor had we intended to include it in our programming. We soon changed our minds. We started with comedy in the Fowler Blast Furnace Room but moved it to the cinemas after we opened. Major comedy acts would appear at the café as the opportunity arose.

HOSPITALITY

By the time we were planning for SteelStacks, Susan Drexinger had made hospitality an essential part of the programming and budget at ArtsQuest. She participated in the design of each part of the building and the campus. As the building took shape and programming began, the only advice I gave to Brogan and Drexinger was that the primary purpose of the building was to present arts programs. When it was not being used as such, rentals were welcome. They worked out a methodology for booking the café and the Blast Furnace Room, including seasonal priorities for concerts and for catering. May and June are the most challenging months: brides versus bands.

In addition to her work at the ArtsQuest Center, Drexinger has worked with Ray Neeb, ArtsQuest's unflappable festival operations guru, to plan the festivals. She has developed the popular Terrace at the new Musikfest main stage, Sands Steel Stage, which offers catering and great seating on both sides of the festival's new main stage at SteelStacks. With her expertise, the revenue from food and beverage sales has become a major factor in the success of ArtsQuest programming.

With food and beverages available to patrons of the Musikfest Café, the Frank Banko Alehouse Cinemas, and the Creativity Commons, as well as a robust hospitality program, we felt confident that we could generate enough revenue to support the expensive operations of the new building, including all that boring stuff—utilities, insurance, security, staff, and maintenance.

We had developed a plan for a performing arts center that would be quite different from those in most communities, especially those in the Rust Belt. Now all we had to do was raise the money to build it.

CHAPTER 25
RAISING MONEY IN A RECESSION

We knew that if we were going to make SteelStacks work, we would need to be creative, aggressive, and lucky. What we did not know when we started in 2007 was that we were about to be hit by the biggest recession since the Great Depression. The individuals and businesses we were hoping would fund the campaign suddenly were watching their business recede and their investments decline. It was not a good time to be asking for major gifts from anyone, including government agencies. By the end of 2008 we had decided to postpone construction of the five-thousand-seat Festival Center building so that we could focus on the ArtsQuest Center and the Public Media Center for our partner, PBS 39. We were counting on the city's redevelopment authority to help make site improvements. But we still needed to raise or borrow $25 million for the ArtsQuest Center, and at least $15 million for the Public Media Center, not to mention money for operating expenses and to support the substantially expanded cultural programming. Yet we believed we would succeed because we knew we were part of a remarkable community.

COMMONWEALTH OF PENNSYLVANIA

The loss of the Bethlehem Steel plant and the consequent challenges to the City of Bethlehem were well known in Harrisburg. While the casino was considered a big "get" for the community, public officials recognized that the development of BethWorks still needed a strong community element. Gaming revenue in 2008 and 2009 allowed the Pennsylvania Legislature to make more money available for the Redevelopment Assistance Capital Program, the state's pot for encouraging urban revitalization. Historically, the governor has distributed half the funds and each house of the legislature controls distribution of a quarter of the money. With Mayor Callahan in the lead, we went to work. With persistent lobbying by Callahan and state senator Lisa Boscola between 2006 and 2010, Governor Rendell agreed to earmark $8 million from his allocation for the ArtsQuest Center and PBS 39.

The Lehigh Valley legislative delegation has not always been aggressive in generating support in Harrisburg. However, with the emergence of the region as the third-largest metropolitan area in the state, and the gradual shift of house and senate districts to the more populous eastern side of the state, the delegation has become more unified. That, and the rise of Pat Browne of Allentown to the senate leadership, gave the region more clout. With the support of Browne and Boscola, as well as assistance from state representative T. J. Rooney, the legislative delegation eventually released another $6 million for SteelStacks, bringing the total for the ArtsQuest Center to $8 million, with $4 million for PBS 39 and an additional $2 million to put toward the deferred five-thousand-seat Festival Center.

Browne recommended that we also consider tapping another legislative program, the Neighborhood Partnership Program, a community revitalization program that grants tax credits to businesses that contribute to it. The south side of Bethlehem met all the demographic and economic criteria for this program. In 2008, when we began the application process, no arts organization had ever qualified for this program. However, ArtsQuest was already serving the south side community through the Banana Factory programs.

Businesses participating in the Neighborhood Partnership Program must commit to $50,000 per year for at least six years and a maximum of ten years. The business receives a 75 to 80 percent tax credit for monies donated to the program. We were able to sign up five companies with a total commitment of more than $4 million. Although we could apply only the first two years of payments directly to the costs of construction, the balance would help pay for the first eight years' operating expenses for programs.

NORTHAMPTON COUNTY

When the state legislature allowed counties in the Lehigh Valley to increase their hotel tax from 3.5 to 4 percent in 2005, Lehigh County pledged the difference to support development in Allentown of Coca-Cola Park, home to the Lehigh Valley Iron Pigs, a AAA team affiliated with the Phillies. Northampton County, which was surprised by the legislature's decision, increased its hotel tax and then increased its grants to nonprofit organizations with programs that supported tourism. We approached County Executive John Stoffa and members of Northampton County Council for $1 million for the ArtsQuest Center and a similar grant for PBS 39. Stoffa and the council set aside a fixed percentage of Northampton County's portion of the hotel tax for construction of SteelStacks; the county expected to provide $2 million over ten years. It was the council's first capital grant to a tourism-related project. Because the new hotels, casino, and additional tourism in the county generated more money than the county anticipated in 2005, it was able to meet its pledge in fewer than eight years.

The county's unprecedented use of hotel tax revenue sent the message to others in the community that SteelStacks was a priority, and it proved to be an important step in our capital campaign.

TAX INCREMENT FINANCING

When Bethlehem Steel and the city agreed to establish a tax increment financing (TIF) district for the Bethlehem Works Redevelopment Area in 2000, no one ever envisioned the district would include a casino. The TIF meant that any additional tax revenue generated by the site would be plowed back into it for infrastructure and public amenities. When the casino opened on May 22, 2009, it became responsible for real estate taxes based on the improved property, which was assessed at $250 million. Because of the TIF, the city, county, and school district sent the increase in real estate tax revenues to the Bethlehem Redevelopment Authority. This revenue gave the redevelopment authority the means to support SteelStacks. Callahan appointed Tony Hanna, his director of community and economic development, as executive director of the redevelopment authority. Hanna's extensive experience in redevelopment and real estate projects was critical to the partnership of the city and SteelStacks.

The redevelopment authority agreed to bear responsibility for all site improvements at SteelStacks outside the walls of the ArtsQuest Center and the PBS 39 buildings. The redevelopment authority also negotiated with Sands BethWorks Retail LLC, the partnership of the original Perrucci group and Sands that owned the land that became SteelStacks, to acquire land directly in front of the blast furnaces for an outdoor concert venue, and the Stock House, the oldest building on the site at the western end of the blast furnaces, for a visitor center. The TIF would pay for all improvements to those properties, as well as parking lots, signs for SteelStacks, running utilities to the properties, and various other expenses. It would also pay for improvements totaling more than $4 million for the space in front of the ArtsQuest Center and the parking lot across the street that is owned by ArtsQuest and now is called PNC Plaza.

With an additional grant of $200,000 from the Pennsylvania Department of Environmental Protection through Northampton County for minor environmental remediation, total government funding for the ArtsQuest portion of SteelStacks was just under $15 million, 40 percent of the money raised for the campaign.

NEW MARKET TAX CREDITS

The New Markets Tax Credit (NMTC), created by Congress in 2000, was designed to increase the flow of capital to businesses in low-income communities by providing private investors with a tax incentive. Congress set an annual cap for the credits, and the U.S. Treasury reviews applications for these complex tax credits, which are extremely competitive, and the mechanism is complicated. Basically, investors put money into a project and get a tax credit in return. SteelStacks was the first such project in the Lehigh Valley. With the help of a team of consultants, lawyers, and accountants, we obtained an allocation of tax credits equal to the total cost of the ArtsQuest Center ($25 million). One out-of-town bank, U.S. Bank, bought all the credits, the full $25 million. The process was long, convoluted, and excruciating. But the New Market Tax Credits yielded a net of almost $5 million, 15 percent of the money raised for the campaign.

FOUNDATIONS AND GRANTS

Despite the wealth that has accrued to Bethlehem residents through the years of industrial might, few foundations serve the community. Neighboring Allentown has the Harry C. Trexler Trust, which supports Allentown's excellent parks system and provides substantial grants to charities throughout Lehigh County. For SteelStacks we had to raise money like never before. But first we approached the R. K. Laros Foundation, the only one in Bethlehem that invests in capital projects. The family foundation focuses on organizations such as St. Luke's Hospital, Moravian College, and the Bethlehem Public Library. It had supported the development of, and improvements to, the Banana Factory. Its early pledge of $100,000 to SteelStacks was important to us and to the success of the projects.

We also approached the Michigan-based Kresge Foundation, which has a national reach for its capital grants in the arts. Kresge had helped fund the Banana Factory and the 2002 expansion. We received a $900,000 grant from Kresge. In all, we received $1.425 million, 4 percent of the money we raised, from foundation grants, including support from the local Keystone Savings Foundation, the Bank of America Foundation, and the Education Foundation of America; the last focuses on renewal of distressed communities.

The National Endowment for the Arts held a special grant competition in 2010 to celebrate the twenty-fifth anniversary of the Mayors' Institute on City Design, the organization whose conference Mayor Callahan had attended. We applied for a grant to pay for a sculpture for the Town Square. Only twenty-one of these grants were issued, and we got one for $200,000 for the sculpture. We were thrilled that we had gained national recognition for the arts aspects of the project and that the special grants were announced in Bethlehem that year. We were becoming the poster child for creative placemaking before we even opened.

CORPORATE SUPPORT

With more than twenty years of relationships with sponsors, we had high expectations for the response of our business community, and they were not misplaced. We sought contributions from our business partners for two needs, construction money and operating funds for SteelStacks once it opened. We knew that many businesses would find it easier to sponsor programs rather than to donate to the capital campaign, because many companies do not include capital campaigns in their philanthropy policies.

Because we were able to offer major donors tax credits through the Neighborhood Partnership Program (NPP), an array of branded sponsorships for programs, and naming opportunities for rooms in the building, we were able to offer donation options that addressed the capabilities, community relations, and marketing needs of many of our current and would-be partners. John McGlade, the CEO of Air Products, a major manufacturer of industrial gases with more than two thousand employees in the Lehigh Valley, has deep roots here. He grew up in Bethlehem and graduated from Lehigh University. As I explained SteelStacks, he became quite enthusiastic. He and his family had attended every Musikfest, and his son was in a band that had often played at Musikfest. McGlade agreed to serve on the leadership team for fund-raising, and he and his wife, Brenda, gave a generous gift.

PNC Bank, also a long-term partner of ArtsQuest, supported SteelStacks as part of its engagement with lower-income communities. The *Morning Call* supported the project with substantial in-kind assistance, which was important for both the capital campaign and the marketing of the new campus in the region. John Walson of Service Electric Cable Television, the family-owned regional cable service, signaled his family's support of ArtsQuest by wiring the entire SteelStacks campus for Internet, telephone, and television and adding a closed fiber optic cable system that connects SteelStacks to the Banana Factory seven blocks away. Chris Martin, the seventh-generation leader of C. F. Martin & Company, continued his company's involvement with ArtsQuest by sponsoring the entryway to the Musikfest Café, the Martin Guitar Lobby.

I had gotten to know Dick Yuengling through Frank Banko. Yuengling is outspoken, even brash, and one of the best people in the world to call a friend. He also makes really good beer. Yuengling beer was available at Musikfest for many years. Like his friend Chris Martin, Yuengling is the seventh-generation owner of his family business, the D. G. Yuengling & Sons Brewery, in Pottsville, Pennsylvania. Yuengling thought I was crazy when he met me at the empty steel plant and I told him what we planned to do. But he was familiar with doing the impossible because he had taken over a small family-owned brewery at a time when big beer was wiping out small breweries and had grown it into a major craft beer distributed in more than twenty states. A year later, as we were walking through the partially built Musikfest Café, he was pleasantly surprised. From then on, it would be the "Musikfest Café Presented by Yuengling."

In all, fifty businesses signed up to support SteelStacks. Their support included the more than $4 million in NPP funds to support construction for two years and then operating costs for as long as eight years; $2.08 million to support the first five years of operating expenses; more than $4.8 million of in-kind capital support, including Sands BethWorks's donation of the property; and $1.665 million in cash support for the building fund. In all, the business community contributed 30 percent of the money raised for the SteelStacks campaign.

INDIVIDUAL GIFTS

In 2006 we had hired the North Group, Halsey and Alice North, to do a feasibility study for a capital campaign for SteelStacks. The firm's expertise and experience in fund-raising for nonprofit arts centers guided our plans. We formed a leadership team and began a long series of conversations, first with those we asked to be on the team, then with those whose support we sought. We had leadership gifts in hand from the Fowlers and Frank Banko, but we knew we had much more to do.

Sam Torrence, then the newly retired CEO of Just Born, the candy company, learned about the SteelStacks project and asked to be involved in the fund-raising. He chaired the ArtsQuest Board of Trustees and the leadership committee. He earned our gratitude for his assistance as we reached out to old and new friends as we sought support for the project. He was joined by Jack Yaissle, founder of Cornerstone Advisors, who became involved with ArtsQuest in the early 2000s by offering support for the Banana Factory and our work with Holy Infancy School. Yaissle, who was a few years ahead of me at Lehigh, is a brilliant business adviser, primarily to family-owned businesses with annual revenues exceeding $50 million. From Torrence and Yaissle the staff received the encouragement and support we needed to forge ahead. And they helped us attract $4.5 million in individual gifts, 14 percent of the money we raised.

At the end of the capital campaign we had commitments totaling $36.75 million (through 2011) to erect the ArtsQuest Center and to support operating programs, not counting what PBS 39 had raised for its building. Of the $36.75 million, almost $10 million comprised pledges for sponsorship of programs or participation in the tax credit program, which had to be used to run programs after the first two years. This was great because we anticipated the need to increase our annual budget from about $12 million to more than $18 million. About $7 million of the $36.75 million was in-kind support—donation of the land, improvements to the Town Square by the redevelopment authority, and space in various media for promoting the campaign. However, these in-kind donations did not count as cash to pay for the building.

Most of the rest of the pledges were to be paid over a period of three to ten years. The state's $8 million was a reimbursement, which meant that we had to temporarily borrow the money (and pay interest) to pay the building costs, architects, engineers, and so forth. The state reimbursed us after we demonstrated that we had paid the money for its intended purpose. The county paid its $1 million donation over seven years. Our organization was well regarded in the community, but vendors insisted on cash, not pledges. All this meant that we had to assume debt, lots of it. We borrowed against the state's pledge for the full $8 million. We borrowed $3.5 million against the Banana Factory to put equity into the project, a loan that we expected to become the long-term debt on the project. And in case the donors did not honor their pledges quickly enough to pay for the project, we borrowed $4 million from a regional loan pool of banks. They had created the pool to support community development projects like SteelStacks. In early 2011, right before we opened SteelStacks, the board of ArtsQuest asked me how much our long-term debt would be after all the dust settled. I responded that if fund-raising continued to go well, I thought it would be about $6 million, perhaps a maximum of $8 million. I was close but no cigar. In February 2017, at the conclusion of the seven-year term of the New Market Tax Credits, ArtsQuest refinanced the debts incurred for construction and initial operation of SteelStacks—they came to $8.14 million.

CHAPTER 26
STEELSTACKS
CAMPUS, STAFF, AND PROGRAMS

Designing the building for ArtsQuest Center was only one piece of the design process. We still had to design the outdoor spaces, including stages, a visitor center, public art, and even parking lots. We were also going to have to add staff to run all of ArtsQuest's new ventures.

In late 2008 Tony Hanna, executive director of the redevelopment authority, led the selection process for the site design team. We chose the Philadelphia-based landscape architecture firm of Wallace Roberts & Todd to design SteelStacks. Hanna, a Lehigh University grad, reads six newspapers daily and has a passion for urban revitalization and an encyclopedic knowledge of state and federal programs. He is also an architect maven. When the mayor asked him to become director of the Bethlehem Redevelopment Authority, he was already directly involved in BethWorks, the tax increment financing (TIF) district, plans for Route 412 (the long-stalled artery between I-78 and the entrance to SteelStacks), and preliminary work on the Bethlehem Commerce Center because he'd been the city's director of community and economic development.

After Hanna introduced us to Wallace Roberts & Todd, we asked the firm to design the "town square of the twenty-first century"; it would become the Air Products Town Square, a space in front of ArtsQuest and PBS, each of which had different concepts for its use. The space needed to be coherent but allow for multiple functions. Two fire sculptures would adorn the plaza, one large steel sculpture that would form an arch from the Town Square over First Street toward the blast furnaces and a smaller sculpture titled *Alchemy* that celebrated Air Products and its mastery of pulling gases, such as oxygen, hydrogen, and helium, out of air. PBS wanted a grassy space from which people could watch the outdoor screen that would carry its broadcast all day. And ArtsQuest wanted a small stage at the west end of the Town Square to feature local bands during warm weather evenings, as well as various types of performances during festivals. We had asked the landscape firm to design a larger stage in front of the blast furnaces that ArtsQuest would use for summer concerts featuring regional and national shows, especially during Musikfest. First Street was straight and ran parallel to the blast furnaces. The only option was to place the stage perpendicular to the furnaces and have audiences sit next to them on a long narrow strip of land. The arrangement was not great for viewing the stacks. But things changed.

LEVITT PAVILION

In January 2009 Philip Horn, executive director of the Pennsylvania Council on the Arts, invited me to be on a panel at the Association of Performing Arts Presenters conference that would discuss how to present free concerts. Among the panelists was Liz Levitt Hirsch. Hirsch's parents, Mortimer and Mimi Levitt, were supporters of an outdoor music pavilion in Westport, Connecticut, near their summer home. When the pavilion needed to be rebuilt, they made a generous donation, and the organization named the venue the Levitt Pavilion. The Levitts were thrilled with the way the outdoor concerts brought the community together. In 1999, when the Levitts sold their business, they put assets into a foundation and began planning a national network of Levitt venues. As I listened to Liz talk about the foundation's requirements for its outdoor pavilions, I felt like peanut butter had just met jelly. To become the site of a Levitt pavilion, a community needs to have a dedicated organization with a volunteer board, a supportive city government, and the fund-raising capacity to make it happen. Levitt lawns must seat at least twenty-five hundred, and the foundation requires the pavilions to offer fifty live free family concerts annually. Seating must be on the lawn—no permanent chairs or benches. That requirement is a great equalizer for a community. Levitt pays a portion of the construction costs and provides a portion of the annual operating expenses.

Within a year the Levitt Foundation, ArtsQuest, and the City of Bethlehem had reached an agreement for the new Levitt Pavilion SteelStacks. The team of landscape architects had a plan to bump out First Street at its intersection with Founders Way, the main entrance to the campus. The pavilion would go up at the base of the blast furnaces, and the audience would face the pavilion. It would have a swooping modern design, with the stage roof made of steel. That arrangement dictated that the backstage functions be placed adjacent to the stage, extending to the concession stand at the far end. Brilliant. The audience, which I join as often as possible, faces a fantastic stage with the illuminated blast furnaces towering over it. In early and late summer the scene changes as the sun sets and the moon and stars slowly reveal themselves. It is a stage like no other.

BETHLEHEM VISITOR CENTER

Given our magnificent historic site, we knew we needed a visitor center. The Stock House at the western end of the blast furnaces was the ideal size and location for one. Working with Hanna, we identified three functions for the building: guest services and site interpretation, restrooms, and offices for ArtsQuest staff to run this massive enterprise.

We were acutely aware of the importance of the site that we were going to occupy and wanted to be as prepared as possible to provide the public with information about Bethlehem Steel. We hired Lou Reda Productions of Easton to create a thirty-minute film about the history of Bethlehem that incorporates the history of the Steel. Over the years Reda has purchased major newsreel libraries, and his company is a major contributor to shows on the History Channel. *Bethlehem—The Christmas City* introduces the city and the site to visitors. We also asked the Historic Bethlehem Partnership, now Historic Bethlehem Museums and Sites, to create a walking tour. It is the only history organization that runs daily scheduled tours in the city.

Gregg Feinberg is a real estate developer whom the redevelopment authority hired to act as owner's representative for construction of the SteelStacks campus. He used to joke that the large number of bathrooms at the visitor center were built just for me. And in fact I was obsessed with generous accommodations because of my decades as a tourist and festivalgoer who often found the availability and cleanliness of bathrooms lacking. I insisted that we have facilities that could handle the large audiences for Musikfest and other events.

PNC PLAZA

At ArtsQuest we always joked that we hated to see an empty park or parking lot. We can erect tents, a stage, and food concessions in no time. Because our plans called for moving some of Musikfest and all of Christkindlmarkt to SteelStacks, and we expected to add other successful festivals at the base of the blast furnaces, we needed flexible space—open and paved, with plenty of power, as well as water and sewer capacity. That space was realized in PNC Plaza, which is covered with pavers and extends from the western end of the blast furnaces between the Visitor Center and the Steel's old Turn and Grind Shop, continuing into macadam that serves as a parking lot when not covered with tents, stages, or other event paraphernalia. At PNC Plaza we could fest to our heart's content.

PUBLIC ART

We could not have an arts campus without public art. With support from the National Endowment for the Arts Mayors Institute grant, we ran a national competition for the design of the large fire sculpture. We wanted a work that reflected the past but also expressed the aspirations of the community. The winner was a concept by the Scranton native Elena Columbo, a simple arch of Corten steel that is seventy-two feet long, incorporating a thirty-seven-foot burner and flame. The arch rises from its base on the Air Products Town Square and reaches toward the blast furnaces. The names of the major bridges, buildings, and ships built by Bethlehem Steel are engraved on the base. The natural gas flame is lighted at the end of major concerts and on other special occasions. Titled *The Bridge,* the sculpture reminds the viewer of the many structures built by Bethlehem Steel and also marks the journey from the past to the future.

When the Air Products team saw the design, they asked Elena to design a smaller fire feature for the interior of the plaza, within view of the first-floor windows of ArtsQuest Center. *Alchemy* is beautiful and practical, offering warmth during spring and fall events on Town Square.

Our public art embraced neon after Stephen Antonakos, known for his abstract neon art on buildings around the world, had an exhibit at Lafayette College in 2008. Antonakos is a native of Greece and lived in New York; most major American museums of modern art collect his work. In the 1920s through the 1950s neon was everywhere on the south side. I thought Antonakos would provide a fitting tribute to this now fading art form, and it would be a great way to add some color to the grays, blacks, and browns that tend to predominate at BethWorks. But Antonakos saw a different opportunity. We invited him to have his way with the main entry facade of the building on Founders Way. He designed simple abstract neon lines in blue and green that highlight the entrance, with an orange elbow that sticks out into the Air Products Town Square to signal visitors that they should explore the other side of the building. In honor of SteelStacks the work is titled *Transformation*.

But our public art doesn't stop there. While Salma Arastu and her husband lived in the Lehigh Valley, she was an artist at the Banana Factory. She was born into a Hindu family in India and later embraced Islam through her marriage. Arastu arrived in this world with the life-defining challenge of a left hand without fingers, but that did not stop her from pursuing her life's passion. Hers is a beautiful soul, and her art reflects it. She approached me soon after SteelStacks was announced to express her desire to create public art. When we had to decide on a piece for the plaza at the visitor center, her work came to mind. The aluminum work with rising figures is titled *Celebration of Life*.

Joe Biondo's spiral staircase, with a vacant circular space in the middle, provided an opportunity for the ArtsQuest Glass Studio. We invited the ArtsQuest glass artists to design a glass piece to extend the three stories of the spiral. John Choi and Dennis Gardner created *The Four Elements*, a 760-piece sculpture of blown and stained glass. It depicts plants, flowers, and rocks at the second floor; at the third floor blue stained-glass panels are water, and white clouds of blown glass represent air; and blown-glass red and orange flames are fire at the fourth floor.

Of course, the mighty blast furnaces are the dominant display. In 2009 the Sands created lighting for the furnaces that paints the structures with colors, which can be changed. The community embraced the illumination, soon requesting green during the Girl Scout cookie drive, red during the Red Cross's annual giving campaign, or blue to mark Autism Month. As anticipated, the furnaces have again become part of the community's daily life, albeit in a much different way than when they created steel for the world.

With the design complete, construction of the campus began in earnest. Our goal was to complete the work by May 2011, when we planned to hold the formal opening for the ArtsQuest Center. And we planned to open the Levitt Pavilion with full programming at the same time (we didn't quite make it and opened on the long July Fourth weekend instead).

ASSEMBLING THE TEAM

Any successful venture requires a team of leaders capable of making the venture a reality. We already had key members of the ArtsQuest team in place, but we realized that we needed additional expertise and that we needed those experts on staff before SteelStacks opened. In 2008 the position of director of sponsor relations for ArtsQuest became open. That led us to Katherine "Kassie" Hilgert of Air Products, who handled community relations there. But she was doing well at Air Products, and ArtsQuest had limited resources to woo her. Somehow we managed to, and Hilgert soon came aboard as the ArtsQuest vice president in charge of sponsorship and marketing. She soon brought in another talent, Curt Mosel. He and his wife had moved to the Lehigh Valley to be near his wife's parents. Our good luck—he had experience marketing for the NBA's Minnesota Timberwolves.

Julie Benjamin came to Bethlehem by way of Spain and Miami. The Ohio native had worked in Seville for ten years before moving to Miami, where she raised money for public television. She came to Bethlehem to handle fund-raising at PBS 39. As the campaign for SteelStacks began, Benjamin was my counterpart at the station and eventually came to work for ArtsQuest, responsible for grants, membership, and coordinating the capital campaign. She was our first senior staff member who was fluent in Spanish. She also became instrumental in managing and establishing a dedicated group of volunteers for the Levitt Pavilion program.

Cindy Karchner and her husband are fans of music and the arts. Their passion is going to concerts and photographing their experiences. Vacations almost always include a special concert by a favorite musician. They live near Allentown, but she was commuting to Reading where she worked in human resources for a manufacturing company. In 2010 she replied to ArtsQuest's ad for an HR person. We desperately needed an HR professional for a staff that was growing to fifty full-time and more than 250 seasonal and part-time employees. Karchner signed on.

Throughout my career I have been blessed with assistants who are smart, good communicators, and quite capable of helping me with time management, my Achilles heel. As SteelStacks came closer to reality, my assistant, a single mother with two children, received an offer she could not refuse and took it. Referring to the 1970s television program *M*A*S*H*, Hilgert said that I needed a Radar O'Reilly, someone who knew what I needed before I did and who could knew how to make it happen. We found her in Joann Lee, the manager of a real estate office who had been cut back to part time during the Great Recession. Lee's energy and capacity quickly filled a void, not just for me but also for other members of the team. She dealt with scheduling issues painlessly, providing me with the time to keep the project moving forward.

Margaret Raymond was a Musikfest volunteer who chaired the Musikfest ball in the 1990s. Her husband, John, is an engineer who had been responsible for building billion-dollar power plants in Turkey and Venezuela, among other assignments. In 2008 Maggie Raymond advised me that her husband had retired but was bored. Direct and a man of few words, he has few filters—bluntness had been an asset in building technical projects in foreign countries where he battled corruption while making sure contracts were fulfilled. We got along famously after he joined ArtsQuest as our owner's representative, the person who represents the owner in dealings with the construction manager, architect, and other members of the construction team.

The Alvin H. Butz Company, based in Allentown, is a large regional construction manager with a history of building projects for nonprofit institutions. Butz had done the Banana Factory construction and became our choice for building the ArtsQuest Center.

We held the formal groundbreaking for SteelStacks on October 28, 2009. Mayor Callahan, Governor Rendell, Linny Fowler, Frank Banko, and more than two hundred guests celebrated how far we had come in a relatively short time. With a growing leadership team, SteelStacks was under way, six years after our visit to the Ruhr Valley.

A FLOCK OF FESTIVALS

As 2010 began and our opening date approached, our to-do list was long. Always at the top was raising more money. With the community slowly recovering from the recession, this was difficult. The deficiencies in our fund-raising would become evident during the next three years, but we were ever hopeful. We operated the largest free music festival in the world, and we were confident that we knew about festivals, music, and our community.

Musikfest

First we had to decide how Musikfest would be incorporated into SteelStacks. Some in the community worried that the entire festival was going to move to SteelStacks and be gated. That would have been antithetical to our mission of revitalization, since removing Musikfest from the north side downtown would have a negative effect on its businesses and economic welfare. Besides, the festival would not fit in the SteelStacks space.

However, PNC Plaza, designed with power, lighting, and running water, would support Musikfest's new Sands Steel Stage, a big temporary stage that we have made Musikfest's main stage. The plaza is ideal for major concerts, a vast improvement over the isolated, difficult-to-use RiverPlace on Sand Island. As a bonus the stage can be placed at the western end of the illuminated blast furnaces, a dramatic backdrop for any performance. And the audience is no more than two hundred feet from the stage, instead of as far as six hundred feet away. With a parking lot right across the street, our VIP guests and those with disabilities have nearby parking.

The second platz to move was Americaplatz. It moved to the new Levitt Pavilion, where Americaplatz music continues with a beautiful stage and a grassy space with some chairs. The residents of New Street near City Center Plaza are able to enjoy Musikfest without enduring the crowds at the old Americaplatz, and the Levitt Pavilion has proved to be a much better site for music, food, and beer.

All other traditional Musikfest platzes have remained where they were. At SteelStacks we added new programming, including concerts in the Musikfest Café, the two cinemas, and on the Air Products Town Square, alternating with Americaplatz shows at Levitt. The only programs we deleted were the ticketed Candlelight Concerts at Moravian College's Foy Hall and the Asa Packer Series at Zoellner Arts Center so that we could focus our efforts on the SteelStacks shows.

Although SteelStacks is only seven blocks from Plaza Tropical, the downtown home base for Latino music, we realized that the distance might be challenging for many festival attendees. We started bus service between the two sites, with a one-way fee of fifty cents or $2 for the day. Volunteers and members use the service for free. We did all this knowing that many people feel great ownership of Musikfest. We hoped that they would embrace the change, given the year-round benefit of SteelStacks.

Christkindlmarkt

When we announced the plan for SteelStacks, we also announced that Christkindlmarkt would be moving there. No longer would that event be subject to freak fall flooding from the Monocacy, poor vendor access, and lousy parking for customers. PNC Plaza's infrastructure provided better accommodations and would allow expansion, again with much better parking access. The downtown merchants had become accustomed to the retail traffic that Christkindlmarkt attracted. In reaction to the loss of the market, they announced that they would operate a new Weihnachtsmarkt (Christmas Market) in the Sun Inn Courtyard. This smaller event with about fifteen booths created some seasonal expansion of the Main Street retail mix and encourages visitors to Christkindlmarkt to be sure to visit Main Street, especially with seasonal trolley service running between the two locations.

Working with Just Born Quality Confections, we created Peeps Fest at the Christkindlmarkt tent in 2009. At SteelStacks we would celebrate Peeps Fest with a New Year's Eve Peeps Fest 5K, two days of family activities inside the ArtsQuest Center (December 30 and 31), using most of the building, and fireworks at 5:15 on the thirty-first, in time to get the children home and in bed at a reasonable hour.

Five New Fests

The sensible thing to do in a new business is to add products gradually. We were not sensible. We got excited about five new festivals so we included them in our plans:

- *RiverJazz*—Each May RiverJazz would feature regional and national jazz artists at our fixed venues at SteelStacks, indoors and out.
- *Sabor ("Taste")*—We worked with local Latino organizations and committees to provide a festival that focuses on a different country's heritage each year. The festival features the food, music, dance, and culture of that year's country.
- *SteelJam*—This festival at the Levitt Pavilion would be for jam band lovers on Labor Day weekend, but unlike the Levitt concerts, we would fence the audience area and charge admission.
- *Blast Furnace Blues*—Set for the lingering days of summer, the second weekend of September, the blues festival would feature a favorite music of the Lehigh Valley and be held indoors and at the Levitt Pavilion, with ticketed admission.
- *Oktoberfest*—The first two weekends of October would be filled with the sound of "Ein Prosit," the smell of bratwurst, and the taste of great beer.

Great ideas all—if only we'd paid attention to the old Yiddish proverb "Man plans and God laughs."

Patriotic Holidays, Markets, and Family Fun

SteelStacks was designed for community celebrations and events. Our plan included special activities for Memorial Day weekend, Independence Day, Veterans Day, and Flag Day.

In the 1990s we had started a farmer's market on the former Broad Street Mall to bring more activity into the downtown. But the ill-fated Marktplatz lasted only two summers. Farmers markets are difficult to organize and run, expensive to market, and subject to weather. So we decided to do it again at SteelStacks and got similar results. Who says we learn from our failures? I still like farmers markets. Fortunately, Easton and Allentown have great farmers markets. We also aspired to an antiques market, but it slipped off the charts as we became overwhelmed with other activities.

Family programming always has been a priority for ArtsQuest. At SteelStacks we planned family shows in the Creativity Commons every Saturday morning, and these have been successful. But family movies, also on Saturday morning, were not successful. We continue to hold family-friendly concerts at the Levitt. Partnerships with school music groups have led to performances at the Capital Blue Cross Creativity Commons every Sunday afternoon, a great opportunity for students to get experience performing in a public place.

CAREENING TOWARD COMPLETION

In late June 2010 we invited our supporters to SteelStacks for the topping-off ceremony. Our guests signed the last beam, which a crane raised into place in the ceiling of the Musikfest Café. It was an emotional moment as the beam, topped with an evergreen tree and an American flag, swung in front of the blast furnaces, then to the top of the building.

We barely noticed as Musikfest 2010 flew by and we approached the last downtown Christkindlmarkt before the SteelStacks opening in May. In a flurry of activity Kassie Hilgert led the development of a new ArtsQuest logo that added Bethlehem Steel's "I-beam" inside the Q, and our colors became orange and blue to reflect the bright orange of the new building. The designers also came up with our tagline, "Imagine that!," which embraces the organization's reputation for creativity.

In the 1990s we had added three volunteer councils, one each for Musikfest, Christkindlmarkt, and the Banana Factory. The role of these councils was to work with the staff to develop and manage our three major programs. With SteelStacks nearly ready to open, we eliminated the councils and created boards for the visual arts, performing arts, and cultural events, each with two representatives on the board of trustees. (The cultural events board was discontinued in 2013 as it struggled to find a role in the organization.) To satisfy the requirements of the national Levitt organization, we created a subsidiary nonprofit, Friends of Levitt Pavilion SteelStacks, which also has two representatives on the ArtsQuest board. Altogether, we had more than seventy-five volunteers on our boards; they represent two thousand volunteers and the community.

One of the biggest decisions we had to make was the selection of a food service company. We had the option of creating a massive food service operation, something with which we had no internal expertise or history. We wisely chose to partner with a food service company. We picked Aramark, which had been our partner for Musikfest hospitality for several years. We knew the organization and its team had been part of the growth of our hospitality revenue. Aramark also had experience working with arts centers, as well as other tourism-related operations. We hoped our relationship would weather some of the challenges we would face in starting a new business.

With each decision and each passing month, we drew closer to opening day. In February, 2011, Patrick Brogan walked into my office one day and proclaimed, "Today is a historic day. For the rest of my tenure here, there will never be a day when we do not have concert tickets on sale. The first Musikfest Café shows go on sale tomorrow." Nor will there be a day when we are not worried about ticket sales, I thought.

MUSIKFEST 2011
North Side Downtown

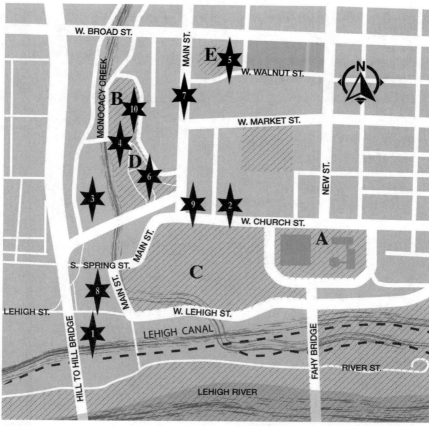

VENUES
1. Banana Island
2. Chamber Series
3. Festplatz
4. Handwerkplatz
5. Liederplatz
6. Lyrikplatz
7. Main Street
8. Plaza Tropical
9. Vesper Concerts
10. Volksplatz

PARKS, PLAZAS, HISTORIC SITES
A. Bethlehem City Center Plaza
B. Johnston Park
C. Moravian College Priscilla Payne Hurd Campus
D. Moravian Colonial Industrial Quarter
E. Sun Inn Courtyard

MUSIKFEST 2011
South Side

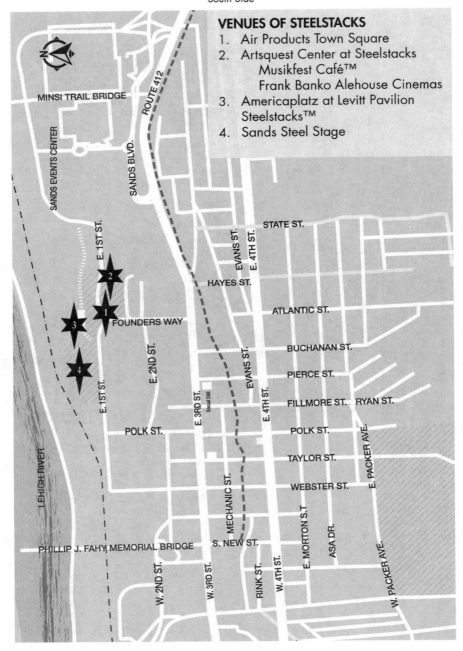

VENUES OF STEELSTACKS
1. Air Products Town Square
2. Artsquest Center at Steelstacks
   Musikfest Café™
   Frank Banko Alehouse Cinemas
3. Americaplatz at Levitt Pavilion
   Steelstacks™
4. Sands Steel Stage

CHAPTER 27
A NEW ERA BEGINS

T he grand opening gala for major supporters of the ArtsQuest Center was held on April 30, 2011, a day before the public grand opening. On a beautiful warm Saturday, five hundred guests celebrated the opening of the ArtsQuest Center with cocktails and hors d'oeuvres in the Air Products Town Square and the Capital Blue Cross Creativity Commons, followed by dinner and a show by the Steve Miller Band in the Musikfest Café Presented by Yuengling. Miller is a friend of Martin Guitar's Dick Boak, who worked with us to arrange the appearance of the rock icon. A new age of live music had dawned in the Lehigh Valley.

The next day the first public concert in the café featured seasoned regional acts led by Craig Thatcher. We wanted to make a statement that while many shows at the café were going to be by people with national reputations, the café also was a new home for regional artists.

For the public grand opening, we wanted something that the Lehigh Valley had never seen, so we booked Mass Ensemble, a Southern California group that plays New Age music with instruments it has created. We put together a weekend residency for the first weekend of May. The group's main instrument is the earth harp, described as a large, architectural stringed instrument. For its appearance in Bethlehem, the group attached the strings to the roof of the four-story ArtsQuest Center, turning the entire building into a harp, with the harpist controlling the strings from a stage set on First Street and facing the building. The audience sat under the harp and was engulfed in the music. Also on the stage was a percussion instrument and a more traditional guitar. The residency included a workshop for students from schools in the area, public lunchtime shows on Friday and Saturday at noon, yoga under the harp on Saturday morning, and an earth harp exhibit and interactive workshop on Sunday afternoon, when we also hosted our first Mother's Day brunch at SteelStacks. The residency went well but was not as well attended as we had hoped. This was something we would have to get used to.

By the time we opened, we had seventy-five shows booked for the café. Sales varied, but were slow overall, as were food and beverage sales during the shows. We told ourselves that sales were slow because the campus was still under construction. The Levitt Pavilion was completed in time for an abbreviated season, opening on Saturday, July 2, just in time for the holiday weekend. Liz Levitt Hirsch and her mother, Mimi Levitt, helped inaugurate the beautiful stage and lawn. The Texas blues singer Marcia Ball performed before an excited audience of several hundred people. We were hopeful that SteelStacks was on its way.

AND THEN THE RAINS CAME

By the end of July SteelStacks was not meeting our projections. We were not just losing money, we were hemorrhaging it. Our budget assumed that Musikfest would have a great year—we figured that the novelty of SteelStacks, as well as a great lineup of shows for the new Sands Steel Stage, would attract audiences. What we did not count on was the rainiest August in many years. It rained six of the ten days of the festival, with the greatest downpour on the second Friday, traditionally one of our biggest nights. After a week of rain Monocacy Creek rose Saturday evening, and we issued evacuation orders for Handwerkplatz and Volksplatz. It did not go well. By 10:00 p.m. the creek was flooding the sites, hitting food stands and the crafters who were still there. By midnight water covered the entire area of Handwerkplatz and most of the food vendors at Volksplatz. For the first time in the history of the festival we were forced to close those two platzes for the final Sunday.

With SteelStacks consuming cash at an alarming rate, and Musikfest bringing in less than we'd counted on because of the rain, this was a crisis. For the first time in our history we decided to ask the public for financial support for Musikfest. We called the campaign Save Our Songs (SOS) and touted it as a way to prevent Musikfest from suffering permanent harm. We sent out emails and advertised. We sent letters to our major supporters. Not everyone was sympathetic. A local barber placed a toilet on his front yard with the lid open and a sign that said DONATIONS FOR JEFF PARKS. I could feel the love. Although the campaign did not reverse the financial slide of 2011, it did raise $100,000 and an additional $100,000 in forgiveness of outstanding bills.

But the rains did not stop with August. We had festivals scheduled for every weekend in September. Rain during Labor Day weekend made SteelJam a big flop. Cool fall weather and lots of competition hurt Blast Furnace Blues, and a partially rainy Oktoberfest did not meet expectations. Musikfest Café audiences were much smaller than the 60 percent attendance we needed to break even, and food and beverage sales were so far below projections that we owed Aramark of more than $200,000. The state has strict requirements for paying its capital assistance grants, which means months of processing before grantees receive partial payments and a final audit of the entire project before they receive the last 5 percent. Meanwhile we were paying interest on the $8 million loan we took out to cover the costs until the grant monies came through. Weekly meetings with Walt Keiper, vice president of finance and administration, became sessions in which we decided which bill to pay first. We cut the ArtsQuest Center's hours to evenings Monday through Thursday, with daytime hours on Friday through Sunday. By January I was forced to make the most difficult decision ever. We had to temporarily reduce the salaries of our full-time staff, by 10 percent for most, 20 percent for senior staff, and 25 percent for the boss.

In December we saw glimmers of hope. Thanks to the bus tour market, we sold more than three thousand meals at the ArtsQuest Center, many to bus groups that had arrived to take in Christkindl-markt and *Christmas 1944*, a theatrical performance geared to the senior market. The café had a few sold-out performances of special holiday programs. The cinema started to break even, and the hospitality team reported that it had booked 112 events for 2012. But none of it was enough to address our cash-flow issues and our growing backlog of unpaid bills. The most encouraging development was that the Kassie Hilgert–Curt Mosel sponsorship team had continued to develop long-term sponsorships for Musikfest and SteelStacks. By the end of 2011 we had multiyear sponsorship agreements, including those signed as part of the SteelStacks campaign, totaling $7.85 million. We couldn't pay the bills, but the future looked bright.

MORE RED INK

In early 2012 we converted Aramark's unpaid bill into an interest-free debt payable over two years. We renegotiated a $3.75 million capital loan from the Lehigh Valley Economic Development Corporation Loan Pool. The original loan required periodic large payments of principal based on capital campaign pledges. Because we were using capital pledges to keep the lights on, it was clear that we would be unable to meet the big payments of principal. The new loan was like a mortgage, with monthly payments of principal and interest on a twenty-five-year schedule except for a balloon payment in five years. We had a reprieve but still had to make the monthly payments.

I spent most of the first four months of 2012 pleading with creditors to reduce or forgive bills, give us advance payment for their sponsorship, apply their bill to future concert ticket purchases, or do anything else they could to forgive or delay payment. We were able to restore full-time salaries by April, but no one got a raise or even a cost-of-living adjustment that year, the first time in the history of ArtsQuest. As anticipated, the first three months of the year were the slowest months at SteelStacks, and that did nothing to help the bottom line. However, payments for SteelStacks and Musikfest sponsorships were due in that quarter, and we were starting to sell concert tickets for Musikfest, so enough cash was coming in to keep going, even if we still could not pay all the bills. Our budget for Musikfest 2012 anticipated a profit sufficient to at least recover a big chunk of the more than $1 million that we had lost in 2011. We eliminated the Jam Band festival and altered other events so they would be less expensive. The blues festival would be an indoor event at the ArtsQuest Center, without an expensive and weather-dependent outdoor component. We cut the number of concerts at the Musikfest Café to 170 per year.

During these years we realized what our two biggest errors in planning had been. First, we were not sufficiently capitalized. We thought we had raised enough money in pledges and sponsorships, but we did not allow for the huge amount of cash we needed on the front end—to buy furniture, fixtures, equipment, and supplies, not to mention wages for workers who were helping us get ready for the opening. Nor did we allow for the full extent of the losses in the first year of operation.

The second big error was having an understaffed finance department. Like any business, we put our major effort into putting out our product, then selling it. The operations and marketing departments took priority over development and finance. Without enough staff to account for the 365 days of revenue and expense, let alone analyze and project, management was flying blind. It is difficult to make decisions without enough information to permit analysis of the situation, something I should have known from the early days of Musikfest. The primary job of the nonprofit CEO, besides representing the organization, raising money, and being the cheerleader, is to allocate resources. That task is much more difficult without the right financial information.

During 2012 a natural disaster and a gamble—introducing new music to our main stage—prevented us from reaching our financial goals. Ticket sales for the main stage at Musikfest were still a leg of Musikfest's financial stool. The first weekend of the festival featured indie rock bands that Patrick Brogan thought would find an audience. (To his credit he was continuing the festival's long-standing tradition of trying new things.) The shows did find an audience, but it was not a big one. Other shows did not sell as well as they should have, and rain and a spectacular thunderstorm interrupted the Thursday evening show. Members of the band Jane's Addiction did a brief acoustic show in the ArtsQuest offices adjacent to the backstage area for a few of our VIP guests, making the evening memorable for more than the bad weather. As we had throughout our history, we relied on Musikfest to pull us out of the red. The festival failed to meet expectations by more than half a million dollars.

Then, in late October 2012, Superstorm Sandy came up the Atlantic coast and stalled off New Jersey. The storm caused major damage throughout New Jersey and New York and some damage in the Lehigh Valley. As a direct result of Sandy, many charter tours were forced to cancel their Christmas trips to Bethlehem, Christkindlmarkt, and SteelStacks. Our December revenue, though good, was less than projected. The year ended with an operating loss of almost $600,000, about half of what we had lost in 2011.

Because we were now relying on our line of credit to address cash-flow needs, we got serious about finding a solution to the short-falls in our operating budget. Based on our pledges and our sponsor-ship contracts, we secured a low-interest $1.45 million loan amor-tized over twenty-five years with a balloon payment due in four years. This brought our total long-term debt to $8.4 million. The loan gave us breathing room, but the new year would have its chal-lenges.

MAKING IT WORK

As 2013 began, we were hopeful that we had stopped digging our financial hole and we would become more stable financially. Steel-Stacks was gaining a local reputation as the place to experiment with arts programming. More community organizations and schools were approaching us about participating in programs, and more business-es were either signing on as sponsors or renting our facilities for meetings and events. The year started slowly, and with the sad loss of our friend and patron Linny Fowler. I would miss her encourage-ment and advice as we continued the SteelStacks adventure.

During January and February our cinema attendance increased, with patrons eager to see Oscar-nominated films before the Acade-my Awards ceremony. Bookings for hospitality also were high. The SteelStacks High School Jazz Band Showcase entered its second year. The event drew eleven talented bands to compete for the honor of appearing at the blues festival in May. The program recognizes the work of students and music teachers in the region. Students at Bethlehem's Liberty and Freedom high schools took a special course called Marketing Musikfest, for which ArtsQuest staff served as classroom resources. The students were given a budget for book-ing shows for a Saturday afternoon at Musikfest. The program was a great success because the students, their friends, and festival patrons attended the shows.

By 2013 our new festivals had begun to take root (with modifica-tions). Blast Furnace Blues started to gain ground as an indoor weekend event, and RiverJazz, sponsored by our accountants, Concannon Miller & Company, grew into a respectable jazz series in May. Sabor!, the Latin festival, gained traction with the Latino community after we added local vendors and booked more prominent Latin shows for the larger Levitt stage.

Musikfest 2013 looked promising, with the comfort-food music of the Lehigh Valley, Styx and Foreigner, and shows by George Thorogood and the Destroyers, Peter Frampton, and KC and the Sunshine Band. Classic rock has been the bread and butter of Musikfest for many years, although country has been gaining fans. The country rocker Darius Rucker, also a local favorite, was in the lineup, which also included Carly Rae Jepson and Ke$ha (pop), One Republic (Indy rock), Avenged Sevenfold (metal), and Skillet (Christian rock) for a great Musikfest mix.

During the summer we realized that the Levitt Pavilion was not only the geographic centerpiece of the campus but also was the key component that made the campus come alive. More than fifty thousand people attended the fifty summer concerts at the site. Hundreds of families, mostly from the south side neighborhoods, attended the new Family Movie Nights, on Wednesday evenings during the summer. Blankets, sodas, popcorn, and a big grassy space for running around created an ideal outing for a summer night. Also during the summer, Mayor Callahan and Tony Hanna announced that the next feature of the SteelStacks campus would be built by summer 2014—the Hoover Mason Trestle Walkway. The trestle, named for the engineers who designed it, was a narrow gauge railroad that carried the limestone, coke, and iron ore for making iron from the Steel's ore yards, where the Sands Casino now sits, to the blast furnaces.

The walkway was supposed to run for a half-mile atop and alongside the elevated railroad tracks between the visitor center and the Sands Hotel. Only the first half of the walkway was built because the casino has suspended all plans for other development between the eastern end of the blast furnaces and the trestle terminus at the entrance to the casino hotel. The walkway has signs that discuss the blast furnaces, noting the people who worked there and the company that built the furnaces. The pedestrian walkway offers a close view of the furnaces and the markings of former workers, as well as a dramatic view of the SteelStacks campus, South Mountain, and St. Michael's Cemetery, where many who worked at Bethlehem Steel are buried. Designed by Wallace Roberts & Todd, the walkway includes three access stairways, an elevator near the visitor center, benches, and a large space that juts out over the lawn of the Levitt Pavilion to allow for gatherings or dramatic artistic presentations in conjunction with the pavilion. To create gardens along the trestle the firm engaged the horticulturalist who did the plantings for New York City's High Line park.

During Musikfest 2013 we had the highest attendance at Steel-Stacks since we opened. We kept the Musikfest Café open until midnight on Fridays and Saturdays. We added shows to the Banko Cinemas, featuring jazz in one theater and a folk music, piano music, vocalists, and guitar music in the other, as well as late-night comedy on Saturdays. On the Town Square the TD Bank Stage featured shows until midnight on weekends. Although revenues from the main stage did not meet our budget expectations, revenues from food, beverages, and hospitality exceeded our goals, particularly during the popular Levitt Pavilion shows. As we had done throughout our history, we adjusted our programs until we found a successful mix.

The year ended with a successful Christkindlmarkt and Peep Drop during Peeps Fest. A ten-foot plastic yellow Peep is dropped promptly from a crane at 5:15 p.m. on New Year's Eve, followed by fireworks. On an operating budget of more than $18 million, we lost only $75,000 in 2013. The tide had turned. Hospitality revenues at SteelStacks were way up, sustaining some of the other programs. The Musikfest Café, now counted among the top two hundred clubs in the world, according *Pollstar Magazine,* was closer to breaking even and, if you counted food and beverage sales, was already in the black.

Despite our fiscal limitations, we did not stop experimenting with new programs and continued our community education and outreach programs. Ryan Hill, the ArtsQuest cinema and comedy programmer, added the Greater Lehigh Valley Filmmakers Festival, to give exposure to regional professional filmmakers. Hill also added the first SteelStacks Improv Festival, drawing more than twenty improv troupes from several states. Patrick Brogan expanded support for local musicians by creating a new partnership with the Greater Lehigh Valley Music Awards. The annual awards are now staged and produced in the Musikfest Café. Dance Now SteelStacks, brought to the campus by the volunteer dance promoter Robin Staff, presents free performances throughout the year as well as two ticketed shows featuring New York dance artists partnering with local college dance students. Lynnie Godfrey, a singer, actor, and director, began a series of play readings related African American history and culture. The LGBT community contributed programs too, including a film series. Open mic nights, hosted by the musician Billy Bauer, have become a Thursday evening tradition. SteelStacks had put the welcome mat out for the local performing arts community, and the community was responding.

By the end of 2013 we knew that SteelStacks would survive. Our anxiety came from unrealistic expectations of instant success, despite the common wisdom that most businesses require three years to break even. SteelStacks would be no different, but it would actually outperform Christkindlmarkt, which took five years to become profitable.

TRANSITION

After SteelStacks opened, I started thinking that it might be time to step aside—I was approaching retirement age—and let others contribute more of their vision and talents. One of my favorite duties was strategic planning, and in late 2012, I asked that Kassie Hilgert become the liaison to the Strategic Planning Committee. I was convinced that she had the chops to become the next CEO of the organization, and this role would make her more visible to our stakeholders. It also was important to have a different eye on the 2014–16 plan to build upon the platform we had created. We had begun using three-year plans in the 1990s and learned that they were the key to getting the organization and all its stakeholders on the same page.

Hilgert spent a great deal of time introducing herself to stakeholders throughout the community. She excelled at designing the 2014–16 Strategic Plan, which reflects the budget limitations imposed by opening the SteelStacks complex but also improves and expands arts programming and community engagement.

The board set up search and selection committees to choose my successor. The goal was to have a candidate in place no later than

October 1, 2014. I was involved only to the extent of reviewing the job description, which included important community engagement and fund-raising responsibilities. We were flattered to receive applications from several states, Canada, and the United Kingdom. In the end the selection committee recommended Hilgert as the next CEO. In June 2014 the board agreed and made the announcement in July, in time for Musikfest.

Through the end of 2014 Hilgert and I worked together to ensure that she had all the information and contacts she needed to be successful in her new role. To make sure that I could not be perceived as meddling, and to make a long-time wish come true for my wife, Susan, we spent the winters of 2015 and 2016 in Florida, where I worked on this book.

TAKING A BOW

By the end of 2013 SteelStacks was well on its way. And 2014 proved to be its breakout year. Oddly it was not an arts event that demonstrated the capacity and attraction of the campus. It was a sports event. Curt Mosel suggested that ArtsQuest host an official viewing party for the FIFA World Cup men's soccer championships. It seemed like a fun thing to do, but none of us anticipated what happened. After months of rigorous efforts to obtain permission from the World Cup's parent organization, we finally became an official viewing site. We arranged to have the games broadcast live on the screen at the Levitt Pavilion, which offered ample seating for most games. From mid-June to mid-July we were surprised by how many local people came out for games between foreign countries, particularly the Latin American countries. When the United States played, we added a large screen on the Town Square. Bolstered by crowd of more than ten thousand for the United States–Portugal game, an estimated fifty thousand people attended the game broadcasts and introduced many new people to the campus.

On another front, Wallace Roberts & Todd nominated Steel-Stacks for the Urban Land Institute's Global Award for Excellence. These prestigious awards are customarily given to large mixed-use real estate development projects throughout the world. SteelStacks was one of the winners in 2014. I accepted the award with Antonio

Fiol-Silva from WRT at the Jacob K. Javits Convention Center in New York. Our project was probably the smallest to receive an award that year, bracketed by winners from London and Singapore—little Bethlehem among the giants.

Musikfest '14 was one of the most successful to date, with great weather and income. The Levitt Pavilion audience continued to grow, to more than seventy thousand, and the cinema and Musikfest Café programs also attracted more people. But the most impressive growth was in catering. As we had hoped, and projected, revenue from catering was now a significant element sustaining SteelStacks and the organization. The food and beverage leg of the stool came into its own. Net income for the organization in 2014 was more than $500,000, enough to start building a much-needed reserve fund.

My retirement dinner was on November 18, 2014, nineteen years to the day the blast furnaces closed down. It was a spectacular affair that filled the Musikfest Café, looking out on the illuminated furnaces and the Hoover Mason Trestle Walkway. Aerialists in the room poured champagne as they swung from the ceiling to a background of jazz. Kassie Hilgert surprised Susan and me with a golden ticket—free tickets for life to any ArtsQuest event. It was the best possible gift. Fireworks ended the evening, surprising the entire city. I was grateful for a career that had gone way beyond my expectations. In the glow of the fireworks, I thought of dear old Helena Clark's looking askance at my decision to go home after law school. I quietly whispered to her: "Yes, Ms. Clark, Bethlehem is one of those very special places, where community is important and creative individuals thrive."

Table 28.1
POPULATION CHANGE 1950-2016
Pennsylvania Cities with Population over 20,000 in 2016

	1950 Population	% Change 1950-80	1980 Population	% Change 1980-2016	2016 Population	% Change 1950-2016
ALLENTOWN	106,757	-3	103,758	16	120,443	13
ALTOONA	77,177	-26	57,078	-22	44,589	-42
BETHLEHEM	66,340	6	70,419	7	75,293	13
CHESTER	66,039	-31	45,794	-26	33,988	-49
EASTON	34,410	-24	26,076	3	26,978	-22
ERIE	130,125	-8	119,123	-17	98,593	-24
HARRISBURG	89,544	-41	53,264	-8	48,904	-45
HAZLETON	35,486	-23	27,318	-10	24,659	-31
LANCASTER	63,774	-14	54,725	8	59,218	-7
LEBANON	28,134	-9	25,711	0	25,726	-9
NEW CASTLE	48,563	-31	33,621	-34	22,142	-54
PHILADELPHIA	2,064,794	-18	1,688,210	-7	1,567,872	-24
PITTSBURGH	673,763	-37	423,938	-28	303,625	-55
READING	109,320	-28	78,686	11	87,575	-20
SCRANTON	125,536	-30	88,117	-12	77,291	-38
WILKES-BARRE	76,826	-33	51,551	-21	40,569	-47
WILLIAMSPORT	44,964	-26	33,401	-14	28,834	-36
YORK	59,953	-26	44,619	-2	43,859	-27
PENNSYLVANIA	10,462,628	13	11,863,895	8	12,784,227	22
USA	151,325,798	50	226,542,199	43	323,127,513	114
Selected Cities with History of Metal Production						
YOUNGSTOWN, OH	168,300	-31	115,510	-44	64,312	-62
BIRMINGHAM, AL	326,037	-13	284,413	-25	212,157	-35
WATERBURY, CT	104,477	-1	103,266	5	108,272	4
PUEBLO, CO	63,700	60	101,690	8	110,291	73

SOURCES: United States Census; American Fact Finder, United States Census Bureau

Table 28.2
ECONOMIC WELLBEING OF COMMUNITY
Pennsylvania Cities with Population over 20,000 in 2016

	Median Household Income $	% Below Poverty Level	Median Residential Property Value $
ALLENTOWN	37,256	27	126,100
ALTOONA	36,741	22	85,400
BETHLEHEM	49,349	17	168,900
CHESTER	27,217	37	66,800
EASTON	45,361	19	127,300
ERIE	35,205	26	86,700
HARRISBURG	32,688	32	83,800
HAZLETON	32,460	25	87,200
LANCASTER	36,233	29	109,300
LEBANON	35,737	26	89,300
NEW CASTLE	31,557	27	61,400
PHILADELPHIA	39,700	26	147,300
PITTSBURGH	42,450	22	100,800
READING	27,247	39	68,400
SCRANTON	38,232	23	104,500
WILKES-BARRE	31,248	30	76,700
WILLIAMSPORT	35,872	28	99,900
YORK	30,068	36	76,100
PENNSYLVANIA	54,895	13	167,700
USA	55,322	15	184,700
Selected Cities with History of Metal Production			
YOUNGSTOWN, OH	24,448	38	43,300
BIRMINGHAM, AL	32,404	29	87,100
WATERBURY, CT	39,681	25	129,500
PUEBLO, CO	35,770	25	116,800

SOURCES: American Fact Finder, United States Census Bureau

Table 28.3
ATTRACTION OF CREATIVE CLASS
Recent College Graduate Settlement Rates
Pennsylvania Cities with Population over 20,000 in 2016

	% of residents Age 25+ with College Degrees	% of residents age 25-34	% of residents Age 25-34 with College Degrees
ALLENTOWN	15	15	17
ALTOONA	17	13	23
BETHLEHEM	27	15	38
CHESTER	10	14	10
EASTON	20	14	24
ERIE	22	16	28
HARRISBURG	18	17	22
HAZLETON	11	13	10
LANCASTER	20	19	26
LEBANON	10	13	9
NEW CASTLE	15	12	22
PHILADELPHIA	26	18	41
PITTSBURGH	41	20	59
READING	9	14	7
SCRANTON	22	13	29
WILKES-BARRE	16	14	19
WILLIAMSPORT	20	15	23
YORK	12	16	15
PENNSYLVANIA	29	13	38
USA	30	14	34
Selected Cities with History of Metal Production			
YOUNGSTOWN, OH	12	13	12
BIRMINGHAM, AL	25	17	33
WATERBURY, CT	15	14	18
PUEBLO, CO	19	14	17

SOURCES: American Fact Finder, United States Census Bureau

CHAPTER 28
BETHLEHEM AT 275

At one of the many events in 2016 that celebrated Bethlehem's founding 275 years earlier, Mayor Robert Donchez paid tribute to the city's resilience. He acknowledged the closing of Bethlehem Steel, an agonizing demise during the late twentieth century that had threatened to hollow out a historic community begun in 1741 by stalwart German immigrants. But the mayor's focus was not on the community's losses. Instead he described a vital community alive with new ventures, a place that had found its strengths in the doldrums of industrial collapse and willed itself to become a model for other struggling Rust Belt cities.

The mayor spoke of diverse industries attracted to the city because of the vision and determination of community leaders—Lehigh Valley Industrial Park's development within the former steel plant, cafés bustling with patrons on Main Street, and new enterprise within the downtown, including a new office building and the Hyatt Place Hotel.

By 2016 Bethlehem was well clear of its history as a one-company town, the mayor noted. Its residents were working in manufacturing, technology, transportation and warehousing, hospitality, finance, insurance, the professions, real estate, health care, education, and the arts and entertainment. Census statistics support Donchez's statements. As table 28.1 shows, Allentown and Bethlehem are the only two Pennsylvania cities with more than twenty thousand people whose populations are bigger than they were in 1950, whereas some of those eighteen cities have lost as as many as 54 percent of their residents. These Pennsylvania cities were centers of industry and many hosted steel mills. The table also lists four cities in New England, the South, Midwest, and West that were historic metals manufacturing cities and how they have fared in comparison. Only one of those cities, Pueblo, Colorado, experienced significant growth, most of which occurred before 1980. The table also shows that since 1980, only five of the Pennsylvania cities experienced growth, because the commonwealth's overall growth has lagged far behind the national increase in population. The growth cities—Allentown, Bethlehem, Easton, Reading, and Lancaster—are on the arc between New York City and Baltimore and can attribute their population growth to Latinos, who now constitute 20 percent (Easton) to 58 percent (Reading) of the cities' populations.

Table 28.2 shows the relative prosperity of these former industrial cities. Bethlehem's median household income is the highest of any of the Pennsylvania cities or the comparison cities, while Bethlehem's is still 13 percent less than the national median household income. Cities nationally have lower prosperity numbers than their suburbs, which in turn raise the national averages, so 13 percent is actually a respectable difference. Seventeen percent of Bethlehem residents live below the poverty level, which is 13 percent higher than the national average but not as severe as the poverty levels seen in all the former industrial cities listed. Although single-family residential property values vary greatly by region, Bethlehem's property values are the highest of the cities in the table, exceeding median residential property values for Pennsylvania as a whole, another remarkable statistic for any city.

For those of us who experienced the brain drain of the late twentieth century as our children and their friends fled for better jobs in vibrant places with great opportunities, the most exciting measure of Bethlehem's success appears in table 28.3. Combining the arts strategies with the traditional economic development strategies of site-ready industrial parks, excellent transportation infrastructure, and a lower tax structure has made the environment hospitable for creative-class professionals, who are returning to the region, especially to Bethlehem. The best measure of that return is the 2016 census assessment of residents twenty-five- to thirty-four-year-olds who have college or graduate degrees. In recent years this group has chosen to either not return to industrial cities or to live in the suburbs if they do return. Of people in this age group who live in the city of Bethlehem, 38 percent have college degrees, surpassing their representation in the two surrounding Lehigh Valley counties, as well as the state and national averages. On this measure Bethlehem lags behind only the state's much bigger cities, Pittsburgh (59.3 percent) and Philadelphia (40.5 percent). Bethlehem is not only benefiting from the economic prosperity of the Lehigh Valley; it is contributing to that prosperity by attracting creative-class workers to a culturally vibrant city.[148]

Many factors have contributed to Bethlehem's success. Laying the groundwork was the visionary work of Bethlehem Steel's Hank Barnette and his team, who steered a dying company while planning for its host community's survival. In 2016 Route 412, the four-lane boulevard that connects SteelStacks and LVIP VII with Interstate 78 and was part of Barnette's check list, opened after much delay. Representatives of the Lehigh Valley Industrial Park announced that a Candlewood Suites Hotel will occupy a prominent spot along the thoroughfare. LVIP also reported that only eight industrial lots remained for sale on the former Bethlehem Steel property and that it was marketing nineteen commercial lots along Route 412. LVIP VII, with over $100 million in infrastructure development, is bigger than all of LVIP's previous parks combined. So much development within twenty years of Bethlehem Steel's closing is testament to the work of Barnette, LVIP, the Lehigh Valley Partnership, Northampton County, and others.

All this has meant that the economic fortunes of Bethlehem, and the SouthSide in particular, have soared. At the same time culture has flourished, lifted by the Banana Factory, SteelStacks, Godfrey Daniels Coffee House, Touchstone Theatre, Lehigh University, Lehigh Valley Charter Arts High School (opened in 2015), and a campus of Northampton Community College. Other signs of prosperity are the multiple facilities operated by St. Luke's University Hospital; the Greenway Commons project of two hundred apartment units, with first-floor retail, under construction on Third Street; and a six-story office and restaurant project across from the Banana Factory. Lehigh University has announced that it intends to increase its student body by one thousand undergraduates and five hundred to eight hundred full-time graduate students and plans to build housing for its expanded population closer to the retail district. The university, led by its new president, John Simon, is coming to the south side development table. Like other colleges it realizes that its students want to be a part of a vibrant community.

Early in 2016 Donchez announced a plan to place directional signs guiding visitors to and from Bethlehem's two retail districts, now known as the SouthSide Arts District and the Moravian Historic District. When completed, the wayfinding system will reinforce the distinctiveness of both parts of the city as cultural tourism, now attracting over 8,000,000 guests to the city each year, continues to grow.[149] In December the U.S. Department of the Interior announced that, through the efforts of Historic Bethlehem Museums and Sites, the federal agency had placed Bethlehem's Moravian National Historic District on the U.S. Tentative List for nomination to the UNESCO World Heritage List.[150] Just a week later a group representing UNESCO stopped in Bethlehem to visit SteelStacks. Group members were familiar with Volklinger Hutte in Germany, the former steel plant that already is a World Heritage site, and were impressed with SteelStacks. Is it possible that one small city could have two World Heritage sites?

Meanwhile Bethlehem's boutique spirits industry continues to grow. Thanks to modifications of Pennsylvania's liquor laws, and the healthy market for locally made beverages, Bethlehem's tradition of alcoholic beverage manufacture is experiencing a rebirth. Social Still near SteelStacks is in the building that once was the bank run by the first woman bank president in Pennsylvania and now houses the first woman-owned distillery (producing bourbon, rye, vodka, rum, and gin) in the state. Social Still is also a bar and restaurant owned by Elaine Pivinski (who also owns Franklin Hill Vineyards), her son Adam Flatt, and his wife, Kate. Just a few blocks away, a couple of actors from New Jersey established Bonn Place Brewery. They found Bethlehem when they performed in *Tony 'n' Tina's Wedding* at Steel-Stacks. On Main Street the Colony Meadery has partnered with the Moravian Book Shop for retail sales of its medieval alcoholic beverages made from honey. The Bethlehem Brew Works continues to thrive, with plenty of sidewalk seating.

My memories of Europe when I was a newly minted college graduate come back as I stroll Main Street on a summer night through the dozen sidewalk cafés filled with people enjoying what we all worked so hard to create. No transcontinental flight is necessary—the experience is two blocks from my home.

ArtsQuest continues its mission of community development. With the support of two generous donors, the organization has hired a director of education, Lisa Harms, who connects the arts and Arts-Quest's community resources with K–12 education throughout the region. ArtsQuest is working with school districts on a variety of arts-related programs. In early 2017 it partnered with the American Society of Civil Engineers to bring more than a thousand students from five school districts and two private high schools to SteelStacks to see the movie *Dream Big* and to discuss with engineers a career in the field. Harms says the area needs an arts preschool program and foresees establishing one at the Banana Factory, among other opportunities.

Although hot weather held down attendance for half of Musikfest 2016, Christkindlmarkt had record attendance, perhaps because the weather was warmer than usual. The Frank Banko Alehouse Cinemas set a monthly attendance record in December 2016 by topping its previous best by 20 percent. Musikfest Café Presented by Yuengling also set a record for attendance and revenue, with shows across the spectrum of contemporary music and comedy. With these program successes, the leaders of ArtsQuest are hoping to move forward with renovating the twenty-six-thousand square feet of the former Bethlehem Steel Turn and Grind Shop, which is adjacent to the SteelStacks Visitor Center. The renovated building would provide indoor space for festivals at SteelStacks and for educational exhibits, sculpture shows, and the latest hot form of entertainment, the cirque. ArtsQuest also is rethinking the Banana Factory after almost twenty years of deferred maintenance and tremendous program growth.

The visibility of the arts impresses visitors to Bethlehem. One eye-catcher is ArtsQuest's hot glass studio, a gamble when it was developed because of its expense and trickiness to run safely but today a major draw. On the first Friday of each month guests swing to a live band playing on the studio floor as teams of glassblowers create a special sculpture for the evening. Everyone, from twelve-year-olds in the ArtSmart afterschool program to high-powered white-collar professionals looking for a creative way to relieve stress, flocks to the studio.

When locals are entertaining guests, they now have many choices—a live music concert or a festival most days of the year, art galleries, a tour of the former steel plant, art house films, or an evening walk for a drink at a craft distillery, dinner at a speakeasy with 1920s music, or dessert at a fine Italian restaurant. They can top off the evening at a concert by local artists against the backdrop of the illuminated blast furnaces. Bethlehem's robust arts scene sets it apart, as visitors soon discover. Many return frequently or even become residents.

Communities always are evolving, and challenges are part of the deal. A case in point is that some former Bethlehem Steel buildings and land adjacent to SteelStacks have yet to be redeveloped, especially for residential use. A report commissioned by SouthSide 2020, a city advisory group, estimates the need for new housing on the SouthSide by 2027 will be 420 to 1,250 units.[151] Nine former steel buildings, including the 1930s-era thirteen-story Steel General Office Building and the grand Number 2 Machine Shop, remain vacant and deteriorating. Several developers have approached the Sands-BethWorks partnership with conceptual plans for multifamily residential and retail development. However, the last new development on the site was an entertainment hall added by the Sands in 2014.

Nevertheless, signs of success continue to sprout. In 2017 the Rudy Bruner Foundation announced that SteelStacks had won the Rudy Bruner Award for Urban Excellence, putting Bethlehem alongside Boston and San Francisco as the only cities in the United States to host a project that has won both the Bruner award and the Urban Land Institute's Global Award for Excellence. Since its inception Bethlehem has welcomed diversity, creativity, and enterprise. Volunteers, public officials, entrepreneurs, business leaders, artists, educators, and community members continue to work together and succeed because, in acting together, they are indeed stronger than steel.

CHAPTER 29
WHY THE ARTS ARE ESSENTIAL TO COMMUNITY DEVELOPMENT

I learned early in life that we humans shy away from difference in favor of fitting in. I was born with a dislocated hip, and by the time I was twelve, my left leg was five inches shorter than my right leg. I suffered the predictable cruelty of other kids, who of course took nasty notice of the specially made balsawood lift I wore on my left shoe. So powerful was the desire to be "normal" that I endured two operations in my teen years to shorten my normal right leg. I did not understand this at the time, but I was letting my difference, and my desperation to be rid of it, define me.

As I look back on a career of creating opportunities for people to gather and celebrate, I realize that my motivation sprang from being that kid with the short leg. My disability gave me two gifts—respect for differences and a desire to bring people together to honor and understand each other.

Americans differ in myriad ways—culture, ethnicity, religion, skin color, sexual orientation, beliefs, abilities, lifestyle, and how we think. Every one of us seeks affirmation, and we often avoid anything that does not provide that affirmation. However, divided communities cannot thrive, either spiritually or economically. Isolation is an enemy. As this story demonstrates, the arts have a significant role to play in overcoming harmful physical and cultural isolation. The payoff literally is money in the bank—thriving businesses, a successful brand, and the growing population vital to continued prosperity.

CREATING ACCESS—WHERE AND HOW THE ARTS ARE PRESENTED

Ensuring access to the arts usually is defined as eliminating barriers to the disabled or lowering the price of a ticket. But museums and performing arts centers pose profound psychological barriers to many, who assume these places are for another generation or society's elite, not them.

Some institutions recognize the problem and have sent art or musical groups into the community or its schools. These programs are admirable but often are not enough to eliminate the emotional barrier to the institution, which its physical structure embodies. Arts organizations that have spent years caring for a facility that has become a community landmark are loath to consider major programs outside their building. Yet public spaces seldom used by arts organizations are where many members of the community feel most at ease. Granted, using outdoor spaces can entail daunting logistical issues. But as creative placemaking—which has been defined as "strengthen[ing] the transformation of a place by being creative, by bringing artists and arts organizations into the fold"—has demonstrated, thinking beyond four walls is a strategy that works.[152] Musikfest and dozens of other ArtsQuest programs prove the point. Musikfest, the Levitt Pavilion, Peeps Fest, the Sabor! Latin Festival, and dozens of other programs introduce people to the artists and the cultures of their community. With physical, psychological, and economic barriers removed, no one need feel left out.

Part of inclusion is recognizing how people consume culture. Most traditional American arts organizations are based on eighteenth-century European models, designed for audiences to sit down, be quiet, and applaud only at the right moments.

Indoor performance space typically has a permanent stage facing permanent seats. But audiences today are engaged with art and artists in drastically different ways than previous generations were. Technology, digital delivery devices, and social networking have heavily influenced cultural trends and created new ways for artists and fans to connect. Several symphony orchestras now set aside seats for tweeters in an effort to become more relevant but also to protect members of the audience who find the practice disruptive of their experience.[153] Mixers at museums are designed to attract young people. Meeting the artist, enjoying drinks, tweeting, and dancing are just some activities that have become part of the arts experience today. However, the majority of traditional arts organizations are not thinking about ways the audience wants to experience the arts. They prefer the old sit-down-and-be-quiet approach, a mind-set that does not develop diverse audiences and leaves these organizations facing an uncertain future.

SOCIAL CAPITAL AND THE ARTS

In their book, *The Smartest Places on Earth,* Antoine van Agtmael and Fred Bakker find commonalities among several Rust Belt communities in the United States and Europe that have emerged as centers of modern industry through the collaboration of business, higher education, and government. These are places with a high amount of social capital. What is difficult to calculate is the contribution of the arts to such community prosperity.

One way is to take a close look at cities like Bethlehem that have demonstrated that the arts, if accessible and relevant, can play a pivotal role in building social capital. In the early 1980s, I used my own supply from a decade of community work to persuade people to invest in the Musikfest concept, which was alien to the community at the time. Once the festival took hold, those who supported Musikfest—the volunteers and people who attended the first festival—amplified its value, which generated more social capital. Since then generations of volunteers, festival vendors, and festivalgoers have gathered, created traditions, and increased community cohesion. Meanwhile, Musikfest became the portal to the rest of what we have achieved, culminating with SteelStacks and its key role in Bethlehem's renaissance.

Critical to the development of social capital is inclusion. The first Musikfest was not culturally diverse. Designed to reflect the Moravian/German heritage of the community, it featured polka, folk, jazz, classical, and a touch of rock music. The audience was virtually all white. We learned as we went, and we changed the event as it grew. We added musical styles that appeal to all sorts of people. With the development of the Banana Factory on the SouthSide and the addition of Plaza Tropical to Musikfest in 2000, along with Puerto Rican and Portuguese foods, the Latino community became engaged in the festival. Gradually the demographics of the festival and its volunteers began to better reflect the community as a whole. I do not pretend that all is perfect in Bethlehem. The Latino community, which now accounts for almost 28 percent of city residents, has the highest poverty rate (30.7 percent) but is increasingly visible in middle-class neighborhoods throughout the city. Bethlehem's low crime rate, better-than-average performance by its urban schools, and diversifying community involvement (two of seven city council members are of Puerto Rican heritage) reflect a place that has developed extensive social capital. An observer can easily see the result by watching the community gather at SteelStacks, particularly during the summer months. As I had always hoped, the arts continue to strengthen Bethlehem's bonds.

BRANDING

We have succeeded in our goal of distinguishing Bethlehem as a place that people and businesses want to move to and that attracts visitors, although it took many years. Beginning in 1985, when the *New York Times* ran an article after the second Musikfest about the steel town's quest to move forward with a new music festival, the arts programs in Bethlehem, and the expanded coverage of these events, have paid enormous dividends.[154] Bethlehem and the ArtsQuest programs frequently make popular best-of lists. Here are some examples:

- Summer stages listed by the *New York Times*—Musikfest 2012, 2013, 2014
- The ten most exciting places in Pennsylvania—*Movoto Blog*, July 2014
- Readers' best summer festivals—*National Geographic*, Musikfest 2014
- Happiest cities in Pennsylvania—CreditDonkey, September 2014
- "Best Christmas Markets Around the World"—*Condé Nast Traveler*, December 2014

- "19 Insanely Weird Concert Venues to Visit Before You Die"—*BuzzFeed*, 2015
- "America's 50 Best Cities in the US to Live"—*Wall Street 24/7*, November 2015
- "15 Incredible Concert Venues Around the World"—*Business Insider*, SteelStacks 2016
- Weirdest object dropped on New Year's Eve—Associated Press, Peeps Fest 2016
- "60 Great Things to See in 2017"—*Chicago Tribune*, Musikfest 2017[155]

My favorite was announced in October 2016, when *Money Magazine* designated Bethlehem as the best place to retire in the Northeast, citing SteelStacks, Musikfest, and the array of arts programs. A few months later *Forbes* included Bethlehem in its top twenty-five places to retire in the country.[156] How clever was I to be living here during my retirement?

As the reputations of Musikfest, Christkindlmarkt, Banana Factory, and SteelStacks have grown, and digital media have expanded, the number of impressions—that is, the number of times people have viewed an image, story, or report—has routinely hit more than one billion, reaching six billion in 2016. According to Meltwater, a private media monitoring service, this is the equivalent of $22 million in paid advertising, a number that major cities strive to achieve. Major media outlets that have included ArtsQuest or its programs in their publications include *Money Magazine*, *Boston Herald*, *US News & World Report*, the *Washington Post*, *Miami Herald*, *Washington Times*, *Chicago Tribune*, *Baltimore Sun*, the website of *CBS This Morning: Saturday*, and *Condé Nast Traveler*.

This coverage has begun to overcome the thirty-year narrative of Bethlehem as a declining steel town.

ATTRACTING RESIDENTS

While walking my little Havanese, Folly, in our downtown neighborhood, at least once a week I meet new residents and spend a few minutes getting their story. One couple told me that when one spouse was transferred from Maine to New Jersey, they found Bethlehem and fell in love with the city. Then I came across empty nesters who were living in New England but could work from anywhere and decided to live closer to their daughters in the New York area; they found Bethlehem and decided this was the place. And a couple living in another state with their young children learned that the husband's Bethlehem-based parents were moving to a house in the Moravian Historic District. The husband quit his great job with a major company and announced that they would purchase his parents' former home in west Bethlehem and he would find a job after they settled in.

As the tables in chapter 28 show, Bethlehem also is attracting millennials. Twenty-five percent of Bethlehem residents are aged twenty to thirty-four and a high percentage have college degrees. Millennials are looking for the vibrant lifestyle that Bethlehem offers, which demonstrates that small cities can compete for young talent. All this has happened without the massive gentrification experienced in other cities and without displacing minority and low-income residents from their neighborhoods. Everyone now has greater access to jobs in the community as well as diverse arts programs.

What the statistics say is that quality of life is important for recruiting and retaining people with skills important for the economic success of a community. Businesses seeking to locate in a community seldom list quality of life in their top five needs when working with economic development officials. But their five most important considerations always include the quality and availability of the workforce they need. It astounds me that more economic development officials do not see the connection between quality of life and quality of the workforce.

But attitudes and approaches are changing. The Lehigh Valley Partnership, which includes the larger businesses, colleges, and health care organizations, now works with an organization, the Lehigh Valley Interregional Networking and Connecting Consortium (LINC), that recruits people for specialized positions. And it helps the people it recruits to find what they need in the community. According to Donna Cornelius, executive director of LINC, whose offices are on Bethlehem's SouthSide, many recruits are not familiar with the Lehigh Valley. The organization's first job is to acquaint them with the regional cultural, recreational, and social offerings. In a recent survey taken at an event for nearly one hundred recruits, 80 percent listed the arts as important when they are choosing a place to live. For many recruits a visit to SteelStacks assures them that the region has a great deal to offer in contemporary performing arts. A frequent comment is "We don't have anything like this in—."

STRATEGIES

Nothing is easy, especially in communities that have suffered deindustrialization. Certainly, the arts are not the only answer to community revitalization. However, traditional economic development strategies can go only so far if the goal is to attract and retain talented individuals, who are the key to sustaining any community. Bethlehem was able to capitalize on the work of many leaders who created industrial parks, developed transportation infrastructure, and established programs like the Ben Franklin Technology Partners. But quality of life plays a significant role in sustaining the businesses in the region. With its attractive quality of life, Bethlehem has been able to support the region's education, health care, and manufacturing businesses by becoming a culturally robust alternative to a suburban lifestyle.

Bethlehem's story may not provide a precise road map for any other community, but the success of arts-related strategies in one community can be inspiration for the development of other communities with similar challenges. In this spirit my message to leaders of small cities is that if a twenty- or thirtysomething approaches you with a crazy idea for a free arts festival in public spaces as a way to rejuvenate Main Street, pay attention. He or she might actually be on to something. What have you got to lose?

ARTS⚲UEST™
imagine that

BANANA FACTORY®

ACKNOWLEDGEMENTS

Collecting the stories of some of my fellow residents of Bethlehem was the most joyous part of the development of this book, as well as the stories of those who have departed but are well remembered by others. I am convinced that our stories are important reflections of our humanity. I am forever grateful for those who shared stories for this book, including: Carole Badman, Curtis "Hank" Barnette, Robert Behney, Joseph Biondo, Michael Bolton, Ross Born, Christopher Bowen (Mr. Beer!), Patrick Brogan, John Callahan, Angelika Cornelius, Don Cunningham, Robert Desalvio, Susan Drexinger, Anne Episcipo (Bert Daday's daughter) Jeffrey Feather, W. Beall Fowler, Ismael Garcia, Marlene Gilley, Jeremy Hachey, Tony Hanna, Carol Henn, Patricia Holetz, Jean Kessler, Bette Kovach, Roland Kushner, Jamie Musselman, Elaine Pavinsky, Michael Perrucci, Ken Rainere, John Raymond, Tony and Judy Sabino, David Shaffer, Ralph Grayson Schwarz, Kenneth Smith, Craig Stefko, Dorothy Stephenson, Richard "Bucky" Szulborski, Donna Taggart, Lorna Velasquez, Rosa Velasquez, Helene Whitaker, Robert Wilkins, Robert "Doc" Windolph, Kerry Wrobel and Sharon Zondag.

It was left for me to tell a part of the stories of individuals who were important to the community and whom I was honored to know and to work with: Marlene O. "Linny" Fowler, Frank Banko, John Walson, Jr., Gordon B. Mowrer, Paul Marcincin and James Delgrosso.

I would like to thank my team of readers and advisers during the writing and production of the book: Merry Sue Baum, Kassie Hilgert, Susan Lawless, Ron Unger, Silagh White, Susan Burdette Ziegler and Sharon Zondag. Special kudos and thanks to my "educator editors" Ardith Hilliard and Polly Kummel. Their support and guidance has made all the difference.

Thanks to Zach Matthei for the use of his beautiful photo of "the stacks" for the cover, Olaf Starorypinsky for his photo of the author and to Lisa Hokans for the design of the book jacket. All great examples of art inspired by SteelStacks.

A heartfelt thank you to two women who have made it possible to do so much with so little time: Iva Ferris and Joann Lee. Bless you both!

To my wife Susan, mother Marilyn and son Jonathan, thanks for supporting me through all of these endeavors.

Last but definitely not least thank you to the thousands of Arts-Quest volunteers, board members and staff along with the business, government and non-profit leaders who believed in their community and made Bethlehem's success, and this book, possible.

NOTES

1. Ann Markusen and Anna Gadwa Nicodemus, *Creative Placemaking*, executive summary of white paper for the Mayors' Institute on City Design, Markusen Economic Research Services and Metris Arts Consulting, 2010.
2. See tables 28.1–28.3.
3. Thomas Kupper, "The End Begins When 'the Steel' Falls Silent," *(Allentown) Morning Call*, special report, October 22–25, 1995, 18.
4. Bette Kovach, interview by author, January 11, 2016, Bethlehem.
5. Ibid.
6. The Historical Society of Pennsylvania, "German Settlement in Pennsylvania: An Overview," n.d., http://hsp.org/sites/default/files/legacy_files/migrated/germanstudentreading.pdf.
7. Chester S. Davis, *Hidden Seed and Harvest: A History of the Moravians* (Winston-Salem, NC: Winston, 1973).
8. W. Ross Yates, *Bethlehem of Pennsylvania, The First Hundred Years, 1741–1841* (Bethlehem, PA: Bethlehem Chamber of Commerce, 1968), 23–29; deed of William Allen to Henry Antes, Moravian Archives, Bethlehem, PA.
9. Kenneth G. Hamilton, *Church Street in Old Bethlehem* (Bethlehem, PA: Author, 1942).
10. Ibid.
11. Historic Bethlehem Museums and Sites, "Colonial Industrial Quarter," 2017, https://historicbethlehem.org/?historic-site=colonial-industrial-quarter.
12. Raymond Walters, *Bethlehem Long Ago and Today* (Bethlehem, PA: Carey Printing, 1923), 102, 106.
13. Yates, *Bethlehem of Pennsylvania*, 158–63.
14. Schwarz Gallery, "View by Artist: Gustavus Johann Grunewald," 2017, http://www.schwarzgallery.com/artist/239/Gustavus-Johann-Grunewald.
15. Christopher Bowen, *Bethlehem Brewed and Distilled,* Exhibit, Historic Bethlehem Museums and Sites, 2014, Bethlehem, PA.
16. Old Breweries, "John Sebastian Goundie Brewery—PA 39B," undated table "Breweries Listed Under Bethlehem, PA 39," http://www.oldbreweries.com/breweries-by-state/pennsylvania/bethlehem-pa-8-breweries/john-sebastian-goundie-brewery-pa-39b/.
17. Frank Whelan, *John Sebastian Goundie, Nineteenth-Century Moravian Entrepreneur* (Bethlehem, PA: Oaks Printing, 1988), 16, 22. A reprint of the book is available at the Historic Bethlehem Visitor Center.
18. Yates, *Bethlehem of Pennsylvania*, 137.
19. Walters, *Bethlehem Long Ago and Today,* 36.

20. Joseph Mortimer Levering, *A History of Bethlehem Pennsylvania, 1741–1892* (Bethlehem, PA: Times Publishing, 1903), 678.

21. R. D. Billinger, "Early Zinc Works in the Lehigh Valley," *Journal of the American Chemical Society*, February 1936, 60.

22. W. Ross Yates, "Samuel Wetherill, Joseph Wharton, and the Founding of the American Zinc Industry," *Pennsylvania Magazine of History and Biography* 98, no. 4 (1974): 485.

23. W. Ross Yates, *Lehigh University, A History of Education in Engineering, Business and the Human Condition* (Bethlehem, PA: Lehigh University Press, 1992), 17–18.

24. W. Ross Yates, *Bethlehem of Pennsylvania: The Golden Years* (Bethlehem, PA: Chamber of Commerce, 1976), 22.

25. Until the 1950s a freight station stood at what is now the Banana Factory Arts Center. The passenger terminal on Second Street was the last union station—one shared by two or more independent railroad companies—built in the United States, shortly before cars, buses, and planes became more popular modes of travel.

26. "First Steel Rails Historical Marker," ExplorePAHistory.com, http://explorepahistory.com/hmarker.php?markerId=1-A-1CA; Terence Bell, "A Short History of Steel," thebalance.com, August 21, 2017, https://www.thebalance.com/a-short-history-of-steel-part-ii-2340103; "Forging America: The Story of Bethlehem Steel," *Morning Call*, December 14, 2003, 22. I am greatly indebted to the work of the *Morning Call*.

27. "Forging America," 26, 22–23; David Colamaria, "The Story of the New Steel Navy," steelnavy.org, 2010, http://www.steelnavy.org/history/exhibits/show/steelnavy/introduction/story.

28. "Forging America," 27, 36.

29. Ibid., 23–25.

30. Ibid., 33; Christopher Gray, "The Late Great Charles Schwab Mansion," *New York Times*, July 8, 2010, http://www.nytimes.com/2010/07/11/realestate/11streets.html.

31. "Forging America," 40.

32. Ibid., 41–42, 45.

33. Ibid., 100.

34. Ibid., 102.

35. Ibid., 64.

36. "Lehigh Valley Silk Mills," National Park Service, n.d., https://www.nps.gov/nr/travel/delaware/sil.htm.

37. Jeremy Hachey, *R. K. Laros, the Patron of Bethlehem* (Bethlehem, PA: R. L. Laros Foundation, 2014).

38. Ibid.

39. Ross Born and David Shaffer, interviews by author, June 16, 2016, Bethlehem, PA.

40. Ibid.

41. Ibid.

42. David Venditta and Ardith Hilliard, eds., *Forging America: The Story of Bethlehem Steel* (Allentown, PA: Morning Call, 2010), , 66. The houses of worship of South Bethlehem remain to tell the story: Holy Infancy Church originally was the first Roman Catholic church, established in 1861, for the Irish community and later was home church for the Portuguese, Mexican, and Puerto Rican communities. It started the wave and was followed by St. Peter's Lutheran (German), Fritz

Memorial Methodist (English); Holy Ghost Roman Catholic (German); St. Joseph's (German, now Puerto Rican); Our Lady of Pompeii (Italian); St. John's African Methodist Episcopal Zion Church (African American); Saints Cyril and Methodius (Slovak); St. John Capistrano Roman Catholic (Hungarian); St. Joseph's Roman Catholic (Slovenian); St. John's Windish Lutheran (Slovenian); St. John's Slovak Lutheran; Cathedral Church of the Nativity (Episcopalian); St. Stanislaus Roman Catholic (Polish); St. Nicholas Greek Orthodox Church; St. Nicholas Russian Orthodox Church (Ukrainian); Congregation Brith Sholom (Jewish, primarily from greater Russia and greater Germany).

43. On Italian immigration see "Italy from 1870 to 1945," *Encyclopedia Britannica*, https://www.britannica.com/place/Italy/Unification#toc27743.

44. Venditta and Hilliard, *Forging America*, 67, 82–83.

45. Ibid., 83.

46. Basilio Huertas, interview by author, June 17, 2015, Bethlehem, PA.

47. Ken Raniere, "South Bethlehem's First Brewery," *Bethlehem Press*, April 10, 2014.

48. Ibid.

49. Raymond Walters, *Bethlehem Long Ago and Today* (Bethlehem, PA: Carey Printing, 1923), 110–11.

50. Ibid., 111–12.

51. Ibid., 115, 116.

52. Federal Highway Administration, "State Motor Vehicle Registration, by Years, 1900–1995," https://www.fhwa.dot.gov/ohim/summary95/mv200.pdf.

53. The other phenomenon they financed was white flight. The federally insured mortgage programs of both the Federal Housing Administration and the VA were designed to lure whites out of public housing and into single-family homes in the suburbs. The government's "explicit program" was not to insure suburban mortgages for African Americans. See Richard Rothstein, "Public Housing: Government-Sponsored Segregation," *American Prospect*, October 11, 2012, http://prospect.org/article/public-housing-government-sponsored-segregation.

54. Bethlehem's population in 1940 was 58,490 and just over sixty-six thousand in 1950. Bureau of the Census, US Department of Commerce, "Population of Pennsylvania by Counties, April 1, 1950," *1950 Census of Population, Preliminary Counts*, September 19, 1950, 8, https://www2.census.gov/library/publications/decennial/1950/pc-02/pc-2-46.pdf.

55. I recently came across a copy of the history of the company, typed on onionskin, in my father's scrapbook and have donated it to the U.S. Army Heritage and Education Center, Carlisle, PA.

56. The first urban planning conference in the United States was held in New York in 1898. Amanda Erickson, "A Brief History of the Birth of Urban Planning," CityLab, August 24, 2012, https://www.citylab.com/life/2012/08/brief-history-birth-urban-planning/2365/.

57. Robinson and Cole, and National Association of Realtors, *Urban Blight: An Analysis of State Blight Statutes and Their Implications for Eminent Domain Reform* (Chicago: National Association of Realtors, 2007), 3, https://www.nar.realtor/smart_growth.nsf/docfiles/blight_study_revised.pdf/$FILE/blight_study_revised.pdf.

58. Ibid., 4.

59. Ibid.

60. Wendell E. Pritchett, "The 'Public Menace of Blight': Urban Renewal and the Private Uses of Eminent Domain," *Yale Law Journal* 21, no .1 (2003), http://digitalcommons.law.yale.edu/ylpr/vol21/iss1/2/.

61. Columbia University Graduate School of Architecture, Planning and Preservation, overview of program leading to an MS in historic preservation, 2017, https://www.arch.columbia.edu/programs/7-m-s-historic-preservation.

62. James Risen, "Another Blow to Flint, Mich.: Auto World Theme Park to Close," *Los Angeles Times,* January 2, 1985.

63. Laura Curtis Gross's first husband was a New York attorney and assistant secretary of the treasury under President Taft. She was known for her hospitality while living in the nation's capital. When she married John Gross and moved to Bethlehem, she converted her Washington home into the 1925 F Street Club, which is in operation today as one of the capital's most exclusive gathering places. Originally a refuge for Republicans during the New Deal, today the club has members of all political affiliations. See "The F Street Club, A Nice Quiet Place," *New York Times,* April 26, 1983.

64. Ralph Schwarz, interview by author, May 31, 2016, Bethlehem.

65. Ibid.

66. Clarke & Rapuano, and Russell VanNest Black, *An Interim Report on the City of Bethlehem,* May 1, 1956. Copies of the report are available at the Lehigh University Library.

67. Schwarz, interview.

68. Ruth Hutchison, "What's Going on in Bethlehem?" *New York Herald Tribune,* October 1, 1961, Sunday suppl., 4.

69. Schwarz, interview.

70. *Bethlehem Globe Times,* November 28, 1967, 1.

71. Ibid., November 29, 1967, 4.

72. Ibid.

73. The report also recommended removing "blighted properties" along the Reading Railroad tracks bisecting the south side and perhaps using some of that land for parking to support the south side business district.

    Pursuant to the report's parking recommendations, the city made spot improvements throughout the city and built the first parking structure in the north side downtown. Bethlehem Steel made improvements to its hotel and built a parking garage overhanging the hillside along the Monocacy Valley.

    The Steel also saw to it that a four-lane controlled access highway from Route 22 to the Hill to Hill Bridge, a major component of the transportation recommendations, was completed in 1966. Unrelated to the city's plans, during the same period the school district developed a new campus with a second high school, middle school, and home for the regional vocational technical school on the border between the city and Bethlehem Township.

74. Ken Raniere, "The Heights—Declaration of Doom," *Bethlehem Press,* September 5, 2013.

75. Clarke & Rapuano, *Center City Bethlehem* (New York: December 1969), 7, Records of the Redevelopment Authority of the City of Bethlehem, Lehigh University Library.

76. *Bethlehem Globe-Times,* March 22, 1976, 3.

77. "Reese Jones, Man of the Decade," editorial, *Bethlehem Globe-Times,* March 22, 1976, A-6.

78. Moravian House 2 with 106 residential units opened in 1977. It, Moravian House 1, and the Bethlehem Housing Authority's Monocacy House provided housing for more than five hundred low- to moderate-income senior citizens and people with disabilities. The downtown now had four of the eight high-rises depicted in the Clarke & Rapuano plan, which had envisioned office towers next to apartments and condominiums that would house the office workers who would live and play in downtown Bethlehem. Instead the city now had one partially filled office tower, a mall with no anchor and few customers, and residents of limited income to support retail, restaurants, and a performing arts center. Construction of these projects traces directly to one man whose commitment and access to resources and community connections made it possible but whose legacy is, at best, mixed.

79. John H. Koch, "Reese Jones and First Valley Bank: Banking on Bigness," *Sunday Call Chronicle*, April 22, 1979, B-1.

80. Before the campaign for the arts center could get under way, Mowrer changed the strategy for Main Street to preservation. That decision, as well as a movement to save the Sun Inn, put an end to the fund-raising effort.

81. Koch, "Reese Jones and First Valley Bank."

82. "Reese Jones, Man of the Decade"; Reese Jones obituary, *Bethlehem Globe-Times*, March 22, 1976, 1; Koch, "Reese Jones and First Valley Bank," B-5.

83. Gordon B. Mowrer, *The Comeback Kid* (Bethlehem, PA: Author, 2010), 59.

84. Urban Land Institute report on Bethlehem, April 2, 1976, 4, Records of the Redevelopment Authority.

85. Ibid., 5.

86. Ibid., 43.

87. On February 20, 2013, the city celebrated improvements to Main Street and a new star of Bethlehem, a graphic representation of the star on South Mountain, embedded at the intersection of Main and Market streets. Mayor John Callahan and Gordon Mowrer unveiled a plaque honoring Mowrer as the "Main Street mayor." It was a fine moment for the Moravian minister, mayor, insurance man, father, and grandfather. Mowrer died on July 19, 2016, leaving an enduring legacy for the people of Bethlehem.

88. Jeffrey Feather and four associates left IBM in 1970 to form a software and services group called Pentamation, which was based in Bethlehem, where IBM had its regional offices, primarily because of Bethlehem Steel. While capital was difficult to find in those days, the startup managed to pull together enough financing to focus on serving three sectors: government, education, and medicine, especially software for hospitals. By 1975 Pentamation was able to take advantage of discounted rates to move into the First Valley Bank tower, which first brought the business to downtown Bethlehem. As the business grew, and the mall was losing tenants, Pentamation rented a former fitness club in the mall to use as a computer center. By 1983 Pentamation had grown even more while the mall had completely failed. Feather and his business partner in Pentamation, Dave Bloys, bought the mall and started using portions of it for Pentamation's offices. Eventually their business used most of the mall for its business needs while renting some space to the Internal Revenue Service and a small convenience store. Jeffrey P. Feather, interview by author, June 17, 2016, Bethlehem.

89. Hughetta Bender obituary, *Morning Call*, March 14, 1995.

90. David Venditta and Ardith Hilliard, eds., *Forging America: The Story of Bethlehem Steel* (Allentown, PA: Morning Call, 2010), 147.

91. Marlene A. Lee and Mark Mather, "U.S. Labor Force Trends," *Population Bulletin*, June 2008, fig. 5, p. 7, http://www.prb.org/pdf08/63.2uslabor.pdf.

92. Alan Mallach, *In Philadelphia's Shadow: Small Cities in the Third Federal Reserve District* (Philadelphia: Federal Reserve Bank of Philadelphia, May 2012), 11, https://www.philadelphiafed.org/-/media/community-development/publications/special-reports/small-cities-in-third-federal-reserve-district.pdf.

93. David Venditta and Ardith Hilliard, eds., *Forging America: The Story of Bethlehem Steel* (Allentown, PA: Morning Call, 2010), 113.

94. John Strohmeyer, *Crisis in Bethlehem* (Pittsburgh: University of Pittsburgh Press. 1986), 114.

95. Ibid.

96. Thomas Kupper, "The End Begins: When 'the Steel' Falls Silent," *Morning Call*, supplement, November 1995, 18.

97. Strohmeyer, *Crisis in Bethlehem*, 114; Venditta and Hilliard, *Forging America*, 147.

98. Strohmeyer, *Crisis in Bethlehem*, 158.

99. John Strohmeyer, "City Services for Musikfest '84 Are Investment in the Future," *Bethlehem Globe Times*, July 3, 1984; Bill Toland, "In Desperate 1983, There Was Nowhere for Pittsburgh's Economy to Go but Up," *Pittsburgh Post-Gazette*, December 23, 2012.

100. David Venditta and Ardith Hilliard, eds., *Forging America: The Story of Bethlehem Steel* (Allentown, PA: Morning Call, 2010), 148.

101. Mary Procter and Bill Matuszeski, *Gritty Cities* (Philadelphia: Temple University Press, 1978).

102. Gregory Ashworth, abstract for "The Instruments of Place Branding: How Is It Done?" *European and Spatial Research Policy* 16, no. 1 (June 2009), doi.org/10.2478/v10105-009-0001-9; Ghazali Musa and T. C. Melwar, "Kuala Lumpur: Searching for the Right Brand," in *City Branding Theory and Cases*, ed. Keith Dinnie (New York: Palgrave Macmillan, 2011), 163.

103. The organizations included the Moravian College, Bach Choir of Bethlehem, Sun Inn Preservation Association, Historic Bethlehem, Inc., Beethoven Choruses, Lehigh Valley Chamber Orchestra, Moravian Museum, Bethlehem Steel, C. F. Martin & Company, Wainwright Travel, Northampton County Tourism Council, and the Bethlehem Chamber of Commerce.

104. Jeffrey A. Parks, *Tourism Task Force on Special Events, Report to the Bethlehem Chamber of Commerce Board of Directors*, June 1983, 2, 3, in the author's files.

105. Pennsylvania law categorizes cities in three classes based on population. Philadelphia is the only first-class city, Pittsburgh the only second-class city; Scranton is classified as 2A (as the runner-up to Pittsburgh), and all the rest are third class—and a bit insulted by the designation.

106. David Venditta and Ardith Hilliard, eds., *Forging America: The Story of Bethlehem Steel* (Allentown, PA: Morning Call, 2010), 148.

107. In the exuberance between the chamber's approval and the garnering of actual support, I added a site to the plan. The short-lived Amerika Platz was to feature American music, such as rock 'n' roll, blues, and country. It was to be located on City Center Plaza. But I had a moment of sanity in December 1983 dropped this platz as a bit too ambitious for the first year of the event.

108. The members of the first board of directors were Carol Henn, director of Institutional Advancement of Moravian College; Anne McGeady, executive director

of the Sun Inn Preservation Association; Jim Davis, executive director of the Bethlehem Chamber of Commerce; Llyena Boylan, executive director of the Lehigh Valley Chamber Orchestra; Janet Goloub, curator, Historic Bethlehem, Inc.; Jean Kessler, chair, Bethlehem Chamber of Commerce Tourism Committee; Gustave K. Skrivanek, Beethoven Choruses; Barbara Caldwell, administrative assistant to the mayor of the City of Bethlehem; Stephanie Katz, executive director of the Northampton County Tourism Bureau; Elizabeth Emslander, manager of the Hotel Bethlehem; Jack Trotter, senior vice president of marketing, First National Bank; Wayne Steeb, vice president of marketing, First Valley Bank; Jeffrey Gordon, public relations manager, First National Bank; Carol Heller, marketing manager, Union Bank and Trust Company; Helene Whitaker, community relations manager, Bethlehem Steel Corporation; Mary Ellen Gallo, president, Banko Beverage of Allentown; James Connell, attorney; Paul Meilinger, merchant and member of the board of the Downtown Bethlehem Association; Barbara M. Stout, public relations professional; Bob Steinmetz, representative of the Stadtkapelle Berching; and Jeffrey A. Parks, attorney. I was the association's president; Henn was vice president, and the board's other officers were McGeady, treasurer, and Davis, secretary.

109. David Venditta and Ardith Hilliard, eds., *Forging America: The Story of Bethlehem Steel* (Allentown, PA: Morning Call, 2010), 148.

110. Roland Kushner, interview by author, December 1, 2015, Bethlehem, PA.

111. The local employment figure is from David Venditta and Ardith Hilliard, eds., *Forging America: The Story of Bethlehem Steel* (Allentown, PA: Morning Call, 2010), 148.

112. John Strohmeyer, "City Services for Musikfest '84 Are Investment in the Future," *Bethlehem Globe Times*, July 3, 1984.

113. Like Musikfest, A Night in Old Vienna offered different foods in its different locations. The Continental Room was serving German specialty foods, German and Austrian wines, and of course beer. The Candlelight Room was the place for dessert—Viennese pastries and exotic coffees.

114. By 1990, the seventh year of Musikfest, sixty food vendors fed the festival, just a few less than we have today. Foods offered that year included shrimp cocktail, crab cake sandwich, chicken éttouffée; smoked turkey legs; peaches and cream (August is the month for local peaches); Belgian waffles; German chocolate cake; swordfish sandwich; homemade fudge; funnel cake (a staple at a Pennsylvania festival); curried rice salad; gyros; pizza; bratwurst; jumbo shrimp scampi; apple, cherry, cheese, and apricot strudels; open-faced rib-eye sandwich; Cornish pasties; potato pancakes; tacos; spinach pies; pancit lo mein; linguini with white clam sauce; egg roll; cabbage and noodles; caldo verde (Portuguese soup with collard greens and sausage); napoleons, cream puffs, and raspberry trifle. The committee wanted to offer an around-the-world food experience and succeeded.

115. Wine sales were modest but gave a big boost to Franklin Hill. Musikfest continued to feature Franklin Hill's wine for several years, but when a major wine company offered an exclusive sponsorship, the festival board accepted. Wine remains only a small part of overall beverage sales. It is not the preferred beverage of summer music festivalgoers.

116. Ticket revenue has rarely covered the entire cost of a show. According to Americans for the Arts, ticket sales for all performing arts (theater, dance, music) account for only 60 percent of the cost of presenting the show. The remainder of the revenue

comes from gifts and memberships from individual donors (25 percent), gifts from corporate donors (3 percent), and foundation and government grants (12 percent). Musikfest created a bold new model by covering a major percentage of the costs by selling food, beverages, and sponsorships.

117. Because Monocacy Creek frequently flooded the Colonial Industrial Quarter, the city removed a Depression-era dam at Johnston Park (Volksplatz) in 2013 and the flooding ceased.

118. For the employment figures see David Venditta and Ardith Hilliard, eds., *Forging America: The Story of Bethlehem Steel* (Allentown, PA: Morning Call, 2010), 148.

119. David Venditta and Ardith Hilliard, eds., *Forging America: The Story of Bethlehem Steel* (Allentown, PA: Morning Call, 2010), 148. Bethlehem Steel also announced in late 1996 that it was forming an entity called Bethlehem Works to "preserve, interpret and redevelop portions of the plant" in Bethlehem (148).

120. Willard G. Rouse III was the nephew of James Rouse, who, with his brother Willard G. Rouse Jr. (father of Willard G. III), developed Faneuil Hall Marketplace in Boston and Harborplace in Baltimore, as well as planned communities like Columbia, Maryland, and many other commercial developments.

121. Curtis "Hank" Barnette, interview by author, November 29, 2016, Bethlehem, PA.

122. Pennsylvania Department of Environmental Protection, "Land Recycling Program," 2017, http://www.dep.pa.gov/BUSINESS/LAND/LANDRECYCLING/Pages/default.aspx.

123. Pennsylvania Department of Environmental Protection, "Program Results: Success Stories," 2017, http://www.dep.pa.gov/Business/Land/LandRecycling/Pages/Program-Results.aspx.

124. The total acreage of the Bethlehem plant was 1,760. Bethlehem Commerce Center, the industrial park, was to include all but the 126 acres set aside for Bethlehem Works. When the dust settled, the 126 acres were conveyed to BethWorks Now; 450 acres had been conveyed to Majestic Realty; and 1,100 went to Lehigh Valley Industrial Park. The remaining 84 acres, which had been intended for the Commerce Center, were deemed too difficult to remediate under Act 2 and were retained by ISG's real estate entity. In 2017 the value of the land had increased so much that a developer bought part of it and immediately began to bring in the required two feet of topsoil to remediate the land for development.

125. Ralph G. Schwarz, Memorandum on Executive Summary of Understanding re Bethlehem Steel Museum, July 6, 1994, in the personal files of Ralph Grayson Schwarz, Bethlehem, PA.

126. Conceptual Design Proposal, Bob Weis Design Island Associates, June 13, 1995, in the personal files of Ralph Grayson Schwarz.

127. Economic Research Associates, "Market Analysis and Evaluation of Warranted Investment for Bethlehem Works, PA," Final Report, San Francisco, CA, 1995, in the personal files of Ralph Grayson Schwarz.

128. Barnette, interview.

129. Ralph Grayson Schwarz, interview by author, May 31, 2016, Bethlehem, PA.

130. For more about Smithsonian Affiliations, see https://affiliations.si.edu/about-us/faq/#toggle-id-1.

131. Thomas Kupper, "Steel Influence Permeates City Debate over Rezoning 160 Acres of Idle Plant Highlights Connections, Steel Ties," *Morning Call*, April 1, 1996.

132. Hugh Bronstein, "Bethlehem Steel Rezoning Plan Cleared," *Morning Call*, April 3, 1996.
133. Barnette, interview.
134. Bronstein, "Bethlehem Steel Rezoning Plan Cleared."
135. The TIF district included properties not owned by Bethlehem Steel to the east and south of the designated Bethlehem Works project. These properties were thought to be good candidates for development that would contribute to the TIF and thus to Bethlehem Works.
136. Don Cunningham, interview by author, January 4, 2017, Bethlehem, PA.
137. "Riverside Arts Park, Bethlehem, PA: A Proposal," March 21, 2003, in the author's files.
138. Ibid. The Sasaki study is no longer in my possession. The quote I have used appears in a footnote in "Riverside Arts Park." The city's Office of Community and Economic Development retains a copy of the study.
139. Peter Zeihan, *The Accidental Superpower: The Next Generation of American Preeminence and the Coming Global Disorder* (New York: Twelve, 2014), 38.
140. Anne Brownley Raines, "Change Through Industrial Culture: Conservation and Renewal in the *Ruhrgebeit*," *Planning Perspectives Journal* 26, no. 2 (2011): 183–207.
141. According to UNESCO, "The Zollverein XII Coal Mine Industrial Complex is an important example of a European primary industry of great economic significance in the 19th and 20th centuries. It consists of the complete installations of a historical coal-mining site: the pits, coking plants, railway lines, pit heaps, miner's housing and consumer and welfare facilities. The mine is especially noteworthy of the high architectural quality of its buildings of the Modern Movement." See UNESCO, "Zollverein Coal Mine Industrial Complex in Essen," http://whc.unesco.org/en/list/975.
142. In fact, the spelling Jonathan suggested was *SteelStax*, which we all agreed was sexier than SteelStacks but turned out to be a potential conflict with rights of the owners of the Stax record company so we changed it.
143. Jeffrey Feather, interview by author, May 18, 2016, Bethlehem, PA
144. Michael Perrucci, interview by author, January 14, 2016, Bethlehem, PA.
145. Michael Perrucci, interview by author, January 14, 2016, Bethlehem, PA.
146. Minutes, Bethlehem City Council, October 3, 2006.
147. See the postings at Film-Tech Cinema Systems, http://www.film-tech.com/ubb/f5/t001340.html.
148. It is important to note that the most prosperous counties in Pennsylvania in terms of median household income are the four Philadelphia suburban counties, Bucks, Chester, Delaware, and Montgomery, which also are attracting young, educated residents.
149. *Wayfinding* "refers to information systems that guide people through a physical environment and enhance their understanding and experience of the space." Society for Experiential Graphic Design, "What Is Wayfinding?" SEGD, n.d., https://segd.org/what-wayfinding. The Sands Casino alone reports 8 million guests per year (some of whom are presumably city residents) and ArtsQuest reports more than 1,500,000 guests per year for Musikfest, Christkindlmarkt and various other events, while many visitors come throughout the year to visit Lehigh University, Moravian College or the various heritage sites. The Hotel Bethlehem, with its prized location in the center of the Moravian Historic District has become a favorite lodging place for guests of regional businesses many of which are

international companies with headquarters in Germany, Japan, Denmark and China.

150. Nicole Radzievich, "Bethlehem Advances in Bid to Be World Heritage Site," *Morning Call*, December 9, 2016, http://www.mcall.com/news/local/bethlehem/mc-bethlehem-world-heritage-nomination-20161209-story.html.

151. 4Ward Planning, Inc., *South Bethlehem Eastern Gateway Study*, March 12, 2014, Philadelphia, 20, available at the Community Action Development Corporation of Bethlehem.

152. Lynne McCormack, "Everything You Ever Wanted to Know about Creative Placemaking," Local Initiatives Support Corporation, June 30, 2016, http://www.lisc.org/our-stories/story/creative-placemaking-q-and-a.

153. Naomi Lewin, "Attraction or Annoyances? Orchestras Invite Audiences to Use Their Smartphones," *WQXR*, March 28, 2012, http://www.wqxr.org/story/194745-attraction-annoyance-orchestras-invite-audiences-use-smartphones/.

154. Lindsey Gruson, "Bethlehem Pins Hopes on Music," *New York Times*, August 25, 1985.

155. Natalie Grigson, "These Are the Ten Most Exciting Places to Live in Pennsylvania," *Movoto Blog*, July 2014, http://www.movoto.com/blog/real-estate-and-more/most-exciting-places-in-pennsylvania/; Megan H. Weiler, "Reader Recs: Best Summer Music Festivals," *National Geographic Travel*, July 17, 2014, http://intelligenttravel.nationalgeographic.com/2014/07/17/reader-recs-best-summer-music-festivals/; Rebecca Lake, "The Best Christmas Markets Around the World," *Condé Nast Traveler*, December 19, 2014, https://www.cntraveler.com/galleries/2014-12-19/the-best-christmas-markets-around-the-world-bryant-park-tivoli-gardens-salzburg/10; Anna Kopsky, "19 Insanely Weird Concert Venues to Visit Before You Die," *BuzzFeed*, July 11, 2015, https://www.buzzfeed.com/annakopsky/incredible-concert-venues-you-must-visit-before-you-die?utm_term=.njPgmOM1Zo#.nxPp8WR2mn; Alexander Kent et al., "America's 50 Best Cities in the US to Live," *Wall Street 24/7*, November 5, 2015, http://247wallst.com/special-report/2015/11/05/americas-50-best-cities-to-live-2-2/; Talia Avakian, "15 Incredible Concert Venues Around the World," *Business Insider,* August 1, 2015, http://www.businessinsider.com/amazing-concert-venues-around-the-world-2015-7/#the-annual-bregenz-festival-which-is-held-in-austria-from-july-through-august-is-known-for-the-incredible-fantasy-like-sets-built-on-its-floating-stage-1; "What Drops on New Year's Eve? Not Just Times Square Ball," Associated Press, December 22, 2016, https://apnews.com/72adc45d4df54abe84b7b65b3682374b/what-drops-new-years-eve-not-just-times-square-ball; Margaret Backenheimer, "60 Great Things to See in 2017," *Chicago Tribune*, December 19, 2016, http://www.chicagotribune.com/lifestyles/travel/ct-big-events-of-2017-travel-0101-20161216-story.html.

156. Sarah Max, "The Best Places to Retire," *Money Magazine Retirement Guide 2016*, http://time.com/money/collection-post/4538894/best-places-retire-2016/; William P. Barrett, "The Twenty-five Best Places to Retire in 2017," *Forbes*, April 20, 2017, https://www.forbes.com/sites/williampbarrett/2017/04/20/the-best-places-to-retire-in-2017/#73e86051f3ad.

INDEX